Mathematical Model Techniques
for Learning Theories

Mathematical Model Techniques for Learning Theories

Gustav Levine

Arizona State University

C. J. Burke

California State College, at Hayward

ACADEMIC PRESS   New York and London

ACADEMIC PRESS, INC.
111 Fifth Avenue, New York, New York 10003

United Kingdom Edition published by
ACADEMIC PRESS, INC. (LONDON) LTD.
24/28 Oval Road, London NW1 7DD

LIBRARY OF CONGRESS CATALOG CARD NUMBER: 79-187221

PRINTED IN THE UNITED STATES OF AMERICA

*To the James McKeen Cattell Fund,
for supporting Levine while he
studied with Burke.*

Contents

Preface

This book was born out of the recognition that there was no single volume containing the mathematical techniques that are needed for the construction of mathematical models of learning. At the present time, such skills are communicated primarily by tutorial relationships, with partial explications scattered through a number of books. Consequently, any book that brings together the bulk of such techniques is most desirable. This book is the outgrowth of that perceived need.

We are aware of the fact that most psychologists have either had very limited mathematical backgrounds, or have forgotten what they had learned, through disuse. Therefore, all that is assumed for readers of this book is a modest knowledge of college algebra. All additional mathematical material that is required is presented as part of the material of the book.

The techniques are presented in the context of specific applications within the learning models literature. It is therefore anticipated that the readers will both learn new skills, and how to apply them.

This book is directed toward students of psychology, and those professional psychologists who are first approaching the mathematical model literature.

It is expected that after having read the text, and having done the exercises, the reader should be able to understand much of the technical literature. In addition, it should be possible for the reader to construct his own mathematical models (with theoretical complexity being a limiting factor, at least initially).

The overriding intent of this text is to develop in the reader the ability to translate a set of verbal statements into mathematical equations. We have presented three major (and several minor) approaches to this translation in this book. One major approach is called the "direct method," and is first presented in Chapter Two. The direct method is the direct translation of verbal-theoretical statements into the probability calculus. The direct method then finds repeated use throughout the text. The next major approach involves the construction of difference equations. Recursive forms of difference equations are first constructed from a recognition of recursive statements or implications in the theory being modeled. Different recursive forms require different solutions. Chapter Three presents some frequently used difference equations and their solutions. Chapter Four presents the Bush and Mosteller learning model, which offers many examples of the use of difference equations. Subsequent chapters offer further examples. In Chapter Five some necessary matrix algebra is introduced. The matrix algebra is then used in Chapter Six, which introduces Markov chain analysis, the third major approach. Markov chain analyses offer predictions about transitions between states. Many psychological theories can be formulated in such terms. Markov chain solutions are offered here to such questions as the expected number of times in any state; the probability of going to any state at least once; the probability of entering any permanent state. These solutions are in the form of matrices, which are then used to obtain other matrices that are useful for further solutions. Chapter Seven then offers examples of Markov chain analysis as applied to some theories of avoidance conditioning. Chapter Eight presents some advanced material that can be quite useful in Markov chain analyses.

There are problems at the ends of all chapters with the exception of Chapters One and Seven. Detailed answers for all of the problems are presented at the back of the book.

Because most of the published mathematical models have been presentations of new theories, mathematical models of learning have sometimes been considered to be a class of learning theories. Actually, mathematical models are most frequently restatements of theories (old or new) which make the theories easier to evaluate. Mathematical models of learning then, are most often representations of theories—all classes of theories—rather than a separate class of learning theories. For this reason, this book is addressed to all psychologists who have any interest in the construction of learning theories, and who have not yet mastered the techniques that are needed for mathematical model construction.

Chapter One

Introduction

Prior to the development of mathematical models in psychology, the similarity between the physical sciences and scientific psychology was primarily one of attitude, in the sense of a recognition of the need for controlled observation. But in the late 1940s and early 1950s quantitative techniques began to be developed that made it possible for theory building in psychology to be analogous to theory building in the physical sciences.

Mathematical Analogies for Learning

To appreciate why the mathematics used for theory building in the physical sciences could not simply be borrowed whole, it is necessary to understand the unique characteristics of psychology's problems. Psychology deals in relationships among events that, within the constraints of current understanding, appear to be of a probabilistic nature. The use of functions with a specifiable outcome mirroring deterministic relationships does not appear to be appropriate to current analyses of psychological processes. Therefore, any equations representing psychological processes appear to require relationships between probabilities, or at the minimum, the use of probabilities as the dependent variable. This requires that mathematical model builders be sophisticated in the probability calculus. Texts explicating the probability calculus in a manner suitable for psychologists as well as mathematicians first became available around the middle of this century [for example, the first edition of Feller's (1968) classic probability text was copyrighted 1950]. Given increasing

1

numbers of psychologists with some sophistication in probability theory, the translation of verbal theoretical statements into equations yielding probabilities became increasingly frequent. Chapter Two attempts to explicate this use of the probability calculus. Further sophistication in such reasoning is obtained with an understanding of set theory, out of which probability theory can be derived, given the proper assumptions. Set theory also became readily, and more readably, available at about this same time.

Experiments in learning phenomena are generally concerned with changes in some evidence of learning as a result of experiences on discrete trials. In most paired-associate learning paradigms the subject's knowledge is tested after every exposure to the correct pairing. In maze running, each trial is a test and, generally, a learning experience as well. In a Skinner box, the rat or pigeon is exposed to potential behavior change at each successful or unsuccessful response. When a number (whether it be a probability value between 0 and 1, or some integer value) changes as a result of discrete opportunities, we are more likely to find accurate mathematical analogies in difference equations than in differential equations. But difference equations were not known to psychologists until this same period: the late 1940s and early 1950s. Combining difference equations with the probability calculus enabled theorists to mirror a probabilistic process that was axiomatized in terms of changes on discrete trials. Those difference equations that are most frequently utilized in psychological model construction are discussed in detail in Chapter Three.

Another body of mathematical techniques useful to psychologists is contained in Markov chain theory. Feller presented this material with his usual skill in his 1950 text (and all subsequent editions). Other texts, at a variety of levels, became available during the 1950s, culminating in the particularly readable *Finite Markov Chains* by Kemeny and Snell (1960). The use of Markov chain techniques is introduced in Chapter Six.

The Theory Generates the Equation

Clark L. Hull (1943) is sometimes considered the first mathematical learning theorist, although there are other, earlier, quantitatively oriented theorists (see Miller, 1964, for a review). The genesis of Hull's model was different from that of current models, and the difference is a critical one. The major mathematical technique used by Hull and his contemporaries was curve fitting. For Hull this meant a somewhat arbitrary selection of one from the many equations whose form would be compatible with previously obtained data. Theory dictated the selection of variables for his equations, but the precise forms of the equations were derived primarily out of attempts to fit the past data. With the new quantitative techniques that have become available, it is now possible to permit the theory to imply the equation form directly, prior to data collection.

The capacity to derive equations from theory, and to see how these theoretically derived equations conform to data patterns, is what is meant by a true analogy between theory building in psychology and theory building in the physical sciences. Explication of the techniques for this translation of verbal theory to mathematical equations constitutes the bulk of this text.

The Theories Are Restricted in Scope

A further change from the past in learning theory that appears to be fairly general in more recent theory building is the abandonment of the belief in a general learning function that should cover all learning situations. More recent thinking recognizes that different theories, and therefore different mathematical functions, might be required for different learning situations. The earlier work assumed that a finding in one laboratory, stemming from one experimental paradigm, could contradict the theory of another experimenter using a different paradigm, with all paradigms assumed to be exploring a similar process. Thus, very general theories of learning were being discussed in the first half of the twentieth century. But the new theories for which mathematical models have been developed generally address themselves to single paradigms or to clearly circumscribed theoretical questions. It is possible to compare sets of assumptions as predictors, for some one paradigm, asking what smallest set of assumptions yields the most accurate predictions. Armed with the best predicting set of assumptions, the issue of further generality to other paradigms and to broadened theoretical issues, with or without additional axioms, can be faced.

Data Collection Is Essential to Mathematical Model Development

It should be clear from the preceding discussion that mathematical models of learning are constructed with a view to explaining at least one particular experimental paradigm. The theory for the paradigm is then supported or disconfirmed by the similarity or dissimilarity between the data and the predictions. Mathematical models of learning in this sense require the running of experiments, and the construction of mathematical models of learning is then the task of an experimental psychologist who uses a mathematical model to generate a large set of quantitative predictions.

The Basic Terms of a Mathematical Model

We shall first present the simplest possible example of an equation in a model of a theory, in order to help to explicate the material in this section.

Assume that a theory (not specified here) indicates that the probability of making an error would decrease by some constant proportion with each trial. Symbolize this proportion as $(1 - a)$, with a being a value between 0 and 1. Symbolize the probability of an error on trial n as $P(E_n)$. Our theory would then imply that

$$P(E_{n+1}) = P(E_n) - (1 - a)P(E_n),$$
$$P(E_{n+1}) = aP(E_n). \tag{1.1a}$$

Equation (1.1a) has the mathematical solution (derived in Chapter Three) shown in Eq. (1.1b).

$$P(E_n) = P(E_1)a^{n-1}. \tag{1.1b}$$

Most of the equations in a mathematical model of learning contain at least one independent variable that is truly variable within any experimental condition. In learning theories, the trial number, such as n in Eq. (1.1b), is an independent variable. Other independent variables can also occur.

There is one dependent variable for each equation, such as $P(E_n)$ in Eq. (1.1b). The dependent variable is generally in the form of a probability, except when we are dealing with summarizing statistics.

For example, we might have an equation for the probability of any particular trial n being the trial of the last error. In the equation the independent variable would be n and the dependent variable would consist of the different probabilities associated with the different values of n.

Our equations will most often include a third quantity, which can be very important for mathematical theory, incorporating terms for events that are not directly observable. We are referring to *parameter values*. The term "parameter" denotes a value that we treat as a constant over some class of experimental conditions or for some set of subjects. Throughout changes in the independent variables, and the resulting changes in the dependent variable, some one, two, or more parameter values remain as constants in the equations. In our Eq. (1.1b), both $P(E_1)$ and a are examples of parameters.

The parameter a in Eq. (1.1b) could be described as a rate of learning parameter. Equating learning with decreasing numbers of errors offers a circular definition with no additional implications. However, the theorist might conceive of further implications for his "learning" construct. He might assume as an axiom of his theory that learning is a process emerging out of continued consistent responding in a constant stimulus environment. According to a theory containing such an axiom, variations in the stimuli from response to response should result in a decreased rate of learning. If this were the case, experimental variation of stimulus conditions should result in a smaller value of $(1 - a)$. This would mean that a would then be a larger value, so that, following Eq. (1.1a), $P(E_{n+1})$ would be closer in value to $P(E_n)$ than if the same stimuli were present on every trial. Additional constructs might be added to the theory. The theorist might introduce a motivational variable, representing it by a new symbol, which would be related to a and $P(E_n)$ by mathematical operations consistent with the additional axioms added to the theory.

However, a parameter does not have to be identified with psychologically significant concepts. It can also be a constant used to bring the values of obtained data into a scale that is manageable, or revealing, or in close accord with empirical distributions. In its most general sense, the parameter of an equation joins with the mathematical operations to relate the independent variables to the dependent variable, and this is what gives the equation its form. In Eq. (1.1b) the independent variable n is related to the dependent variable $P(E_n)$ by two parameters and a mathematical operation. That is, by the learning parameter a, the initial trial error probability $P(E_1)$, and the multiplication operation.

In a verbalized theory, each term of the theory will have some verbalizable meaning, or at the minimum, a symbolic designation. If a term that is at times constant has some verbalizable relations, then its occasional variability under specifiable experimental conditions should be predictable within the theory. This would be the case for our hypothetical theorist's learning construct, represented by the parameter a. With controlled experimental variations, a theorist could then keep check on hypothetical intervening phenomena that are represented by parameters. He could then speak of intervening events, add explanatory constructs to a theory, and have a way of keeping track of, or validating, the predictive value of otherwise elusive or invisible constructs. This is one of the important gains from the development of mathematical models of verbalized theories. It is probably a contributing factor in the recent revival of speculative cognitive theorizing.

A Theory's Theorems and a Model's Equations

Ideally, a theory is constructed to account for all of the possible outcomes of an experiment and all conceivable analyses of the data. Consequently, the axioms of a theory should be combined in every conceivable way, and all implications of the theory's axioms, which are called *theorems*, should be revealed. A theorist cannot be expected to achieve a complete listing of all the theorems implied by a theory. Rather, it is something toward which he aims. Later theorists and experimenters will find additional implications of his theory to test. A theory supported by today's data may well be disconfirmed by later data, which will test different theorems.

A mathematical model that analogizes a theory can be manipulated, algebraically, for example, and its resulting probabilistic statements and expected values will constitute the quantitative implications of additional theorems of the theory. Therefore, a mathematical model is a way of exploring a theory's implications. The mathematical statements of a theory's implications, in the form of equations, will generally be less ambiguous than verbalizations of these implications.

The Use of the Term "Model"

The term "model" has a number of overlapping meanings which can cause confusion. The most common meaning encountered in the vernacular is the reference to the simulation of the physical appearance of an object, generally on a different physical scale. A more relevant meaning for our purposes is duplication of the operating principles of a system, rather than duplication of its physical appearance. For example, we might visually examine the flow of colored water in a system through which air normally flows, in order to understand the conditions under which the air would flow in different directions. The water system would be a working model of the principles involved in the air system, and would help to reveal what occurs in the air system.

A still more relevant meaning has to do with the "as if" analysis of a system. A scientist might state that in a little unidentified black box he has noted that increases in temperature increase the pressure readings on the sides of the box. He might then verbalize an "as if" model, stating that the box operates as though perfectly elastic submicroscopic billiard balls existed inside it, with the balls responding to increased temperature with increased movement. This conceptualized (as opposed to constructed) model presents a circumstance with known principles, which acts as a generator of principles in the theorist's thinking. The laws, or operating principles, in the model are assumed to hold for the system that we call upon the model to help to explain. If we can list the laws in the model, we shall then have the laws that, we assume, govern the system being modeled. The laws for the system being modeled constitute the theory. In the model as a physical analogy, we would have the model giving us the theory.

It is also possible to go further, and assume that the physical constitution of the unknown circumstance requiring a theory is actually similar to that of the model, perhaps only different in size. This was the case in the submicroscopic billiard ball analogy that we used in our last example. Scientists did indeed postulate existential status for such submicroscopic elements in gases, prior to obtaining confirming evidence.

The use of either hypothetical physical systems or analogous physical systems allows for rich conjecture, which in turn allows more powerful theories to emerge. The analogy of the physical model builds the theory for the theorist, or if he recognizes that he has only a partial analogy in his model, the model at least contributes some axioms to his theory.

It is possible to build theories without conceptual or physical models and still obtain the same theoretical end results. The advantage of the conceptual or physical model is that it usually makes theoretical development easier. It is also more likely that the axioms making up the new theory are consistent with each other if they are borrowed whole from a functioning physical system.

THE MATHEMATICAL MODEL AS DISTINCT FROM OTHER MODELS

The mathematical model for a rationalized theory generally does not precede the theory, but rather follows it. It does not generally develop the theory, but makes the theory's quantitative implications manifest. However, it is still a model in the sense of its being a system that can be manipulated analogously to the system being modeled (algebraically, or with changing parameter values, as two examples). Thus, outcomes of the system being modeled can be seen and predicted through the abstract mathematical manipulations, to the degree that the mathematical model is a proper analogy for the system that it models.

Just as it is possible (though usually difficult) to bypass conceptual model construction on the way to a theory, it is also possible to bypass verbalized theory on the way to mathematical model construction. We would then have a mathematical theory, rather than a mathematical model of a verbalized theory. This would occur if the theorist had an insight into the quantitative relations of a system and either did not require, or did not wish to express, analogous verbal imagery, or if he eschewed speculations on underlying physical possibilities. Clearly, then, a mathematical model and a mathematical theory (as differentiated from a verbalized theory) are one and the same. If a verbalized theory exists, however, the mathematical expression of that theory can be seen to function as a mathematical model of that theory. Most generally, among contemporary mathematical models of learning, we are dealing with mathematical models of theories. The theories are attempts to "explain" some incidents of learning by suggesting principles that could be responsible for the learning. For this reason, a purely mathematical theory might predict, but it would do so without explanatory content.

Three Submodels

A model takes its meaning and significance from its relation to something else. It is therefore critical that there be clarity on what it is that the model builder is trying to model. In mathematical models of learning there is a natural source of confusion. Three related submodels can often be implied within the structure of a mathematical model of learning.

1. There can be a mathematical model of the data.
2. There can be a verbal model (a theory) of the subject's behavior.
3. There can be a mathematical model of the verbal model.

The Mathematical Model of the Data

The mathematical model of the data stems from some insight into a set of mathematical assumptions that would generate patterns of values, such as the data patterns that are generated by some specified experimental paradigms. An equation for a curve is a model of a particular pattern of relationships between varying values of two variables. This is the limited sense in which curve fitting might be called model building. However, theorists are generally concerned with a need to predict many distributions emanating from a single experiment. Therefore, the mathematical insight has to be more broadly encompassing than that which is generally implied by a single curve. The theorist often looks for a reasonable psychological process that might offer some unifying element for this larger set of mathematical statements. At the minimum of psychological assumption we would have something like the Bush and Mosteller (1955) linear operator model. This is almost exclusively a mathematical model, with the barest nod to theoretical commitment. The inspiration for this model appears to have come from combining an acceptance of a gradual learning assumption with the assumption that all trial-to-trial changes can be analogized with linear operators (discussed in Chapter Four). In more recently developed models with minimal commitments to intervening psychological processes, theorists have also tried to discover a set of mathematical assumptions that would predict data distributions similar to the empirically derived distributions. There is now a sufficient backlog of data to impose immediate mathematical restrictions on most new theories (see Bjork, 1970, for some clearly stated specific examples). When a mathematical model is found that fits previous data, it is of course then tested on data from new experimental situations.

Obtaining a mathematical insight from a perusal of data patterns requires some mathematical skill and experience. The techniques and examples in this book should provide some initial degree of sophistication.

Models can begin with a mathematical model of the data. More often, theorists begin with either a verbal model of behavior or a verbal model of behavior coupled with a mathematical insight.

The Verbal Model of Behavior

The verbal model of the subject's behavior patterns in an experimental situation often stems from some insight into a hypothetical structure or process within the organism that could generate the observed behavior patterns. A hypothetical physiological event, or intervening processing mechanism, could be postulated by the theorist.

The verbal model can also postulate an intervening process that does not refer to inner processes, thereby avoiding any physiological or cognitive implications. For example, Bower's (1959) theory of vicarious trial and error in choice behavior (discussed later in Chapter Six) postulated minute alternations in physical orientation at the choice point as an intervening process.

The distinguishing characteristic of the verbal model is its set of postulates attempting to generate the observed behavior through some psychological rationale, either cognitively or behaviorally oriented. A verbal model of behavior is really just a psychological theory.

A mathematical model of the data, described in the immediately preceding section, is detailed in its quantitative statements, but can also have some small psychological commitment within its axioms. Conversely, the verbal model of behavior has its maximum commitment to psychological rationale, but can also have some minimal references to quantitative commitments. However, the full quantitative significance embodied in, or desired for, a psychological theory, requires a mathematical restatement of the verbal model of behavior. This restatement into mathematical language is the process of creating a mathematical model of a verbal model.

A MATHEMATICAL MODEL OF THE VERBAL MODEL

The mathematical model of the verbal model is a direct translation of the verbal statements into the probability calculus or some other mathematical form. Throughout this book, we stress this aspect of model construction. The most direct form of this translation is introduced in Chapter Two and is identified as the *direct method*. An example of its implementation is the frequent use of addition for " or " and multiplication for " and." We also have the difference equations, introduced in Chapter Three, which are generally related to verbalizations through a recursive statement in need of projection to an nth instance. A recursive statement is a statement about trial-to-trial changes (more generally, a statement relating consecutive events in any sequence). Equation (1.1a) has a form that could analogize some recursive statements. Its mathematical solution, given in Eq. (1.1b), could be translated back to a verbalization about a particular (nth) trial. Another medium for translating verbal statements into mathematical equations is Markov chain theory, introduced in Chapter Six. The word "states" as used in "states of learning," for example, generally corresponds directly to the word "states" as used in Markov chain theory. Consequently, Markov chain theory can be used to develop equations analogizing statements about the probabilities of moving from one state to another.

FORMAL VERSUS PROCESS MODELS

A distinction is sometimes made between a formal model and a process model. A formal model is a model constructed with a minimal number of postulates referring to psychological processes. It conforms to our designation of a mathematical model of the data, discussed on page 8.

A process model (sometimes called a *structural model*) is a model that can be dichotomized into two submodels, the verbal model of behavior and a mathematical model of the verbal model. It assumes some commitment to a psychological process, which in turn has some quantitative implications suggesting a mathematical form.

When we think of a psychological theory with some attendant mathematization that makes clear-cut parametric predictions, we are thinking of a process model. The stimulus sampling theory models, with their assumptions of intervening stimulus sampling behavior (discussed in Chapter Three), constitute process models. The definition of a mathematical model of learning as a mathematical model of a theory is appropriate for a process model, but not for a formal model. The belief that development of a mathematical model of learning is primarily a mathematical enterprise is correct with reference to a formal model, but not with reference to a process model.

The trichotomy of models suggested in the previous section clearly overlaps with the more common dichotomy of formal versus process models. What we are suggesting with our trichotomization is a second dichotomy of the process models into two sets of axioms. One set, constituting the verbal model of behavior, is enlarged upon or otherwise altered, due to psychological considerations. The other set, constituting our mathematical model of the verbal model, is enlarged upon or otherwise altered to give greater specificity to the mathematical implications of the verbal model. The two sets of axioms are combined to produce the axioms of the overall process model.

The isolation of different kinds of modeling within a single model can allow for intellectual pauses and determination of whether some or all aspects of a model's requirements have been met.

The Purpose of This Book

A good mathematical model presents many features or many predictions of the data; that is, a good mathematical model is one in which many dependent variables are expressed through functions. Of course, this statement assumes that the predictions are valid. The latter point is generally realized in only a relative fashion, in comparison to alternative models.

Psychology is still a young science. It has a long way to go in the development of a large body of functional theory. Therefore, each mathematical model builder has had to be a theory builder, as well as a mathematician with skills to enable him to express his theory in equation form, as well as an experimenter to obtain parameter estimates and to test his theory. This book is dedicated to helping the theoretically interested psychologist develop the mathematical skills needed for expressing a theory as a mathematical model.

Chapter Two

Probability Theory and the Direct Method

Mathematical models of learning most characteristically (though not exclusively) attempt to answer questions about discrete trial processes. These are models of situations in which subjects have been exposed to a sequence of discrete events, each of which constitutes a learning opportunity (such as the pairings in a paired-associate paradigm).

The outcomes of individual trials constitute a probabilistic sequence. That is, the outcome of an individual trial cannot be known with certainty prior to the actual outcome. The various possible outcomes of an experiment can be arbitrarily categorized for the convenience of the experimenter. It is only necessary to establish criteria for differentiating experimental outcomes in some mutually exclusive and exhaustive way. For example, we could dichotomize the possible outcomes into correct and incorrect responses.

Random Variables

It is profitable, from the point of view of managing predictions, to give a unique numerical designation to each possible mutually exclusive outcome. These numerical designations are called *random variable values*. Each random variable value would have some probability of occurrence, and we would be able to draw up a graph giving the probability distribution for these random variable values. That is, the random variable values would be presented on the axis of the abscissa and the relative probabilities of each value would be represented as the height of each point on the graph, on the axis of the ordinate.

As a sequence of trials was observed, different random variable values would appear, or rather, different experimental outcomes would be observed, each having a random variable value. A sequence of such random variable values (for example, over trials) is called a *stochastic process*.

Any convenient set of real numbers can be used as the random variable values. For example, we might be interested in an experiment dichotomized according to whether the subject did or did not remember some information. We could then assign the values 0 and 1, respectively, to the two possible outcomes. Or we might use numbers related to the categorization of the outcomes for the random variable values. For example, we could observe, as our stochastic process, the trial number of the first correct response for each subject in some learning task. Our random variable values might then be the conceivable number of trials that it might take for the first correct response to occur (probably the values 1 to whatever number of trials the experimenter would be willing to run for a subject that was not learning).

The major function of theories of learning accompanied by mathematical models is to predict the probability distributions of random variable values. The mathematical model is a model of the stochastic process.

The totality of possible random variable values in the set is represented by a single symbol, which is generally an arbitrarily selected capital letter. This is a random variable, and it is said to take on the values that we have designated as random values. For example, we could define a random variable L, which could assume any of the values corresponding to the possible trials on which a subject could commit his last error in some experimental task. The probability that a subject will commit his last error on some trial r would then be symbolized as $P(L = r)$.

Expected Values

We can conceive of an average value for the random variable over several observations. Empirically, this value would simply be the sum of all of the actually obtained values divided by the number of such values. (For example, if the trial of the last error were obtained for three subjects, the results being 5, 6, and 7, and if we assume that this is a good representation of the values to be obtained by other subjects, the expected value would be 6.)

If the individual probability of each value occurring is known, we can obtain a predicted average value, denoted the *expected value* (of a random variable). To compute the expected value, we would multiply each possible value of the random variable by its individual probability of occurrence, and then sum all of these products. This procedure can be intuitively appreciated as reasonable if we first express our probabilities as fractions the denominator of which would be the total number of the hypothetical observations to be made. For example, if the random variable can take on any of the values 5, 6, or 7 with respective probabilities of .25, .25, and .50, and if we use 8 as the hypothetical number of observations to be made, we would anticipate twice as many 7's as either 5's or 6's, and the average value of the random variable would be intuitively computed in the following way:

$$\frac{5 + 5 + 6 + 6 + 7 + 7 + 7 + 7}{8} = \left(5 \cdot \frac{2}{8}\right) + \left(6 \cdot \frac{2}{8}\right) + \left(7 \cdot \frac{4}{8}\right)$$

$$= 6.25.$$

This is equivalent to multiplying each random variable value by the fraction of the total number of times that it would occur, that is, in this case, with weightings $\frac{2}{8}$, $\frac{2}{8}$, and $\frac{4}{8}$. These fractions, each being an expected or empirical relative frequency, are the usual operational definitions of probability.

Imagine a large revolving drum containing a great many slips of paper, from which individual slips are selected blindly at regular intervals. We assume that each of the slips of paper has written on it the number 5, 6, or 7. We further assume that there are twice as many slips of paper bearing the number 7 as bear the number 6, and an equal number of slips bearing the number 5 as bear the number 6. We conceive of this as a random process, since it is not known which of the three possible values will appear on any one trial and there is no consistent factor influencing the selection of one slip of paper rather than another. By combining our slips into classes, in this instance into classes according to the numbers that they bear, we can speak of the different probabilities of individual classes being selected ($\frac{1}{4}$, $\frac{1}{4}$, and $\frac{1}{2}$). If we use the letter X to represent our random variable, we can symbolize our probabilities in the following way:

$$P(X = 5) = .25,$$
$$P(X = 6) = .25,$$
$$P(X = 7) = .50.$$

In any one sampling, we get an actual average value. When we speak of the expected value, we assume a hypothetical infinitely large sampling. The expected value is the anticipated average if such an infinite sampling were undertaken. It then becomes our best guess for a small sample, and this best guess is our expected value. It is computed as the sum of the products obtained by multiplying each possible random variable value by its respective probability.

PROBABILITY

If we wish to know the probability of each member of some set of events, where only one of these events could occur on any one trial, we are really concerned with relative frequencies. Since on any one trial some event will occur, its occurrence would end speculation, and the probabilities would become irrelevant. However, we ask such questions with a long-term view, with an implicit understanding of wanting to know what chance each of the values has of occurring on any one trial, where probability is operationally understood as the relative frequency of each event given a long series of repetitions of such trials. Another way of saying this is that we want to know the fraction of times that each of the events should occur. It is consequently convenient to think of the complete set of probabilities (one for each event) as a unit quantity, some one large pie, where if one slice (one probability) is increased, the remainder must be decreased.

The Three Basic Axioms of Probability

A simple mathematical analog of relative occurrence, where the increase of one probability implies a decrease in at least one other probability, is found in the notion of the total of the probabilities summing to a constant. If one is increased, there has to be an equal decrease elsewhere, in order to keep the sum constant. The most convenient constant is the number one, so we make the following two assumptions (the first two axioms of probability).

Axiom 1. The probability of any event is between 0 and 1 inclusive.

$$0 \le P(A) \le 1, \tag{2.1}$$

where A is any event in the sample space.

Axiom 2. The sum of all of the probabilities equals 1.

$$P(A_1) + P(A_2) + \cdots + P(A_j) + \cdots + P(A_n) = 1, \tag{2.2}$$

where A_j is one of n mutually exclusive and exhaustive events in the sample space.

We call the complete set of all of the possible events the *sample space*. Still assuming that only one event can occur on any one trial, we might conceivably be interested in the question whether, out of some larger pool of possibilities (the sample space), one event from a smaller subset of the larger pool might occur (without being interested in identifying the unique member of the subset that does occur). For example, we might want to know whether our subjects make any errors at all. We have then expressed an interest (within our sample space, which includes 0 errors) in a subset that excludes 0. We phrase our problem as, "What is the probability that our subject makes at least one error?" We can calculate this probability by enumerating the probabilities of each of the alternative events within the subset of acceptable events [one or more errors, that is, $P(X = 1)$ or $P(X = 2)$ or $P(X = 3)$ or ...], and then using the following axiom to draw conclusions as to the probability of some undifferentiated member of this subset occurring.

Axiom 3. The probability of any among a subset of mutually exclusive events occurring is the sum of the probabilities of each of the members of the subset.

$$P(A_1 \text{ or } A_2 \text{ or } \cdots \text{ or } A_j \text{ or } \cdots \text{ or } A_n)$$
$$= P(A_1) + P(A_2) + \cdots + P(A_j) + \cdots + P(A_n), \qquad (2.3)$$

where A_j is any one of n mutually exclusive events in the sample space.

THE "OR" RELATION

Axiom 3 offers a mathematical analog for any theoretical statement about mutually exclusive outcomes where individual probabilities are known, but it is the probability of a class of events that is desired. It is the mathematical equivalent of the verbal statement of an "or" relation. It is used when we wish to know the probability of an event that is defined by results A_1, or A_2, or A_3, etc.

COMPLEMENTARY EVENTS AND THE "NOT" RELATION

An alternative way of solving some summation problems covered by Axiom 3 is to seek the complement of the probability of the events not in the subset.

The complement of a probability $P(X = r)$ is $1 - P(X = r)$. The complement is equivalent to "the probability that X does not equal r," since

$$1 - P(X = r)$$

is the probability of the set of all events other than X equal to r.

$$P(X \neq r) = 1 - P(X = r). \qquad (2.4)$$

Equation (2.4) can be proved by the use of Axioms 2 and 3.

Since an event either does or does not occur, $P(X = r)$ or $P(X \neq r)$ together constitute a complete partition of the sample space; that is, their enumeration exhausts all alternatives. From Axiom 3 we have

$$P(X = r \text{ or } X \neq r) = P(X = r) + P(X \neq r).$$

From the fact that this exhausts all possibilities, Axiom 2 suggests that

$$P(X = r) + P(X \neq r) = 1.$$

Subtracting $P(X = r)$ from both sides of this simple equation, we have Eq. (2.4). This theorem [Eq. (2.4)] presents a mathematical analog for theoretical statements about the probability of events *not* occurring.

If only one member of the sample space is excluded in the selection of a subset, the probability of a member of the subset occurring is often more easily arrived at by taking the complement of the excluded member than by enumerating and summing all of the members of the subset. For example, if the random variable could assume any value from 0 to infinity in our sample space of possible totals of errors, calculating the probability of at least one error from $1 - P(X = 0)$ might be simpler than taking the sum of the probabilities of all possible numbers of errors from 1 to infinity.

Conditional Probability

Our previous discussion utilized an assumption of some specific pool of possible events (the sample space), with the focus on some one event having an assigned probability that reflected the fact that the probability was relative to the other members of the total sample space. This can be symbolized as $P(X = r \mid S) = Y$, where S equals the sample space and the vertical line means "given," so that the resulting statement is "The probability that the random variable X equals some number r, given the sample space S, is Y."

If the sample space is clear and the random variable is clear, we can simply have $P(X = r \mid S) = P(X = r) = P(r) = Y$, signifying that the probability of r equals Y.

If we were to change the sample space, perhaps removing half of the possible events, it should be clear that the probability of the focal event would change. Axiom 3 required our looking at subsets of the whole sample space in grouping separate events and summing them to obtain the probability of this subset of events. It is also conceivable that we would be interested in the probability of a particular event, or further limited subset of events, relative to a reduced sample space, that is, relative to some subset of the whole sample space. For example, we might be interested in the probability of a subject making a particular number of errors, say 6, given that he made at least 1 error. The original sample space would contain all possible outcomes for individual subjects, 0, 1, ..., n errors (with n the total number of trials, therefore limiting the total number of errors possible). We could symbolize this as $P(X = 6 \mid S) = P(X = 6) = P(6)$. Defining the probability via relative frequency, we would have

$$P(6) = \frac{f(6)}{f(0) + f(1) + f(2) + \cdots + f(n)}.$$

If there were 100 subjects, and 30 had made 6 errors, the relative frequency of 6 errors would be

$$P(6) = \tfrac{30}{100} = \tfrac{3}{10},$$

giving us the probability of a subject in that population having made 6 errors. However, if we wanted the conditional probability of the subject having made 6 errors, given that he made at least 1 error, we would have a new probability, provided that some subjects had actually had 0 errors. Let us assume that 10 subjects had 0 errors. This would give us a reduced population of 90 subjects, by excluding those that made 0 errors. That is, the relative frequency definition of probability would give us a decreased denominator:

$$P(X = 6 \mid E) = \frac{f(6)}{f(1) + f(2) + \cdots + f(n)} = \frac{30}{90} = \frac{1}{3}. \tag{2.5}$$

Joint Events

In the example just given, our sample space was reduced through a consideration of admissible scores on the critical variable (the outcomes whose probabilities we were examining). We constructed our new sample space from a subset of the original sample space on the basis of errors, using the criterion of at least one error to establish a new reduced sample space. We then examined the probabilities of particular numbers of errors in this reduced sample space. It is also possible to find subsets on the basis of the subjects' performance on other tasks, or scores on other dimensions, or the occurrence of certain variable experimental conditions, etc. For example, suppose that the subjects were reinforced on some trials but not on others, and we were interested in whether subjects had a different probability of being correct, depending on whether or not they had been reinforced on the previous trial. We would then want the probability based on a new sample space limited to trial outcomes that were immediately preceded by a reinforced trial. We shall identify the additional event qualifying our sample space as the *conditional* event and symbolize it as C. We shall assume that the occurrence of the conditional event will limit the number of ways that the other event (symbolized O) can occur. The new sample space will be limited to the original sample space or a smaller subset. This means that in a relative frequency interpretation of probability, the conditional probability $P(O \mid C)$, would have a probability constructed from the frequency with which there is a joint occurrence of these two events $f(OC)$ divided by the reduced sample space consisting of the total number of occurrences of C, that is, $f(C)$. In equation form,

$$P(O \mid C) = \frac{f(OC)}{f(C)}. \tag{2.6}$$

To be able to deal in terms of probabilities on both sides of Eq. (2.6), we divide the numerator and denominator of the right-hand side of Eq. (2.6) by the size of the original sample space, the total number of all outcomes, which gives us

$$P(O|C) = \frac{P(OC)}{P(C)}. \tag{2.7}$$

To define $P(OC)$, we simply multiply both sides of Eq. (2.7) by $P(C)$, obtaining

$$P(OC) = P(O|C) \cdot P(C). \tag{2.8}$$

We define $P(OC)$ as the probability that O has occurred, given that C has occurred, times the probability that C actually occurred. Its meaning is simply the probability that they have both occurred, which implies that

$$P(OC) = P(CO). \tag{2.9}$$

Analogously to Eq. (2.7), we have

$$P(C|O) = \frac{P(CO)}{P(O)} \tag{2.10}$$

and

$$P(CO) = P(C|O) \cdot P(O). \tag{2.11}$$

Combining Eqs. (2.8), (2.9), and (2.11) we have

$$P(O|C) \cdot P(C) = P(C|O) \cdot P(O), \tag{2.12}$$

although we see from Eqs. (2.7) and (2.10) that, in general,

$$P(O|C) \neq P(C|O) \tag{2.13}$$

unless $P(C) = P(O)$.

INDEPENDENCE

We can think of a conditional probability as a probability following from some "additional" information about the event in question. There might be one probability of a correct response on trial $n + 1$, $P(S_{n+1})$, and a different probability $P(S_{n+1}|S_n)$, given the knowledge that the subject had been correct on the previous response. Our previous discussion of conditional probability indicated that we cannot automatically assume an equality between $P(O|C)$ and $P(O)$.

An inequality between a conditional and an unconditional probability of the same event suggests that being in possession of information about the conditional event requires changing our expectation as to the probabilities of outcomes of the event. Conversely, having the conditional and unconditional probabilities equal suggests that knowledge of the outcome of the event on which the probability is conditional does not change the predictions (probabilities). In other words, when knowledge of the outcome of one event does not change our predictions about the likelihood of another event, these two events are *independent*. In summary form, we have the following definition of independence.

Events O and C are independent if

$$P(O|C) = P(O). \tag{2.14}$$

THE "AND" RELATION

Our defining equation for $P(OC)$, Eq. (2.8), when combined with Eq. (2.14), which defines independence, gives us the equality

$$P(OC) = P(O) \cdot P(C) \tag{2.15}$$

if events O and C are independent.

Equation (2.15) gives us the important and often used theorem that *the probability of the joint occurrence of independent events is simply the product of their individual probabilities of occurrence*. We then have the probability theory analog for the conjunctive relation in our verbalized theory, with the implication that a theoretical statement of an " and " relation (the probability that O *and* C occur) is analogous mathematically to multiplication, provided that the events are independent.

When the events are not independent, we simply return to Eq. (2.8), which defines the joint event, which holds with or without independence [since, given independence, it reduces to (2.15)]. If we had to deal with more than two events, where independence could not be assumed, we could extend Eq. (2.8) in the following way:

$$P(OCD) = P(O|CD) \cdot P(CD),$$
$$P(OCD) = P(O|CD) \cdot P(C|D) \cdot P(D), \tag{2.16}$$
$$P(OCDE) = P(O|CDE) \cdot P(CDE),$$
$$P(OCDE) = P(O|CDE) \cdot P(C|DE) \cdot P(D|E) \cdot P(E), \tag{2.17}$$
$$\vdots$$

Given the definition of independence in Eq. (2.14), and extending it so that it includes events whose probabilities are conditional upon several events, we can extend Eq. (2.15) the following way:

$$P(OCD) = P(O) \cdot P(C) \cdot P(D) \tag{2.18}$$

if events O, C, and D are all independent of each other, individually and collectively.

$$P(OCDE) = P(O) \cdot P(C) \cdot P(D) \cdot P(E) \qquad (2.19)$$

if events O, C, D, and E are all independent of each other, individually and collectively.

THE "OR" RELATION WITH JOINT EVENTS

Given that we had the probabilities of all of the joint events that are possible in some situation, we could use a theorem analogous to Axiom 3 to obtain the probability of the one common event between them. We sum the probabilities of each of the ways that some event can occur (each time in conjunction with some other event) until we have summed all of the ways in which the common event could occur, and this gives us the probability of the common event occurring. The common event can occur either one way, or another way, or another, etc., until all of the possible ways that it can occur have been exhausted.

Suppose that we run two different strains of rats in an experiment, maze-bright and maze-dull rats. The experimental situation utilizes a Skinner-box discrimination. We randomly select a rat from either of the two groups, with a probability $P(B) = \frac{1}{2}$ of obtaining a maze-bright rat and a probability $P(D) = \frac{1}{2}$ of obtaining a maze-dull rat. We wish to know the probability of their succeeding in making a response during a brief time interval during which a discriminative stimulus is present. Let us speak of the probability of a correctly timed response $P(C)$ and the probability of an incorrectly timed response $P(I)$. There are then two ways in which a correctly timed response could occur: A maze-bright rat is selected and responds correctly (CB) and a maze-dull rat is selected and responds correctly (CD). The probability of a correctly timed response is then $P(C) = P(CB) + P(CD)$. If maze-bright and maze-dull rats perform equally well in this Skinner-box discrimination, this discrimination performance is independent of breeding for maze performance, and using Eq. (2.15) for the joint probabilities, we have

$$P(C) = P(B) \cdot P(C) + P(D) \cdot P(C). \qquad (2.20)$$

In general, with any number of ways in which an event X can happen, say K ways, we have

$$P(X) = P(XA_1) + P(XA_2) + \cdots + P(XA_K). \qquad (2.21)$$

Whether we use Eq. (2.15) or Eq. (2.8) to define each joint probability depends on whether or not we can assume independence.

We can illustrate the difference between independent and dependent instances of our maze-bright and maze-dull rats in a Skinner box by the use of a tree diagram. Figures 2.1 and 2.2 illustrate the alternatives, and their respective probabilities, at each point in the sequence of possible outcomes.

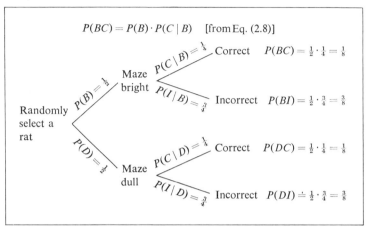

Figure 2.1. Independence.
$P(B) = P(D) = \frac{1}{2}$, $P(C|B) = P(C|D) = \frac{1}{4}$, $P(I|B) = P(I|D) = \frac{3}{4}$.

To obtain $P(C)$ in Figure 2.1, we use Eq. (2.21), summing the two probabilities of the two ways that a correct response could occur (that is, via a maze-bright or a maze-dull rat). Thus,

$$P(C) = P(BC) + P(DC),$$
$$P(C) = \tfrac{1}{8} + \tfrac{1}{8} = \tfrac{1}{4}.$$

We can see from the tree diagram that $P(C|B) = \frac{1}{4}$ and that $P(C|D) = \frac{1}{4}$. In fact, without regard to the previous event, $P(C) = \frac{1}{4}$, meeting the criterion of independence in Eq. (2.14).

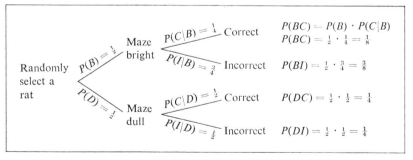

Figure 2.2. Dependence.
$P(B) = P(D) = \frac{1}{2}$, $P(C|B) = \frac{1}{4}$, $P(I|B) = \frac{3}{4}$, $P(C|D) = P(I|D) = \frac{1}{2}$.

Using Eq. (2.21) again, we can see that in Figure 2.2,

$$P(C) = \tfrac{1}{8} + \tfrac{1}{4} = \tfrac{3}{8},$$

and this does not equal $P(C|B)$ or $P(C|D)$. Here we have a case of dependence. With no information on the first event, we would determine the probability of a correct response to be $\frac{3}{8}$. If we had a maze-bright rat, we would assume the probability of a correct response to be $\frac{1}{4}$, if a maze-dull one, $\frac{1}{2}$.

Note that in both Figure 2.1 and Figure 2.2, the probability of the joint event at the end of any one branch of the tree is the product of the probabilities along the branch. Although the probability of being correct is conditional upon the previous events along that branch in the dependent case, in the case of independence, a particular outcome probability at a point in the process is independent of the branch in which it occurs. In both cases the outcome is a product of the sequence of probabilities, but with dependence, conditional probabilities are used.

We have been speaking in terms of sequences of events. However, the time dimension is not a necessary factor. It is really only important to distinguish those instances in which determination of one event changes the probability of a second event, from those situations where such knowledge does not affect predictions. The event designated "second" depends on which is the event being predicted and which is the event for which some information is obtainable. The actual sequence of the events is not relevant here.

The "And/Or" Relationship

In our original mathematical formulations of an " or " relation, Eq. (2.3), we were restricted to a set of mutually exclusive probabilities. That is, A_1, or A_2, or A_3, etc., with no possibility of both A_1 and A_2. However, we shall encounter instances in which we have an " or " relationship to be mathematically analogized, but where a joint occurrence is not necessarily excluded. We term this an *and/or* relationship.

Our discussion of joint events has given us the tools necessary for estimating the probabilities of the joint event alternatives, so we can now present the mathematical equivalent of an " and/or " statement. The proof can be found in most elementary discussions of probability theory, and utilizes set theory. It can also be intuitively appreciated with the use of Venn diagrams. We shall merely present the correct formula here.

$$P(A_1 \text{ and/or } A_2) = P(A_1) + (A_2) - P(A_1 A_2). \tag{2.22}$$

If the two events turn out to actually be mutually exclusive, then $P(A_1 A_2)$ equals 0, and we again have Eq. (2.3).

Extending Eq. (2.22) to an instance with three possible events, we have

$$\begin{aligned} P(A_1 \text{ and/or } A_2 \text{ and/or } A_3) \\ = P(A_1) + P(A_2) + P(A_3) - P(A_1 A_2) \\ - P(A_1 A_3) - P(A_2 A_3) + P(A_1 A_2 A_3). \end{aligned} \tag{2.23}$$

PROBABILITY DISTRIBUTIONS

Before proceeding with the direct application of the foregoing axioms and theorems of probability to the generation of mathematical model formulas, it will probably be helpful to examine the concept of a distribution of probabilities.

We shall examine the graphical and statistical aspects of probability distributions. On the statistical side, we shall concern ourselves with the mean and variance of distributions, the word "statistics" here connoting a term that singly represents a collection of data, or some aspect of the data (such as central tendency, or the degree of variability around that central tendency).

Unique Shapes of Probability Distributions

If a set of possible random variable values were placed on the x axis of a graph, with the probability of each random variable value plotted parallel to the y axis, we would have a graph of a probability distribution of the possible values. For example, the probability of the first trial as the trial of the last error in a difficult task would be less than the probability of some later trial as the trial of the last error. However, given an easy task, such as a paired-associate learning task with only two responses possible, so that every stimulus is associated with either the number one or the number two, each item might be very quickly learned. We might find no errors, or the first trial might be the most likely trial of the last error for a particular stimulus, with subsequent trials less probable as the trial of the last error. Figure 2.3 is an example of such a distribution, taken from Bower (1961, p. 272).

Assume that we were to graph a variety of such probability distributions, having the possible random variables on the x axis, and their individual probabilities plotted parallel with the y axis. A line drawn between the various probability values to give some continuous appearance to the probability distribution would probably assume a different shape for each different experimental situation or each different aspect of a constant experimental situation. We would then compare data with theory at each point in this distribution to see how good our theory is as a predictor.

When developing these distributions, it will be convenient to recognize certain frequently recurring distributions for which distribution formulas have already been developed.

Recurrent Probability Distributions

There are a number of distribution shapes that occur with high frequency and that have readily ascertainable statistical properties. That is, the mean, the variance, and other characteristic values of the distribution can be deter-

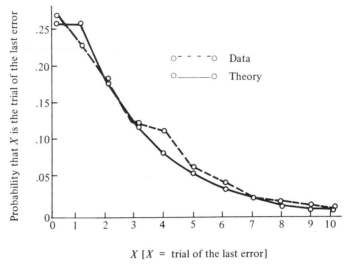

X [X = trial of the last error]

Figure 2.3.[1]

mined from formulas containing the same parameters as the distribution formula, but having different forms.

The two most common distributions in the mathematical models of learning literature are the *binomial* and the *geometric* distributions. They are, in fact, so convenient to use that it is often desirable to recategorize data and redefine sample spaces, so that the newly categorized or defined events will be expected to occur with frequencies characteristic of the binomial or geometric distributions.

Since the binomial distribution is exemplified in, and frequently identified with, the probability distribution for the number of successes in a sequence of Bernoulli trials, and the geometric distribution can be similarly identified with the probability distribution for the first success in a series of Bernoulli trials, it will be helpful to look at the concept of Bernoulli trials.

BERNOULLI TRIALS

Whenever outcomes of trials evolve as each trial takes place, the outcome of any one trial being individually unpredictable, we have a stochastic (random) process. If there are only two possible outcomes on any one trial of a stochastic series, so that the probability of success is the complement of the probability of failure, and if the probabilities of each of these possible outcomes each remains constant from trial to trial, we have a series of Bernoulli trials. The outcome on any one trial is *independent* of the outcome on all other trials.

[1] From Bower (1961). By permission of the Psychometric Society.

Repartitioning Sample Spaces into Dichotomies

Although a sequence of events conforming to these probabilistic requirements may appear to be rare, it is actually frequently possible to repartition a sample space of possible outcomes so that the necessary assumptions for a Bernoulli trials process are met (given that we are initially dealing with a stochastic process).

The necessary dichotomy is obtained by simply considering some one outcome to constitute success, and all else, that is, any other outcome, to constitute failure (or, conversely, the one outcome is called failure and all else is called success, the principle being a dichotomization into one identifiable outcome versus all other possibilities). We can speak of avoidance versus escape from shock (rather than the continuous categorization of time from signal to jumping a barrier), or correct versus incorrect recall of an item in its correct sequence in the rote memorization of a list of words (rather than the sequential number of the word recalled), etc.

Constancy of Probabilities

The more difficult assumption to meet is that of a constant probability of success (and its complement, failure). Where this is seen to vary during an experiment, it is sometimes seen to vary as the direct result of some particular event. For example, we might expect that the probability of a correct response in some discrimination learning task, or dichotomous choice problem, etc., would be the same all the while that a subject in an experiment is guessing, but that it might cease to be that same value after some learning has occurred. The principle, then, where there is some specific reason to assume a change in some event's probability, is to identify a limited set of circumstances during which the probabilities remain constant. In this way, we would speak of a Bernoulli trials process during guessing, and another Bernoulli trials process after some specifiable state of learning has been reached or after new experimental conditions are introduced, etc. When we cannot identify the variables, or points in time, at which the probabilities of success or failure change, at least theoretically, then we are unable to use such an analysis fruitfully. Since there are models for dealing with continuous changes in probability, all is not lost, but these would not use Bernoulli trial processes as the central analytic conception (see Chapter Four).

Once we have defined the circumstances that would represent a Bernoulli trials process, our next question would be directed toward identifying the specific single probability value that constitutes the probability of "success" and its complement, the probability of "failure." For the moment, let us identify these two probabilities as p and q, respectively, so that we have the probability of success as

$$p = 1 - q.$$

The Binomial Distribution

Identifying the probability of success on any one trial in a Bernoulli distribution as p, let us look at the probability of two successes in two consecutive trials. This would be p times p or p^2. That is, following Eq. (2.15), the probability of the joint occurrence of two independent events is the product of their individual probabilities of occurrence. The probability of two failures in two consecutive trials follows as q^2. But what about the probability of one success and one failure? This can occur in two different ways, either as a success and then a failure, or a failure and then a success, the former having a probability pq and the latter having the equivalent probability qp. From Eq. (2.3) we have the probability of one success and one failure in two consecutive trials as $pq + qp = 2pq$. We could pursue this to any specific number of consecutive trials, and all of its possible outcomes with their individual probabilities. For three consecutive trials, we would have three successes as having probability p^3, two successes as having probability $ppq + pqp + qpp = 3qp^2$, one success as having probability $qqp + qpq + pqq = 3pq^2$, and zero successes as having probability q^3.

We can recognize the binomial expansion as the generator of the appropriate probabilities for each of the possible outcomes. [The binomial expansion is the sum of terms equivalent to a term $(p + q)^n$ when the term in parentheses has been raised to the nth power.]

$$(p + q)^1 = p + q,$$
$$(p + q)^2 = p^2 + 2pq + q^2,$$
$$(p + q)^3 = p^3 + 3p^2q + 3pq^2 + q^3.$$

The right-hand equivalence for $(p + q)^3$ then offers, in sequence, the probability of three successes, two successes, one success, and zero successes, in three trials.

In general, we would find that

$$(p + q)^n = \sum_{j=0}^{n} \binom{n}{j} p^j q^{n-j},$$

where

$$\binom{n}{j} = \frac{n!}{j!(n-j)!}. \tag{2.24a}$$

The formula for a particular number of successes, say j, in n trials of a Bernoulli series is consequently

$$B(j; n, p) = \binom{n}{j} p^j q^{n-j}. \tag{2.24b}$$

Since $p + q = 1$ we have $(p + q)^n = 1$ for any n, and so we meet the assumption of probability Axiom 2 that the probabilities of all of the possible outcomes (for a particular number of trials) sum to 1.

We now have an interesting result. Any sequence of n trials with only one of two outcomes possible on any one trial, and with a constant probability of p for one of the events, will have the same probability distribution regardless of the actual nature of the events that have been dichotomously categorized. The ease with which events can generally be categorized into success or failure makes this a simple way to convert data into a very general statement for which formal systems of analysis have been worked out independently of the experimental particulars. Mathematicians have examined the binomial distribution and have created formulas relating to it that we can take advantage of, given that the data have been cast into this distribution.

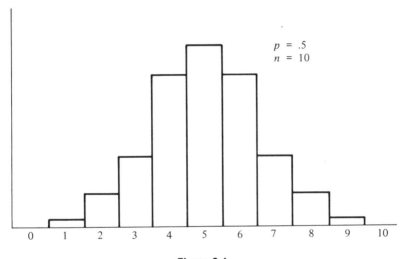

Figure 2.4.

Assume a very frequent repetition of a series of n Bernoulli trials with probability of success p. On any one such series, there can be any number of successes from 0 to n, and over many repetitions of the series, a relative frequency for each number of successes. The relative frequencies offer a graph of the binomial distribution with probability p and n trials. In Figure 2.4 we see a graph of the binomial distribution with $p = .5$ and $n = 10$. We can see that 0 and 10 successes occur very seldom relative to the others, whereas 5 occurs most frequently. In fact, we speak of 5 as the expected value over the long run of series of 10 trials, and therefore the expected value and best single prediction for any one such series. Figure 2.5 has the same value for p, but a smaller n, that is, $n = 6$. Here we see that the least expected values, the

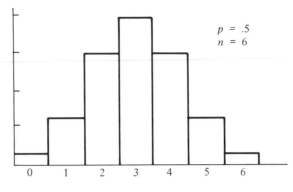

Figure 2.5.

most extreme values possible in a series of six (0 and 6 successes), still occur with some measurable frequency. With a series of 10, the most extreme values (0 and 10) are very rare. However, the expected number of successes, the most probable on any one trial, with $n = 6$ and $p = .5$, is 3.

If we look at Figure 2.6 we see that changing the value of p (the probability of success) changes the shape of the graph more drastically than does a

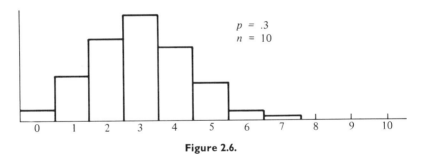

Figure 2.6.

change in n. We now see, in comparing Figures 2.4 and 2.6, that decreasing p decreases the probability of a large number of successes, and now the expected number of successes is 3, with 8, 9, and 10 all very unlikely numbers of successes (in 10 trials with the probability of success .3).

We can see that the binomial distribution offers a family of distributions, where each distribution is a function of both n and p. We call n and p the parameters of the distribution. Any general formulas of expectations for the binomial distribution will have to include these parameters, to identify which member of the family of binomial distributions is being examined.

Let us look at the expected number of successes for the binomial distribution. We shall use the capital letter E for "expectation," the capital sigma $\sum$ for "sum" and T_j for "Trial j."

The expectation on any one trial, we saw in our discussion of expected values, is the sum of the products of the probability of each random variable value times each one's respective probability. But what random variable values should we use? On any one trial, a success does or does not occur. If it does, it will add 1 to our later summation of successes; if it does not, it will add 0. We therefore give a success the random variable value 1 and a failure 0. For any trial j, we have

$$E(T_j) = 1 \cdot P(1) + 0 \cdot P(0),$$
$$E(T_j) = P(1).$$

This gives us the expectation on any one trial. But we wish the expected sum over n trials, rather than the random variable value expectation on one trial. We therefore sum this expectation over all n trials:

$$E \sum_{j=1}^{n} (T_j) = \sum_{j=1}^{n} E(T_j) = \sum_{j=1}^{n} P(1).$$

Since $P(1)$ is a constant, we sum n of this constant, which gives us n times the constant, so

$$E \sum_{j=1}^{n} (T_j) = np,$$
$$\text{mean} = np \tag{2.25}$$

for a binomial distribution with probability of success p and n trials.

Since the expected sum over n trials is the expected value, this is the mean value for that binomial distribution with probability of success p and n trials.

We have thus derived the formula for the expected number of successes in a binomial distribution, and the formula is sufficiently flexible to reflect the different expectations for distributions with different n and p values.

Just as we have derived the expected number of successes, the mean, for the binomial distribution, we can also derive the variance for the binomial distribution. This would be seen to be

$$\sigma^2 = npq \tag{2.26}$$

for a binomial distribution with probability of success p and n trials.

The Geometric Distribution

Whereas the binomial distribution is concerned with numbers of successes in some finite number of n trials (limiting the actual number of successes to n), the geometric distribution assumes the possibility of an infinite number of trials. It maps the probability of the first success occurring on any trial from 1 to infinity. We could graph the probability of the first success occurring on trial 1, and the probability of it occurring on trial 2, and on trial 3, etc., up through any conceivable number. Clearly, if the probability p of success on any one trial is large, the probability of later trials being the trial of the first success is small. If p is quite small, then an early trial is unlikely to be the trial of the first success, and some later trial is more likely. Clearly, the relevant parameter for this distribution's expectations is p. In keeping with this fact, we find that the formulas for the mean and variance of the geometric distribution contain only the parameter p (and q, which equals $1 - p$).

$$\text{Mean} = \frac{1}{p} \tag{2.27}$$

for a geometric distribution with probability of success p.

$$\sigma^2 = \frac{q}{p^2} \tag{2.28}$$

for a geometric distribution with probability of success p.

To concretize this probability distribution, we can look at the probability distribution for the first correct response in a series of Bernoulli trials where the probability of success $p = .5$.

The probability of any trial n being the trial of the first correct response would simply be $(.5)^n$ [from Eq. (2.15)]. The probability distribution's graph would begin with the first probability (the one above $x = 1$) as .5, the next (the one above $x = 2$) as .25, the next as .125, etc., quickly approaching 0 probability for later trials as the trial of the first correct response. The expected trial of the first correct response, that is, the mean of the trials of the first correct response if we were to repeat this data gathering for many subjects (all having the same p value), would be $1/.5 = 2$, and the variance would be $.5/(.5)^2 = .5/.25 = 2$ [from Eqs. (2.27) and (2.28), respectively].

If the probability of success was, say $p = .9$, the probabilities for $x = 1, 2, 3,$ and 4 would be, respectively, $(.9) \cdot (.1)^0 = .9; (.9) \cdot (.1)^1 = .09; (.9) \cdot (.1)^2 = .009;$ and $(.9) \cdot (.1)^3 = .0009$. The power to which $(.1)$ is raised represents the number of trials in which an error occurs before the first success (with probability $1 - p = q = 1 - .9 = .1$ for each such unsuccessful trial). The expected trial of the first correct response, the mean over many repetitions of the experiment, would be $1/.9 = 1.1$, with the variance equal to $.1/.9^2 = .1/.81 = .12$. This small variance would appear to be correct from the apparent difference in the probabilities for the first and subsequent trials. That is, the first trial would almost always be the trial of the first correct response.

Reversing the probabilities of p and q, with p now equal to .1, we would have as the probabilities of the trial of the first success (beginning with $x = 1$): $(.1) \cdot (.9)^0 = .1; (.1) \cdot (.9)^1 = .09; (.1) \cdot (.9)^2 = .081; (.1) \cdot (.9)^3 = .072;$ etc. The first success, when the probability of success is equal to .1, would probably come after many trials. The expected trial of the first success would be $1/.1 =$ 10 and the variance would be $.9/.1^2 = .9/.01 = 90$. This very large variance can be seen as reasonable, given the very small probability of any one trial being the trial of the first success. (Note that we speak of the probability of a correct response on any single trial as being constant, but that the probability of being the *first* correct response is not constant over trials, since the probability of the correct response may be constant, but the probability of no previous correct responses will be different, depending on the length of the preceding series of trials.)

We can see from the particular examples of the geometric distribution that we have presented that the general formula is

$$P(X = n) = p \cdot q^{n-1} \tag{2.29}$$

for trial n as the trial of the first success in a Bernoulli series with a probability of success p.

We have called the dichotomization success and failure, although it should be clear that any verbal dichotomy would do. The geometric distribution is frequently described as a distribution of waiting times, since it maps the probability of waiting $n - 1$ times before a given event first occurs.

THE USE OF DISTRIBUTION FORMULAS

The experimenter can take some representative of a relevant distribution (such as its mean or variance) and equate this with an empirical value. The formula will contain some parameter values, and by the theoretical and empirical equivalence he can usually obtain values for the parameters within the formula. These same parameters will also appear in the formula for individual points in the distribution, allowing the experimenter to then predict the entire distribution. For example, the mean of the binomial distribution is np, and we also know that the individual distribution points (each identified as some jth point on the x axis) would be $\binom{n}{j}p^j(1 - p)^{n-j}$. Having the value of np from an empirical mean value, we can obtain the value of the parameter p (n is usually an experimentally controlled constant). This distribution can also offer insights into other distributions of the same theory. Equations for predicted distributions of the same theory generally have many, or most, parameters in common. Establishing values for one distribution can therefore usually aid in the establishment of values for another.

THE DIRECT METHOD

We have to build our distributions, and obtain our expected mean values and other statistics, by translating our verbalized theory into mathematical equations. For this reason we were careful earlier in the chapter to point out the mathematical analogies to such relational terms as "or" and "and." We use the probability calculus because the events with which we deal are all probabilistic. In fact, one method that we use for developing equations for probability distributions is simply a direct translation of our verbalized theory into the language of probability. We therefore identify this method as the *direct method*. Since our theories tend to be couched even informally in probabilistic terms, the translation is not a difficult one conceptually. In later sections of this text we shall introduce methods that are less direct. In these other methods we obtain our equation forms by recognizing analogies between classes of equations and the verbalizations in our theories. With the direct method, we apply the mathematical operations implied by our theory's axioms to the variables of the theory, and the result is some useful equations.

Bower (1961) developed a theory to which the direct method may be readily applied. The theory itself is a tour de force in the use of a minimum of assumption and a maximum of prediction. In this early state of theoretical development in psychology, our theories will most frequently be over-simplifications of the principles obtaining in natural circumstances. We therefore do not introduce this model for its substantive importance. Rather, it represents an extraordinarily good example of how far insightful mathematical model development can take even the simplest of theoretical systems. The substantive simplicity makes it easier to discern the mathematical ingenuity involved, and consequently makes it the best single example for pedagogical purposes. We shall therefore rely heavily on this theory and its model for examples in this chapter and in Chapter Six.

We shall now look at Bower's theory and use the method of direct translation from verbalizations into probabilistic equations to which we alluded earlier.

The Theory Underlying Bower's One-Element Model

Let us assume a paired-associate learning paradigm where the responses are a small number of already familiar items, such as the numbers one and two. Since on each trial the stimulus item is present for the subject, the only thing that he has to learn is which of the two responses goes with each of the stimuli. In Bower's theory, it is assumed that the "connection" between each stimulus and each response is learned as an all-or-none phenomenon. Once learning of a particular pair takes place, there is no further learning and no loss of learning. Thus, for each stimulus–response pair, we can think of a dichotomy of possibilities. The stimulus–response pair is either conditioned or not conditioned. If the pair is conditioned, it is assumed that the subject always responds correctly to that item. If the pair is not conditioned (which is the only other possibility), then it is assumed that the subject can only be correct by guessing. The model makes the further assumption that the probability of a correct guess in the nonconditioned state is a constant, $1/N$, where N is the number of alternative responses, the probability of an incorrect guess then being $1 - 1/N$ (here equaling one half). The only other variable to be considered is a parameter that would have to be estimated from the data and is symbolized by the letter c. This is the probability of going from the nonconditioned state to the conditioned state, that is, the probability of the all-or-none learning taking place on any one trial. It is assumed that the subject begins in the nonconditioned state for each stimulus–response pair. The axioms of the theory loosely stated above are taken from the theory that Bower modeled and that we now present more formally.

AXIOMS OF THE THEORY UNDERLYING BOWER'S MODEL

Axiom 1. Each item may be represented by a single stimulus element which is sampled on every trial (that is, on every run through of the paired-associate list).

Axiom 2. The stimulus element is in either of two states: C (conditioned to the correct response) or G (not conditioned).

Axiom 3. On each trial, the probability of a transition from G to C is a constant $c > 0$ (and is thus independent of the trial number and outcomes of previous trials). The probability of remaining in the conditioned state is 1; that is, once in the conditioned state, that stimulus stays in that state.

Axiom 4. If the element is in state C, then the probability of a correct response is 1 (and therefore the probability of an error is 0). If the element is in state G, the probability of a correct response is $1/N$, where N is the number of response alternatives [and therefore the probability of an error is $1 - 1/N = (N - 1)/N$].

Axiom 5. The subject begins in the guessing state on Trial 1, with reference to each stimulus. (Although the probability of being in the guessing state on the first trial is 1, the probability of being in the guessing state on the following trial is $1 - c$, that is, 1 minus the probability of entering the only other state possible, the conditioned state, as implied in Axiom 3.)

REINFORCEMENT IN BOWER'S THEORY

It might be helpful to note that the term "reinforcement" is used very broadly here. It is not used to denote a stimulus whose presence would tend to increase the frequency of only a previously emitted response (as it would be, for example, in an operant frame of reference). Rather, the reinforcement is seen as effective for a particular response regardless of the response just previously emitted.

THE ROLE OF THE RESPONSE IN THE BOWER MODEL

The response is seen as an indication of learning. It is not a participant in the learning process, but a result of the learning.

LIMITATIONS OF BOWER'S THEORY

It should be apparent from Axiom 3 that forgetting is not a possibility within the Bower theory. You may be disturbed by the apparent limitations of such a theory, in that there are not many situations in which we can make the assumption of no forgetting. However, it is not the purpose of this theory to explain or describe all learning situations, or even all paired-associate learning paradigms. The model stemming from this theory, like all current mathematical models of learning, attempts to predict some limited describable circumstances. If the predictions are successful, the model can always be extended through the introduction of additional, or altered, axioms into the theory. The question is, does the theory predict the probabilities (that is, the relative frequencies) of events in a realizable learning situation that does fit the axiomatic limitations?

Application of the Direct Method to Bower's Theory

In this paired-associate paradigm, we can dichotomize any trial as resulting in either an error or a success.

Let us symbolize the random variable taking on different values for success or error as Q_n, where n represents the particular trial under consideration. The random variable values can be 1 (for error) or 0 (for success), so that we can later sum the random variable values accumulated over trials to determine the total number of errors for a subject.

$P(Q_n = 1) =$ the probability of an error on trial n.

$P(Q_n = 0) =$ the probability of success on trial n.

Note that if we knew the state that the subject was in for a particular stimulus, that is, conditioned or not conditioned, these two probabilities would be identifiable without regard to the trial number, from Axiom 4 of Bower's theory, allowing us to dispense with n. When we do not know which state the subject is in relative to a particular stimulus, then we require the value of n, in order to incorporate the probability of each state.

Developing Probabilistic Equations for Theoretical Statements

We first define and symbolize some probability statements, such as the probability of an error on trial n. We illustrate this in the following paragraphs, combining simple statements into complex statements using the previously discussed "or," "and," "and/or," and "not" rules, as well as other useful equivalences from the probability calculus.

The Probability of an Error on the nth Trial

On the nth trial, the subject is in either the conditioned state C or the nonconditioned state G (the guessing state). There are thus two conditional probabilities of making an error, one given the conditioned state $[P(Q_n = 1 | C_n)]$ and one given the nonconditioned state $[P(Q_n = 1 | G_n)]$. Equations (2.8) and (2.21) suggest the equivalence

$$P(Q_n = 1) = P(Q_n = 1 | C_n) \cdot P(C_n) + P(Q_n = 1 | G_n) \cdot P(G_n). \qquad (2.30)$$

Having restated an implication (a theorem) of the theory in general mathematical form in Eq. (2.30), we can now attempt greater specificity for our symbols in the equation in order to obtain specific parameter representations.

Since the probability of making an error while in the conditioned state is 0 (Axiom 4 of Bower's theory), the first component on the right-hand side of Eq. (2.30) is 0. The second component includes the probability of an error in the nonconditioned state, $P(Q_n = 1 | G_n)$, which yields the equivalence (again from Axiom 4)

$$P(Q_n = 1 | G_n) = 1 - \frac{1}{N}. \qquad (2.31)$$

This second component also includes the probability of being in the nonconditioned state on trial n, $P(G_n)$, which requires some discussion.

If the subject has been conditioned to the particular hypothetical stimulus at any time before trial n, the subject would still be in the conditioned state (Axiom 3 of Bower's theory). Consequently, $P(G_n)$ requires that the subject be in the nonconditioned state on all previous trials.

He is in the nonconditioned state on the first trial with probability 1, but remains there on the second trial with probability $1 - c$ (from Axiom 3 of Bower's theory, as discussed in Axiom 5). All future trials keep him in the guessing state with the same $1 - c$ on each additional trial. Extending Eq. (2.8) as we did in Eqs. (2.16) and (2.17), we would obtain

$$
\begin{aligned}
P(G_n G_{n-1} &\cdots G_2 G_1) \\
&= P(G_n | G_{n-1} \cdots G_2 G_1) \cdot P(G_{n-1} | \cdots G_2 G_1) \cdots P(G_2 | G_1) \cdot P(G_1) \\
&= (1 - c)^{n-1} \cdot 1 \\
&= (1 - c)^{n-1},
\end{aligned}
$$

which is the probability that the subject is in the guessing state on the nth trial, which implies that

$$P(G_n) = (1 - c)^{n-1}. \tag{2.32}$$

In essence, we have used the fact that a probability of 1 of entering the first trial in the guessing state, times the probability $(1 - c)$ of entering the second trial in the guessing state, times the probability $(1 - c)$ of entering the third trial in the guessing state from a guessing state in the second trial, etc., yields a product of $(1 - c)$ multiplied against itself $n - 1$ times (for an "and" relation).

We can now write a parameter value equivalent of Eq. (2.30), which will give us the probability of the subject making an error on the nth trial in terms of parameter values. To do this, we merely substitute Eqs. (2.31) and (2.32) appropriately into Eq. (2.30), remembering that the first component in the sum in Eq. (2.30) is eliminated as a result of having been multiplied by 0. We then have

$$P(Q_n = 1) = \left(1 - \frac{1}{N}\right) \cdot (1 - c)^{n-1}.$$

Let us assume that E_n represents an error on trial n. Thus

$$P(E_n) = \left(1 - \frac{1}{N}\right) \cdot (1 - c)^{n-1}. \tag{2.33}$$

The Probability of an Error Being Made on Trials n and n + k

If we wanted the probability that an error will be made on trial n and will be followed by an error k trials later, we could symbolize this as $P(E_{n, n+k})$.

In order for an error to occur on any trial, Axiom 4 indicates that the subject must be in the nonconditioned state on that trial (with reference to that particular stimulus). In fact, in this instance, it is necessary that the subject be in the nonconditioned state specifically on trial $n + k$, and Axiom 3 indicates that this would imply that the subject had been in the nonconditioned state on all previous trials. Thus, establishing the probability that the subject was in the nonconditioned state on trial $n + k$ would also establish it for trial n. The probability of an error on trial n or on trial $n + k$, given that the subject is in the nonconditioned state, is in each case a conditional probability, and can be symbolized

$$P(Q_n = 1 \mid G_n) \quad \text{and} \quad P(Q_{n+k} = 1 \mid G_{n+k}),$$

respectively. But we know from Axiom 4 that this is constant, independent of trial number and previous events (given the nonconditioned state). We therefore have two independent events, and we want the probability of their both occurring, given the nonconditioned state. Axiom 4 tells us that it is $1 - 1/N$ for one trial, and Eq. (2.15) indicates that it is then

$$P(E_{n,\,n+k}|G_{n+k}) = \left(1 - \frac{1}{N}\right)^2. \tag{2.34}$$

We require the probability of a joint event, that is, both the pair of errors $(E_{n,\,n+k})$ and a nonconditioned state on trial $n + k$. Equation (2.8) defined the joint event for us in terms of conditional probabilities, and using the symbols of this section, we would have the joint event

$$P(E_{n,\,n+k},\,G_{n+k}) = P(E_{n,\,n+k}|G_{n+k}) \cdot P(G_{n+k}). \tag{2.35}$$

Using Eqs. (2.32) and (2.34), we can restate Eq. (2.35) as the equality

$$P(E_{n,\,n+k},\,G_{n+k}) = \left(1 - \frac{1}{N}\right)^2 \cdot (1 - c)^{n+k-1}.$$

But the occurrence of an error assumes the nonconditioned state. We can restate the left-hand side of the equality, so that we have

$$P(E_{n,\,n+k}) = \left(1 - \frac{1}{N}\right)^2 \cdot (1 - c)^{n+k-1}. \tag{2.36}$$

This is the probability of an error on the nth trial along with an error on the $(n + k)$th trial. If $k = 1$, then we have Eq. (2.36) as the probability of two consecutive errors at any specified point n.

The Probability of Two Consecutive Successes

There are three different ways in which a success can occur on two consecutive trials $(S_{j,\,j+1})$.

(1) The subject could have guessed correctly on both trial n and $n + 1$, if he was in the guessing state on both trial n and trial $n + 1$. This would require the simultaneous events of his having remained in the guessing state for $n + 1$ trials, having guessed correctly on both the nth trial and the $(n + 1)$st trial [symbolizable as having the probability $P(S_n, S_{n+1}, G_{n+1})$]. These events must all occur, suggesting an "and" relationship of the type suggested by Eq. (2.16). That is, we multiply the three probabilities, some of which are conditional.

$$P(S_{n,\,n+1}) = P(S_n,\,S_{n+1},\,G_{n+1}),$$
$$P(S_{n,\,n+1}) = P(S_n|S_{n+1},\,G_{n+1}) \cdot P(S_{n+1}|G_{n+1}) \cdot P(G_{n+1}).$$

Since the success on trial n is not affected by success on $n + 1$, this can be restated as

$$P(S_{n,\,n+1}) = P(S_n|G_{n+1}) \cdot P(S_{n+1}|G_{n+1}) \cdot P(G_{n+1}), \tag{2.37}$$

assuming guessing correctly for both successes.

(2) It is also possible that the subject guessed correctly on the first success, but that the second success was the result of having been conditioned (which Axiom 4 indicates yields a success with probability 1). Here we would need to symbolize the probability of having remained in the guessing state until the nth trial, having successfully guessed at that point, and then having been conditioned during the nth trial so that the $(n + 1)$st trial is entered in the conditioned state. This combination of three probabilities would appear as

$$P(S_{n, n+1}) = P(S_n, C_{n+1}, G_n),$$
$$P(S_{n, n+1}) = P(S_n | C_{n+1}, G_n) \cdot P(C_{n+1} | G_n) \cdot P(G_n),$$
$$P(S_{n, n+1}) = P(S_n | G_n) \cdot P(C_{n+1} | G_n) \cdot P(G_n), \tag{2.38}$$

assuming guessing correctly for only the first success.

(3) The third way in which we could have two consecutive successes is if the subject had been in the conditioned state on the nth trial. Since Axiom 3 of Bower's theory says that once in the conditioned state, the subject remains there (for the particular stimulus), all that would be required for this alternative probability of obtaining two consecutive successes is the probability of having been conditioned by the nth trial.

$$P(S_{n, n+1}) = (C_n), \tag{2.39}$$

assuming having been conditioned as the basis of both successes.

We shall now find parameter equivalents for Eqs. (2.37)–(2.39). Axiom 4 of Bower's theory tells us that the probability of a success, given the guessing state, is $1/N$, regardless of the trial number. The first two terms then, in the right-hand product of Eq. (2.37) combine as $(1/N)^2$. The last term in the product of Eq. (2.37) we previously obtained as Eq. (2.32). We can now restate Eq. (2.37) in terms of parameters as

$$P(S_{n, n+1}) = \left(\frac{1}{N}\right)^2 \cdot (1 - c)^n, \tag{2.40}$$

assuming guessing correctly for both successes.

For Eq. (2.38), we require one less guessing, since the inclusion of the probability of being conditioned on the nth trial precluded anything but a success on the $(n + 1)$st trial. Axiom 3 indicates that the probability of transition to the conditioned state on any trial on which the subject is in the guessing state is c. This allows us to restate Eq. (2.38) in terms of parameters as

$$P(S_{n, n+1}) = \left(\frac{1}{N}\right) \cdot (1 - c)^{n-1} \cdot c, \tag{2.41}$$

assuming guessing correctly for only the first success. The parameter equivalents for Eq. (2.39) can best be obtained by conceiving of our problem as determining a "not" relation in the manner suggested by Eq. (2.4). That is, we want the probability of the subject being in the conditioned state on trial n. But this could have occurred by his having been conditioned on the just previous trial, or the trial before that, etc., since once in the conditioned state, the subject remains in that state. Instead of summing all of the alternative probabilities involved in this large "or" relation, the number of which would change with each value of n, we look at the only other alternative, the probability of being in the guessing state on trial n, a value already expressed in parameters for us in Eq. (2.32). Since on trial n the subject is either in the conditioned or the guessing state, we can obtain the probability of being in the conditioned state by trial n as the probability of not being in the guessing state on trial n, which is formed as the complement of Eq. (2.32).

$$P(S_{n, n+1}) = [1 - (1 - c)^{n-1}], \qquad (2.42)$$

assuming having been conditioned as the basis of both successes.

To obtain the probability of two consecutive successes, regardless of the way in which they have come about, we simply add the alternative probabilities with which this event can happen [Eqs. (2.40), (2.41), and (2.42)], this being an "or" relation involving mutually exclusive alternatives. This would yield

$$P(S_{n, n+1}) = \left(\frac{1}{N}\right)^2 \cdot (1 - c)^n + c \cdot \left(\frac{1}{N}\right) \cdot (1 - c)^{n-1} + [1 - (1 - c)^{n-1}].$$
$$(2.43)$$

Formula (2.43) can be consolidated somewhat by removing the common factor $(1 - c)^{n-1}$, to obtain the equivalent equation

$$P(S_{n, n+1}) = 1 - (1 - c)^{n-1} \left[1 - \left(\frac{1}{N}\right)^2 (1 - c) - \frac{c}{N}\right]. \qquad (2.44)$$

We have succeeded in transforming three general statements (the probability of an error on trial n, the probability of an error on trials n and $n + k$, and the probability of two consecutive successes) into symbolic statements compatible with the probability calculus, and then converting these three symbolic statements into equations in terms of parameter values [for example, Eq. (2.30) into (2.33) and Eq. (2.35) into (2.36)].

All of these equations were in terms of N and c. We know what N is in this model. It is the number of alternative responses, and we decided that we would empirically have only two responses, so $N = 2$. The value of c will have to be estimated from the data, and a way in which this can be done will be illustrated in a later section.

We began our illustrations of the finding of parameter equivalents to probabilistic statements with the equation for the probability of an error on the

nth trial, Eq. (2.30). We then presented the steps to the development of Eq. (2.33). Using Eq. (2.33), we could find a different probability value for each value of n, that is, for each trial number for which we computed the value of $P(E_n)$. We could, in fact, draw a probability distribution of all possible trial numbers. Trial number would be on the x axis and theoretical probability, from Eq. (2.33), would be on the y axis (assuming that we have an estimate of the value of c).

We have here arbitrarily assigned the value of 1 to the random variable value, leaving the axis of the abscissa free to identify the trial number (each having a particular probability for the value 1). At other times, for example, when dealing with total number of errors or other random variable values that need no trial number identification, we shall use the axis of the abscissa to identify particular values of the random variable. In such instances, the probability distribution would map the different probabilities for the different random variable values (rather than for different trial numbers).

We would also like to obtain statistics representing such distributions (such as the mean and variance). Such statistics would simplify empirical versus theoretical comparisons by allowing us to use summarizing values in our comparisons. In order to do this, however, we shall have to summate series of values [for example, our Eq. (2.33)] over all values of a variable (such as n). We shall therefore pause to explicate a general summation technique for the class of equations we shall meet most frequently. These are equations that are raised to the power of some variable that takes on only integer values [such as $(n - 1)$ in Eq. (2.33)].

SUMS OF GEOMETRIC SERIES

Assume that the probability of learning in any one trial is .3, and that the probability of not learning is .7, in a Bernoulli series of trials (implying constant probabilities and independence). The probability of learning on the first trial is then .3. The probability of not learning on the first trial, but learning on the second, is then .7 × .3 (this being an independent "and" relation). The probability of not learning for two trials and learning on the third is .7 × .7 × .3. In summary, the probability of learning on the nth trial is .3 × .7^{n-1}. (We can see that this is a geometric series.) If we wish to know the probability of learning in any of trial 1 through trial n, this would be a question of mutually exclusive "or" relations, and Eq. (2.3) would suggest that we add the probabilities of the event's occurrence on trials 1, and 2, and 3, etc., up to trial n, since it can happen on trial 1 *or* 2 *or* 3, etc., and satisfy the requirements for the occurrence of the event (success on trial 1, or 2, or 3, etc.). This summation of a series of terms, each progressively increased by a unit power of the same term (in this example, .7), is a summation of a power series. A more general term, including the multiplication of the series of terms each by a constant (in this case .3), is the term "geometric series," which implies only a constant ratio between adjacent terms in the series of terms being added, which is always true when a power series is multiplied by a constant. We symbolize the foregoing geometric series as

$$\sum_{k=1}^{n} (.3)(.7)^{k-1} = (.3) \sum_{k=1}^{n} (.7)^{k-1} = .3[1 + .7 + .49 + .343 + \cdots + (.7)^{n-1}].$$

If we wished to know the probability of learning on any trial from trial 1 through trial 4, the answer would be .3(2.533) = .7599.

We now present a more general statement of the example above, so that when we deal with equations in which our parameters are not yet specified by a numerical value (but will be solved for at a later point), we can still find solutions (in terms of the as yet unsolved parameters).

Finite Series

Our summations will generally be over some series in which some value, symbolized as C or $(1 - c)$ or $A(1 - c)$, etc., will represent a common factor, and the series will look like one of the following.

$$S = \sum_{k=1}^{n} C^{k-1} = 1 + C + C^2 + C^3 + \cdots + C^{n-1},$$

$$S = \sum_{k=1}^{n} (1 - c)^{k-1} = 1 + (1 - c) + (1 - c)^2 + (1 - c)^3 + \cdots + (1 - c)^{n-1},$$

$$S = \sum_{k=1}^{n} A(1 - c)^{k-1} = A + A(1 - c) + A(1 - c)^2 + \cdots + A(1 - c)^{n-1},$$
$$\vdots$$

To find the sum, we spell out the terms in the summation twice, once in the original form, and then in the new form obtained by multiplying the entire series by its common factor in the power series [such as C or $(1 - c)$], as indicated in Figure 2.7 for the case of $S = \sum_{k=1}^{n} C^{k-1}$. We then subtract this second series from the first (see Figure 2.7). Note that we carry out the subtraction on both sides of the equality. We then extract a factor on the left side that would isolate the symbol for the sum that we desire (S in our illustration), and divide both sides of the equality by that extracted factor (see Figure 2.7). The result is an equality between our symbol for the sum S and a new simplified statement of the summation. We can now insert in that new statement any value of C and any value of n, for the specific instance. (The summation techniques outlined in this and the following section require $-1 < C < +1$.)

$$\begin{aligned} S &= 1 + C + C^2 + C^3 + \cdots + C^{n-1} \\ CS &= C + C^2 + C^3 + \cdots + C^n \\ \hline S - CS &= 1 - C^n \\ S(1 - C) &= 1 - C^n \\ S &= \frac{1 - C^n}{1 - C} \end{aligned}$$

Figure 2.7. Summation technique for $S = \sum_{k=1}^{n} C^{k-1}$.

Figure 2.8 gives the summation when the exponent is k rather than $k - 1$. If we were to recognize that

$$\frac{C - C^{n+1}}{1 - C} = \frac{C(1 - C^n)}{1 - C},$$

we would see that $\sum_{k=1}^{n} C^k = C \sum_{k=1}^{n} C^{k-1}$ (comparing Figures 2.7 and 2.8). In general,

$$\sum_{k=j}^{n} C^k = C \sum_{k=j}^{n} C^{k-1}. \tag{2.45}$$

$$\begin{aligned} S &= C + C^2 + C^3 + \cdots + C^n \\ CS &= C^2 + C^3 + \cdots + C^{n+1} \\ \hline S - CS &= C - C^{n+1} \\ S(1 - C) &= C - C^{n+1} \\ S &= \frac{C - C^{n+1}}{1 - C} \end{aligned}$$

Figure 2.8. Summation technique for $S = \sum_{k=1}^{n} C^k$.

We could also begin at $k = 0$, if the exponent were k rather than $k - 1$. This is illustrated in Figure 2.9.

We present a table of finite summations of power series (Table 2.1), which can all be obtained by the identical algorithm presented in Figures 2.7–2.9. We juxtaposed $\sum_{k=j}^{n} C^{k-1}$ and $\sum_{k=j}^{n} C^k$ to make clear the relationship given in Eq. (2.45). To obtain the first equality in Table 2.1, $\sum_{k=0}^{n} C^{k-1}$, we used the algorithm of Figure 2.9 to solve for $C \sum_{k=0}^{n} C^{k-1} = \sum_{k=0}^{n} C^k$ [from Eq. (2.45)], and then divided both sides by C, for $\sum_{k=j}^{n} C^{k-1}$. For the geometric series $\sum_{k=j}^{n} AC^k$, we simply multiply the solution of $\sum_{k=j}^{n} C^k$ by A. For example, in

$$
\begin{aligned}
S &= 1 + C + C^2 + C^3 + \cdots + C^n \\
CS &= C + C^2 + C^3 + \cdots + C^{n+1} \\
\hline
S - CS &= 1 - C^{n+1} \\
S(1 - C) &= 1 - C^{n+1} \\
S &= \frac{1 - C^{n+1}}{1 - C}
\end{aligned}
$$

Figure 2.9. Summation technique for $S = \sum\limits_{k=0}^{n} C^k$.

TABLE 2.1

Summations from $k = 0$, 1, or 2 to n with Exponents k and $k - 1$

$$\sum_{k=0}^{n} C^{k-1} = \frac{1 - C^{n+1}}{C(1 - C)} \qquad\qquad \sum_{k=0}^{n} (1 - c)^{k-1} = \frac{1 - (1 - c)^{n-1}}{(1 - c)c}$$

$$\sum_{k=0}^{n} C^{k} = \frac{1 - C^{n+1}}{1 - C} \qquad\qquad \sum_{k=0}^{n} (1 - c)^{k} = \frac{1 - (1 - c)^{n+1}}{c}$$

$$\sum_{k=1}^{n} C^{k-1} = \frac{1 - C^{n}}{1 - C} \qquad\qquad \sum_{k=1}^{n} (1 - c)^{k-1} = \frac{1 - (1 - c)^{n}}{c}$$

$$\sum_{k=1}^{n} C^{k} = \frac{C(1 - C^{n})}{1 - C} \qquad\qquad \sum_{k=1}^{n} (1 - c)^{k} = \frac{(1 - c)[1 - (1 - c)^{n}]}{c}$$

$$\sum_{k=2}^{n} C^{k-1} = \frac{C(1 - C^{n-1})}{1 - C} \qquad\qquad \sum_{k=2}^{n} (1 - c)^{k-1} = \frac{(1 - c)[1 - (1 - c)^{n-1}]}{c}$$

$$\sum_{k=2}^{n} C^{k} = \frac{C^{2}(1 - C^{n-1})}{1 - C} \qquad\qquad \sum_{k=2}^{n} (1 - c)^{k} = \frac{(1 - c)^{2}[1 - (1 - c)^{n-1}]}{c}$$

[a] Note the way that the exponent in the right-hand statement of the equality decreases with increasing values of the initial sum ($k = 0$, 1, or 2) on the left of the equality. Note also the way in which the common factor in the power series is multiplied against the sum, with increasing powers (C^{-1}, C^{0}, C^{1}, C^{2}) as the exponent in the left-hand statement of the equality is increased, if the initial value of k is kept constant.

our previous illustration of a geometric series, we would have $A = .3$, and $C = .7$. We would then duplicate our numerical solution with the general solution of Figure 2.7 multiplied by .3.

$$\frac{.3(1 - .7^4)}{1 - .7} = 1 - .7^4 = .7599.$$

Infinite Series

It is conceivable that we would have the trial number as the exponent in a power series, where the common factor is a probability (between 0 and 1) representing, perhaps, the probability of an error on a specific trial. Then, if the probability of an error decreased according to an integer-stepped power function, each trial's probability of an error would be less than the previous one, and would gradually approach 0 as n increased. If we wanted to obtain the probability of at least one error having occurred over the total number of trials, we would want to summate all probabilities of an error over all trials, from the first to infinity, since this would be an "or" relation. This would mean the summation of a power series C^k from k equals 1 to infinity, symbolized as $S = \sum_{k=1}^{\infty} C^k$. If for some reason we wished to represent the probability of an error on the first trial as equaling 1 (unlikely with the foregoing question, but often encountered with other questions), we would perhaps express the sum as $\sum_{k=1}^{\infty} C^{k-1}$.

For infinite summation, we proceed in a manner similar to the algorithm for a finite summation. However, here we take advantage of the fact that if the common factor C is between 0 and 1, then as the exponent goes toward infinity, the value of C^k, or C^{k-1}, would tend to 0 and would no longer contribute, at some point, to the value of the continued summation from 1 to infinity. That is, the series will converge toward some finite value, because at some point in the value of k, increasing k by 1 and adding this new C^{k+1} to the summation will effectively add only 0. Therefore, when we spell out our summation, beginning, let us say, with C^0 and continuing on until we reach C^{∞}, if we then multiply the sum by C, we would begin with C^1 and continue again to C^{∞}. In subtracting this second sum from the first (as we did for the finite sum algorithm), our difference would consist only of an initial value of the first sum.

Figures 2.10 and 2.11 offer two examples of the algorithm of infinite summation.

If we wanted $\sum_{k=1}^{\infty} C^{k-1}$, we could again go through the algorithm, or else we could recognize that

$$\sum_{k=1}^{\infty} C^k = C \sum_{k=1}^{\infty} C^{k-1}$$

$$S = 1 + C + C^2 + C^3 + \cdots + C^\infty$$
$$CS = C + C^2 + C^3 + \cdots + C^\infty$$
$$S - CS = 1$$
$$S(1 - C) = 1$$
$$S = \frac{1}{1 - C}$$

Figure 2.10. Summation technique for $S = \sum_{k=0}^{\infty} C^k$.

$$S = C + C^2 + C^3 + \cdots + C^\infty$$
$$CS = C^2 + C^3 + \cdots + C^\infty$$
$$S - CS = C$$
$$S(1 - C) = C$$
$$S = \frac{C}{1 - C}$$

Figure 2.11. Summation technique for $S = \sum_{k=1}^{\infty} C^k$.

TABLE 2.2

Infinite Summations from $k = 0$, 1, or 2 with Exponents k and $k - 1$

$$\sum_{k=0}^{\infty} C^{k-1} = \frac{1}{C(1 - C)} \qquad \sum_{k=0}^{\infty} (1 - c)^{k-1} = \frac{1}{(1 - c)c}$$

$$\sum_{k=0}^{\infty} C^k = \frac{1}{1 - C} \qquad \sum_{k=0}^{\infty} (1 - c)^k = \frac{1}{c}$$

$$\sum_{k=1}^{\infty} C^{k-1} = \frac{1}{1 - C} \qquad \sum_{k=1}^{\infty} (1 - c)^{k-1} = \frac{1}{c}$$

$$\sum_{k=1}^{\infty} C^k = \frac{C}{1 - C} \qquad \sum_{k=1}^{\infty} (1 - c)^k = \frac{1 - c}{c}$$

$$\sum_{k=2}^{\infty} C^{k-1} = \frac{C}{1 - C} \qquad \sum_{k=2}^{\infty} (1 - c)^{k-1} = \frac{1 - c}{c}$$

$$\sum_{k=2}^{\infty} C^k = \frac{C^2}{1 - C} \qquad \sum_{k=2}^{\infty} (1 - c)^k = \frac{(1 - c)^2}{c}$$

and therefore divide the sum obtained in Figure 2.11 by C, which gives us

$$\sum_{k=1}^{\infty} C^{k-1} = \frac{1}{1-C}.$$

In Table 2.2 we present a number of useful infinite summations.

We shall often wish to obtain mean values of trial numbers of particular significance, such as the average trial number (over all subjects) of the last error, or the average trial number of the first correct response. These often can theoretically be any trial from 1 to infinity. Since expectations are obtained as the sum of products of random variable values times their respective probabilities, if the probability of the event was a power function of the trial number, such as C^k with C any constant and k the trial number, we could symbolize the sum that would lead to the expectation as

$$\text{expectation} = \sum_{k=1}^{\infty} kC^k. \tag{2.46}$$

We shall therefore frequently find ourselves dealing with sums with the variable as both an exponent and a multiplier. At such times, we shall sometimes find that carrying out the algorithm does not produce a solution. We then repeat the algorithm, and find that a solution eventually becomes apparent, although three or four repetitions of the algorithm may be required. We illustrate repeated applications of the algorithm in Figures 2.12 and 2.13.

$$S = 1 + 2C + 3C^2 + 4C^3 + \cdots$$
$$CS = C + 2C^2 + 3C^3 + 4C^4 + \cdots$$

$$S - CS = 1 + C + C^2 + C^3 + \cdots$$
$$S(1-C) = 1 + C + C^2 + C^3 + \cdots$$
$$CS(1-C) = C + C^2 + C^3 + \cdots$$

$$S(1-C) - CS(1-C) = 1$$
$$S(1-C)(1-C) = 1$$
$$S(1-C)^2 = 1$$

$$S = \frac{1}{(1-C)^2}$$

Figure 2.12. Summation technique for $S = \sum_{k=1}^{\infty} kC^{k-1}$.

$$S = 1 + 4C + 9C^2 + 16C^3 + 25C^4 + \cdots$$
$$CS = C + 4C^2 + 9C^3 + 16C^4 + \cdots$$

$$S(1 - C) = 1 + 3C + 5C^2 + 7C^3 + 9C^4 + \cdots$$
$$CS(1 - C) = C + 3C^2 + 5C^3 + 7C^4 + 9C^5 + \cdots$$

$$S(1 - C)^2 = 1 + 2C + 2C^2 + 2C^3 + 2C^4 + \cdots$$
$$CS(1 - C)^2 = C + 2C^2 + 2C^3 + 2C^4 + 2C^5 + \cdots$$

$$S(1 - C)^3 = 1 + C$$

$$S = \frac{1 + C}{(1 - C)^3}$$

Figure 2.13. Summation technique for $S = \sum_{k=1}^{\infty} k^2 C^{k-1}$.

In Table 2.3 we present some infinite summations involving the variable as a multiplier as well as an exponent.

TABLE 2.3

Infinite Summations from $k = 1$, with Variables k and $k - 1$ as both Exponents and Multipliers[a]

$$\sum_{k=1}^{\infty} kC^{k-1} = \frac{1}{(1 - C)^2} \qquad \sum_{k=1}^{\infty} k(1 - c)^{k-1} = \frac{1}{c^2}$$

$$\sum_{k=1}^{\infty} kC^k = \frac{C}{(1 - C)^2} \qquad \sum_{k=1}^{\infty} k(1 - c)^k = \frac{1 - c}{c^2}$$

$$\sum_{k=1}^{\infty} (k - 1)C^{k-1} = \frac{C}{(1 - C)^2} \qquad \sum_{k=1}^{\infty} (k - 1)(1 - c)^{k-1} = \frac{1 - c}{c^2}$$

$$\sum_{k=1}^{\infty} (k - 1)C^k = \frac{C^2}{(1 - C)^2} \qquad \sum_{k=1}^{\infty} (k - 1)(1 - c)^k = \frac{(1 - c)^2}{c^2}$$

$$\sum_{k=1}^{\infty} k^2 C^{k-1} = \frac{1 + C}{(1 - C)^3} \qquad \sum_{k=1}^{\infty} k^2(1 - c)^{k-1} = \frac{2 - c}{c^3}$$

$$\sum_{k=1}^{\infty} k^2 C^k = \frac{C(1 + C)}{(1 - C)^3} \qquad \sum_{k=1}^{\infty} k^2(1 - c)^k = \frac{(1 - c)(2 - c)}{c^3}$$

[a] With k as a multiplier, if the initial value of k is 0 rather than 1, the summation remains the same, since it would merely add 0.

SUMMATIONS IN COMPUTING A MEAN AND VARIANCE

We saw that we could use the summation technique in the form of Eq. (2.46) to obtain the mean of a distribution of scores containing integer values from $k = 1$ to ∞, each with probability C^k. Table 2.3 indicates that the solution of that sum is

$$\text{expectation} = \sum_{k=1}^{\infty} kC^k = \frac{C}{(1-C)^2}. \tag{2.47}$$

Just as we used the summation technique to obtain a mean value, we could also use the summation technique to obtain a variance. It can be shown that the variance of a distribution of values of some random variable K is equivalent to

$$\sigma^2 = \sum_{j=1}^{\infty} k_j^2 p(k_j) - \left[\sum_{j=1}^{\infty} k_j p(k_j) \right]^2, \tag{2.48}$$

where $p(k_j)$ is the probability of the jth value of k, and j can take on any value from 1 to ∞, so that all possible values of k are included (see Freund, 1962, pp. 94–96, or any text on mathematical statistics). Instead of $p(k)$, let us use our previous notation of some sort of probability value C^k, which we assume changes as a power function of k (which happens to be a frequently occurring function).

$$\sigma^2 = \sum_{k=1}^{\infty} k^2 C^k - \left(\sum_{k=1}^{\infty} kC^k \right)^2. \tag{2.49}$$

Looking at Table 2.3, we find the solution to be

$$\sigma^2 = \frac{C(1+C)}{(1-C)^3} - \frac{C^2}{(1-C)^4} = \frac{C(1-C^2-C)}{(1-C)^4}. \tag{2.50}$$

Thus, if C^k was the probability of trial k being the trial of the last error, we would use Eq. (2.47) to find the expected trial of the last error over all of our subjects, and we would use Eq. (2.50) to find the variance of the distribution of trials of the last error.

Applications of Summation of Geometric Series in Bower's Model

We previously indicated that in order to obtain an expected value of a random variable, we have to sum each product of each value of the random variable times its probability. If we had dichotomized our random variable values into 1 and 0, then the average value for one trial would be 1 times the probability of an error plus 0 times the probability of a success, which reduces arithmetically to the probability of an error. If the probability was $\frac{1}{2}$ for each random variable value, for example, in tossing a coin where a head was 1 and a tail was 0, we would have an expected value of $\frac{1}{2}$ per trial, and therefore an expectation of $\frac{1}{2}$ a head per trial. Although an expectation of $\frac{1}{2}$ a head per trial would not appear sensible on a single-trial basis, we could take the expected value for one trial and sum this over all trials in order to obtain the expected sum over all trials (which would here be $n/2$).

We can restate Eq. (2.25) for the mean of a binomial distribution, so that it can include a series of dichotomous event trials with changing probabilities. Assuming that we know what the probability would be at each trial k, and symbolizing the expected number of successes in n trials as $E(T)$, we would have

$$E(T) = \sum_{k=1}^{\infty} p_k. \qquad (2.51)$$

For the average number of total errors for a subject, we generally are dealing with an experimental paradigm that runs subjects to some criterion of errorless performance. It is then assumed that were the trials to continue beyond this point an infinite number of times, there would no longer be any errors. An equation analogous with this would require us to sum the probabilities of errors over all trials from 0 to ∞ for the expected total number of errors for an average subject in an experiment.

EXPECTED NUMBER OF ERRORS

In Eq. (2.33) we obtained the probability of an error on trial n as $P(E_n) = (1 - 1/N)(1 - c)^{n-1}$. Still categorizing errors as having random variable value 1 and successes as 0, if we wished the expected total number of errors for an average subject (the mean number of errors), we could sum the probabilities over all trials. The expected number of errors per subject then, in Bower's model, is, from Eqs. (2.51) and (2.33).

$$\sum_{n=1}^{\infty} P(E_n) = \left(1 - \frac{1}{N}\right) \sum_{n=1}^{\infty} (1 - c)^{n-1}$$
$$= \frac{(1 - 1/N)}{c}. \qquad (2.52)$$

Estimation of a Parameter Related to a Hypothetical State

Since mathematical models are analogs of theories, it is quite common for the models to contain variables that represent the probability of entering states that are not directly observable. We have just developed a formula, Eq. (2.52), relating c, the probability of entering the conditioned state, to both N (the number of alternative responses), a known value, and the average total number of errors per subject, an empirically obtainable value. We can use this formula [Eq. (2.52)] and the empirical information to obtain an estimate of the value of c, which is the probability of entering this hypothetical conditioned state.

This would represent an example of parameter estimation. (When we then develop other formulas for other predictions of results from the model, we could simply "plug in" the value of c and observe how closely the new formulas, with the parameters now estimated in advance, can predict empirical results.)

Equation (2.52) is a particularly simple example, because we have one unknown and one equation. Under such conditions, we simply use algebra to solve for the value of the unknown. As an example, let us assume that we have observed the average number of errors per subject to be 3, and there are two response alternatives, making $N = 2$. Estimation of c would then proceed as follows.

$$\text{Expectation} = \frac{(1 - 1/N)}{c} = \frac{.5}{c},$$

$$3 = \frac{.5}{c},$$

$$c = .167.$$

THE PROBABILITY OF k ERRORS BEFORE THE FIRST SUCCESS

Let us compute another expected value in the Bower model. If we wanted the average number of trials before the first success, this expectation would represent an average taken over subjects, with each subject producing some specific value of the random variable, namely, the trial of his first success. The probability for each of the values that the random variable could take would be constructed by using the direct method (of translating verbalized theory into probabilistic equations). Then we would use the summation technique to sum the products of the random variable values (trial number of the first success) times their individual probabilities. We thus need the probability of each trial as the trial of the first success.

For a success on the first trial the probability of guessing correctly is simply $1/N$, since by assumption we begin in the guessing state (Axiom 5 of Bower's theory). Beyond the first trial, there are two ways that the first success can occur on any one trial. A success can occur either by the subject guessing correctly while in the guessing state or by the subject having been conditioned on the previous trial, assuring a success on the next response.

Since only errors or successes can occur, we can speak of trials before the first success as error trials. We can then symbolize the probability of k error trials before the first success as $P(E = k)$, and we indicated earlier that $P(E = 0) = 1/N$ (for the probability of a success on the first trial). For $P(E = k)$ with $k > 0$, regardless of which of the two ways the first success occurs (that is, in the guessing or the conditioned state), we have to assume that the subject was unconditioned in all previous trials and had kept guessing incorrectly. For trials 1 to k this incorrect guessing would have occurred with probability $(1 - c)^{k-1}(1 - 1/N)^k$. The rationale is that conditioning does not take place on trial 1, and then continues not to take place on any of the other of the $k - 1$ trials through trial $k - 1$ with probability $(1 - c)^{k-1}$. In addition, with the probability of an error on trial n symbolized as $P(Q_n = 1)$, the axiom on the probability of an error in the guessing state states that $P(Q_n = 1 | G_n) = 1 - 1/N$, regardless of n. Since we want the probability of an error on all trials 1 through k inclusive, while remaining in the guessing state, we have the resulting $(1 - c)^{k-1}(1 - 1/N)^k$. (The use of k and $k - 1$ might be confusing. A subject moves into a conditioned state or nonconditioned state during some trial $k - 1$, and this can influence his ability to be incorrect or not on the *following* trial. Thus, for guessing to take place up through trial k, we would only require no conditioning up through trial $k - 1$.) Given that the subject has had only errors up through trial k, there are two ways that he can have his first correct response on trial $k + 1$: Either conditioning has taken place on trial k; or, given no conditioning on trial k, the subject guesses correctly on trial $k + 1$.

$$P(E = k) = \left(1 - \frac{1}{N}\right)^k (1 - c)^{k-1} \cdot c + \left(1 - \frac{1}{N}\right)^k (1 - c)^{k-1} \cdot (1 - c)\left(\frac{1}{N}\right)$$
$$= \left(1 - \frac{1}{N}\right)^k (1 - c)^{k-1}\left(c + \frac{1 - c}{N}\right) \qquad (2.53)$$

(probability of k errors before the first correct response).

The Average Number of Errors before the First Success

For the expected value of E, that is, the theoretical expectation of trials before the first success, we would sum each value of E times its probability of occurrence (this would theoretically include $E = 0$, but the latter would in fact not contribute to the sum because that probability would be multiplied by 0). The expected value for E from Eq. (2.53) would be

$$\left(1 - \frac{1}{N}\right)\left(c + \frac{1-c}{N}\right)\sum_{k=1}^{\infty} k\left[(1-c)\left(1 - \frac{1}{N}\right)\right]^{k-1}$$

[to maintain a common exponent, we factor out $(1 - 1/N)$]

$$= \left(1 - \frac{1}{N}\right)\left(c + \frac{1-c}{N}\right) \cdot \frac{1}{[1 - (1-c)(1 - 1/N)]^2}$$

$$= \left(\frac{N-1}{N}\right)\left(\frac{Nc + 1 - c}{N}\right)\frac{1}{[(Nc + 1 - c)/N]^2}$$

$$= \frac{(N-1)(Nc + 1 - c)}{(Nc + 1 - c)^2}$$

$$= \frac{N-1}{Nc + 1 - c}.$$

THE PROBABILITY OF NO MORE ERRORS AFTER THE FIRST CORRECT RESPONSE

In certain experimental designs, it is not unusual for a subject to make no more errors to a particular stimulus after his first correct response to that stimulus (for example, in our previous paired-associate paradigm, with any one of two responses possible for any stimulus). We might wish to see if the model can predict the probability of this event, that is, the proportion of the times that this will in fact occur. Let us state this as " the probability that there are no more errors after the first correct response (to some stimulus), " and for simplicity, symbolize it as P_1.

There are two ways that we can have no more errors after a correct response. If the first correct response did not occur by guessing, that would mean that the subject was conditioned, and in Bower's model, once the subject is conditioned, there are no more errors. The second way that the first correct response would be followed by 0 errors is more complex. Let us begin by creating a symbol, b, for the probability of no more errors after a first correct *guess*. If we also symbolize the probability of a first correct response by guessing as g_1, the probability of no more errors after the first correct response would look like

$$P_1 = (1 - g_1) + g_1 b,$$

which represents the situation where there are no more errors if the first correct response occurred in a way other than guessing, *or* if the first correct response occurred by guessing (g_1) *and* there were no more errors after the first correct guess (b).

The Probability That the First Correct Response Occurs by Guessing (g_1)

The probability of a first correct response by guessing g_1 requires that there be no conditioning until after the first correct response. For each trial on which the first correct response by guessing occurs, there must be no correct responses in all of the previous trials. It would appear to be a series like the following:

$$g_1 = \frac{1}{N} + \left[\left(1 - \frac{1}{N}\right)(1 - c)\right]\frac{1}{N} + \left[\left(1 - \frac{1}{N}\right)^2(1 - c)^2\right]\frac{1}{N} + \cdots.$$

That is, we have a summation, because the first correct response occurring by guessing can occur in any of these mutually exclusive ways. To obtain g_1, then, we would have to carry out the summation of this "or" relationship.

$$g_1 = \frac{1}{N} \sum_{k=0}^{\infty} \left[\left(1 - \frac{1}{N}\right)(1 - c)\right]^k = \frac{1}{N[1 - (1 - 1/N)(1 - c)]} = \frac{1}{Nc + 1 - c}.$$

The Probability of No More Errors Given That the Subject Is in the Guessing State

We now need the value of b, the probability of no more errors after a guess (which happens to be a correct guess). In order for a guess to occur, the subject must still be in the guessing state. But if the subject is in the guessing state, the probability of an error in that state is always $(1 - 1/N)$, and the probability of his being in the conditioned state on the *next* trial is the constant c. This is precisely the subject's status at the very first trial. Therefore, if after a trial a subject is still in the guessing state, the probabilities of any future events are just as they were at the first trial. This is sometimes verbalized as "the guessing state resets the system." This allows b to be independent of the trial on which the first correct guess actually occurs. Given that it has just occurred, the different ways in which no more errors will occur can be represented by the series

$$b = c + (1 - c)\frac{1}{N} \cdot c + (1 - c)^2\left(\frac{1}{N}\right)^2 \cdot c + (1 - c)^3\left(\frac{1}{N}\right)^3 \cdot c + \cdots,$$

$$b = c \sum_{k=1}^{\infty} \left[\frac{1 - c}{N}\right]^{k-1} = \frac{c}{1 - (1 - c)/N} = \frac{Nc}{N - 1 + c}.$$

The series represents the fact that during the trial of the first correct guess, the subject may have been conditioned, with probability c (resulting in no more errors), or he may have not been conditioned, but may nevertheless have guessed correctly again on the following trial, during which time he was conditioned [with probability $(1 - c)1/N \cdot c$], and so on through different numbers of correct guesses prior to conditioning.

We can now completely construct P_1.

$$P_1 = (1 - g_1) + g_1 b,$$

$$P_1 = \left(1 - \frac{1}{Nc + 1 - c}\right) + \frac{1}{Nc + 1 - c} \cdot \frac{Nc}{N - 1 + c},$$

$$P_1 = 1 - \frac{1}{Nc + 1 - c}\left(1 - \frac{Nc}{N - 1 + c}\right) = \begin{array}{l} \text{the probability of no more errors} \\ \text{after the first correct response.} \end{array}$$

We shall again return to the direct method, helping the reader to see it in some practical contexts, in later sections. For the moment, it is important to realize that this represents an intuitively obvious and overt method for translating probabilistic statements of the theoretical model into probability distributions, from which theoretical curves can be drawn or expected values computed. Of course, becoming accustomed to translating the theoretical statements into equations that take advantage of the theorems of probability requires some practice. Deciding to first compute the additional probabilities, as in the last example, where two probabilities had to be computed to obtain a third, obviously requires experience with these techniques and these kinds of problems.

Problems

1. In Chapter Two we found (a) the distribution for the probability of k errors before the first success, in Bower's one-element model, predicted to be

$$P(E = k) = \left(1 - \frac{1}{N}\right)^k (1 - c)^{k-1}\left(c + \frac{1 - c}{N}\right);$$

(b) the average number of errors before the first success in Bower's model, predicted to be

$$\sum_{k=1}^{\infty} k[P(E = k)] = \frac{N - 1}{Nc + 1 - c}.$$

Using (a) and (b), construct the variance for the number of errors before the first success. (Carry out the summation in the answer.)

2. Present the distribution of probabilities of each number as the trial of the last error for Bower's one-element model.

Hint 1: We already have the probability of no more errors after a guess as

$$b = \frac{Nc}{N - 1 + c}.$$

Hint 2: The guessing state "resets the system" so that *the probability of no more errors* is the same from any trial n on, given that the subject is in the guessing state. It is the same regardless of whether the subject had an error or a correct guess on trial n.

3. Present the expectation for the distribution obtained for Problem 2. (Carry out the summation in the answer.)

4. Present the distribution of the number of errors between the first and the second success (for Bower's one-element model).

This can be a difficult question without any suggestions for proceeding, since it is most easily done by first defining another probability. Fortunately, we already have this definition at the end of Chapter Two. That is, you will need the probability of a first correct response occurring by guessing g_1. You may also find it convenient to symbolize the probability of an error while not being conditioned:

$$\left(1 - \frac{1}{N}\right)(1 - c) = \alpha.$$

This also implies its complement

$$c + \frac{1 - c}{N} = 1 - \alpha,$$

which is the sum of the probabilities of either being conditioned or not being conditioned while guessing correctly.

With g_1 and the α terms or their equivalents you should be able to construct the probability distribution for k errors between the first and second success. An additional suggestion is that you define the probability of 0 errors between the first and second success differently than for $k > 0$.

5. Present the mean of the distribution obtained for Problem 4.

6. Assume a conditioned subject responding in a discrete trial experimental situation, where the conditions for trials have just changed from reinforcement on every trial to extinction. The experimenter has a theory that predicts the gradually decreasing probability of a response over the nonreinforced trials. This decreasing probability of a response on any trial n trials into extinction is, according to his theory,

$$P(R_n) = P(R_1)[(1 - e)(1 - s)d]^{n-1},$$

where $P(R_1)$ is the probability of a response on the first trial into extinction and e, s, and d are parameters of the theory.

What is the average number of responses anticipated by the theory over an infinitely long sequence of extinction trials?

Chapter Three

Difference Equations

We shall now examine a technique of particular importance in mathematical models of learning. In our use of the direct method, we used our theoretical axioms' implications as to the effect of each trial to generate an equation that could give us the probability of an event, given the number of trials that had taken place up to the point in question. For example, in determining the probability of the occurrence of an error on some trial n in Bower's model, we had to determine the probability of being in the guessing state on trial n. We noted that, according to our theoretical axioms, the probability of remaining in the guessing state on the next trial was a constant, independent of trial number. Given that the subject was in the guessing state on the first trial (a theoretical assumption), there were then $n - 1$ times that a metaphorical coin had to come up "guessing state," for the subject to still be in that state on the nth trial (since, having left it once, it would not have been possible to return). Recognizing this as an "and" relationship, we concluded that

$$P(G_n) = (1 - c)^{n-1} \cdot P(G_1),$$

as indicated in Eq. (2.32), although in our special case $P(G_1) = 1$, so that we had previously omitted $P(G_1)$.

We can approach the foregoing example as an instance of a more general statement. We can call any equality between one step in a series and a function on the previous step in that series a *difference equation*. When the steps in the series are integer steps (as is the case with the trial number n), and our equality is between one step in the series and a function on the previous step in the series, we have the *recursive* form of the difference equation. The simplest

56

example would be

$$X_{n+1} = A \cdot X_n, \tag{3.1}$$

where A is any constant and X_n is the nth value in a series of X values, changing (moving along the series) as a function of n according to the recursive rule of Eq. (3.1). Thus, if $X_1 = 4$ and $A = 3$, then X_2 would equal 12 and X_3 would equal 36, etc. (Note the necessity of X_1 being given.)

Since we are interested in probabilities that change as a function of trials, we can suggest probability values with such notation as

$$P(X_{n+1}) = A \cdot P(X_n).$$

Since probability values are between 0 and 1, it is likely that A will be less than 1 and that $P(X_n)$ will be less than 1 for most values of n. If we were to consider X_n to be the probability of a guess on trial n, we could symbolize it as $P(G_n)$. If we decided that A were equal to $(1 - c)$, we could restate Eq. (3.1) as

$$P(G_{n+1}) = (1 - c) \cdot P(G_n). \tag{3.2}$$

If we began with $n = 1$, we would find that

$$P(G_2) = (1 - c) \cdot P(G_1),$$
$$P(G_3) = (1 - c) \cdot P(G_2)$$
$$= (1 - c) \cdot (1 - c) \cdot P(G_1)$$
$$= (1 - c)^2 \cdot P(G_1)$$
$$P(G_4) = (1 - c) \cdot P(G_3)$$
$$= (1 - c)^3 \cdot P(G_1),$$
$$\vdots$$

until we conclude by induction that

$$P(G_n) = (1 - c)^{n-1} \cdot P(G_1), \tag{3.3}$$

as we reasoned in Eq. (2.32). We call Eq. (3.3) the solution to the difference equation (3.2).

We referred earlier to conclusions by induction. It will be helpful to stop and demonstrate the general technique of mathematical induction. This will allow you to follow the proofs for our solutions to the difference equations that we shall examine in this text and to check your attempts to develop solutions to difference equations.

Mathematical Induction

We begin with concern for some sequence of values. The sequence must, in some fashion, be a function of integer steps. Thus, the sequence (1), (1 + 2), (1 + 2 + 3), etc., would constitute such a sequence, as would (2), (4), (6), etc., or (C^0), (C^1), (C^2), etc. We develop, either by trial and error or by guessing, some general statement that holds for all members of the sequence. For example, we might state that for the sequence (1), $(1 + 2)$, $(1 + 2 + 3)$, ..., $(1 + 2 + 3 + \cdots + n)$, each of the values in the sequence (the sum in each set of parentheses) is equal to $[n(n + 1)]/2$ when we identify n as the last number in the particular summation. We turn to mathematical induction as a technique for proving our general statement about the members of a sequence. We now use this technique to prove the statement in our example.

To prove:

$$1 + 2 + 3 + \cdots + n = \frac{n(n + 1)}{2}.$$

We first verify that this is true for some initial value.

STEP 1.   *We verify the following:*

For $n = 1$, $1 = \dfrac{1(2)}{2}$.

For $n = 2$, $1 + 2 = \dfrac{2(3)}{2}$.

STEP 2.   *Assume that for $n = k$*

$$1 + 2 + 3 + \cdots + k = \frac{k(k + 1)}{2}.$$

STEP 3a.   *Operate on the kth term in the series* to produce the $(k + 1)$st term in the series (on the left-hand side of the equation in Step 2), and then apply the same operation to the general statement (on the right-hand side in Step 2).

$$1 + 2 + 3 + \cdots + k + (k + 1) = \frac{k(k + 1)}{2} + (k + 1).$$

STEP 3b.   *Algebraically manipulate the operation on the general statement to see if it is equivalent to the general statement in Step 2, with k changed to $k + 1$. If the form of the general statement is maintained (but with $n = k + 1$ instead of $n = k$), the resulting implication is that n can equal $k + 1$ and be true if it can equal k and be true.*

$$1 + 2 + 3 + \cdots + k + (k + 1) = \frac{k(k + 1)}{2} + (k + 1)$$

$$= \frac{k(k + 1) + 2(k + 1)}{2}$$

$$= \frac{k^2 + 3k + 2}{2}$$

$$= \frac{(k + 1)(k + 2)}{2},$$

yielding

$$1 + 2 + 3 + \cdots + k + (k + 1) = \frac{(k + 1)(k + 2)}{2}.$$

STEP 4.   *Conclusion.* We can see that

$$\frac{(k + 1)(k + 2)}{2} = \frac{n(n + 1)}{2},$$

when $n = (k + 1)$, so that the equality assumed at $n = k$ is maintained at $n = (k + 1)$.

We have therefore shown that if the general statement is true for $n = k$ (our assumption of Step 2), then it is also true for $n = (k + 1)$, as shown in Step 3. Note that we were careful to show first that it was true for the lowest values of n, in Step 1. We then demonstrated that it remains true at each reassignment of a new larger value to n. We have consequently demonstrated that it is true for all values of n.

Instead of spelling out the sum, we could have stated it as

$$\sum_{j=1}^{n} j = \frac{n(n + 1)}{2}.$$

By using a defining equation

$$S_n = \sum_{j=1}^{n} j,$$

we can express our general statement about the terms in the series as

$$S_n = \frac{n(n + 1)}{2}.$$

We could then restate our proof of the general statement by using S_1 and S_2 in our Step 1 verification, S_k for Step 2, and S_{k+1} for Step 3. This use of a symbol for the value in the series, recovered through a defining equation, will be helpful to us in our use of such terms as $P(G_n)$. Such probabilities will indeed change with each value of n, and our theories will suggest the trial-by-trial values, in the form of defining equations in recursive form, such as Eq. (3.2).

Let us use the method of mathematical induction to examine the adequacy of the general statement about the sequence $P(G_n)$ contained in Eq. (3.3), which we have offered as the solution to Eq. (3.2).

Instead of the specific parameter $(1 - c)$, let us express our equation more generally, using A for $(1 - c)$ and X_n for $P(G_n)$.

To prove:

$$X_n = A^{n-1}X_1 \quad \text{(the general statement).} \tag{3.4}$$

Defining equation:

$$X_{n+1} = AX_n. \tag{3.5}$$

STEP 1.   *We verify the following:*

For $n = 1$, $X_1 = A^{1-1}X_1 = A^0 X_1 = X_1$.

(Although X_1 cannot be independently defined by our equations, we can see that it does not contradict our general statement.)

For $n = 2$, $X_2 = AX_1$,

which is correct according to our defining equation and agrees with our general statement.

For $n = 3$, $X_3 = ?$

Our defining equation tells us that

$$X_3 = AX_2,$$

but we have just seen that $X_2 = AX_1$, so that we have $X_3 = AAX_1$, or

$$X_3 = A^2 X_1,$$

which also agrees with our general statement. Having now accounted for X_1 through X_3, and thus having established that for $n =$ some k ($k = 1, 2$, and 3) the general statement $X_n = A^{n-1}X$ can be true, we now attempt to prove that if it is true for any $n = k$, it is also true for $n = k + 1$, and therefore, by step-by-step induction, true for all n.

STEP 2.   *Assume that for $n = k$*

$X_k = A^{k-1}X_1$.

STEP 3a.   *Operate on the kth term in the series* [according to the defining
           equation (3.5)] to produce the $(k + 1)$st term in the series, applying
           the operation to both sides of the equation in Step 2. The equation
           in Step 2 then becomes

$$AX_k = AA^{k-1}X_1,$$

$$X_{k+1} = AA^{k-1}X_1. \tag{3.6}$$

STEP 3b.   *Algebraically manipulate the operation on the right-hand side,*
           and see if the form of the general statement is maintained, but with
           $n = k + 1$ instead of $n = k$.

$$A \cdot A^{k-1} = A^k;$$

           therefore, we can restate Eq. (3.6) as

$$X_{k+1} = A^k X_1.$$

STEP 4.   *Conclusion.* If any $X_k = A^{k-1}X_1$, then

$$X_{k+1} = A^k X_1.$$

But some X_k does equal $A^{k-1}X_1$ (Step 1), so the general statement is true for
$n = $ any k.

   We now apply this general insight, Eq. (3.4), to the particular instance of
Eq. (3.2). With $P(G_{n+1}) = X_{n+1}$, $P(G_1) = X_1$, and $(1 - c) = A$, we shall find
Eq. (3.3) as the correct solution to Eq. (3.2).

DIFFERENCE EQUATION SOLUTION TO $X_{n+1} = AX_n + B$

   We could conceive of a different operation, a transforming function,
different from Eq. (3.2), for the recursive form of the difference equation
taking us along the sequence of values in the series. For example, at each trial
some false information might be gained by the subject, which would cumulate
and lessen the likelihood of the subject being conditioned. We would then
have to add some probability of remaining in the guessing state at each trial.
On the other hand, the correct information would also be provided, in some
consistent fashion, at each "reinforcement" following each trial. We would
then be postulating a factor adding to the probability of remaining in the
guessing state plus a factor reducing the probability of remaining in the
guessing state at each trial. We could represent this as a simple additive
factor B, with $0 < B < 1$, in the recursive equation, along with multiplication
by a value A, with $0 < A < 1$, times whatever the last probability was. In the
recursive form, it might appear as

$$X_{n+1} = AX_n + B, \tag{3.7}$$

where X_n would be the probability of being in the guessing state on trial n, and both A and B would be greater than 0 but less than 1. If we had $-1 < B < 0$, then both factors A and B would represent aids toward reaching the conditioned state.

To solve Eq. (3.7), we can begin by following the first few values of the series, using the recursive equation (3.7) repetitively. We shall assume that X_1 has no theoretical solution, but must be estimated empirically.

$$X_2 = AX_1 + B \qquad \text{[directly from Eq. (3.7)]};\tag{3.8}$$

$$X_3 = A(AX_1 + B) + B \qquad \text{[from Eqs. (3.7) and (3.8)]}$$
$$= A^2 X_1 + B(A + 1);\tag{3.9}$$

$$X_4 = A[A^2 X_1 + B(A + 1)] + B \qquad \text{[from Eqs. (3.7) and (3.9)]}$$
$$= A^3 X_1 + B(A^2 + A + 1);\tag{3.10}$$

$$X_5 = A[A^3 X_1 + B(A^2 + A + 1)] + B \qquad \text{[from Eqs. (3.7) and (3.10)]}$$
$$= A^4 X_1 + B(A^3 + A^2 + A + 1).$$

We can see that part of the general solution may be

$$X_n = A^{n-1} X_1 \cdots.\tag{3.11}$$

The remaining component of the tentative solution appears to be a series with a consistent pattern of change with changing values of n. We can therefore pause and sum this series, for a general term as a function of n. We use our summation technique for the sum $S = \sum_{k=0}^{n-2} A^k$.

$$S = 1 + A + A^2 + A^3 + \cdots + A^{n-3} + A^{n-2},$$
$$AS = A + A^2 + A^3 + \cdots + A^{n-2} + A^{n-1},$$

$$S(1 - A) = 1 - A^{n-1},$$

$$S = \frac{1 - A^{n-1}}{1 - A}.$$

In our tentative solution, implied by Eqs. (3.8)–(3.10), this series is multiplied by B, so that the full tentative solution appears to be

$$X_n = A^{n-1} X_1 + B \frac{(1 - A^{n-1})}{1 - A}.\tag{3.12}$$

which can also be expressed as

$$X_n = A^{n-1}\left(X_1 - \frac{B}{1 - A}\right) + \frac{B}{1 - A}.\tag{3.13}$$

We now use the technique of mathematical induction to check this solution.

To prove: $\quad X_n = A^{n-1}\left(X_1 - \dfrac{B}{1-A}\right) + \dfrac{B}{1-A}$ $\qquad$ (general statement).

Defining equation:

$$X_{n+1} = AX_n + B$$

STEP 1. *We verify the first couple of values in the sequence.*

For $n = 1$, $X_1 = X_1$ (since X_1 is a given). Putting $n = 1$ into our general statement, we find

$$X_1 = A^0\left(X_1 - \frac{B}{1-A}\right) + \frac{B}{1-A}$$

$$= X_1 - \frac{B}{1-A} + \frac{B}{1-A},$$

$$X_1 = X_1,$$

indicating that X_1 does not create any inconsistencies for our general statement, Eq. (3.13).

For $n = 2$, $X_2 = AX_1 + B$ (from the defining equation). Putting $n = 2$ into our general equation, we find

$$X_2 = A^{2-1}\left(X_1 - \frac{B}{1-A}\right) + \frac{B}{1-A}$$

$$= AX_1 - \frac{AB}{1-A} + \frac{B}{1-A}$$

$$= AX_1 + \frac{B(1-A)}{1-A}$$

$$= AX_1 + B,$$

the defining equation, thus verifying the general statement for $n = 2$.

STEP 2. *Assume that for $n = k$*

$$X_k = A^{k-1}\left(X_1 - \frac{B}{1-A}\right) + \frac{B}{1-A}. \qquad (3.14a)$$

STEP 3a.   *Operate on the kth term in the series.*

$$X_{k+1} = A\left[A^{k-1}\left(X_1 - \frac{B}{1-A}\right) + \frac{B}{1-A}\right] + B$$

by using the defining equation to obtain the operation on Eq. (3.14a) that represents the general statement.

STEP 3b.   *Algebraically manipulate the operation on the right-hand side.*

$$X_{k+1} = A^k\left(X_1 - \frac{B}{1-A}\right) + \frac{AB}{1-A} + B$$

$$= A^k\left(X_1 - \frac{B}{1-A}\right) + \frac{AB + B(1-A)}{1-A}$$

$$= A^k\left(X_1 - \frac{B}{1-A}\right) + \frac{AB + B - AB}{1-A},$$

$$X_{k+1} = A^k\left(X_1 - \frac{B}{1-A}\right) + \frac{B}{1-A}. \tag{3.14b}$$

STEP 4.   *Conclusion.* If Eq. (3.14a) is true for k any value, then Eq. (3.14b) is true. Therefore, for n equal any k,

$$X_n = A^{n-1}\left(X_1 - \frac{B}{1-A}\right) + \frac{B}{1-A}.$$

We have succeeded in speculating upon a possible solution to a difference equation of the form of Eq. (3.7), and then proving that our speculation was correct. At any time, then, that we were to find a situation where the relationship between one trial's probability and the next was of the form of Eq. (3.7), where X_n stood for the nth trial's probability, and A and B were constants, however complex in form, the solution would be Eq. (3.13). This means that given the values of the probability for the first trial and the values of A and B, the nth trial probability can be found.

We could proceed along the same lines with any recursive equation that we might encounter. However, the road of inductive speculation can be a long and tedious one, and always has to be followed by the proof through mathematical induction. Fortunately there are some algorithms for arriving at solutions to difference equations, and these can simplify the process. We shall examine two of these solution techniques. With some equations, one technique is easier to use than the other. Also, one can be used as a check on the other. For either or both, the technique of mathematical induction can always be called upon as a definitive check on the solution.

We shall first examine an algorithm which we shall identify as the *summation technique* for the solution of difference equations.

The Summation Technique for Solving Difference Equations

In pursuing a solution to an algebraic identity, such as

$$3x + 2 = 5 \qquad (3.15)$$

or

$$3x - 6 = 0, \qquad (3.16)$$

we often refer to the specific value of x that satisfies the equality as the *root* of the equation. The root of Eq. (3.15) would be 1, and of Eq. (3.16) would be 2. We shall use the term "root" similarly in our solutions of difference equations. A second term that we will use is *homogeneous*, which merely refers to that form of an equation in which the identity is with zero. Thus, Eq. (3.15) would not be a homogeneous equation in its current form, but if changed to $3x - 3 = 0$, it would be a homogeneous equation. Equation (3.16) is already a homogeneous equation.

In addition to the terms "root" and "homogeneous" we shall require the concept of an *operator*. We have defined a difference equation as an equality between one step in a series and a function on the previous step in that series. Along with the definition, we presented the simplest example of the recursive form of such an equation, Eq. (3.1):

$$X_{n+1} = A X_n.$$

In this example, the "function" transforming the value on step or trial n to its value on trial $n + 1$ is simply multiplication by A. In Eq. (3.7),

$$X_{n+1} = A X_n + B,$$

we saw a slightly more complex function doing the transformation to the next step in the sequence. We shall call the algebraic operation describing the rules for the transformation an *operator*. Applying an operator will mean changing the value at the nth step to its value at the $(n + 1)$st step in the sequence by applying the algebraic operations given in the recursive form of the difference equation. If the operator is applied twice, it will transform the value from the nth value in the sequence to the $(n + 2)$nd value in the sequence.

We now present the steps in the summation technique solution, using Eq. (3.7) for the example.

STEP 1. $X_{n+1} = A X_n + B$

is *the recursive equation* to be solved.

STEP 2. $X_{n+1} - AX_n = 0$

represents changing the equation to a *homogeneous form* by dropping all terms in the equation other than the value of the *n*th step and its coefficient (which is moved to the other side of the equation).

STEP 3. $\mathbf{D}X_n - AX_n = 0$

represents *changing to operator notation*, where the use of operator symbol $\mathbf{D}$ implies the next step in the sequence for the term for which it is a coefficient.

STEP 4. $(\mathbf{D} - A)X_n = 0,$

    Root $= A,$

reveals the root of the equation. Here $\mathbf{D}$ is treated as a variable, the value of which would make the equality true. It generally involves factoring out the *n*th-step value of the sequence in the way shown here.

STEP 5. $X_n = A^{n-1}C\cdots$

represents the *general solution of the homogeneous equation*. We take advantage of a mathematical theorem which states that the solution of a difference equation requires that we include the root to some specifiable power times a constant (for which we solve at a later step). The power of the root depends on the number of times that the coefficient of the *n*th step value has to be applied to reach the final *n*. [See Eqs. (3.8)–(3.10), leading to Eq. (3.11).] When we begin the sequence with X_1, the number of theoretical applications of the recursive equation is $n - 1$ to reach the *n*th step, and therefore the power is $n - 1$. If we denoted the first step in the sequence as X_0, then *n* applications of the recursive equation would be required to reach the step in the sequence notated as X_n, and the solution would have A (that is, the coefficient here symbolized as A) to the *n*th power times C.

We have now obtained the *general* solution for the *homogeneous* equation. To solve for the *complete* equation, as opposed to the homogeneous equation, we solve for whatever parts of the equation were omitted to obtain the homogeneous equation. When we solve for these temporarily excluded parts of the original equation, we add all of these solutions together to form the complete solution. Having the solutions to these additional parts of the equation all gathered into the equation, it is possible to solve for the constant C, which then gives us the correct complete *particular* solution, as opposed to the complete general solution.

We shall now solve for the formerly excluded term B. We shall use, as an operator, the term $(\mathbf{D} - A)$ from the fourth step in our solution. Representing the solution for the constant B by the symbol k, we shall ask, in Step 6, what value of the constant k, when operated on by the term $(\mathbf{D} - A)$, will yield the constant B. (This enables the root of the general solution to the homogeneous equation to enter into the solution for the omitted terms.)

STEP 6. $(\mathbf{D} - A)k = B$

represents *solving for an excluded term.*

STEP 7. $k - Ak = B$

represents *carrying out the operation of the term yielding the root,* on the excluded term. (Note that operating on a constant with $\mathbf{D}$ simply yields the constant. For example, $\mathbf{D}k = k$.)

STEP 8. $k(1 - A) = B$,

$$k = \frac{B}{1 - A},$$

represents the *algebraic clarification of the value of k.*

STEP 9. $X_n = A^{n-1}C + \dfrac{B}{1 - A}$

represents the *general solution of the complete equation* (obtained by adding the solutions of all of the parts of the equation).

We now solve for the constant C. To do this, we must isolate C, which requires eliminating its coefficient. We do this by equating the general solution of the complete equation with the value in the sequence that will reduce A^{n-1} to 1. That would be X_1, since $A^{1-1} = 1$. If the exponent of the root were n, we would have to use X_0. (The value used is generally the first value in the sequence, and with probabilities can often be estimated from the data. The value of X_0 or X_1 obtained in this way becomes a parameter of the model.) The algebra that follows this isolation of C is then standard, and is exampled in Step 10.

STEP 10. $X_1 = A^0 C + \dfrac{B}{1 - A}$,

$$C = X_1 - \frac{B}{1 - A}$$

represents *solving for the constant coefficient of the root* (here C).

STEP 11. $X_n = A^{n-1}\left(X_1 - \dfrac{B}{1-A}\right) + \dfrac{B}{1-A}$

represents the *particular solution of the complete equation* (obtained by substituting the solution of C from Step 10 into the general solution of the complete equation of Step 9).

STEP 12. $X_n = \dfrac{B}{1-A} - \left(\dfrac{B}{1-A} - X_1\right)A^{n-1}$

represents *the asymptotic solution*. This is identical to the complete particular solution of Step 11, but is sometimes restated this way to make clear the value of the solution as n goes to infinity. That is, since the root A is always a value between 0 and 1 in our literature, it approaches 0 as n approaches infinity, eliminating the second term in the solution.

Table 3.1 summarizes the preceding steps.

TABLE 3.1

Summation Technique Solution of the Difference Equation $X_{n+1} = AX_n + B$[a]

STEP 1.	$X_{n+1} = AX_n + B$	The recursive equation
STEP 2.	$X_{n+1} - AX_n = 0 \cdots$	Homogeneous form
STEP 3.	$\mathbf{D}X_n - AX_n = 0$	Changing to operator notation
STEP 4.	$(\mathbf{D} - A)X_n = 0$	Revealing the root of the equation
STEP 5.	$X_n = A^{n-1}C \cdots$	General solution of the homogeneous equation
STEP 6.	$(\mathbf{D} - A)k = B$	Solving for an excluded term
STEP 7.	$k - Ak = B$	Carrying out the operation of the term yielding the root
STEP 8.	$k(1 - A) = B, \quad k = \dfrac{B}{1-A}$	Algebraic clarification of the value of k
STEP 9.	$X_n = A^{n-1}C + \dfrac{B}{1-A}$	General solution of the complete equation
STEP 10.	$X_1 = A^0 C + \dfrac{B}{1-A}$ $C = X_1 - \dfrac{B}{1-A}$	Solving for the constant coefficient of the root
STEP 11.	$X_n = A^{n-1}\left(X_1 - \dfrac{B}{1-A}\right) + \dfrac{B}{1-A}$	Particular solution of the complete equation
STEP 12.	$X_n = \dfrac{B}{1-A} - \left(\dfrac{B}{1-A} - X_1\right)A^{n-1}$	The asymptotic solution

[a] See text for additional comments on steps.

Application of the Summation Technique for Solving Difference Equations

Stimulus sampling theory provided the most frequently used frame of reference in the early development of mathematical models of learning (Burke, Estes, & Hellyer, 1954; Estes, 1950, 1955; Estes & Burke, 1952; Estes & Straughan, 1954). There have been a number of different models beginning with the basic stimulus sampling assumptions. The different models have had in common the assumptions of chance variability in the sampling of stimuli, experimentally influenced variability in the associations of stimuli to responses, and behavioral variability based on stimulus impingement. [See Estes (1959) for a review of stimulus sampling theory history; Atkinson (1963) and Kintsch (1970, Ch. 3) for reviews of types of stimulus sampling models and their assumptions.]

We shall now explore one such model, which will be particularly helpful in explicating the use of difference equations.

A STIMULUS SAMPLING THEORY MODEL

We shall think of an organism as being reinforced for responding with a particular response, called A_1. The probability of the organism responding with this response on the nth trial will be symbolized as $P(A_{1_n})$. If we assume that the probabilities of the organism's responses are controlled by the stimulus properties of the environment, we shall assume some indeterminate number of undefined stimulus elements in the environment, each having some potential of impinging on the organism. For simplicity, we assume that the elements are initially indistinguishable for purposes of eliciting responses from the organism. That is, the environment is just a collection of equal-valence stimuli, some limited proportion of which impinges on the organism at any one time. At the point at which we observe behavior, we assume that every stimulus element has somehow become committed to one or another response. We further assume that it is readily dislodged from one stimulus–response association to another on any one trial, under conditions indicated below. We conceive of the organism responding with the response A_1 as a function of the stimuli that have just impinged. Specifically, the probability of response A_1 occurring is a function of the percentage of stimuli in the environment that are attached to A_1. Since the organism is generally confronted by only a proportion of the environment at any one time, he may happen to confront only stimuli that are connected to response A_1 prior to one trial, ensuring then the occurrence of that particular response. Or there may be no A_1-connected stimuli impinging just prior to the response, ensuring the non-occurrence of the A_1 response. More frequently, there will be some combination of stimuli, where the proportion of stimuli attached to the A_1 response would determine the probability of response A_1 on that trial. Assuming random sampling of the complete population of stimuli in the environment on each trial, in the long run the probability of response A_1 would reflect the status of stimulus attachments in the general population of available stimuli. However, on any one trial, for one subject, the response would reflect the proportions in the immediately preceding sample only.

We indicated that the stimuli have no special response predetermination; that is, the class of response that each stimulus evokes can be changed. This requires some axioms in the model specifying the basis for stimulus–response attachment and change.

The basis for such attachment and change is simply the appearance of the stimulus in the sample immediately prior to the reinforcement of some one class of response. That is, stimuli are attached to responses as a result of stimulus–*reinforcement* juxtapositions. In this model, no statement is made as to the necessity of the response that is reinforced being made. This type of model developed with the aid of paired-associate learning paradigms, where reinforcement can be viewed as a form of information presentation at each trial. The subject, even if he has made an incorrect response, can be informed as to the correct response when the correct response appears on the rotating drum after he has made his guess. In this model, then, each trial consists of some stimulus sampling by the organism, followed by a response that can inform the experimenter of the relative balance of stimuli attached to a response class in the last stimulus sample. The response is then followed by a reinforcement that can affect the stimulus–reponse associations by attaching all of the stimuli that were just present to the reinforced response. If some stimuli present were already attached to the response class of the upcoming re-inforcement, they remain attached to the same response (the response that the reinforcement indicates is correct). If the antecedent stimuli are attached to some other response, they are immediately attached to the new response.

We shall assume only two classes of response, A_1 and A_2, with only A_1 being reinforced. We then have responses A_1 and A_2 with reinforcements E_1 and E_2, respectively, but in this initial version of the model we shall assume that only E_1 will occur. We also have an environment consisting of N stimuli. On any one trial, some proportion of these N stimuli impinge on the organism. We symbolize the proportion as θ, and consider that the stimulus elements are sampled on a random basis for each trial.

SOME DIFFERENCE EQUATIONS IN A STIMULUS SAMPLING MODEL

In order to be able to describe the trial-by-trial changes in the probability of some selected response (in this case response A_1), we build our equations as difference equations in recursive form, with trial number as the integer variable. We go about this in much the same way that we built equations using the direct method. That is, we symbolize, and then mathematize, the implications of the theory.

Working with a Single Operator

On a single trial, the number of elements impinging on the organism are θN, since there are N elements in the population of possible stimuli and the proportion of these stimuli impinging on each trial is θ. Since we assume that the characteristics of this random sample of stimuli are in the long run representative of the whole population of N stimuli, we assume that the same proportion of stimuli are attached to response A_1 in the sample as there are in the whole population of N stimuli [symbolized (p_{1n})].

To obtain the total number of stimuli attached to response A_1 on trial n, we multiply the proportion of stimuli attached to A_1 by the number of stimuli in the population N. This means that the number of all stimuli attached to response A_1 on trial n is Np_{1n}.

We now wish a statement of the number of stimlui on trial $n + 1$ attached to A_1 as a function of the stimuli attached to A_1 on trial n, in order to develop a recursive equation. We noted previously that the stimuli on a trial that are already attached to the response being reinforced on that trial do not change their attachments. Thus, the number of stimuli Np_{1n} already attached on trial n is not changed by trial n (given E_1 reinforcement), and specifically the θNp_{1n} such A_1 attached stimuli sampled on that trial remain attached to A_1.

What about those stimuli that are not attached to response A_1 on trial n? There are $\theta N(1 - p_{1n})$ of them. Trial n increases the number of stimuli attached to A_1 by precisely this amount, since these are the number of stimuli present but not attached to the reinforced response at the beginning of trial n. At the end of trial n, given a reinforcement of response A_1, these stimuli are added to the total number of stimuli attached to A_1. If we add the total number of stimuli attached to response A_1 at the beginning of trial n, which is Np_1, to the amount increased during trial n, which is $\theta N(1 - p_{1n})$ we have

$$Np_{1n+1} = Np_{1n} + \theta N(1 - p_{1n}). \tag{3.17}$$

However, N represents an unknown number. It is clear that many additional axioms would be required to attempt to state the exact number of stimuli into which the environment should be divided for best prediction. Consequently, we remove N, and thereby remove the problem of its estimation, by dividing both sides of Eq. (3.17) by N. This will leave us with proportions, rather than numbers, but according to our theory, the proportion of stimuli attached to a response suggests the probability of that response, which is precisely that which was desired. We then carry out the division by N, which gives us the following recursive statement of probability (proportion) changes from trial n to trial $n + 1$.

$$p_{1n+1} = p_{1n} + \theta(1 - p_{1n}), \tag{3.18}$$

which, when multiplied through, gives

$$p_{1n+1} = p_{1n} + \theta - \theta p_{1n},$$

and, equivalently,

$$p_{1n+1} = p_{1n}(1 - \theta) + \theta. \tag{3.19}$$

We have rearranged Eq. (3.18) to Eq. (3.19) so that we would have a difference equation in the recursive form of Eq. (3.7), where p_{1n} is equivalent to X_n, $(1 - \theta)$ is equivalent to A, and θ is equivalent to B.

We can insert these equivalent symbols into Eq. (3.13), and then have a solution to Eq. (3.19), which we find to be

$$p_{1n} = 1 - (1 - p_{11})(1 - \theta)^{n-1}. \tag{3.20}$$

However, we shall go through the algorithm for the summation technique of solving difference equations, as shown in Table 3.1, to illustrate the technique again in Table 3.2.

TABLE 3.2

Summation Technique Solution of the Difference Equation $p_{1n+1} = p_{1n}(1 - \theta) + \theta$

PART I.	*Obtaining the Root*
1. $p_{1n+1} = p_{1n}(1 - \theta) + \theta$	The recursive equation
2. $p_{1n+1} - (1 - \theta)p_{1n} = 0$	The homogeneous form
3. $Dp_{1n} - (1 - \theta)p_{1n} = 0$	Changing to operator notation
4. $[D - (1 - \theta)]p_{1n} = 0$	Revealing the root of the equation
$\text{Root} = (1 - \theta)$	
5. $p_{1n} = (1 - \theta)^{n-1} C \cdots$	General solution of the homogeneous equation
PART II.	*Obtaining Values for the Constants*
6. $[D - (1 - \theta)]k = \theta$	Solving for an excluded term
7. $k - k + k\theta = \theta$	Carrying out the operation of the term yielding the root
8. $k\theta = \theta$	Algebraic clarification of the value of k
$k = 1$	
9. $p_{1n} = (1 - \theta)^{n-1}C + 1$	General solution of the complete equation
10. $p_{11} = (1 - \theta)^{0}C + 1$	Solving for the constant coefficient of the root
$C = p_{11} - 1$	
11. $p_{1n} = (1 - \theta)^{n-1}(p_{11} - 1) + 1$	Particular solution of the complete equation
12. $p_{1n} = 1 - (1 - p_{11})(1 - \theta)^{n-1}$	The asymptotic solution[a]

[a] Note that the asymptotic probability of a correct response, according to these equations, is 1.

Working with Two Operators

Suppose that instead of reinforcing only response A_1 on every trial, we now reinforce some other response A_2 as well. What would happen to the probability of response A_1 on trials that have been reinforced by E_2? Following the previous analysis for E_1 reinforcement, we would have some number Np_{1n} of stimuli conditioned to response A_1 at the beginning of trial n. Some proportion θ of these would appear in the sample of stimuli during trial n, which would then change their attachments from A_1 to A_2, following the E_2 reinforcement. That is, after trial n, the number of stimuli attached to A_1 should be $Np_{1n} - \theta Np_{1n}$. Again, dividing by N to get the proportion of stimuli attached to response A_1 (but this time after reinforcement E_2), we would have

$$p_{1n+1} = p_{1n} - \theta p_{1n};$$

using the notation of conditional probability, this would be $\{P(A_{1n+1}|E_{2n})\}$. Making the recursive form manifest, we would have

$$p_{1n+1} = (1 - \theta)p_{1n}, \tag{3.21}$$

given reinforcement condition E_2.

To obtain the solution of Eq. (3.21), we can go through the algorithm for the summation technique (going from Step 5 in Table 3.1 or 3.2 directly to Step 10). More simply, we can use the solution implied by Eq. (3.4), where $(1 - \theta)$ replaced A and p_{1n} replaced X_n. The solution is then

$$p_{1n} = (1 - \theta)^{n-1}p_{11}, \tag{3.22}$$

given reinforcement condition E_2.

We now have two difference equations giving the probability of response A_1 on any trial. In one case [Eq. (3.20)] we are given that the A_1 response was reinforced on each previous trial; in the other one [Eq. (3.22)], we are given that the A_2 response was reinforced on each previous trial.

Let us now assume that the experimenter wishes to reinforce both responses, but each one some predetermined percentage of the time. That is, regardless of the particular response sequences that the subject emits, some proportion is followed by E_1 and the complementary proportion is followed by E_2. We shall need to distinguish the trial number of a particular reinforcement, so we shall include a second subscript on the reinforcement symbols E_{1n} and E_{2n}, indicating, respectively, a reinforcement of response A_1 on trial n and a reinforcement of response A_2 on trial n.

We can see from probability equations (2.8) and (2.21) in Chapter Two that

$$P(A_{1n+1}) = P(A_{1n+1}|E_{1n})P(E_{1n}) + P(A_{1n+1}|E_{2n})P(E_{2n}). \quad (3.23a)$$

We can more conveniently symbolize $P(E_{1n})$, the probability of the occurrence of E_1 on trial n, as π_1. [Assuming that $P(E_{1n})$ is constant for all n obviates the necessity for the addition of n to π_1.] Similarly, we have π_2 for $P(E_{2n})$. We then have π_1 and π_2 as the percentage of times, respectively, that A_1 responses and A_2 responses were reinforced. Using recursive equations (3.19) and (3.21) in Eq. (3.23), and using π_j for $P(E_{jn})$, we would have

$$p_{1n+1} = [(1 - \theta)p_{1n} + \theta]\pi_1 + [(1 - \theta)p_{1n}]\pi_2. \quad (3.23b)$$

Rearranging this equation so that its recursive features are manifest gives

$$p_{1n+1} = [(1 - \theta)p_{1n}](\pi_1 + \pi_2) + \theta\pi_1.$$

Since E_1 and E_2 are the only reinforcements that are possible, their probabilities are complementary; that is, $\pi_1 + \pi_2 = 1$, yielding

$$p_{1n+1} = (1 - \theta)p_{1n} + \theta\pi_1. \quad (3.24)$$

This is the recursive form of the probability of response A_1 given the predetermined probabilities π_1 and π_2 for reinforcements E_1 and E_2. This is called the noncontingent form of this model, since the probability of a particular reinforcement is not contingent on the subject's response, but is preset by the experimenter as π_1 and π_2. An alternative assumption is discussed by Estes (1957). We can solve Eq. (3.24) in the way that we solved Eq. (3.19), that is, with the algorithm of Table 3.1 or 3.2, or by simply using Eq. (3.13) as a model. You should attempt this for yourself. You will find the answer to be, at Step 11 in Tables 3.1 and 3.2,

$$p_{1n} = (1 - \theta)^{n-1}(p_{11} - \pi_1) + \pi_1. \quad (3.25)$$

Changing to the asymptotic form (Step 12), you should have

$$p_{1n} = \pi_1 - (\pi_1 - p_{11})(1 - \theta)^{n-1}. \quad (3.26)$$

Equation (3.26) [and Eq. (3.25)] gives us the probability distribution for the value of a particular random variable. This is a random variable with only two possible values, 1 or 0. We give the value of 1 to the focal event, in this case response A_1, and 0 to its nonoccurrence. We then ask, what is the probability of the random variable having the value of 1 on some trial n? At each point n there is some different probability value, giving a distribution of values, and this distribution is obtainable from Eq. (3.26) [or Eq. (3.25)] by using different values of n from trial 1 to the last trial run in the experiment. We can look at a graph obtained through Eq. (3.26), or make the computations at any particular point n, and have a theoretical probability of the occurrence of response A_1 on that trial.

We could then have a distribution of probability values, one for each trial, for a dichotomous event, response A_1 or not response A_1. As indicated in Chapter Two, Eq. (2.51), we can sum the probabilities of a dichotomous event, such as response A_1, over a series of, say, m trials to obtain the expected number of occurrences of A_1 in m trials. From Eq. (3.26) we have

$$\sum_{n=1}^{m} p_{1n} = \sum_{n=1}^{m} [\pi_1 - (\pi_1 - p_{11})(1 - \theta)^{m-1}]$$

$$= m\pi_1 - (\pi_1 - p_{11}) \sum_{n=1}^{m} (1 - \theta)^{m-1} .$$

(The sum of a constant is simply the number of times that the constant is summed times the constant, which is the reason that $\sum_{n=1}^{m} \pi_1 = m\pi_1$.) We carry out the summation of the exponential term as suggested in Chapter Two (see Table 2.2). This gives us

$$\sum_{n=1}^{m} p_{1n} = m\pi_1 - (\pi_1 - p_{11}) \left[\frac{1 - (1 - \theta)^m}{\theta} \right]. \tag{3.27}$$

Equation (3.27) offers us the average number of A_1 responses that the theory predicts in m trials, with noncontingent E_1 and E_2 reinforcements.

You might try computing values for the probability of an A_1 response on trials 4, 6, and 8 by using Eq. (3.26), the parameter values $\theta = .2$ and $\pi_1 = .5$, and the probability of the correct response on the first trial, $p_{11} = 0$. (The answers should be .25, .34, and .40, respectively.) You might also compute the total *number* of correct responses expected to occur by each of these trials, using Eq. (3.27) and these same parameters. (The answers should be .6, 1.15, and 1.92.)

The Contingent Case

There are times when it might be desirable to assume that the reinforcement probabilities are contingent on the response (Estes, 1957). That is, a probability of reinforcing response A_1, given that A_1 has occurred, might be some probability π_{11}, whereas the probability of reinforcing response A_1 given that A_2 has just occurred might be some other probability π_{21}. This is always possible in a paradigm in which reinforcement is really informational (rather than stimuli with drive-reducing, or hedonistic, implications). For example, in a guessing task (such as "which of two lights will occur next?"), we could think of an electronically controlled program that scheduled a different probability of reinforcement on a particular trial, depending on which response had occurred. (The subject could press either a left or a right button for his choice.) Then

$$P(E_1|A_1) = \pi_{11} \tag{3.28}$$

might be different than

$$P(E_1|A_2) = \pi_{21}, \tag{3.29}$$

causing us to distinguish two π_1 values, one after response A_1 and the other after response A_2. [In the noncontingent case, $\pi_{11} = \pi_{21}$ and $\pi_{22} = \pi_{12}$. With $P(E_1|A_1) = P(E_1|A_2)$ we have $P(E_1) = P(E_1|A_j)$ for all j. Therefore, we have independence, as defined in Eq. (2.14), between the probability of an error on any trial and reinforcement or nonreinforcement on the previous trial.] Despite these possible inequalities among the four possible trial outcomes in the contingent case, we have the following equalities:

$$\pi_{11} = 1 - \pi_{12} \tag{3.30}$$

and

$$\pi_{22} = 1 - \pi_{21}. \tag{3.31}$$

Equation (3.30) is due to the fact that $\pi_{11} + \pi_{12}$ constitute the two complementary alternatives, given that the subject responds with response A_1. That is,

$$P(E_{1n}|A_{1n}) + P(E_{2n}|A_{1n}) = 1. \tag{3.32}$$

Equation (3.32) comes from Eq. (2.2), since the terms in the left-hand sum are mutually exclusive and exhaustive probabilistic alternatives. Equation (3.32) can also be shown to be correct by multiplying both sides of the equality by $P(A_{1n})$ to obtain

$$P(E_{1n}|A_{1n})P(A_{1n}) + P(E_{2n}|A_{1n})P(A_{1n}) = P(A_{1n}),$$

which yields from Eqs. (2.8) and (2.9),

$$P(A_{1n}E_{1n}) + P(A_{1n}E_{2n}) = P(A_{1n}),$$

which is equivalent to the valid Eq. (2.21).

With similar rationale, we can obtain

$$P(E_{1n}|A_{2n}) + P(E_{2n}|A_{2n}) = 1. \tag{3.33}$$

Substituting π_{ij} for $P(E_{jn}|A_{in})$, we can obtain Eqs. (3.30) and (3.31), respectively, from Eqs. (3.32) and (3.33).

Let us now examine the contingent case, and derive a desired distribution of response probabilities. We have previously stated [Eq. (3.23)]

$$P(A_{1n+1}) = P(A_{1n+1}|E_{1n})P(E_{1n}) + P(A_{1n+1}|E_{2n})P(E_{2n})$$

for the noncontingent case. But in the contingent case, $P(E_{jn})$ will be different, conditional upon the previous response. We again use Eqs. (2.8) and (2.21), this time to construct

$$P(E_{1n}) = P(E_{1n}|A_{1n})P(A_{1n}) + P(E_{1n}|A_{2n})P(A_{2n}). \tag{3.34}$$

On any one trial, say trial n, the subject can only produce either response A_1 or response A_2, so that

$$P(A_{2n}) = 1 - P(A_{1n}).$$

We can then restate Eq. (3.34) as

$$P(E_{1n}) = P(E_{1n}|A_{1n})P(A_{1n}) + P(E_{1n}|A_{2n})[1 - P(A_{1n})]. \tag{3.35}$$

Using Eqs. (3.28)–(3.30), we can restate Eq. (3.35) as

$$P(E_{1n}) = (1 - \pi_{12})P(A_{1n}) + \pi_{21}[1 - P(A_{1n})],$$

from which we can obtain

$$P(E_{1n}) = P(A_{1n})(1 - \pi_{12} - \pi_{21}) + \pi_{21}. \tag{3.36}$$

For later use, we can note at this point that since on a particular trial n either an E_1 or an E_2 reinforcement (but not both) will occur, we have

$$P(E_{2n}) = 1 - P(E_{1n}). \tag{3.37}$$

At this point, it will be helpful to equate components of, and juxtapose, some previously presented equations:

$$P(A_{1n+1}|E_{1n}) = p_{1n}(1 - \theta) + \theta = p_{1n+1}, \tag{3.19}$$

given an E_1 reinforcement on the previous trial;

$$P(A_{1n+1}|E_{2n}) = p_{1n}(1 - \theta) = p_{1n+1}, \tag{3.21}$$

given an E_2 reinforcement on the previous trial;

$$P(A_{1n+1}) = P(A_{1n+1}|E_{1n})P(E_{1n}) + P(A_{1n+1}|E_{2n})P(E_{2n}) = p_{1n+1}. \quad [3.23]$$

We now restate Eq. (3.23), using the preceding equivalences:

$$p_{1n+1} = [p_{1n}(1 - \theta) + \theta]P(E_{1n}) + [p_{1n}(1 - \theta)][1 - P(E_{1n})]$$

[restating (3.23) with the aid of (3.19), (3.21), and (3.37)]

$$\begin{aligned}
p_{1n+1} &= p_{1n}(1 - \theta)[P(E_{1n}) + 1 - P(E_{1n})] + \theta P(E_{1n}) \\
&= p_{1n}(1 - \theta) + \theta P(E_{1n}) \\
&= p_{1n}(1 - \theta) + \theta[p_{1n}(1 - \pi_{12} - \pi_{21}) + \pi_{21}] \quad \text{[from Eq. (3.36)]} \\
&= p_{1n}[(1 - \theta) + \theta(1 - \pi_{12} - \pi_{21})] + \theta\pi_{21},
\end{aligned}$$

$$p_{1n+1} = p_{1n}[1 - \theta(\pi_{12} + \pi_{21})] + \theta\pi_{21}. \tag{3.38}$$

Equation (3.38) is the recursive form for the probability of an A_1 response in the case of response-contingent reinforcement probabilities. You should attempt to solve this with the steps previously outlined for the summation technique for solving difference equations in Tables 3.1 and 3.2. It can also be solved by using Eq. (3.13) as a model, with $p_{1n} = X_n$, $A = [1 - \theta(\pi_{12} + \pi_{21})]$ and $B = \theta\pi_{21}$. The answer in either case will be

$$p_{1n} = [1 - \theta(\pi_{12} + \pi_{21})]^{n-1}\left(p_{11} - \frac{\pi_{21}}{\pi_{12} + \pi_{21}}\right) + \frac{\pi_{21}}{\pi_{12} + \pi_{21}} \tag{3.39}$$

and, in asymptotic form,

$$p_{1n} = \frac{\pi_{21}}{\pi_{12} + \pi_{21}} - \left(\frac{\pi_{21}}{\pi_{12} + \pi_{21}} - p_{11}\right)[1 - \theta(\pi_{12} + \pi_{21})]^{n-1}. \tag{3.40}$$

Up to this point, we have solved only recursive difference equations of the form

$$X_{n+1} = AX_n \quad \text{and} \quad X_{n+1} = AX_n + B.$$

The summation technique applied to two additional possible recursive forms,

$$X_{n+1} = AX_n + LB^{n-1}, \tag{3.41}$$

and

$$X_{n+1} = AX_n + B^{n-1} + L, \tag{3.42}$$

are presented in Tables 3.3 and 3.4, respectively.

TABLE 3.3

Summation Technique Solution of the Difference Equation $X_{n+1} = AX_n + LB^{n-1}$, $B \neq A$

STEP 1.	$X_{n+1} = AX_n + LB^{n-1}$	The recursive equation
STEP 2.	$X_{n+1} - AX_n = 0$	Homogeneous form
STEP 3.	$DX_n - AX_n = 0$	Changing to operator notation
STEP 4.	$(D - A)X_n = 0$ $\text{Root} = A$	Revealing the root of the equation
STEP 5.	$X_n = A^{n-1}C \cdots$	General solution of the homogeneous equation
STEP 6.	$(D - A)\lambda k^{n-1} = LB^{n-1}$	Solving for an excluded term[a]
STEP 7.	$\lambda k^n - A\lambda k^{n-1} = LB^{n-1}$	Carrying out the operation of the term yielding the root[b]
STEP 8.	$\lambda k^{n-1}(k - A) = LB^{n-1}$ $\lambda k^{n-1} = \dfrac{LB^{n-1}}{B - A}$	Algebraic clarification[c] of the value of λk^{n-1}
STEP 9.	$X_n = A^{n-1}C + \dfrac{LB^{n-1}}{B - A}$	General solution of the complete equation
STEP 10.	$X_1 = A^0 C + \dfrac{LB^0}{B - A}$ $X_1 = C + \dfrac{L}{B - A}$ $C = X_1 - \dfrac{L}{B - A}$	Solving for the constant coefficient of the root
STEP 11.	$X_n = A^{n-1}\left(X_1 - \dfrac{L}{B - A}\right) + \dfrac{LB^{n-1}}{B - A}$ $= \left(X_1 + \dfrac{L}{A - B}\right)A^{n-1} - \dfrac{LB^{n-1}}{A - B}$	Particular solution of the complete equation (For simpler comparison with other tables)

[a] We assume the same trial-dependent form for symbolizing the solution, λk^{n-1}, as for the excluded term of the recursive form, LB^{n-1}.

[b] Although a term $D(\lambda k) = \lambda k$, a term $D(\lambda k^{n-1}) = \lambda k^n$. This is true because a constant having an exponent incorporating the subscript indexing recursion (n) will have its exponent changed with each change in the subscript (n).

[c] Note that on the right-hand side of the equality, $k = B$.

TABLE 3.4

Summation Technique Solution of the Difference Equation $X_{n+1} = AX_n + B^{n-1} + L$, $A \neq 1, A \neq B$

STEP 1.	$X_{n+1} = AX_n + B^{n-1} + L$	The recursive equation
STEP 2.	$X_{n+1} - AX_n = 0$	Homogeneous form
STEP 3.	$\mathbf{D}X_n - AX_n = 0$	Changing to operator notation
STEP 4.	$(\mathbf{D} - A)X_n = 0$ Root $= A$	Revealing the root of the equation
STEP 5.	$X_n = A^{n-1}C \cdots$	General solution of the homogeneous equation
STEP 6a.	$(\mathbf{D} - A)k^{n-1} = B^{n-1}$	Solving for an excluded term (See footnote a to Table 3.3.)
STEP 7a.	$k^n - Ak^{n-1} = B^{n-1}$	Carrying out the operation of the term yielding the root (See footnote b to Table 3.3.)
STEP 8a.	$k^{n-1}(k - A) = B^{n-1}$ $k^{n-1} = \dfrac{B^{n-1}}{B - A}$	Algebraic clarification of the value of k^{n-1} (On the right-hand side of the equality, $k = B$.)
STEP 6b.	$(\mathbf{D} - A)k = L$	Solving for an excluded term (This is the second such term.)
STEP 7b.	$k - Ak = L$	Carrying out the operation of the term yielding the root
STEP 8b.	$k(1 - A) = L$ $k = \dfrac{L}{1 - A}$	Algebraic clarification of the value of k
STEP 9.	$X_n = A^{n-1}C + \dfrac{B^{n-1}}{B - A} + \dfrac{L}{1 - A}$	General solution of the complete equation
STEP 10.	$X_1 = A^0 C + \dfrac{B^0}{B - A} + \dfrac{L}{1 - A}$ $X_1 = C + \dfrac{1}{B - A} + \dfrac{L}{1 - A}$ $C = X_1 - \dfrac{1}{B - A} - \dfrac{L}{1 - A}$	Solving for the constant coefficient of the root
STEP 11.	$X_n = A^{n-1}\left(X_1 - \dfrac{1}{B - A} - \dfrac{L}{1 - A} \right)$ $+ \dfrac{B^{n-1}}{B - A} + \dfrac{L}{1 - A}$	Particular solution of the complete equation
STEP 12.	$X_n = \dfrac{L}{1 - A} - \dfrac{B^{n-1}}{A - B}$ $- \left(\dfrac{L}{1 - A} - \dfrac{1}{A - B} - X_1 \right) A^{n-1}$	The asymptotic solution

The Multiple-Operator Technique for Solving Difference Equations

We shall now look at another algorithm for solving difference equations. In this method, we do not need to assume a homogeneous form to begin the solution. Rather, repeated applications of one or several operators gives us a homogeneous equation form. We begin by explicating the meaning of an equation in which a second or third operator appears.

The Meaning of Higher-Order Difference Equations

We have been working with first-order equations, that is, equations stating equalities between one step in a sequence and a function on the immediately preceding step, such as

$$X_{n+1} = AX_n + B.$$

In psychology, we are generally interested in effects of individual trials, and in changes from one trial to the immediately following one. We could conceive of a second-order equation, in which the equation states a relation between three successive trials rather than the two successive trials of a first-order equation. If n represented some arbitrary trial number, we might represent some sequence of probabilities as

$$P_{n+2} = 4P_{n+1} - 4P_n,$$

which can be restated as

$$P_{n+2} - 4P_{n+1} + 4P_n = 0.$$

Thinking of the operator $\mathbf{D}$ as moving the value of P to the next trial's P value, we might express this equation in the following way:

$$\mathbf{D}^2 P_n - 4\mathbf{D}P_n + 4P_n = 0, \tag{3.43}$$

which can be restated as

$$(\mathbf{D}^2 - 4\mathbf{D} + 4)P_n = 0. \tag{3.44}$$

The difference between the lowest and the highest n value gives the order of the equation. This, then, is a second-order equation. It is possible to have third-order, fourth-order, or even higher-order equations.

FINDING THE HOMOGENEOUS FORM WITH MULTIPLE OPERATORS

You are probably familiar with the quadratic equation

$$X^2 - aX + b = 0$$

from high-school algebra. This equation will have two nonzero roots, $+j$

and $+k$, that will constitute its solution. That is,

$$(X - k)(X \quad j) = X^2 - aX + b$$
$$= 0.$$

We can think of the operator $\mathbf{D}$ as we would of a variable X, and find the roots to our equation (3.43). Using the form of Eq. (3.44)

$$(\mathbf{D}^2 - 4\mathbf{D} + 4)P_n = 0$$

and assuming that P_n is not zero, we look for an analogous "characteristic" equation. This would be $X^2 - 4X + 4$, which would be equal to $(X - 2) \times (X - 2)$. Substituting $\mathbf{D}$ for X, we would have

$$(\mathbf{D} - 2)(\mathbf{D} - 2)P_n = (\mathbf{D}^2 - 4\mathbf{D} + 4)P_n, \tag{3.45}$$

which could be confirmed by carrying out the multiplication on the left side. The advantage of reexpressing Eq. (3.44) as (3.45) is that the value of $\mathbf{D}$ that would make the equality with zero true is more obvious in the form $(\mathbf{D} - 2)(\mathbf{D} - 2)$ than it is in $(\mathbf{D}^2 - 4\mathbf{D} - 4)$. That is, if we substitute the value of 2 for $\mathbf{D}$, we would have

$$(\mathbf{D} - 2)(\mathbf{D} - 2) = 0$$
$$= (\mathbf{D}^2 - 4\mathbf{D} - 4).$$

The values that, when substituted for $\mathbf{D}$, make the equality with zero true are called the roots of the equation. Since, $\mathbf{D}$ by definition, cannot have any value, we use the analogous form of a characteristic equation in X as a conceptual aid. But the mechanics of the solution do not require the substitution of an X.

Let us examine another equation.

$$2P_{n+2} = 6P_{n+1} - 4P_n.$$

We would divide each of the coefficients (that is, the entire equation) by the coefficient of the highest-order operator, in this case 2, obtaining

$$P_{n+2} = 3P_{n+1} - 2P_n.$$

Proceeding as before, we would have

$$P_{n+2} - 3P_{n+1} + 2P_n = 0,$$
$$(\mathbf{D}^2 - 3\mathbf{D} + 2)P_n = 0. \tag{3.46}$$

Since

$$(X - 1)(X - 2) = X^2 - 3X + 2,$$

we would have

$$(\mathbf{D} - 1)(\mathbf{D} - 2) = \mathbf{D}^2 - 3\mathbf{D} + 2,$$
$$(\mathbf{D} - 1)(\mathbf{D} - 2) = 0,$$

given proper substitutions for $\mathbf{D}$, so that the roots of Eq. (3.46) are 1 and 2. We hold in abeyance the question what to do with these roots.

Choice of Roots

At this point, it is important to become acquainted with the bases for choice of roots. In the past the root was mechanically determined. For example, in working with Eq. (3.7)

$$X_{n+1} = AX_n + B,$$

we simply transposed AX_n to the left-hand side and dropped B, whereupon the root emerged from the expression $(\mathbf{D} - A)$. That is,

$$X_{n+1} - AX_n = (\mathbf{D} - A)X_n.$$

However, we now wish initially to retain B, and by judicious choice of a second root, to eliminate B.

Remembering that $\mathbf{D}$ times a constant results in only the constant, we proceed as follows:

$$X_{n+1} = AX_n + B,$$
$$X_{n+1} - AX_n = B,$$
$$(\mathbf{D} - A)X_n = B,$$
$$(\mathbf{D} - 1)(\mathbf{D} - A)X_n = (\mathbf{D} - 1)B$$
$$= B - B$$
$$= 0,$$

yielding the roots 1 and A.

We can now see how the use of multiple operators can bring us to a homogeneous equation. We begin as for the summation technique, but when confronted with a remaining constant, symbolized as k, we select a value y for a particular value of k such that $(\mathbf{D} - y)k = 0$, and y is then the second root.

Multiple Roots

We shall now deal with the question what to do with the roots in the multiple operator technique. In the foregoing example, using Eq. (3.7), we found the roots to be 1 and A. In the summation technique, we used a theorem which said that the solution to the difference equation begins with the root taken to some appropriate power (generally n or $n - 1$) times some constant. In the multiple operator technique, we similarly take each root to the same appropriate power and multiply each root by a constant. As the roots may or may not be different, so, similarly, and independently of root similarity, the coefficients may or may not be different. We then add the two terms (each a product of a root to some power and a coefficient). For Eq. (3.7), the solution would require an equation of the form

$$X_n = C_1 1^{n-1} + C_2 A^{n-1}$$
$$= C_1 + C_2 A^{n-1}.$$

Solving for Constants

To solve an equation with two unknowns (the unknowns here are C_1 and C_2, since we assume that A is a number that we have merely symbolized as A) we need two equations in these same unknowns. Our equations hold true through all trials of n, so we simply select two appropriately simple instances, generally the earliest trials, and proceed to solve for C_1 and C_2 as with any simultaneous equation problem. In our example, we would have

$$\begin{aligned} X_2 &= C_1 + C_2 A, \\ X_1 &= C_1 + C_2, \end{aligned} \qquad (3.47)$$

$$\begin{aligned} X_2 - X_1 &= C_2 A - C_2 \\ &= C_2(A - 1), \end{aligned}$$

$$C_2 = \frac{X_2 - X_1}{A - 1}. \qquad (3.48)$$

It would appear that we could enter Eq. (3.47) with the value of C_2 as expressed in Eq. (3.48) and could then solve for C_1. But our solutions to the value of both C_1 and C_2 would require a knowledge of the value of both X_1 and X_2. Since X_1 is generally some initial trial value prior to the introduction of experimental variables, we are generally willing to estimate this value from the data (for example, X_1 might refer to the proportion of subjects making errors on the first trial, or the proportion of correct responses on the first trial, etc.). But X_2 would already reflect part of the process that we are hoping to predict, so for that reason alone we would prefer to avoid having to obtain that value empirically; that is, we would prefer to predict it. In addition, it is important to minimize the absolute number of empirically obtained values, so as to be able to maximize the amount of independent predictions in the model. We thus follow a procedure that can generally permit us to obtain expressions for our constants that are only in terms of numerical constants, such as A and the initial trial value X_1. We do this by taking advantage of the fact that we have two expressions for the value of each X_n. We have the recursive form expression, such as Eq. (3.7), and the form for the general solution of the complete equation, such as Eq. (3.47). We can therefore find two values for a term like $X_2 - X_1$. One of these would be obtained by subtracting one recursive expression from the other, and another by subtracting one general solution expression from another. In arranging such subtractions, it is possible to use the fact that by repeated applications of the recursive form, it is possible to express any value in terms only of X_1; that is, in Eq. (3.7), we can have

$$X_1 = X_1,$$
$$X_2 = AX_1 + B,$$
$$X_3 = A^2 X_1 + AB + B,$$
$$\vdots$$

Therefore, we can arrange a value of $X_2 - X_1$ purely in terms of X_1. This value is then equated with the general solution equivalent, as is seen in Step 9 of Table 3.5. Table 3.5 gives the complete set of steps for solving Eq. (3.7) with the multiple operator technique.

In the example of Table 3.5, Step 7 resulted in the elimination of C_2 and the isolation of C_1 within the expression $X_2 - X_1$. There are times when this will not occur with simple subtraction of X_1 from X_2. In those instances, either X_1 or X_2 (or both, if necessary) is multiplied by whatever value will allow the elimination of either C_1 or C_2, but not both. An example of this is presented in Steps 7 and 8 of Table 3.6.

MULTIPLE OPERATOR TECHNIQUE WITH EQUAL ROOTS

We shall also occasionally find that we have two or three roots that are equal. For example, for an equation such as

$$X_{n+1} = AX_n + BA^{n-1}, \tag{3.49}$$

our first few steps with the multiple operator technique would look like

$$X_{n+1} - AX_n = BA^{n-1}$$
$$(\mathbf{D} - A)X_n = BA^{n-1}$$
$$(\mathbf{D} - A)(\mathbf{D} - A)X_n = (\mathbf{D} - A)BA^{n-1}$$
$$= BA^n - BA^n$$
$$= 0,$$

giving us two roots, both equal to A.

Stating our solution in the general solution form, we would have

$$X_n = C_1 A^{n-1} + C_2 A^{n-1}.$$

TABLE 3.5

Multiple Operator Technique Solution of a Difference Equation
with Two Roots $X_{n+1} = AX_n + B$, $A \neq 1$

STEP 1.	$X_{n+1} = AX_n + B$	The recursive equation
STEP 2.	$\mathbf{D}X_n - AX_n = B$	Changing to operator notation
STEP 3.	$(\mathbf{D} - A)X_n = B$ First root $= A$	Revealing first root of the equation
STEP 4.	$(\mathbf{D} - 1)(\mathbf{D} - A)X_n = (\mathbf{D} - 1)B$ Second root $= 1$	Revealing second root of the equation[a]
STEP 5.	$(\mathbf{D} - 1)(\mathbf{D} - A)X_n = B - B$ $= 0$	Multiplying out the operator of the previous step to obtain a homogeneous equation
STEP 6.	$X_n = C_1 A^{n-1} + C_2 1^{n-1}$ $= C_1 A^{n-1} + C_2$	General solution of the complete equation
STEP 7.	$X_1 = C_1 + C_2$ $X_2 = C_1 A + C_2$ $X_2 - X_1 = C_1 A - C_1 + C_2 - C_2$ $X_2 - X_1 = C_1(A - 1)$	Stating as many values of X_n as there are roots, in general solution form; then subtracting
STEP 8.	$X_1 = X_1$ $X_2 = AX_1 + B$ $X_2 - X_1 = AX_1 - X_1 + B$ $X_2 - X_1 = X_1(A - 1) + B$	Stating as many values of X_n as there are roots, in recursive form; then subtracting
STEP 9.	$X_2 - X_1 = X_2 - X_1$ $X_1(A - 1) + B = C_1(A - 1)$	Equating the values as defined in recursive form (Step 8) with those as defined in general solution form (Step 7)
STEP 10.	$C_1 = X_1 + \dfrac{B}{A - 1}$ $= X_1 - \dfrac{B}{1 - A}$[b]	Solving the equality of previous step for C_1
STEP 11.	$X_1 = C_1 + C_2$ $X_1 = X_1 - \dfrac{B}{1 - A} + C_2$ $C_2 = \dfrac{B}{1 - A}$	Using solution of C_1 in simplest general solution formula to obtain value of C_2
STEP 12.	$X_n = \left(X_1 - \dfrac{B}{1 - A} \right) A^{n-1} + \dfrac{B}{1 - A}$	Putting values of C_1 and C_2 from Steps 10 and 11 into general solution of Step 6 to obtain the particular solution of the complete equation
STEP 13.	$X_n = \dfrac{B}{1 - A} - \left(\dfrac{B}{1 - A} - X_1 \right) A^{n-1}$	Asymptotic form

[a] In this case it is 1, but it would always be whatever value substituted for the leftmost $\mathbf{D}$ in Step 5, would produce a value of 0.

[b] For simpler comparison with previous tables.

TABLE 3.6

Multiple Operator Technique Solution of a Difference Equation
with Two Roots $X_{n+1} = AX_n + LB^{n-1}$, $A \neq B$

STEP 1.	$X_{n+1} = AX_n + LB^{n-1}$	The recursive equation
STEP 2.	$\mathbf{D}X_n - AX_n = LB^{n-1}$	Changing to operator notation
STEP 3.	$(\mathbf{D} - A)X_n = LB^{n-1}$ First root $= A$	Revealing first root of the equation
STEP 4.	$(\mathbf{D} - B)(\mathbf{D} - A)X_n = (\mathbf{D} - B)LB^{n-1}$ Second root $= B$	Revealing second root of the equation
STEP 5.	$(\mathbf{D} - B)(\mathbf{D} - A)X_n = LB^n - LB^n$ $= 0$	Multiplying out the operator of the previous step to obtain the homogeneous equation (See footnote b to Table 3.3)
STEP 6.	$X_n = C_1 A^{n-1} + C_2 B^{n-1}$	General solution of the complete equation
STEP 7.	$BX_1 = C_1 B + C_2 B$ $X_2 = C_1 A + C_2 B$ $X_2 - BX_1 = C_1 A - C_1 B$ $X_2 - BX_1 = C_1(A - B)$	Stating as many values of X_n as there are roots, in general solution form, then subtracting[a]
STEP 8.	$BX_1 = BX_1$ $X_2 = AX_1 + L$ $X_2 - BX_1 = AX_1 - BX_1 + L$ $X_2 - BX_1 = X_1(A - B) + L$	Stating as many values of X_n as there are roots, in recursive form, then subtracting[b]
STEP 9.	$X_2 - BX_1 = X_2 - BX_1$ $X_1(A - B) + L = C_1(A - B)$	Equating the values as defined in recursive form (Step 8) with those defined in general solution form (Step 7)
STEP 10.	$C_1 = X_1 + \dfrac{L}{A - B}$	Solving the equality of the previous step for C_1
STEP 11.	$X_1 = C_1 + C_2$ $X_1 = X_1 + \dfrac{L}{A - B} + C_2$ $C_2 = -\dfrac{L}{A - B}$	Using solution of C_1 in the simplest general solution formula to obtain C_2
STEP 12.	$X_n = \left(X_1 + \dfrac{L}{A - B}\right)A^{n-1} - \dfrac{LB^{n-1}}{A - B}$	Putting values of C_1 and C_2 from Steps 10 and 11 into the general solution of the complete equation of Step 6 to obtain the particular solution of the complete equation

[a] In subtracting X_1 from X_2, we would obtain an answer in both C_1 and C_2, which necessitated our using BX_1 rather than X_1.

[b] We would normally begin with X_1 rather than BX_1. However, having found that BX_1 was necessary in Step 7, we use BX_1 also in this step.

TABLE 3.7

Multiple Operator Technique Solution of a Difference Equation
with Equal Roots $X_{n+1} = AX_n + BA^{n-1}$, $A \neq 0$

STEP 1.	$X_{n+1} = AX_n + BA^{n-1}$	The recursive equation
STEP 2.	$\mathbf{D}X_n - AX_n = BA^{n-1}$	Changing to operator notation
STEP 3.	$(\mathbf{D} - A)X_n = BA^{n-1}$	Revealing first root of the equation
	First root $= A$	
STEP 4.	$(\mathbf{D} - A)(\mathbf{D} - A)X_n = (\mathbf{D} - A)BA^{n-1}$	Revealing second root of the equation
	Second root $= A$	
STEP 5.	$(\mathbf{D} - A)^2 X_n = BA^n - BA^n$	Multiplying out the operator of the
	$= 0$	previous step to obtain the homo-geneous equation
STEP 6.	$X_n = C_1 A^{n-1} + (n-1)C_2 A^{n-1}$	General solution of the complete equation[a]
STEP 7.	$X_1 = C_1 A^0 + (0)C_2 A^0$	Stating as many values of X_n as there
	$X_1 = C_1$	are roots, in general solution form,
	$X_2 = C_1 A + C_2 A$	then subtracting
	$X_2 - X_1 = C_1(A - 1) + C_2 A$	
	Unacceptable, since it includes both C_1 and C_2; therefore:	
	$AX_1 = C_1 A$	
	$X_2 = C_1 A + C_2 A$	
	$X_2 - AX_1 = C_2 A$	
STEP 8.	$AX_1 = AX_1$	Stating as many values of X_n as
	$X_2 = AX_1 + B$	there are roots, in recursive form,
	$X_2 - AX_1 = B$	then subtracting[b]
STEP 9.	$X_2 - AX_1 = X_2 - AX_1$	Equating the values as defined in
	$B = C_2 A$	recursive form (Step 8) with those as defined in general solution form (Step 7)
STEP 10.	$C_2 = \dfrac{B}{A}$	Solving the equality of the previous step for C_2
STEP 11.	From the initial try in Step 7, we see that	We would normally use the solution to C_2, in the general solution form
	$C_1 = X_1$	of X_1, to obtain C_1, but C_1 was already isolated
STEP 12.	$X_n = C_1 A^{n-1} + (n-1)C_2 A^{n-1}$	Putting values of C_1 and C_2 from
	$X_n = X_1 A^{n-1} + (n-1)\dfrac{B}{A} A^{n-1}$	previous steps into the general solution of the complete equation of
	$X_n = X_1 A^{n-1} + (n-1)BA^{n-2}$	Step 6 to obtain the particular
	$X_n = [X_1 A + (n-1)B]A^{n-2}$	solution of the complete equation

[a] We use the form of Eq. (3.52), since that will allow us to eliminate C_2 in part of the next step.

[b] The previous step suggested the necessity for AX_1 rather than X_1, so that a useful equality could be maintained in the next step.

With such a general form for all values of n, it would be impossible to eliminate C_1 and C_2 from an equation separately, even using the extra multiplication step in Table 3.6. Fortunately, it is possible to reexpress the general form as either

$$X_n = C_1 A^{n-1} + nC_2 A^{n-1},$$

or

$$X_n = C_1 A^{n-1} + (n-1)C_2 A^{n-1}.$$

In general, with k equal roots (and symbolizing the equal roots as A and any unequal roots as U), we can use the forms

$$X_n = C_1 A^{n-1} + nC_2 A^{n-1} + n^2 C_3 A^{n-1} + \cdots$$
$$+ n^{k-1} C_k A^{n-1} + C_{k+1} U^{n-1} + \cdots, \quad (3.50)$$

$$X_n = C_1 A^{n-1} + nC_2 A^{n-1} + n(n-1)C_3 A^{n-1} + \cdots$$
$$+ n(n-1)(n-2)(n-3) \cdots [n-(k-2)]C_k A^{n-1} + C_{k+1} U^{n-1} + \cdots, \quad (3.51)$$

$$X_n = C_1 A^{n-1} + (n-1)C_2 A^{n-1} + (n-1)(n-2)C_3 A^{n-1} + \cdots$$
$$+ (n-1)(n-2)(n-3)(n-4) \cdots [n-(k-1)]C_k A^{n-1} + C_{k+1} U^{n-1} + \cdots.$$
$$(3.52)$$

Note that C_1 through C_k are constants for the equal roots, with any number of unequal roots in addition, as coefficients for C_{k+1}, C_{k+2}, etc.

Our choice of a particular alternate form from Eqs. (3.50)–(3.52) is based on the advantages that each offers for eliminating terms conveniently during the simultaneous equation solution part of the algorithm.

In Table 3.7 we present the multiple operator technique applied to the solution of an equation with two equal roots:

$$X_{n+1} = AX_n + BA^{n-1}. \quad (3.53)$$

MATHEMATICAL INDUCTION AS A DEFINITIVE CHECK

In examining the applications of the algorithms of the summation and multiple operator techniques, it can be seen that these have to be modified in terms of number of steps or in terms of the particular algebraic problems encountered in solving a specific equation. When working with equation forms that have not been presented in this text, you may experience some doubt as to the validity of your conclusion. In those instances, you will find that since you will already have a tentative solution, you can apply the technique of mathematical induction to check your solution. You should carry out the steps of confirmation for our solution to Eq. (3.53) if you are not yet comfortable in the use of mathematical induction.

In Table 3.8 we summarize the solutions to the recursive forms of some of the difference equations that we have examined in this chapter. Solutions take interesting, and at times helpfully simplified, forms when the same parameters appear at more than one point in the recursive form, as can be seen by comparing (3.41) and (3.53). Other such equations to be found in the text are Eq. (3.19), (3.24), and (3.38), the solutions to which are found in Eq. (3.20), (3.26), and (3.40), respectively.

TABLE 3.8

Solutions to Some Difference Equations

Equation number	Recursive form	Solution
(3.5)	$X_{n+1} = AX_n$	$X_n = X_1 A^{n-1}$
(3.7)	$X_{n+1} = AX_n + B$	$X_n = \dfrac{B}{1-A} - \left(\dfrac{B}{1-A} - X_1\right)A^{n-1}$
(3.41)	$X_{n+1} = AX_n + LB^{n-1}$	$X_n = \left(X_1 + \dfrac{L}{A-B}\right)A^{n-1} - \dfrac{LB^{n-1}}{A-B}$
(3.42)	$X_{n+1} = AX_n + B^{n-1} + L$	$X_n = \dfrac{L}{1-A} - \dfrac{B^{n-1}}{A-B}$ $- \left(\dfrac{L}{1-A} - \dfrac{1}{A-B} - X_1\right)A^{n-1}$
(3.53)	$X_{n+1} = AX_n + BA^{n-1}$	$X_n = [X_1 A + (n-1)B]A^{n-2}$

We shall now examine an article from the literature of mathematical models of learning that for the most part does not require skills beyond those presented so far. The article is "A Model with Neutral Elements," by David LaBerge (1959).

This model is in the general frame of reference of stimulus sampling theory, so that you can refer back to the explication of this frame of reference earlier in this chapter if reorientation is necessary. LaBerge has presented a variation on the more usual stimulus sampling approach. In general, the early stimulus sampling models conceived of all of the stimuli in the environment as committed to some response. It was therefore not surprising to find later models, such as Restle's (1955) and LaBerge's, positing the existence of neutral stimulus elements. However, each such model proffered a different role for these neutral stimuli.

LaBerge divided the possible responses in the experimental situation into two classes: the recorded responses, in which the experimenter has some interest, labeled R responses; and the nonrecorded responses, which the experimenter chooses to ignore and which include a class of no response. That is, there are times when an animal samples his stimulus environment and then makes no response, perhaps repeating this sequence several times before producing a recordable response. This set of nonrecorded or non-recordable responses LaBerge labeled type N responses.

Corresponding to these two types of responses are two types of stimuli. There is nothing inherently different about these two types of stimuli; it is just that while the stimuli are attached to one or another type of response, they are classified in keeping with the response to which they are attached. As in the familiar stimulus sampling models, the subject samples a proportion θ of the stimulus population on each trial, and the proportion of elements connected to each response type determines the type of response that will occur following that sampling. If type N (neutral) stimuli were more numerous in a sample, then no response (or a nonrecorded response) would occur on that sampling trial. From the point of view of the experimenter, however, the trial does not terminate until a recorded response occurs. Therefore, although the subject organism may sample, and make a type N response, it is assumed that he will continue to sample the stimulus environment, with the stimulus–response attachments unchanged, since no reinforcement is offered until a recorded response occurs. After a recorded response, some reinforcement takes place, which, in keeping with the usual stimulus sampling model, results in all of the stimuli present just prior to this recorded response becoming attached to the *reinforced* response. This means that neutral stimuli present just before the type R response will now be attached to a type R response, the response that was reinforced (regardless of the type R response that actually occurred). In addition, all type R stimuli present in the sample that were attached to type R responses other than the one reinforced will now be attached to the reinforced response.

Neutral stimuli are not seen as having any effect on a response (other than the effect of delaying a recorded response in those cases when neutral stimuli are sufficiently numerous to make a recorded response improbable). Given that the majority of the stimuli in a stimulus sample are type R stimuli, the particular type R response that occurs will be a function of the relative proportions of the different type R stimuli.

The foregoing suppositions suggest that this model will yield different predictions than the previous stimulus sampling models during early trials only, since given continued sampling and repeated reinforcement, all of the neutral stimuli should eventually become attached to type R responses. This would leave only stimulus elements all of which are attached to recordable responses, and the laws of change of stimulus–response attachment would not differ from the traditional Burke–Estes model.

In addition to the type N and type R responses and stimuli, the sampling parameter θ, response A_i, and reinforcement E_i, with $P(E_i) = \pi_i$, we symbolize the set of neutral stimuli on trial n as C_{0n}, with the number of elements in that set as c_{0n}. Similarly, the set of type R stimuli attached to response A_i on trial n, denoted as C_{in}, contains c_{in} elements. We can assume that the probability of response A_i on trial n, symbolized as p_{in}, is

$$p_{in} = \frac{c_{in}}{\sum_{i=1}^{k} c_{in}}, \tag{3.54}$$

where we assume k different recordable responses. Neutral elements would play a part only in the probable number of unrecorded resamplings by the subject, and not in the eventual choice of a type R response.

Solving Difference Equations in LaBerge's Model

We would first attempt to obtain a recursive expression of Eq. (3.54), equating the probability of an event on trial $n + 1$ with some transformation of the probability of the event on trial n. In the foregoing instance, this is best done by constructing separate recursive expressions for the numerator and then for the denominator. The difference equation solution for numerator and denominator would also be taken separately, using recursive expressions.

Our reasoning at this point would be similar to our reasoning earlier in the chapter. Given an E_i event on trial n, the number of stimuli attached to the A_i response on the following, or $(n + 1)$st, trial would be the number attached just preceding trial n, that is, c_{in}, plus the number of stimuli sampled on trial n that are not attached to A_i. This latter number would be $\theta(N - c_{in})$, where N is the total number of stimuli in the environment. Therefore, given E_{in},

$$c_{in+1} = c_{in} + \theta(N - c_{in}),$$
$$c_{in+1} = (1 - \theta)c_{in} + \theta N. \tag{3.55}$$

Similarly, an E_j $(i \neq j)$ event on trial n would result in trial $n + 1$ occurring with the number of elements attached to A_i on trial n depleted by the number θc_{in} lost to A_j. Therefore, given E_{jn}

$$c_{in+1} = c_{i1} - \theta c_{in},$$
$$c_{in+1} = (1 - \theta)c_{in}. \tag{3.56}$$

We would weight Eq. (3.55) and (3.56) by the respective probabilities of E_i and E_j events, that is, by π_i and π_j. Assuming only two types of R responses, we would have

$$\pi_j = 1 - \pi_i$$

and

$$
\begin{aligned}
c_{in+1} &= \pi_i[(1 - \theta)c_{in} + \theta N] + (1 - \pi_i)(1 - \theta)c_{in} \\
&= \pi_i c_{in} - \pi_i \theta c_{in} + \pi_i \theta N + c_{in} - \pi_i c_{in} - \theta c_{in} + \pi_i \theta c_{in} \\
&= c_{in} - \theta c_{in} + \pi_i \theta N, \\
c_{in+1} &= (1 - \theta)c_{in} + \pi_i \theta N.
\end{aligned}
\tag{3.57}
$$

Equation (3.57) would give us the mean number of elements connected to A_i on trial $n + 1$, given that we had the number of elements attached to response A_i on trial n. This is the numerator term in Eq. (3.54), in recursive form. We then solve Eq. (3.57) to take us a step closer to solving Eq. (3.54). Using the form of Eq. (3.7) with $A = (1 - \theta)$ and $B = \pi_i \theta N$, we would have, from Eq. (3.14),

$$
\begin{aligned}
c_{in} &= \frac{\pi_i \theta N}{1 - (1 - \theta)} - \left[\frac{\pi_i \theta N}{1 - (1 - \theta)} - c_{i1}\right](1 - \theta)^{n-1}, \\
c_{in} &= \pi_i N - (\pi_i N - c_{i1})(1 - \theta)^{n-1}.
\end{aligned}
\tag{3.58}
$$

In order to obtain the solution to the denominator term of Eq. (3.54), a summation over all i would be required. [We have specified only two possible recordable responses, i and j, for working with Eqs. (3.55) and (3.56), in which case the k in Eq. (3.54) would equal 2. However, the summation could be carried out over any number we desired, so at this point we keep it non-specific.] The numerator and denominator of Eq. (3.54) are identical except for the summation, so that we can use the already obtained recursive form of the numerator, Eq. (3.57), but sum it, to obtain the recursive form of the denominator.

$$
\begin{aligned}
\sum_{i=1}^{k} c_{in+1} &= (1 - \theta) \sum_{i=1}^{k} c_{in} + \theta N \sum_{i=1}^{k} \pi_i \\
&= (1 - \theta) \sum_{i=1}^{k} c_{in} + \theta N,
\end{aligned}
$$

where $\sum_{i=1}^{k} \pi_i = 1$, since one or another response is always reinforced.

This is again a recursive equation in the form of Eq. (3.7), and can be solved as an analog of Eq. (3.14) with $A = (1 - \theta)$ and $B = \theta N$.

$$
\begin{aligned}
\sum_{i=1}^{k} c_{in} &= \frac{\theta N}{1 - (1 - \theta)} - \left[\frac{\theta N}{1 - (1 - \theta)} - \sum_{i=1}^{k} c_{i1}\right](1 - \theta)^{n-1}, \\
\sum_{i=1}^{k} c_{in} &= N - \left(N - \sum_{i=1}^{k} c_{i1}\right)(1 - \theta)^{n-1}.
\end{aligned}
\tag{3.59}
$$

We can now return to Eq. (3.54) with the difference equation solutions to both the numerator and denominator having been obtained as Eqs. (3.58) and (3.59). We shall combine these solutions below.

$$p_{1n} = \frac{\pi_i N - (\pi_i N - c_{i1})(1 - \theta)^{n-1}}{N - (N - \sum_{i=1}^{k} c_{i1})(1 - \theta)^{n-1}}. \qquad (3.60)$$

Dividing the numerator and denominator of Eq. (3.60) by N, we have

$$p_{1n} = \frac{\pi_i - [\pi_i - (c_{i1}/N)](1 - \theta)^{n-1}}{1 - [1 - (\sum c_{i1}/N)](1 - \theta)^{n-1}}. \qquad (3.61)$$

We can see that in Eq. (3.61) we have almost, but not quite, eliminated N. It still appears as a denominator to c_{i1} and $\sum c_{i1}$. But, since both c_{i1} and $\sum c_{i1}$ are numbers from the set of N possible events (stimuli), these fractions will give us proportions, which are a very desirable form for us.

A proportion of special interest in this model is the proportion of neutral stimuli,

$$u_n = \frac{c_{0n}}{N}. \qquad (3.62)$$

Recognizing that the total number of stimuli N can be conceptualized dichotomously as

$$N = c_{0n} + \sum_{i=1}^{k} c_{in},$$

we can state that

$$u_n = \frac{c_{0n}}{c_{0n} + \sum_{i=1}^{k} c_{in}}$$

and, specifically,

$$u_1 = \frac{c_{01}}{c_{01} + \sum_{i=1}^{k} c_{i1}}.$$

It follows that

$$1 - u_1 = 1 - \frac{c_{01}}{c_{01} + \sum c_{i1}}$$

$$= \frac{c_{01} + \sum c_{i1} - c_{01}}{c_{01} + \sum c_{i1}}$$

$$= \frac{\sum c_{i1}}{c_{01} + \sum c_{i1}},$$

$$1 - u_1 = \frac{\sum c_{i1}}{N}, \qquad (3.63)$$

from which we can state that

$$u_1 = 1 - \frac{\sum c_{i1}}{N}. \tag{3.64}$$

Now we can substitute Eq. (3.63) into Eq. (3.61), which gives us

$$p_{1n} = \frac{\pi_i - [\pi_i - (c_{i1}/N)](1 - \theta)^{n-1}}{1 - u_1(1 - \theta)^{n-1}}. \tag{3.65}$$

We now wish to restate the term c_{i1}/N in Eq. (3.65). This term is the relative number of stimuli attached to response A_i on trial 1 over all stimuli, including the neutral stimuli. If we wished to symbolize the probability of response A_i on trial 1, we would have a similar fraction, but omit the neutral stimuli; that is,

$$p_{i1} = \frac{c_{i1}}{\sum_{i=1}^{k} c_{i1}},$$

from which we can state that

$$p_{i1} \sum_{i=1}^{k} c_{i1} = c_{i1}.$$

Dividing through by N, we would have

$$p_{i1} \frac{\sum_{i=1}^{k} c_{i1}}{N} = \frac{c_{i1}}{N}. \tag{3.66}$$

Equation (3.66) gives us an equality with the term we wished, c_{i1}/N. Looking at the left side of Eq. (3.66), we can see that the coefficient of p_{i1} is actually $1 - u_1$ [from Eq. (3.63)]. We can then state that

$$\frac{c_{i1}}{N} = p_{i1}(1 - u_1). \tag{3.67}$$

Placing Eq. (3.67) into Eq. (3.65), we finally have the probability of response A_i on any trial n, in terms of accessible parameters.

$$p_{1n} = \frac{\pi_i - [\pi_i - (1 - u_1)p_{i1}](1 - \theta)^{n-1}}{1 - u_1(1 - \theta)^{n-1}}. \tag{3.68}$$

With considerable algebraic manipulation, we would find this equal to

$$p_{1n} = \pi_i - [(1 - u_1)(\pi_i - p_{i1})]\frac{(1 - \theta)^{n-1}}{1 - u_1(1 - \theta)^{n-1}}. \tag{3.69}$$

If u_1, the proportion of neutral stimuli on Trial 1, were equal to 0, then Eq. (3.68) would reduce to our previous equation (3.26) for the stimulus sampling model where no neutral stimuli were assumed.

Since θ is a proportion with value between 0 and 1, $(1 - \theta)^{n-1}$ will approach 0 as n increases. Equation (3.68) can therefore be seen to have an asymptote of π_1, the probability of reinforcing response A_i on any trial. If u_1 on Trial 1 equaled 1, then $1 - u_1$ would equal 0, and the equation would reach its asymptote on the very first trial. This can be contrasted with the case where $u_1 = 0$, in which case the asymptote is only reached slowly. It can be seen that, for this model, the greater the proportion of neutral elements in the population on the first trial, the greater the rate of learning that is predicted. Specifically, $(1 - \theta)^{n-1}$ and its coefficient will approach zero faster, with a smaller coefficient. The rate of learning is then faster, with a smaller coefficient, and the coefficient of $(1 - \theta)^{n-1}$ is smaller when u_1, the proportion of neutral stimuli on the first trial, is larger [as can be seen by examining Eq. (3.69)].

AN EXPERIMENTAL TEST OF LABERGE'S MODEL

LaBerge suggested a simple test of his model. He stated that by using a π_i of .50 in a simple two-choice experiment, after a sufficient number of trials, there should be no preference for one response over the other. Continuing this experiment, but with one series of trials continuing for a longer time on $\pi_i = .50$, the experimenter would eventually switch to a π_i value of .90. Since in one series there would have been a greater opportunity for a decrease in neutral elements than in the other, the rate of learning in the two series after the change in π_i should be different. LaBerge made these comparisons and found that the model was reasonably accurate in its predictions. However, the actual procedure was slightly more complicated, and its implications somewhat weakened, in that θ had been found to vary with π_i, so that separate estimates had to be made of θ for the two different values. Any such additional considerations represent additional assumptions to obtain data fits, and as such can weaken the argument for a model. The stimulus sampling parameter θ has in general had a somewhat disappointing history, from the point of view of stability over subjects, experiments, and conditions, in the stimulus sampling models. This has been an important factor in changing stimulus sampling theory from a major theory of learning to an analytic approach to the development of new theories of learning in particularized experimental situations.

PARAMETER ESTIMATION IN LABERGE'S MODEL

We stated earlier that Eqs. (3.68) and (3.69) had accessible parameters. We take a portion of the data that are obtained after many, many trials, so that we assume that at that point, $u_n = 0$. We take some arbitrary trial at that point and " begin " the experiment there, in the sense of recording data from some trial m to some trial n. As we had previously indicated, with no neutral stimuli the data obtained should appear as they do for the Burke–Estes model, expressed in Eq. (3.26). We would then cumulate that equation, summing from trial m to n. Equation (3.26) looked like

$$p_{1n} = \pi_i - (\pi_i - p_{i1})(1 - \theta)^{n-1},$$

and summing the probabilities over trials m to n, we would have

$$\sum_{j=m}^{n} p_{ij} = \sum_{j=m}^{n} \pi_i - (\pi_i - p_{im}) \sum_{j=m}^{n} (1 - \theta)^{j-1}. \tag{3.70}$$

Calling $j = m$ the first trial, n now equal to $n - m$, that is, the number of trials in this trial block, we could restate Eq. (3.70) as

$$\sum_{j=1}^{n} p_{ij} = \sum_{j=1}^{n} \pi_i - (\pi_i - p_{i1}) \sum_{j=1}^{n} (1 - \theta)^{j-1},$$

which from Table 2.1 can be seen to be equal to

$$\sum_{j=1}^{n} p_{ij} = n\pi_i - (\pi_i - p_{i1}) \left[\frac{1 - (1 - \theta)^n}{\theta} \right]. \tag{3.71}$$

We can estimate this special p_{i1} from the data, that is, from the proportion of subjects on this trial (actually trial m) that make response A_i on that trial. Since π_i is determined by the experimenter, this leaves only one parameter, θ, which can be obtained by comparing the summed proportions of response A_i from trial m to trial n with Eq. (3.71), and solving for θ.

We then return to Eq. (3.69), for which we now have θ, along with π_i, but lack the actual first trial p_{i1}, along with u_1. We simply estimate p_{i1} from the proportion of A_i responses on the actual first trial, so we have solved everything in Eq. (3.69) except u_1. This can then be solved for in an equality between the empirical proportion of A_i responses for a group of subjects on any trial n and Eq. (3.69).

Problems

1. Derive the nth value of the following equation, using the procedures of Table 3.1. Present both the particular solution to the complete equation (Step 11) and the asymptotic solution (Step 12).

$$p_{n+1} = \alpha p_n + (1 - \alpha).$$

2. Let us assume that there are two states involved in remembering previously learned material: a "reminiscence state" and a "forgetting state." A theory adapted from Murdock (1970) includes the following axioms.

> If the subject is in the reminiscence state on any trial n, the subject will remain in that state for trial $n + 1$ with probability equal to α.

If the subject is in the reminiscence state on any trial n, the subject will move to the forgetting state for trial $n + 1$ with probability equal to $(1 - \alpha)$.

If the subject is in the forgetting state on any trial n, the subject will move to the reminiscence state on trial $n + 1$ with probability equal to $(1 - \beta)$.

If the subject is in the forgetting state on any trial n, the subject will remain in that state for trial $n + 1$ with probability equal to β.

(a) Given this little theory, what would be the appropriate recursive equation for the probability of being in the reminiscence state on trial $n + 1$?

(b) Assuming that we could obtain the probability of being in the reminiscence state on the first trial empirically, what would be the general formula for being in the reminiscence state on any trial n?

3. Derive the nth value of the following equation.

$$p_{n+1} = (\alpha + \beta)^2 p_n + (\alpha + \beta).$$

Use the procedures of Table 3.5. Present both the particular solution of the complete equation (Step 12) and the asymptotic solution.

4. Solve

$$p_{n+1} = (\alpha\beta)^2 p_n + \beta^2$$

by equating appropriate components of Eq. (3.7) and the solution of Eq. (3.7) given in Step 11 of Table 3.1. [That is, instead of going through the steps of either Table 3.1 or Table 3.5, use the substitution in the analogous Eq. (3.7) that has already been solved as Eq. (3.14) and as Step 11 in Table 3.1.]

5. Using mathematical induction, prove the correctness of the solution to Eq. (3.53) in Table 3.8.

6. Solve the recursive equation

$$p_{n+1} = \alpha p_n + \beta\gamma^{n-1} + \delta$$

using the summation technique.

In the example in the text of Eq. (3.7)

$$X_{n+1} = AX_n + B,$$

the equation

$$(\mathbf{D} - A)k = B$$

was utilized in determining the appropriate term to add to the general solution. When dealing with an equation that has an additive component to some power of n, such as $\beta\gamma^{n-1}$, the representation of the additive component by a simple constant such as k would not lead to a solution. We need a value to be added to the general form of the equation that will be influenced by n in a manner similar to the way in which $\beta\gamma^{n-1}$ might be influenced. Therefore, attempt the solution of

$$p_{n+1} = \alpha p_n + \beta\gamma^{n-1} + \delta$$

by representing $\beta\gamma^{n-1}$ with a term bk^{n-1}. That is, begin finding the first appropriate additive component with

$$(\mathbf{D} - \alpha)bk^{n-1}.$$

Remembering also to solve for a proper term for a second additive component, stemming from having δ in the recursive equation. The complete solution, then, will be the sum of three solutions.

For Problems 7 through 11 we shall first present a brief theory. Answer the questions with reference to this theory. The solution will require material from Chapter Two or Chapter Three, or from both; these problems are a good but difficult test of your understanding of the material to this point. Maximum benefit can be obtained by checking the detailed answer in the back of the book for Problem 7 immediately after attempting to solve the problem. This should provide hints for handling Problem 8, the answer to which should then be checked before you go on to Problem 9. Knowing the answers to Problems 7 and 8, you should not find Problem 9 difficult.

The paradigm: Subjects are given a long paired-associate list to learn. After the subject gives his response on each trial, he is exposed to the correct response for that stimulus. There is some probability that the subject will not learn the response, though exposed to it. The subject is instructed to say "no response" rather than to guess if he does not know the correct answer.

The theory: Learning the response is assumed to involve placement from some short-term perceptual store (when looking at the response) into some long-term memory store. However, it is possible for forgetting to occur, with the item being lost from long-term memory. This can even occur on the very same trial on which the item has entered the long-term memory store, so that the item is not seen as having been learned until learned again.

Let us symbolize the following:

$P(C_{0n})$ = the probability of the subject being in the unlearned state on trial n.

$P(C_{1n})$ = the probability of the subject being in the learned state on trial n.

Axiom 1. Given that the subject is in the unlearned state on any trial n, the probability of the subject learning the correct response for trial $n + 1$ is some probability value $= c$. The probability, therefore, of his not learning it is some probability $(1 - c)$ on some one exposure.

Axiom 2. The response having been learned on some *n*th trial's response exposure, the probability of the subject forgetting the correct response before trial $n + 1$ is some probability $= f$. The probability of the subject not forgetting the correct response, having just learned it, is therefore $(1 - f)$.

Axiom 3. Given that the subject is in the learned state while being tested (and therefore giving a response), the probability of his leaving the learned state by the next trial $= f$. That is, once in the learned state, he will remain in that state on each trial with a probability $= (1 - f)$.

Axiom 4. The subject will always refuse to give a response (will say "no response") if he is in the unlearned state. He will always answer with a response when he is in the learned state (and confronting a stimulus).

Axiom 5. The subject will be assumed to begin in the unlearned state on trial 1, and therefore will not respond to that first trial.

Answer Problems 7 through 11 with reference to the foregoing paradigm and theory.

7. What is the probability of the subject refusing to answer on any trial n?
8. We have assumed that the first trial will be one on which the subject will refuse to answer (Axiom 5). We wish to know the probability of any trial n being the trial of the second refusal to answer.

   We will define a random variable R_2, taking on the values $n = 1$ to ∞, representing trial numbers of the second refusal to answer.

   It will be helpful to tabulate the equations as

$$P(R_2 = n) \begin{cases} 0, & n = 1, \\ ?, & n = 2, \\ ?, & n > 2. \end{cases}$$

   As implied in this suggested partitioning of the distribution, the probability of the second trial as the trial of the second refusal to answer has a different form than the probability for $n > 2$. It may be easier for you first to obtain the probability for occurrence on the second trial, and to go from there to the more general formula for $n > 2$.
9. What is the probability, on any trials n and $n + 1$, of two consecutive refusals to answer?
10. Returning to Problem 7, what is the expected number of refusals to answer in m trials?
11. Returning to Problem 8, what is the expected trial of the second refusal to answer?

Chapter Four

Linear Operator Models

In Chapter Two we examined the Bower model of paired-associate learning. It was a model that assumed one-trial all-or-none learning. In Chapter Three we examined two versions of stimulus sampling theory in which individual elements again were learned or not learned on single trials. In the latter two models, however, a gradual appearance of learning even for individual subjects is possible. This is because many different proportions of elements could be learned at any one point in time, and increasing proportions of elements being learned could appear behaviorally as different probabilities of correct responding.

In this chapter we look at the general case of gradual learning. We do not assume any special component basis or psychological theory as the generator of a gradual learning curve. Rather, we assume gradual change in the probability of the recorded behavior, and investigate a particular mathematical analogy that describes the pace of this learning.

In our previous work, we used the direct method to generate the form of our equations, even when we used difference equation techniques for solutions. We symbolized the terms of the theory and then juxtaposed and operated on these terms in accordance with the probabilistic implications of the theory. Thus, we had a theory based on some a priori assumptions, such as hypothetical changes in states, assumed sampling proportions, or stimulus–response bonding. These assumptions implied relations between the terms of the theory, and the relations were analogized with mathematical operations. The theory was always overtly probabilistic in implication, leading directly to the use of the probability calculus to frame our basic equations. We then simply took advantage of the difference equation technique when our probabilistic statements led to a recursive form for an equation. It was frequently possible to conceive of "operating" on a subject during a learning trial via reinforcement as analogous to the notion of mathematical operators creating trial-by-trial changes in (difference) equation values. However, the operator notion was not the route by which we reached either the use of, or the form for, the difference equations. We began with a verbalized theory in which we could recognize a trial-to-trial form of change that analogized recursive forms, which then would allow for difference equation solutions. But we can now see that the operator concept represents so direct an analogy to the behavior-modifying events of some learning situations that it is also possible to develop a learning model by using the mathematical model as the inspiration for the theory, rather than the converse. We call this particular mathematically inspired model a *linear operator* model. Using the mathematical form as a "given," we can examine the most general implications of a model that uses the linear operator analogy for gradual learning. Specific theories using this form (such as some versions of stimulus sampling theory) then imply specific restrictions, and offer special cases of the general linear operator model.

The most thorough exploration of the general linear operator model was undertaken by Bush and Mosteller (1955). Much of the material of this chapter is an abstraction and restatement of material from the Bush and Mosteller volume.

Mathematical Implications of a Single-Operator Model

We can use the recursive form

$$p_{n+1} = \alpha p_n + a$$

as the starting point of our linear operator analysis. We can further assume that our formulation will represent transformations of probabilities. This suggests that the asymptotic values of p_n can be no greater than 1 nor less than 0. We shall be describing learning processes in changing values of p_n, so whether we are focusing on error reduction or correct response increase, we shall always be at some stage of learning with a maximal possible increase given by our current distance from the asymptote.

Assume for the moment a learning situation where we are focusing on the anticipated increasing probability of some one continually reinforced response. Let us further assume that at some point the probability of the correct response will approach 1. We then know that each trial will bring the probability closer to the asymptote of 1, moving in steps that are each some proportion of the distance of p_n from 1.

We can recognize the difference equation in its recursive form as corresponding to the foregoing verbal description, by going through the following steps:

$$p_{n+1} = p_n + k(1 - p_n), \qquad 0 < k < 1, \tag{4.1}$$

$$\begin{aligned} p_{n+1} &= p_n + k - kp_n, \\ p_{n+1} &= (1 - k)p_n + k. \end{aligned} \tag{4.2}$$

Were we to assume that only two responses were possible, we would have to assume that their probabilities were complementary; that is, the probability of the nonreinforced response would have to be

$$q_n = 1 - p_n.$$

Then, to see the fate of q_n after a reinforcement of the continually reinforced response, we would restate Eq. (4.2) as

$$\begin{aligned} 1 - q_{n+1} &= (1 - k)(1 - q_n) + k, \\ 1 - q_{n+1} &= 1 - q_n + kq_n, \\ q_{n+1} &= q_n - kq_n, \\ q_{n+1} &= (1 - k)q_n. \end{aligned} \tag{4.3}$$

Equation (4.3) represents a trial-by-trial change in q_n, the probability of the nonreinforced response on trial n. Examples of learning situations where Eq. (4.2) and (4.3) might be applicable are a paired-associate paradigm where only two responses are possible, and the subject is always " reinforced " by the presentation of the correct response, or a light prediction experiment with two lights, only one of which is ever lighted.

We can see that, given Eq. (4.2) as the single equivalence for p_{n+1} and the knowledge that only two responses are possible, the recursive form of the nonreinforced response's probability is given by mathematical considerations.

We can also recognize that this is a one operator model; that is, one transforming equation provides all of our predictions of response probabilities. Looking back at our stimulus sampling model, where we began with some theoretical considerations, including a stimulus sampling parameter θ, we can see that by replacing θ with a theoretically noncommittal k, we can derive the same recursive equations without the substantive theoretical rationale that we coupled to our derivation of Eq. (3.21). Equation (3.21) is identical to Eq. (4.3) in that both map the changes in the probabilities of the nonreinforced response. However, Eq. (3.21) was rationalized through a discussion of theoretical assumptions, whereas with the derivation of Eq. (4.3) we show that our verbalizations were gratuitous. Equation (3.21) follows mathematically from Eq. (3.19), just as Eq. (4.3) follows mathematically from Eq. (4.2).

The solutions to recursive Eqs. (4.2) and (4.3) are of course identical to those obtained for the analogous equations in the stimulus sampling model.

We now abandon the assumption of an asymptote of 1 and designate the asymptote as some number x. For the reinforced response p_n from Eq. (4.1) we then have

$$p_{n+1} = p_n + k(x - p_n),$$
$$p_{n+1} = p_n - kp_n + kx,$$
$$p_{n+1} = (1 - k)p_n + kx, \qquad 0 < k < 1, \quad 0 \le x \le 1. \tag{4.4}$$

For the alternative nonreinforced response, from Eq. (4.4), we have

$$1 - q_{n+1} = (1 - k)(1 - q_n) + kx,$$
$$1 - q_{n+1} = 1 - k - q_n + kq_n + kx,$$
$$q_{n+1} = k - q_n - kq_n - kx,$$
$$q_{n+1} = (1 - k)q_n + k(1 - x). \tag{4.5}$$

Setting x equal to 1 in Eqs. (4.4) and (4.5), we would obtain Eqs. (4.2) and (4.3), the equations with an asymptote of 1. If we were to set x equal to 0 (for example, in some paradigm using shock as a negative reinforcer), we would find p_{n+1} in Eq. (4.4) decreasing, in keeping with the same equation as q_{n+1} in Eq. (4.3), and q_{n+1} in Eq. (4.5) increasing, in keeping with p_{n+1} in Eq. (4.2). This might appear to imply that an experiment using shock would have the same probability distribution for the negatively reinforced response as a positive reinforcement paradigm would have for the nonreinforced response in a sequence of trials. It is likely, however, that the constant k in these two situations would not have the same value.

A Multiple-Operator Model

In the foregoing we assumed that the probabilities of the two responses on any trial were complementary and that the transformations over trials were in the form of a single linear operator with a specifiable asymptote. We also assumed that there was only one possible outcome on any trial, the reinforcement of the one prespecified response. At no point, therefore, was it necessary to construct more than one operator. We could also examine the mathematical implications of a model containing two operators. We can rationalize the existence of two operators in this same paradigm by assuming that the reinforcement had a different effect on the subject when he guessed incorrectly, as opposed to when he guessed correctly. If we thought that there was some psychological difference in the effectiveness of a reinforcer, given that the subject was either incorrect or correct in his guess, then we would

require two different operators for these two events. Given the usual reinforcement of the one response, say the turning on of the right light in a prediction
experiment, we would have, from Eq. (4.2),

$$p_{n+1} = (1 - k)p_n + k$$

if the subject guessed correctly, and

$$p_{n+1} = (1 - k')p_n + k'$$

if the subject guessed incorrectly. The two different equivalences for p_{n+1}
would then provide a two operator model. (There would also be two operators
for the fate of q_{n+1}, but they would each be derivable from an equivalence
with $1 - p_{n+1}$.)

The logical necessity for an additional operator would be further advanced
by having the always "given" reinforcement only sporadically available,
occurring or not occurring as a function of the subject's responses. An
animal in a maze, turning right when food was in the left goal box, would
not consistently be exposed to the consistently "available" reinforcement.
The animal's response would, in such a paradigm, be even more certain to
have some influence on the effects of the one reinforcing event occurring in
the experiment. Two operators might consequently be necessary to describe
the two different outcomes that would be possible, even though there would
only be a single reinforcing event.

If it were possible for the experimenter to reinforce either response, we
would be faced with the possibility of requiring four independent operators
to describe the complete set of possible transitions. (We are still focusing
only on p_{n+1}, the probability of a response A_1, knowing that q_{n+1}, the probability of a response A_2 on trial $n + 1$, can be obtained from p_{n+1}.) We can
have four response–reinforcement juxtapositions as outcomes on trial n:
$A_1 E_1, A_1 E_2, A_2 E_1$, and $A_2 E_2$, with A_j the jth response and E_j the reinforcement of the jth response. We could require a different operator to analogize
the different affects that each such combination of events (different outcomes
on trial n) might have on the probability of response A_1 on trial $n + 1$.

Control of Experimental Outcome

It is possible to classify models in many different ways. Bush and Mosteller
(1955) used a trichotomous classification, considering models as experimenter
controlled, subject controlled, or experimenter–subject controlled. Their
classification is a very useful one for revealing mathematical implications of
different assumptions. In this section we shall discuss their trichotomous
classification, using the term "outcome" as suggested by Sternberg (1963).

When reinforcements can impinge whenever the experimenter wishes them to, and assuming that he then arranges for these reinforcements to occur at his discretion, we can describe the trial outcomes as *experimenter-controlled outcomes*. The distinguishing feature of this class of models is that the subject always receives the reinforcement programmed by the experimenter, regardless of the subject's response. In the stimulus sampling models, experimenter-controlled outcomes are identified as the noncontingent case. Experimenter-controlled outcomes are most frequent in cases of information reinforcement, such as paired-associate learning and prediction experiments where the subject predicts which of two lights is expected to be lit at each trial. We also classify maze learning experiments *with correction procedures* in this way. One or more operators could be applicable, each corresponding to an outcome. The experimenter can then determine in advance what the sequence of operators would be.

Situations in which the experimenter's decision about the probability of reinforcement and the subject's choice of a response both determine the availability of the reinforcement to the subject are designated experimenter–subject-controlled outcomes. The T maze without correction procedure, in our previous reference to a four operator model, is the prototypical experimental situation for this classification. In stimulus sampling theory, this would be identified as the contingent case. Mathematically, the experimenter–subject-controlled situation is short on general solutions, unless special simplifying assumptions are made. However, the stimulus sampling theory example does include the necessary simplifying assumptions, and this was what allowed us to formulate the equation for the mean probability value for any trial, in Chapter Three, although at that time we did not point out these assumptions. In the experimenter–subject-controlled situation, there is again an operator corresponding to each experimental outcome. However, the experimenter cannot determine the sequence of operators in advance, because of the subject's part in determining the sequence.

A third situation, designated *subject-controlled outcomes*, can be recognized. It is the instance of experimenter–subject control in which one operator is always applied, given a particular response. The subject's response will be the sole determiner of the reinforcement outcome. In a sense, the subject-controlled outcome can be seen as the experimenter–subject-controlled outcome in which the experimenter relinquishes his control by making his contribution perfectly predictable. The experimenter's mark is then in the design of the situation, rather than in his trial-by-trial sampling from some hypothetical hat filled with "reinforce" and "do not reinforce" slips of paper. An example would be always reinforcing only one side of a T maze. There are times, however, when two responses both bring reinforcement, but the reinforcements differ in some way. The crucial aspect that maintains this as a subject-controlled event is that the subject's response is what determines which reinforcement occurs. An example would be the alternative events of either avoidance of shock or escape from shock in an experimental situation where either event is possible (via a warning buzzer and an adjoining shock-free compartment). We could focus on one of these eventualities, most probably avoidance of shock (making this our A_1 response). We could assume that successfully avoiding the shock would have a different effect on the probability of future avoidance of shock than would escape from shock. Thus, two operators would be formulated, each transforming the current probability of shock avoidance (the A_1 response) with its own parameters, and each being applied depending on which response the subject emits on a particular trial. Once the experiment begins, the experimenter has no control over which operator will occur on any trial. Although this is not as mathematically tractable as the experimenter-controlled outcome, it is a little simpler than the experimenter–subject-controlled outcome.

COMPUTING EXPECTATIONS FOR THE LINEAR OPERATOR MODEL

We shall first examine experimenter-controlled outcomes, since the problems this situation raises are all solvable without special assumptions. This will expedite the analysis and allow the other two classes of models to be examined as variations of the simplest case.

Assume an experiment in which on any trial either light could be selected by the experimenter. The two operators, one for each light, could occur in some prearranged sequence. If we focused on one response, say the right light, designating prediction of the right light by the subject as response A_1, our probability of that response on some trial $(n + 1)$ might be something like

$$\mathbf{D}_1 \mathbf{D}_2 \mathbf{D}_1 \cdots \mathbf{D}_1 \mathbf{D}_2 p_0,$$

where $\mathbf{D}_1$ would be the operator for changes in the probability of response A_1 after the occurrence of one light ("reinforcement" by the right light), $\mathbf{D}_2$ the operator for changes in the probability of response A_1 after the occurrence of the other light, and p_0 the initial probability of response A_1. The exact sequence of operators would depend on the exact sequence of light occurrences (reinforcements).

It is possible that the number of applications of each operator would be only one of two factors in the eventual probability, of response A_1. It is also possible for the sequence of operators to be relevant. When the sequence does not affect the eventual probability, we say that the operators "commute." We shall discuss the conditions under which operators do and do not commute in a later section. At the moment, we just accept the fact that different sequences might create different probabilities. Therefore, if we wished to test the model using these operators, we would want all possible sequences represented. Consequently, rather than having one sequence for all subjects, the experimenter would have different proportions of subjects receiving different sequences of the two operators. This would be arranged through a prespecified probability, on any trial, of a particular operator occurring. That is, on any trial, there would be some prespecified probability π_1 of the right light coming on, with the complementary probability $(1 - \pi_1) = \pi_2$ for the other light. In Figure 4.1 we see the various sequences possible, up to the

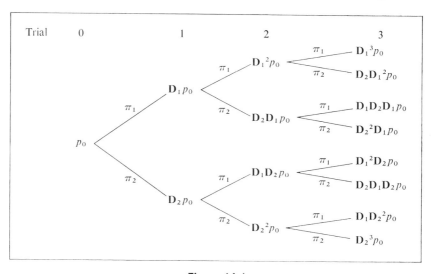

Figure 4.1.[1]

third trial past the initial trial, with two operators, D_1 and D_2. We symbolize the initial trial probability of a correct response as p_0. Numbers designating subsequent trials then refer to a number of operators applied up to that point in the square. With probability π_1 the subject has, as his trial 1 probability of a response A_1, the new probability $D_1 p_0$, and with probability π_2 he has, as his trial 1 probability of response A_1, the new probability $D_2 p_0$. At any particular trial number, the probability of a particular sequence having occurred is the product of the π_j values passed through in the sequence. The probability of response A_1 at the end of any sequence of operators is the initial probability of A_1, which is p_0, transformed by the sequence of operators through which it has passed. The overall probability of response A_1 among all subjects on some trial n can then be derived as a sum of the following products: each sequence-generated probability of response A_1 times the prob-

[1]Adapted from Bush, R. R. and Mosteller, F. *Stochastic models for learning*, Fig. 3.2, p. 70. New York: Wiley, 1955. By permission of John Wiley & Sons, Inc.

ability of that sequence summed over all possible sequences. This can be recognized as an expectation if the probability of response A_1 at the end of any one sequence is seen as the value of a random variable, and the probability of each sequence occurring is seen as the probability of a particular value of the random variable. This would then give us the first expectation that we want, the average probability of response A_1 on trial n. To estimate this in advance for the model on some trial n could require spelling out all 2^n paths, then applying the operators in the sequence of each path, and then weighting the probability of each sequence by the product of the intervening π_j values. Rather than do this sequence by sequence, we shall apply each operator in proportion to its probability of occurrence, repeating this procedure for each trial, in difference equation form. We shall consequently require a recursive form, but instead of an operator applied at each trial, we shall have two operators, each weighted by its π_j value. Let us specify the operators as

$$\mathbf{D}_1 p_n = \alpha_1 p_n + a_1 \tag{4.6}$$

and

$$\mathbf{D}_2 p_n = \alpha_2 p_n + a_2. \tag{4.7}$$

Thus, for $\bar{p}_{n+1}$, the average probability of response A_1 on trial $n + 1$, we have

$$\begin{aligned}
\bar{p}_{n+1} &= \pi_1 \mathbf{D}_1 \bar{p}_n + \pi_2 \mathbf{D}_2 \bar{p}_n \\
&= \pi_1(\alpha_1 \bar{p}_n + a_1) + \pi_2(\alpha_2 \bar{p}_n + a_2) \\
&= \pi_1 \alpha_1 \bar{p}_n + \pi_2 \alpha_2 \bar{p}_n + \pi_1 a_1 + \pi_2 a_2,
\end{aligned} \tag{4.8}$$

$$\bar{p}_{n+1} = (\pi_1 \alpha_1 + \pi_2 \alpha_2)\bar{p}_n + (\pi_1 a_1 + \pi_2 a_2). \tag{4.9}$$

Since the terms in the parentheses are all constant, it will be convenient to simplify their symbolization.

$$\bar{\alpha} = (\pi_1 \alpha_1 + \pi_2 \alpha_2), \tag{4.10}$$

$$\bar{a} = (\pi_1 a_1 + \pi_2 a_2). \tag{4.11}$$

Consequently, we can restate Eq. (4.9) as

$$\bar{p}_{n+1} = \bar{\alpha} \bar{p}_n + \bar{a}. \tag{4.12}$$

(Note that $\bar{\alpha}$ and $\bar{a}$ represent weighted averages of the α_j and a_j values of the two operators contributing to the recursive equation.)

We can solve Eq. (4.12) as we solved Eq. (3.7) in Chapter Three. The solution in asymptotic form, from Table 3.1, is

$$\bar{p}_n = \frac{\bar{a}}{1 - \bar{\alpha}} - \left(\frac{\bar{a}}{1 - \bar{\alpha}} - \bar{p}_0\right)\bar{\alpha}^n. \tag{4.13}$$

(Note that we have adjusted the exponent in keeping with an initial probability of $\bar{p}_0$ rather than $\bar{p}_1$.) We can see that the solution as given in Eq. (4.13) has an asymptote of $\bar{a}/(1 - \bar{\alpha})$. If we now symbolize the asymptote of Eq. (4.13) as

$$\bar{\lambda} = \frac{\bar{a}}{1 - \bar{\alpha}}, \tag{4.14}$$

we can restate Eq. (4.13) as

$$\bar{p}_n = \bar{\lambda} - (\bar{\lambda} - \bar{p}_0)\bar{\alpha}^n,$$
$$\bar{p}_n = \bar{\alpha}^n p_0 + (1 - \bar{\alpha}^n)\bar{\lambda}. \tag{4.15}$$

The only variables present in Eq. (4.15) are the rate of learning parameter $\bar{\alpha}$, the initial probability p_0, and the asymptote $\bar{\lambda}$, the latter being the fixed point toward which the equation tends. This is called the fixed-point form of the equation for the probability of a correct response on trial n.

We can also state the original equations (4.6) and (4.7) in a fixed-point form. To do this, we symbolize the asymptote and then include the asymptote in the recursive equation. For Eq. (4.6), we would have

$$p_{n+1} = \alpha_1 p_n + a_1. \tag{4.16}$$

The solution in asymptotic form to Eq. (4.16) would be

$$p_n = \frac{a_1}{1 - \alpha_1} - \left(\frac{a_1}{1 - \alpha_1} - p_0\right)\alpha_1{}^n.$$

Symbolizing the asymptote as

$$\lambda_1 = \frac{a_1}{1 - \alpha_1}, \tag{4.17}$$

which implies

$$a_1 = (1 - \alpha_1)\lambda_1,$$

we would have the fixed-point form of Eq. (4.16) as

$$p_{n+1} = \alpha_1 p_n + (1 - \alpha_1)\lambda_1. \tag{4.18}$$

Similarly, for Eq. (4.7) we would have

$$p_{n+1} = \alpha_2 p_n + a_2. \tag{4.19a}$$

The solution in asymptotic form would be

$$p_n = \frac{a_2}{1 - \alpha_2} - \left(\frac{a_2}{1 - \alpha_2} - p_0\right)\alpha_2{}^n. \tag{4.19b}$$

Symbolizing the asymptote as

$$\lambda_2 = \frac{a_2}{1 - \alpha_2}, \tag{4.20}$$

we would have the fixed-point form of Eq. (4.19a) as

$$p_{n+1} = \alpha_2 p_n + (1 - \alpha_2)\lambda_2. \tag{4.21}$$

COMMUTATIVITY

We alluded earlier to the fact that order of application of operators can make a difference in the resulting probability of a response. It is a relatively easy matter to determine under just what quantitative conditions the order of the operators would or would not make a difference. We simply compare $\mathbf{D}_1\mathbf{D}_2 p_n$ with $\mathbf{D}_2\mathbf{D}_1 p_n$ and see under what conditions they are equal.

From Eqs. (4.18) and (4.21) we would have

$$\mathbf{D}_1\mathbf{D}_2 p_n = \alpha_1[\alpha_2 p_n + (1 - \alpha_2)\lambda_2] + (1 - \alpha_1)\lambda_1,$$
$$\mathbf{D}_1\mathbf{D}_2 p_n = \alpha_1\alpha_2 p_n + \alpha_1(1 - \alpha_2)\lambda_2 + (1 - \alpha_1)\lambda_1, \tag{4.22}$$

and

$$\mathbf{D}_2\mathbf{D}_1 p_n = \alpha_2[\alpha_1 p_n + (1 - \alpha_1)\lambda_1] + (1 - \alpha_2)\lambda_2,$$
$$\mathbf{D}_2\mathbf{D}_1 p_n = \alpha_2\alpha_1 p_n + \alpha_2(1 - \alpha_1)\lambda_1 + (1 - \alpha_2)\lambda_2. \tag{4.23}$$

Comparing Eqs. (4.22) and (4.23), we would find

$$\mathbf{D}_1\mathbf{D}_2 p_n - \mathbf{D}_2\mathbf{D}_1 p_n = \alpha_1\lambda_2 - \alpha_1\alpha_2\lambda_2 + \lambda_1$$
$$- \alpha_1\lambda_1 - \alpha_2\lambda_1 + \alpha_2\alpha_1\lambda_1 - \lambda_2 + \alpha_2\lambda_2,$$

which can be restated as

$$\mathbf{D}_1\mathbf{D}_2 p_n - \mathbf{D}_2\mathbf{D}_1 p_n = (1 - \alpha_1)(1 - \alpha_2)(\lambda_1 - \lambda_2). \tag{4.24}$$

We can see that if any of the factors on the right-hand side of Eq. (4.24) is equal to zero, then the complete right-hand side equals zero. Given the equality of Eq. (4.24), a right-hand side equivalence with zero would mean a difference of zero in the effects of different operator sequences. The three conditions for a right-hand side equivalence with zero would be

$$\alpha_1 = 1, \tag{4.25}$$

$$\alpha_2 = 1, \tag{4.26}$$

or

$$\lambda_1 = \lambda_2. \tag{4.27}$$

If either Eq. (4.25) or Eq. (4.26) is true, then one of the operators Eq. (4.18) or Eq. (4.21)

$$p_{n+1} = \alpha_i p_n + (1 - \alpha_i)\lambda_i$$

is an identity operator. That is,

$$p_{n+1} = p_n.$$

This might be the case, for example, if one operator were equivalent to a reinforcement (that is, say, the right light would go on) and the other operator were equivalent to simply no light being lit (no information on that trial).

If Eq. (4.27) were true, then the two operators would move the probablity toward the same asymptote, although this might be at different rates. An example of this might be two different delays to reinforcement, although both reinforcements were reinforcements of the same response.

MOMENTS FOR STATISTICS

We previously (in Chapter Two) defined the expectation of a set of random variables $\{x_j\}$ as

$$E(x) = \sum_j x_j p(x_j). \tag{4.28}$$

If the random variable values are raised to some mth power, the resulting value

$$E(x)^m = \sum_j x_j{}^m p(x_j) \tag{4.29}$$

is called the mth moment about the origin of the distribution of the random variable x.

The second moment has special implications for us in that

$$\sigma^2 = \sum_j x_j{}^2 p(x_j) - [\sum_j x_j p(x_j)]^2,$$

as indicated in Eq. (2.48).

We shall find it advantageous to work with moments of distributions in discussing solutions for the different types of models.

The Mean and Variance of p_n in the Experimenter-Controlled Model

To obtain the expected probability on trial n, $\bar{p}_n$ in Eqs. (4.13) and (4.15), we applied the two operators in proportion to their respective probabilities of occurrence. Prior to that, we had suggested the possibility of deriving the value of $\bar{p}_n$ by summing the products of each probability of a probability times that probability. We shall now develop an equation for $\bar{p}_n$ that is equivalent to such a sum of products, and that in addition will be helpful in obtaining the variance of p_n.

Given $\bar{p}_n$, we have two p_{n+1} values possible. They are $\mathbf{D}_1 \bar{p}_n$ and $\mathbf{D}_2 \bar{p}_n$, each occurring with respective probabilities π_1 and π_2. A sum consisting of each of the possible random values $\mathbf{D}_j \bar{p}_n$ times its respective probability value π_j gives the expected value on trial $n + 1$, as indicated in Eq. (4.8), where

$$\bar{p}_{n+1} = \sum_j \pi_j \mathbf{D}_j \bar{p}_n. \tag{4.30}$$

Recognizing that the many sequences presented in Figure 4.1 can be divided into those which are expected to have had an A_1 response reinforced on trial n and those that are expected to have had an A_2 response reinforced on trial n, we can symbolize their respective proportions as $\pi_1 \sum_k P_{kn}$ and $\pi_2 \sum_k P_{kn}$, where P_{kn} is the proportion of the total number of subjects in the kth sequence on the nth trial. For each proportion $\pi_j P_{kn}$ there will be a new probability, either $\mathbf{D}_1 p_{kn}$ or $\mathbf{D}_2 p_{kn}$, of an A_1 response on trial $n + 1$. We can consequently restate the probability of an A_1 response on trial $n + 1$ as

$$\bar{p}_{n+1} = \sum_{k=1}^{2^n} (\mathbf{D}_1 p_{kn})\pi_1 P_{kn} + \sum_{k=1}^{2^n} (\mathbf{D}_2 p_{kn})\pi_2 P_{kn} = \sum_j \pi_j \mathbf{D}_j \bar{p}_n. \qquad (4.31)$$

We know that on trial n there are 2^n possible sequences, so we have indexed the sum from 1 to 2^n.

We wish to introduce a notation that indicates moments of distributions. We therefore restate the left side of Eq. (4.31) as

$$V_{1,n+1} = \sum_k (\mathbf{D}_1 p_{kn})\pi_1 P_{kn} + \sum_k (\mathbf{D}_2 p_{kn})\pi_2 P_{kn} \qquad (4.32)$$

for the first moment. This is equivalent to

$$V_{1,n+1} = \bar{\alpha} V_{1,n} + \bar{a} \qquad (4.33)$$

from Eqs. (4.12), (4.31), and (4.32).

The mth moment is

$$V_{m,n+1} = \sum_k (\mathbf{D}_1 p_{kn})^m \pi_1 P_{kn} + \sum_k (\mathbf{D}_2 p_{kn})^m \pi_2 P_{kn}, \qquad (4.34a)$$

which, from Eqs. (4.6) and (4.7), equals

$$V_{m,n+1} = \pi_1 \sum_k (\alpha_1 p_{kn} + a_1)^m P_{kn} + \pi_2 \sum_k (\alpha_2 p_{kn} + a_2)^m P_{kn}. \qquad (4.34b)$$

We can now use the binomial expansion, discussed in Chapter Two, where, from Eq. (2.24a),

$$(X + Y)^m = \sum_{l=0}^{m} \binom{m}{l} X^{m-l} Y^l.$$

We apply this to the mth-power terms in Eq. (4.34b),

$$V_{m,n+1} = \pi_1 \sum_k \sum_l \binom{m}{l} a_1^{m-l}(\alpha_1 p_{kn})^l P_{kn} + \pi_2 \sum_k \sum_l \binom{m}{l} a_2^{m-l}(\alpha_2 p_{kn})^l P_{kn},$$

which we then rearrange as

$$V_{m,n+1} = \pi_1 \sum_l \binom{m}{l} a_1^{m-l} \alpha_1^l \sum_k (p_{kn})^l P_{kn} + \pi_2 \sum_l \binom{m}{l} a_2^{m-l} \alpha_2^l \sum_k (p_{kn})^l P_{kn}. \qquad (4.35)$$

On trial n, we have a probability of an A_1 response that is p_{kn} for any kth sequence, with an overall probability of an A_1 response of $\sum_k p_{kn}$. But there are possibly different proportions of subjects in each kth sequence. The proportion in each is P_{kn}. Therefore, $\sum_k p_{kn} P_{kn}$ is the expected probability of an A_1 response on trial n. It is also the first moment of $\sum_k (p_{kn})^l P_{kn}$. Consequently, we restate Eq. (4.35) by substituting,

$$\sum_k (p_{kn})^l P_{kn} = V_{l,n},$$

which yields

$$V_{m,n+1} = \pi_1 \sum_l^m \binom{m}{l} a_1^{m-l} \alpha_1^l V_{l,n} + \pi_2 \sum_l^m \binom{m}{l} a_2^{m-l} \alpha_2^l V_{l,n}. \tag{4.36}$$

We now carry out the binomial expansion of the second moment in Eq. (4.36), setting $m = 2$.

$$V_{2,n+1} = \pi_1 \left[\binom{2}{0} a_1^2 V_{0,n} + \binom{2}{1} a_1 \alpha_1 V_{1,n} + \binom{2}{2} \alpha_1^2 V_{2,n} \right]$$
$$+ \pi_2 \left[\binom{2}{0} a_2^2 V_{0,n} + \binom{2}{1} a_2 \alpha_2 V_{1,n} + \binom{2}{2} \alpha_2^2 V_{2,n} \right],$$
$$V_{2,n+1} = \pi_1 a_1^2 + 2\pi_1 a_1 \alpha_1 V_{1,n} + \pi_1 \alpha_1^2 V_{2,n}$$
$$+ \pi_2 a_2^2 + 2\pi_2 a_2 \alpha_2 V_{1,n} + \pi_2 \alpha_2^2 V_{2,n}$$

(note that $V_{0,n}$ has been dropped as a coefficient because it is equal to 1; that is, $V_{0,n} = \sum_k p_{kn}^0 P_{kn} = \sum_k P_{kn} = 1$);

$$V_{2,n+1} = (\pi_1 a_1^2 + \pi_2 a_2^2) + 2(\pi_1 a_1 \alpha_1 + \pi_2 a_2 \alpha_2) V_{1,n} + (\pi_1 \alpha_1^2 + \pi_2 \alpha_2^2) V_{2,n}. \tag{4.37}$$

Equation (4.37) now gives us an equation with $V_{2,n+1}$ on the left of the equal sign and $V_{2,n}$ on the right. If we could replace $V_{1,n}$ in Eq. (4.37) with a constant, we would have a recursive equation from which we could obtain a solution. We shall achieve this by restating $V_{1,n}$ in terms of $V_{1,0}$, which is the mean on the first trial, and $V_{1,\infty}$, which is the expected asymptote. Equation (4.14) offers the asymptotic solution to $\bar{p}_n$, which is equal to $V_{1,\infty}$; that is,

$$\lambda = \bar{p}_\infty = V_{1,\infty}.$$

In addition, $V_{1,0}$ is the initial trial probability; that is, by definition consistent with our symbolism and consistent with Eq. (4.13),

$$V_{1,0} = \bar{p}_0.$$

We can therefore restate Eq. (4.13) as

$$V_{1,n} = V_{1,\infty} - (V_{1,\infty} - V_{1,0})\bar{\alpha}^n. \tag{4.38}$$

This offers us a third form for the mean of $\bar{p}_n$. It is equivalent to both Eq. (4.13) and Eq. (4.15). It offers a restatement of $V_{1,n}$ in terms of constants, and therefore helps us to obtain a recursive form for the second moment. We now insert the solution to $V_{1,n}$ as given in Eq. (4.38) into Eq. (4.37), obtaining

$$V_{2,n+1} = (\pi_1 a_1{}^2 + \pi_2 a_2{}^2) + 2(\pi_1 a_1 \alpha_1 + \pi_2 a_2 \alpha_2)$$
$$\times [V_{1,\infty} - (V_{1,\infty} - V_{1,0})\bar{\alpha}^n] + (\pi_1 \alpha_1{}^2 + \pi_2 \alpha_2{}^2)V_{2,n},$$

which can be restated as

$$V_{2,n+1} = (\pi_1 a_1{}^2 + \pi_2 a_2{}^2) + 2(\pi_1 a_1 \alpha_1 + \pi_2 a_2 \alpha_2)V_{1,\infty}$$
$$- [2(\pi_1 a_1 \alpha_1 + \pi_2 a_2 \alpha_2)(V_{1,\infty} - V_{1,0})]\bar{\alpha}^n + [\pi_1 \alpha_1{}^2 + \pi_2 \alpha_2{}^2]V_{2,n}.$$
$$\tag{4.39}$$

In Eq. (4.39) let us identify the entire first term on the right-hand side by the symbol C_1. Note that C_1 is a constant. We can identify everything within the brackets of the second term by the symbol C_2, and everything within the brackets of the third term as C_3. This yields the symbolically simplified equation

$$V_{2,n+1} = C_1 - C_2 \bar{\alpha}^n + C_3 V_{2,n}, \tag{4.40}$$

where

$$C_1 = (\pi_1 a_1{}^2 + \pi_2 a_2{}^2) + 2(\pi_1 a_1 \alpha_1 + \pi_2 a_2 \alpha_2)V_{1,\infty},$$
$$C_2 = [2(\pi_1 a_1 \alpha_1 + \pi_2 a_2 \alpha_2)(V_{1,\infty} - V_{1,0})],$$

and

$$C_3 = (\pi_1 \alpha_1{}^2 + \pi_2 \alpha_2{}^2).$$

Equation (4.40) is a recursive equation in $V_{2,n}$, almost identical in form to Eq. (3.42), which we solved in Chapter Three. The difference is that the covert coefficient 1 in (3.42) is replaced here with C_2, and $n-1$ is replaced with n as the power of the second term. We can therefore use the solution as given in Step 11 of Table 3.4. In this chapter we begin our recursive sequence with zero ($V_{2,0}$) rather than one ($V_{2,1}$), so we adjust for this as well in our solution. The solution to Eq. (4.40) is then

$$V_{2,n} = \left(V_{2,0} + \frac{C_2}{\bar{\alpha} - C_3} - \frac{C_1}{1 - C_3}\right)C_3{}^n - \frac{C_2 \bar{\alpha}^n}{\bar{\alpha} - C_3} + \frac{C_1}{1 - C_3}. \tag{4.41}$$

This gives us the second moment at some trial n. For the variance at trial n, we use Eqs. (2.48), (4.38), and (4.41) to obtain

$$\sigma_n{}^2 = V_{2,n} - (V_{1,n})^2. \tag{4.42}$$

We can obtain the second moment at asymptote rather easily. We note that as n goes to infinity, we have

$$V_{2, \infty} = \frac{C_1}{1 - C_3},$$

and so for the variance at asymptote we have

$$\sigma_\infty^2 = V_{2, \infty} - (V_{1, \infty})^2. \tag{4.43}$$

The Expected Total Number of Correct Responses, and Its Variance, for the Experimenter-Controlled Model

We have examined the experimenter-controlled model with our focus on $\bar{p}_n$, the probability of response A_1 on any one trial. This would give us an expected proportion of some number of subjects that we would expect to respond with the A_1 response on each trial. In order to obtain the expected total of A_1 responses in n trials for any one subject, we would sum all of the probabilities. That is, responding or not responding is a dichotomous event, and so, as indicated in Chapter Two, with Eq. (2.51) for the mean of a distribution of dichotomous events with changing probabilities, we simply sum all of the individual trial probabilities to obtain the expected total of A_1 responses per subject. We consequently sum Eq. (4.38).

$$\sum_{k=1}^{n} V_{1, k} = \sum_{k=1}^{n} [V_{1, \infty} - (V_{1, \infty} - V_{1, 0})\bar{\alpha}^n]. \tag{4.44}$$

Carrying out the summation in Eq. (4.44), we would have

$$\sum_{k}^{n} V_{1, k} = nV_{1, \infty} - \frac{(V_{1, \infty} - V_{1, 0})(1 - \bar{\alpha}^n)}{(1 - \bar{\alpha})}, \tag{4.45}$$

which is the expected number of A_1 responses per subject in n trials, in the experimenter-controlled model.

Both Eq. (4.45) and Eq. (2.51),

$$E(T) = \sum_{k}^{n} p_k,$$

are analogous to the binomial distribution Eq. (2.25)

$$E(T) = np$$

except that there is no assumption of a constant probability in Eqs. (4.45) and (2.51). We can similarly use the variance formula for the binomial [Eq. (2.26)]

$$\sigma^2 = npq$$

to obtain the variance for the total number of correct responses, by substituting $\sum_k^n p_k$ for np, which yields

$$\sigma^2 = \sum_k^n p_k q_k$$

with

$$q_k = 1 - p_k,$$

and taking $\sum p_k$ from Eq. (4.44). The result is

$$\sigma^2 = \sum_{k=1}^n [V_{1,\infty} - (V_{1,\infty} - V_{1,0})\bar{\alpha}^k]\{1 - [V_{1,\infty} - (V_{1,\infty} - V_{1,0})\bar{\alpha}^k]\}.$$

Multiplying out

$$\sigma^2 = \sum_k^n [V_{1,\infty} - (V_{1,\infty} - V_{1,0})\bar{\alpha}^k] - \sum_k^n [(V_{1,\infty})^2 - 2V_{1,\infty}(V_{1,\infty} - V_{1,0})\alpha^k$$
$$+ (V_{1,\infty} - V_{1,0})^2\bar{\alpha}^{2k}]$$

and rearranging, we have

$$\sigma^2 = \sum [V_{1,\infty}(1 - V_{1,\infty})] - \sum [(1 - 2V_{1,\infty})(V_{1,\infty} - V_{1,0})\bar{\alpha}^k]$$
$$- \sum [(V_{1,\infty} - V_{1,0})^2\bar{\alpha}^{2k}].$$

Carrying out the summation, we have the variance for the average number of A_1 responses,

$$\sigma^2 = n[V_{1,\infty}(1 - V_{1,\infty})] - \frac{(1 - 2V_{1,\infty})(V_{1,\infty} - V_{1,0})(1 - \bar{\alpha}^n)}{(1 - \bar{\alpha})}$$
$$- \frac{(V_{1,\infty} - V_{1,0})^2(1 - \bar{\alpha}^{2n})}{(1 - \bar{\alpha}^2)} \qquad (4.46)$$

in the case of experimenter-controlled events.

We have now extended our information from means and variances of probabilities of correct responses on individual trials to expected total number of correct responses, and their variances, over all trials of an experiment. We have also derived asymptotic probabilities of response $\bar{\lambda}$, as well as the variance of the asymptote. We have therefore accumulated knowledge of characteristics that the model predicts over individual trials, over all trials, and at the end of a sufficiently long set of trials to approach some relatively stable condition (asymptotic performance). The initial probability $\bar{p}_0$ can be most simply defined as the average over all subjects on the first trial.

The Mean and Variance of $\bar{p}_n$ in the Subject-Controlled Model

We again have an operator $\mathbf{D}_1$ applied to some probability p_{kn} (of response A_1 on trial n following some kth sequence of operators), giving us

$$\mathbf{D}_i p_{kn} = \alpha_i p_{kn} + a_i.$$

Assuming two such operators, we need the probability of each occurring. With experimenter-controlled outcomes, the experimenter determines each experimental constant π_i. But with subject-controlled outcomes, the probability of an operator is no longer a constant. It is a function of the response probabilities, which are themselves changing values if learning is taking place. The difference between the two models is presented in Table 4.1.

TABLE 4.1

Difference between Experimenter-Controlled and Subject-Controlled Models[a]

Values of p_{kn+1}	P_{kn+1}	
	Experimenter control	Subject control
$\mathbf{D}_1 p_{kn} = \alpha_1 p_{kn} + a_1$	$\pi_1 P_{kn}$	$p_{kn} P_{kn}$
$\mathbf{D}_2 p_{kn} = \alpha_2 p_{kn} + a_2$	$\alpha_2 P_{kn}$	$(1 - p_{kn})P_{kn}$

[a] We use p_{kn} to symbolize the probability of response A_1 on trial n, and P_{kn} for the probability of being in the kth group on the nth trial ($k = 1$ to 2^n).

To obtain the equation for moments in the subject-controlled model we shall use Eq. (4.34a) for the experimenter-controlled events, replacing the P_{kn+1} values for experimenter control with those of subject control from Table 4.1.

$$\begin{aligned} V_{m,n+1} &= \sum_{k=1}^{2^n} (\mathbf{D}_1 p_{kn})^m p_{kn} P_{kn} + \sum_{k=1}^{2^n} (\mathbf{D}_2 p_{kn})^m (1 - p_{kn})P_{kn} \\ &= \sum_k (a_1 + \alpha_1 p_{kn})^m p_{kn} P_{kn} + \sum_k (a_2 + \alpha_2 p_{kn})^m P_{kn} \\ &\quad - \sum_k (a_2 + \alpha_2 p_{kn})^m p_{kn} P_{kn}. \end{aligned}$$

From the binomial expansion

$$V_{m,n+1} = \sum_{k=1}^{2^n} \sum_{l=0}^{m} \binom{m}{l} a_1^{m-l}(\alpha_1 p_{kn})^l p_{kn} P_{kn} + \sum_{k=1}^{2^n} \sum_{l=0}^{m} \binom{m}{l} a_2^{m-l}(\alpha_2 p_{kn})^l P_{kn}$$

$$- \sum_{k=1}^{2^n} \sum_{l=0}^{m} \binom{m}{l} a_2^{m-l}(\alpha_2 p_{kn})^l p_{kn} P_{kn}$$

$$= \sum_{k} \sum_{l} \binom{m}{l} a_1^{m-l} \alpha_1^{\,l} p_{kn}^{l+1} P_{kn} + \sum_{k} \sum_{l} \binom{m}{l} a_2^{m-l} \alpha_2^{\,l} p_{kn}^{l} P_{kn}$$

$$- \sum_{k} \sum_{l} \binom{m}{l} a_2^{m-l} \alpha_2^{\,l} p_{kn}^{l+1} P_{kn}$$

$$= \sum_{l=0}^{m} \binom{m}{l} a_1^{m-l} \alpha_1^{\,l} V_{l+1,n} + \sum_{l=0}^{m} \binom{m}{l} a_2^{m-l} \alpha_2^{\,l} V_{l,n} - \sum_{l=0}^{m} \binom{m}{l} a_2^{m-l} \alpha_2^{\,l} V_{l+1,n},$$

$$V_{m,n+1} = \sum_{l=0}^{m} \left[\binom{m}{l} a_1^{m-l} \alpha_1^{\,l} V_{l+1,n} + \binom{m}{l} a_2^{m-l} \alpha_2^{\,l}(V_{l,n} - V_{l+1,n}) \right]. \tag{4.47}$$

We now set $m = 1$ in Eq. (4.47) to obtain the first moment.

$$V_{1,n+1} = \binom{1}{0} a_1 V_{1,n} + \binom{1}{1} \alpha_1 V_{2,n} + \binom{1}{0} a_2(V_{0,n} - V_{1,n}) + \binom{1}{1} \alpha_2(V_{1,n} - V_{2,n})$$

$$= a_1 V_{1,n} + \alpha_1 V_{2,n} + a_2(1 - V_{1,n}) + \alpha_2(V_{1,n} - V_{2,n}),$$

$$V_{1,n+1} = a_2 + (a_1 - a_2 + \alpha_2)V_{1,n} + (\alpha_1 - \alpha_2)V_{2,n}. \tag{4.48}$$

Again, from Eq. (4.47), setting $m = 2$ for the second moment, we obtain

$$V_{2,n+1} = \binom{2}{0} a_1^2 V_{1,n} + \binom{2}{1} a_1 \alpha_1 V_{2,n} + \binom{2}{2} \alpha_1^2 V_{3,n} + \binom{2}{0} a_2^2(V_{0,n} - V_{1,n})$$

$$+ \binom{2}{1} a_2 \alpha_2(V_{1,n} - V_{2,n}) + \binom{2}{2} \alpha_2^2(V_{2,n} - V_{3,n})$$

$$= a_1^2 V_{1,n} + 2a_1 \alpha_1 V_{2,n} + \alpha_1^2 V_{3,n} + a_2^2(1 - V_{1,n}) + 2a_2 \alpha_2 V_{1,n}$$

$$- 2a_2 \alpha_2 V_{2,n} + \alpha_2^2 V_{2,n} - \alpha_2^2 V_{3,n},$$

$$V_{2,n+1} = a_2^2 + (a_1^2 + a_2^2 + 2a_2 \alpha_2)V_{1,n} + (2a_2 \alpha_1 - 2a_2 \alpha_2 + \alpha_2^2)V_{2,n}$$

$$+ (\alpha_1^2 - \alpha_2^2)V_{3,n}. \tag{4.49}$$

We can see that in the equation for the first moment, Eq. (4.48), we have a solvable recursive form going from $V_{1,n}$ to $V_{1,n+1}$, if we can eliminate $V_{2,n}$. We also find, in the equation for the second moment, Eq. (4.49), that we have a solvable recursive form going from $V_{2,n}$ to $V_{2,n+1}$, if we can eliminate $V_{3,n}$ and find a solution for $V_{1,n}$. All of these things can be accomplished by assuming that $\alpha_1 = \alpha_2$. That is, $V_{2,n}$ in Eq. (4.48) then has a coefficient of 0, eliminating $V_{2,n}$ from the equation, enabling us to solve Eq. (4.48). We then substitute this solution in Eq. (4.49), and with $\alpha_1 = \alpha_2$ also eliminating $V_{3,n}$, we can solve Eq. (4.49) for the second moment.

We now rewrite Eqs. (4.48) and (4.49) with the equal alpha assumption.

$$V_{1,n+1} = a_2 + (a_1 - a_2 + \alpha)V_{1,n}, \qquad (4.50)$$

$$V_{2,n+1} = a_2^2 + (a_1^2 + a_2^2 + 2a_2\alpha)V_{1,n} + \alpha(2a_1 - 2a_2 + \alpha)V_{2,n}. \quad (4.51)$$

Equation (4.50) is in a most familiar form [Eq. (3.7)], and is easily solved as

$$V_{1,n} = \frac{a_2}{1 - (a_1 - a_2 + \alpha)} - \left[\frac{a_2}{1 - (a_1 - a_2 + \alpha)} - V_{1,0}\right](a_1 - a_2 + \alpha)^n. \qquad (4.52)$$

Recognizing that as n goes to infinity, Eq. (4.52) becomes

$$V_{1,\infty} = \frac{a_2}{1 - (a_1 - a_2 + \alpha)},$$

and symbolizing

$$\beta = (a_1 - a_2 + \alpha), \qquad (4.53)$$

we have, as a restatement of Eq. (4.52),

$$V_{1,n} = V_{1,\infty} - (V_{1,\infty} - V_{1,0})\beta^n. \qquad (4.54)$$

Substituting this solution for $V_{1,n}$ into Eq. (4.51) and symbolizing

$$B_1 = a_1^2 + a_2^2 + 2a_2\alpha, \qquad B_2 = \alpha(2a_1 + 2a_2 + \alpha),$$

we obtain

$$V_{2,n+1} = a_2^2 + B_1[V_{1,\infty} - (V_{1,\infty} - V_{1,0})\beta^n] + B_2 V_{2,n},$$

$$V_{2,n+1} = (a_2^2 + B_1 V_{1,\infty}) - [B_1(V_{1,\infty} - V_{1,0})]\beta^n + B_2 V_{2,n}. \quad (4.55)$$

Symbolizing the constants contained in the brackets

$$C_1' = [a_2^2 + B_1 V_{1,\infty}],$$

$$C_2' = [B_1(V_{1,\infty} - V_{n,0})],$$

and

$$C_3' = B_2,$$

we can restate Eq. (4.55) as

$$V_{2,n+1} = C_1' - C_2'\beta^n + C_3' V_{2,n}. \qquad (4.56)$$

We can recognize the identity in form between Eq. (4.56) and Eq. (4.40), which we solved earlier as Eq. (4.41) when discussing experimenter-controlled outcomes. The analogous solution, then, to Eq. (4.56) is

$$V_{2,n} = \left(V_{2,0} + \frac{C_2'}{\beta - C_3'} - \frac{C_1'}{1 - C_3'}\right)C_3'^n - \frac{C_2'\beta^n}{\beta - C_3'} + \frac{C_1'}{1 - C_3'}. \quad (4.57)$$

We have therefore obtained both the mean [Eq. (4.54)] and the second moment [Eq. (4.57)] for the subject-controlled model, under the assumption that $\alpha_1 = \alpha_2$. We can obtain the variance with the mean (the first moment) and the second moment, precisely as we did, for example, when constructing Eq. (4.42). That is,

$$\sigma^2 = V_{2,n} - (V_{1,n})^2.$$

The Mean and Variance of $\bar{p}_n$ in the Experimenter–Subject-Controlled Model

In the case of experimenter–subject-controlled outcomes, the subject's probability of response and the experimenter's probability of reinforcing a particular response both affect the probability of a subject's receiving a reinforcement. These probabilities would consequently both enter into the probability of a particular operator being applied in the model. The probability of a particular sequence of operators is reflected in P_{kn}, the probability of a subject going through the kth sequence to trial n. For the next trial, instead of either a π value (experimenter's reinforcement probability) or a p_{kn} value (a subject's response probability) modifying the probability of a particular sequence (for a new P_{kn+1}), we have the condition of both of these factors affecting P_{kn}. This is detailed in Table 4.2.

TABLE 4.2

Probabilities of Operators in Experimenter–Subject-Controlled Model[a]

Response–reinforcement sequences possible	Values of p_{kn+1}	P_{kn+1} in experimenter–subject control
$A_{1n}E_{1n}$	$\mathbf{D}_{11}p_{kn} = \alpha_{11}p_{kn} + a_{11}$	$\pi_{11}p_{kn}P_{kn}$
$A_{1n}E_{2n}$	$\mathbf{D}_{12}p_{kn} = \alpha_{12}p_{kn} + a_{12}$	$\pi_{12}p_{kn}P_{kn}$
$A_{2n}E_{1n}$	$\mathbf{D}_{21}p_{kn} = \alpha_{21}p_{kn} + a_{21}$	$\pi_{21}(1 - p_{kn})P_{kn}$
$A_{2n}E_{2n}$	$\mathbf{D}_{22}p_{kn} = \alpha_{22}p_{kn} + a_{22}$	$\pi_{22}(1 - p_{kn})P_{kn}$

[a] Sequences are symbolized as:
 A_{in} = response i on trial n, E_{jn} = reinforcement j on trial n;
 π_{ij} = the conditional probability of reinforcement j, given response i;
 p_{kn} = the probability of response A_1 on trial n in the kth of 4^n possible sequences;
 P_{kn} = the probability of the occurrence of the kth of 4^n possible sequences, to trial n.

We again develop an equation similar in form to Eq (4.34a) for the mth moment $V_{m,n+1}$. However, our P_{kn+1} values are now taken from Table 4.2 rather than Table 4.1. In addition, since there are four alternative operators (although still only two reinforcements possible), there are 4^n possible sequences on trial n.

$$
\begin{aligned}
V_{m,n+1} &= \sum_{k=1}^{4^n} (\mathbf{D}_{11} p_{kn})^m \pi_{11} p_{kn} P_{kn} + \sum_{k=1}^{4^n} (\mathbf{D}_{12} p_{kn})^m \pi_{12}\, p_{kn} P_{kn} \\
&\quad + \sum_{k=1}^{4^n} (\mathbf{D}_{21} p_{kn})^m \pi_{21}(1 - p_{kn}) P_{kn} + \sum_{k=1}^{4^n} (\mathbf{D}_{22}\, p_{kn})\pi_{22}(1 - p_{kn}) P_{kn} \\
&= \sum_{k=1}^{4^n} \big[\pi_{11}(a_{11} + \alpha_{11} p_{kn})^m p_{kn} P_{kn} + \pi_{12}(a_{12} + \alpha_{12}\, p_{kn})^m p_{kn} P_{kn} \\
&\qquad + \pi_{21}(a_{21} + \alpha_{21} p_{kn})^m P_{kn} - \pi_{21}(a_{21} + \alpha_{21} p_{kn})^m p_{kn} P_{kn} \\
&\qquad + \pi_{22}(a_{22} + \alpha_{22}\, p_{kn})^m P_{kn} - \pi_{22}(a_{22} + \alpha_{22}\, p_{kn})^m p_{kn} P_{kn} \big].
\end{aligned}
$$

$$ (4.58) $$

We again use the binomial expansion, and the fact that

$$
\sum_k (p_{kn})^l P_{kn} = V_{l,n},
$$

to obtain

$$
\begin{aligned}
V_{m,n+1} &= \sum_{k=1}^{4^n} \sum_{l=0}^{m} \bigg[\pi_{11}\binom{m}{l} a_{11}^{m-l}\alpha_{11}^l p_{kn}^{l+1} P_{kn} + \pi_{12}\binom{m}{l} a_{12}^{m-l}\alpha_{12}^l\, p_{kn}^{l+1} P_{kn} \\
&\qquad + \pi_{21}\binom{m}{l} a_{21}^{m-l}\alpha_{21}^l p_{kn}^{l} P_{kn} - \pi_{21}\binom{m}{l} a_{21}^{m-l}\alpha_{21}^l p_{kn}^{l+1} P_{kn} \\
&\qquad + \pi_{22}\binom{m}{l} a_{22}^{m-l}\alpha_{22}^l p_{kn}^{l} P_{kn} - \pi_{22}\binom{m}{l} a_{22}^{m-l}\alpha_{22}^l p_{kn}^{l+1} P_{kn} \bigg],
\end{aligned}
$$

$$
\begin{aligned}
V_{m,n+1} &= \sum_{l=0}^{m} \bigg[\pi_{11}\binom{m}{l} a_{11}^{m-l}\alpha_{11}^l V_{l+1,n} + \pi_{12}\binom{m}{l} a_{12}^{m-l}\alpha_{12}^l V_{l+1,n} \\
&\qquad + \pi_{21}\binom{m}{l} a_{21}^{m-l}\alpha_{21}^l V_{l,n} - \pi_{21}\binom{m}{l} a_{21}^{m-l}\alpha_{21}^l V_{l+1,n} \\
&\qquad + \pi_{22}\binom{m}{l} a_{22}^{m-l}\alpha_{22}^l V_{l,n} - \pi_{22}\binom{m}{l} a_{22}^{m-l}\alpha_{22}^l V_{l+1,n} \bigg].
\end{aligned} \quad (4.59)
$$

For the mean, we set $m = 1$.

$$V_{1,n+1} = \pi_{11}\left[\binom{1}{0}a_{11}V_{1,n} + \binom{1}{1}\alpha_{11}V_{2,n}\right]$$

$$+ \pi_{12}\left[\binom{1}{0}a_{12}V_{1,n} + \binom{1}{1}\alpha_{12}V_{2,n}\right]$$

$$+ \pi_{21}\left[\binom{1}{0}a_{21}V_{0,n} + \binom{1}{1}\alpha_{21}V_{1,n}\right]$$

$$- \pi_{21}\left[\binom{1}{0}a_{21}V_{1,n} + \binom{1}{1}\alpha_{21}V_{2,n}\right]$$

$$+ \pi_{22}\left[\binom{1}{0}a_{22}V_{0,n} + \binom{1}{1}\alpha_{22}V_{1,n}\right]$$

$$- \pi_{22}\left[\binom{1}{0}a_{22}V_{1,n} + \binom{1}{1}\alpha_{22}V_{0,n}\right].$$

$$V_{1,n+1} = (\pi_{21}a_{21} + \pi_{22}a_{22})$$
$$+ (\pi_{11}a_{11} + \pi_{12}a_{12} - \pi_{21}a_{21} - \pi_{22}a_{22} + \pi_{21}\alpha_{21} + \pi_{22}\alpha_{22})$$
$$\times V_{1,n} + (\pi_{11}\alpha_{11} + \pi_{12}\alpha_{12} - \pi_{21}\alpha_{21} - \pi_{22}\alpha_{22})V_{2,n}. \qquad (4.60)$$

Since $\pi_{ij} = P(E_{jn}|A_{in})$, we have

$$\pi_{i1} + \pi_{i2} = P(E_{1n}|A_{in}) + P(E_{2n}|A_{in}),$$

and therefore, from Eq. (3.33),

$$\pi_{i1} + \pi_{i2} = 1. \qquad (4.61)$$

If we make the assumption of equal alphas for all four operators, as we did for the two operators in the subject-controlled model, and combine this with Eq. (4.61), the figures in parentheses in the last sum of Eq. (4.60) can be simplified in the following way:

$$(\pi_{11}\alpha_{11} + \pi_{12}\alpha_{12} - \pi_{21}\alpha_{21} - \pi_{22}\alpha_{22}) = \alpha(\pi_{11} + \pi_{12} - \pi_{21} - \pi_{22})$$
$$= \alpha(1 - 1) = 0.$$

This eliminates $V_{2,n}$ in Eq. (4.60), and gives us our desired solvable recursive equation in $V_{1,n}$ and $V_{1,n+1}$ for the first moment for the experimenter–subject-controlled model.

$$V_{1,n+1} = (\pi_{21}a_{21} + \pi_{22}a_{22}) + (\pi_{11}a_{11} + \pi_{12}a_{12} - \pi_{21}a_{21} - \pi_{22}a_{22} + \alpha)V_{1,n}.$$
$$(4.62)$$

Note also that in this simplified version of Eq. (4.60), we have reduced $\pi_{21}\alpha_{21} + \pi_{22}\alpha_{22}$ to α, on the basis of Eq. (4.61) and the equal α assumptions. Again taking advantage of simplified symbolization of constants

$$\bar{a}_1 = (\pi_{11}a_{11} + \pi_{12}a_{12}),$$
$$\bar{a}_2 = (\pi_{21}a_{21} + \pi_{22}a_{22}),$$
$$\gamma = (\bar{a}_1 - \bar{a}_2 + \alpha),$$

we can now express as Eq. (4.62)

$$V_{1,n+1} = \bar{a}_2 + (\bar{a}_1 - \bar{a}_2 + \alpha)V_{1,n},$$
$$V_{1,n+1} = \bar{a}_2 + \gamma V_{1,n}.$$

This familiar form is again easily solved as

$$V_{1,n} = \frac{\bar{a}_2}{1-\gamma} - \left(\frac{\bar{a}_2}{1-\gamma} - V_{1,0}\right)\gamma^n,$$
$$V_{1,n} = V_{1,\infty} - (V_{1,\infty} - V_{1,0})\gamma^n. \tag{4.63}$$

The second moment can be obtained by setting $m = 2$ in Eq. (4.59) and adding the equal alpha assumption. The variance can then be obtained as before, in Eq. (4.42).

SIMILARITY BETWEEN THE CONTINGENT CASE AND THE EXPERIMENTER–SUBJECT-CONTROLLED MODEL

We can examine the similarity between the contingent case in the stimulus sampling model and the general case of the experimenter–subject-controlled linear operator model. From Eqs. (3.23) and (3.34) we have, for the stimulus sampling model,

$$P(A_{1n+1}) = P(A_{1n+1}|E_{1n})P(E_{1n}) + P(A_{1n+n}|E_{2n})P(E_{2n}),$$
$$P(E_{1n}) = P(E_{1n}|A_{1n})P(A_{1n}) + P(E_{1n}|A_{2n})P(A_{2n}).$$

Therefore

$$P(A_{1n+1}) = P(A_{1n+1}|E_{1n})[P(E_{1n}|A_{1n})P(A_{1n}) + P(E_{1n}|A_{2n})P(A_{2n})]$$
$$+ P(A_{1n+1}|E_{2n})[P(E_{2n}|A_{1n})P(A_{1n}) + P(E_{2n}|A_{2n})P(A_{2n})]. \tag{4.64}$$

We can note the following symbolic equivalence in the two models:

$$\sum_k \mathbf{D}_{ij}p_{kn} = P(A_{1n+1}|E_{jn}A_{in}),$$
$$\pi_{ij} = P(E_{jn}|A_{in}),$$
$$\sum_k p_{kn}P_{kn} = P(A_{1n}),$$
$$\sum_k (1 - p_{kn})P_{kn} = P(A_{2n}).$$

The following juxtaposition will show the identity between stimulus sampling equation (4.64) and Eq. (4.58) of the general linear model.

$$P(A_{1,n+1}) = P(A_{1n+1}|E_{1n})P(E_{1n}|A_{1n}) \, P(A_{1n})$$
$$V_{1,n+1} \qquad \sum_k \mathbf{D}_{11}p_{kn} \qquad \pi_{11} \qquad \sum_k p_{kn}P_{kn}$$

$$+ \, P(A_{1n+1}|E_{1n})P(E_{1n}|A_{2n}) \quad P(A_{2n})$$
$$\sum_k \mathbf{D}_{21}p_{kn} \qquad \pi_{21} \qquad \sum_k (1-p_{kn})P_{kn}$$

$$+ \, P(A_{1n+1}|E_{2n})P(E_{2n}|A_{1n}) \, P(A_{1n})$$
$$\sum_k \mathbf{D}_{12}p_{kn} \qquad \pi_{12} \qquad \sum_k p_{kn}P_{kn}$$

$$+ \, P(A_{1n+1}|E_{2n})P(E_{2n}|A_{2n}) \quad P(A_{2n}).$$
$$\sum_k \mathbf{D}_{22}p_{kn} \qquad \pi_{22} \qquad \sum_k (1-p_{kn})P_{kn}$$

The equal alpha assumption required for the solution of Eq. (4.60) was incorporated in the stimulus sampling model solution by specifying the operators in the original recursive equations as having equal alphas (all equal to $1 - \theta$).

SEQUENTIAL ANALYSES OF RESPONSES

A useful theorem for sequential analyses of responses has been derived by Bush (1959). This theorem affords a means of developing equations for the expected number of error runs of all sizes.

We shall define three terms that have subtle but important distinctions. The three terms R_n, r_{jn}, and u_{jn} are interrelated in a helpful way. You should take pains to understand their differences.

We begin by defining a random variable $x = 1$ or $x = 0$, the value of which is dependent on which of two mutually exclusive and exhaustive responses occurs on a particular trial. We then conceive of a sequence, over n trials, of such random variables

$$x_1, x_2, x_3, \ldots, x_n,$$

which is equivalent to a sequence of 1's and 0's. As an example, assume six trials, where an error has the random variable value 1. In the sequence

$$1 \quad 1 \quad 0 \quad 1 \quad 0 \quad 1$$

we can see that we have two "runs" of precisely one error in length and one run of precisely two errors in length. We symbolize these two counts of runs as $r_{16} = 2$ and $r_{26} = 1$, where

r_{jn} = the number of sequences of precisely length j in n trials. (4.65)

The total number of runs, including runs of all lengths, is

$$R_n = \sum_{j=1}^{n} r_{jn}.$$ (4.66)

That is, R_n gives us the number of runs of all sizes, where each x_i is counted in only one run. Note that there is no overlap in the runs of different sizes when counting R_n.

To understand u_{jn}, we return to the concept of a sequence of trials, each having the random variable value $x = 1$ or $x = 0$, depending on which response occurs. For any sequential number of trials j, we can form a product of all of the random variable values. If response A_1, defined as an error, is given the random variable value $x = 1$, then all j trials would have to be errors in order for the product of the j random variable values to be equal to 1. That is,

$$x_i \cdot x_{i+1} \cdot x_{i+2} \cdots x_{i+j-1} = 1 \qquad \text{iff all } j \text{ values of } x = 1.$$ (4.67)

We can examine a large series of n trials, $n > j$, but abstract out j sequential trials and form a product of these j trials as in Eq. (4.67). We can do this for all possible j sequential trials in the total of n trials, and then add the sum of these products. We would take the first j of the n trials and form a product. It would contribute 1 to the sum if the first j of the n random variable values were all equal to 1, and 0 otherwise. We would then begin with the second x value, taking the product of that value times its $j - 1$ adjacent values, again obtaining a product of j adjacent random variable values. We would be able to form $n - j + 1$ products in this way, each product excluding the first x of the last product, replacing it by moving along in the sequence. The last product would be the one including the nth trial as the last factor in the product. The sum of these products would give the number of sets of j adjacent random variable values where all j of them are equal to 1, equivalent to the number of runs of j consecutive A_1 responses. Symbolically stated, it would be

$$u_{jn} = \sum_{i=1}^{n-j+1} x_i \cdot x_{i+1} \cdot x_{i+2} \cdots x_{i+j-1}.$$ (4.68)

As a general example, let $j = 2$, and $n = 5$ with the sequence

$$1 \quad 1 \quad 1 \quad 0 \quad 1.$$

This would yield

$$u_{25} = 1 \cdot 1 + 1 \cdot 1 + 1 \cdot 0 + 0 \cdot 1 = 2.$$

With $j = 3$ and $n = 5$ for the same sequence, we would have

$$u_{35} = 1 \cdot 1 \cdot 1 + 1 \cdot 1 \cdot 0 + 1 \cdot 0 \cdot 1 = 1.$$

The symbol u_{jn} in each instance gives the number of runs of size j, without regard to whether or not they overlap. To see the way in which u_{jn}, R_n, and r_{jn} are related, we shall examine a specific sequence, five consecutive errors in five trials

$$1 \quad 1 \quad 1 \quad 1 \quad 1.$$

In this instance

$$u_{15} = 1 + 1 + 1 + 1 + 1 = 5.$$

For the same sequence,

$$r_{15} = 0$$

(that is, there are no runs of a single error), while

$$r_{55} = 1$$

(that is, there is one run of five errors). This suggests that

$$u_{15} = 5r_{55}.$$

Comparing all different u_{jn} and r_{jn} values, with n constant, we would find the following useful relations:

$$u_{1n} = r_{1n} + 2r_{2n} + 3r_{3n} + \cdots + nr_{nn}, \tag{4.69}$$

$$u_{2n} = \qquad r_{2n} + 2r_{3n} + \cdots + (n-1)r_{nn}, \tag{4.70}$$

$$u_{3n} = \qquad\qquad r_{3n} + \cdots + (n-2)r_{nn},$$
$$\vdots$$

By subtraction, we find Eqs. (4.69) and (4.70) to imply

$$u_{1n} - u_{2n} = r_{1n} + r_{2n} + r_{3n} + \cdots + r_{nn},$$

$$u_{1n} - u_{2n} = \sum_{j=1}^{n} r_{jn}. \tag{4.71}$$

Combining Eqs. (4.66) and (4.71), we have

$$R_n = u_{1n} - u_{2n}. \tag{4.72}$$

Analogous to the specific Eq. (4.71), we have the more general

$$u_{jn} - u_{j+1,n} = r_{jn} + r_{j+1,n} + \cdots + r_{nn}. \tag{4.73}$$

We can isolate r_{jn} in Eq. (4.73).

$$r_{jn} = u_{jn} - u_{j+1,n} - (r_{j+1,n} + r_{j+2,n} + \cdots + r_{nn}). \tag{4.74}$$

The term in parentheses in Eq. (4.74) is $u_{j+1,n} - u_{j+2,n}$, from Eq. (4.71), since j is an arbitrary value. Therefore

$$r_{jn} = (u_{jn} - u_{j+1,n}) - (u_{j+1,n} - u_{j+2,n}),$$
$$r_{jn} = u_{jn} - 2u_{j+1,n} + u_{j+2,n}. \tag{4.75}$$

All of this complexity is warranted by the greater ease with which the

u_{jn} can often be computed, which leads to the generally more meaningful r_{jn} values, via Eq. (4.75).

Sequential Analyses in the Bush and Sternberg Single Operator Model

As an example of the use of Eqs. (4.68) and (4.75), we shall use the Bush and Sternberg single operator model (1959). The single operator in the model is

$$p_{n+1} = \alpha p_n, \tag{4.76}$$

with p_n equal to the probability of an error on the nth trial. In the Bush and Sternberg article (1959) the first trial is symbolized as p_1 rather than p_0 as in the other sections of this chapter. We shall maintain their symbolism. The solution then, to Eq. (4.76) is

$$p_n = \alpha^{n-1} p_1. \tag{4.77}$$

As an example, we might think of a very simple task, say trying to toss a penny into a cigar box 10 feet away. Very few people would get the penny into the box the first time. Therefore, the probability p_1 of an error on the first trial would probably be close to 1. With practice, the error rate might approach 0. (Using one operator, we would have to assume that every trial contributed the same proportion of improvement over the last performance. Therefore, trials when the subject hit the box and trials when he missed would all be expected to contribute the same proportionate gain in skill. If this was not anticipated, we would have to use two operators, one for hit trials and one for error trials. This would then become a subject-controlled model.)

To obtain the total number of errors anticipated in this single operator model, we would simply sum the probability of an error on any one trial over all n trials in the experiment. That is, we would sum Eq. (4.77). The rationale for this would be identical to that for Eqs. (2.51) and (4.44). For the variance of the expected total errors, we would proceed as we did in constructing Eq. (4.46). The mean and variance would appear as in Eqs. (4.78) and (4.79).

$$\text{Mean total} = \sum_i^n p_i = p_1 \sum_i^n \alpha^{i-1},$$

$$E(T_n) = \frac{p_1(1 - \alpha^n)}{1 - \alpha}. \tag{4.78}$$

$$\text{Variance of the total} = \sum_i^n [(\alpha^{i-1} p_1)(1 - \alpha^{i-1} p_1)],$$

$$\sigma^2 = \sum_i^n \alpha^{i-1} p_1 - \sum_i^n \alpha^{2(i-1)} p_1^2,$$

$$\sigma^2 = \frac{p_1(1 - \alpha^n)}{1 - \alpha} - \frac{p_1^2(1 - \alpha^{2n})}{1 - \alpha^2}. \tag{4.79}$$

If we ran the subjects to some strong criterion, where we could assume no further additions of errors, then we would have an empirical equivalent of the asymptotic value for total errors. We could equate this with the summation of Eq. (4.77) from 1 to ∞, which would give us

$$E(T_\infty) = \frac{p_1}{1 - \alpha}. \tag{4.80}$$

We could then use Eq. (4.80) to determine the value of α in our experiment. The simplest way of doing this would be to assume that p_1 is equal to the empirically obtained proportion of correct responses over subjects on the first trial. Let us assume that we ran 10 subjects in this experiment and only one of them got the penny into the box on the first trial; that is, we had 9 out of 10 errors. We would then consider

$$p_1 = .9 \quad \text{(empirical)}$$

and place this value in Eq. (4.80). Let us assume, for our hypothetical example, that the average total of errors for subjects (at the point where they had reached some stringent criterion of continuous correct responding) was 4.5 errors per subject. That is,

$$E(T_\infty) = 4.5 \quad \text{(empirical)}.$$

We can then equate Eq. (4.80) with the value 4.5 to obtain α.

$$4.5 = \frac{.9}{1 - \alpha},$$

$$4.5 - 4.5\alpha = .9,$$
$$4.5\alpha = 4.5 - .9,$$
$$4.5\alpha = 3.6,$$
$$\alpha = .8.$$

We now have the two parameters of the model,

$$p_1 = .9 \quad \text{and} \quad \alpha = .8,$$

so in developing additional equations we would have specific predictions, because the parameters would have specific values. We could then see how closely the empirical and theoretical values compared. Putting the parameter values into Eq. (4.78), for example, would give us theoretically expected totals, which we could compare to the empirical total number of errors per subject (or averaged over subjects) at each trial number. Table 4.3 offers the theoretical values for Eq. (4.78), with our hypothetical parameter values.

TABLE 4.3

Theoretical Values for Eq. (4.78) with Hypothetical
Parameter Values $p_1 = .9$ $\alpha = .8$

n	$E(T_n) = \dfrac{p_1(1 - \alpha^n)}{1 - \alpha}$
1	.90
2	1.60
3	2.20
4	2.66
5	3.03
6	3.32
7	3.56
8	3.75
9	3.90
10	4.02

We now return to Eqs. (4.68) and (4.75) and see how we would develop them for use in the Bush and Sternberg model. The formula for r_{jn} depends on u_{jn}. We therefore begin with Eq. (4.68) for u_{jn}.

$$u_{jn} = \sum_{i=1}^{n-j+1} x_i \cdot x_{i+1} \cdot x_{i+2} \cdots x_{i+j-1},$$

where x_i is the random variable value 1 or 0, depending on whether there is an error or success on that trial. This is a sum of values of products. However, the products will only equal either 1 or 0. This is, then, a dichotomous event, equivalent to the binomial examples in Chapter Two, but with changing probabilities (for different trial numbers used in each product), having the mathematical solution of Eq. (2.51). The expectation of u_{jn}, then, would be

$$E(u_{jn}) = \sum_{i}^{n-j+1} \text{Prob}[(x_i \cdot x_{i+1} \cdot x_{i+2} \cdots x_{i+j-1}) = 1],$$

which is a sum of probabilities of obtaining the random variable value 1 on *all* of a sequence of trials where each sequence is j trials long. If the probability of obtaining $x_i = 1$ on some trial i is p_1, then the probability of obtaining a 1 on all j trials of a particular sequence beginning on trial i would be

$$p_i \cdot p_{i+1} \cdot p_{i+2} \cdots p_{i+j-1}.$$

The expectation of u_{jn} would then be the sum

$$E(u_{jn}) = \sum_{i=1}^{n-j+1} p_i \cdot p_{i+1} \cdot p_{i+2} \cdots p_{i+j-1}. \tag{4.81}$$

From Eq. (4.77) we restate Eq. (4.81) as

$$E(u_{jn}) = \sum_{i}^{n-j+1} \alpha^{i-1} p_1 \cdot \alpha^i p_1 \cdot \alpha^{i+1} p_1 \cdots \alpha^{i+j-2} p_1. \tag{4.82}$$

Let us assume that we have run the subjects to a strong criterion of continuous successes. We can then equate our empirical results with asymptotic performance. That is, we would assume that $n = \infty$. We can restate Eq. (4.82) as

$$\overbrace{\qquad\qquad\qquad\qquad}^{(j \text{ items being multiplied for each term of the sum})}$$

$$E(u_{j\infty}) = \sum_{i}^{\infty} \alpha^{i-1} p_1 \cdot \alpha^i p_1 \cdot \alpha^{i+1} p_1 \cdots \alpha^{i+j-2} p_1,$$

$$E(u_{j\infty}) = \sum_{i}^{\infty} \alpha^{j(i-1)} p^j [\alpha^0 \cdot \alpha^1 \cdot \alpha^2 \cdots \alpha^{j-1}]. \tag{4.83}$$

A sum of terms

$$0 + 1 + 2 + 3 + 4 + \cdots,$$

where there are j such terms [including the 0 term, so that the largest positive integer is the $(j-1)$st term] gives the equation

$$\sum_{n=0}^{j-1} n = \frac{j(j-1)}{2}.$$

Therefore, we can restate Eq. (4.83) as

$$E(u_{j\infty}) = \sum_{i}^{\infty} \alpha^{j(i-1)} p^j \alpha^{j(j-1)/2},$$

$$E(u_{j\infty}) = \alpha^{j(j-1)/2} p^j \sum_{i}^{\infty} (\alpha^j)^{i-1},$$

$$E(u_{j\infty}) = \frac{\alpha^{j(j-1)/2} p^j}{1 - \alpha^j}. \tag{4.84}$$

Now we can enter Eq. (4.84) into Eq. (4.75).

$$r_{j\infty} = \frac{\alpha^{j(j-1)/2} p^j}{1 - \alpha^j} - \frac{2\alpha^{j(j+1)/2} p^{j+1}}{1 - \alpha^{j+1}} + \frac{\alpha^{(j+1)(j+2)/2} p^{j+2}}{1 - \alpha^{j+2}}. \tag{4.85}$$

We now set the parameters in Eq. (4.85) equal to our hypothetical parameters for α and p_1.

$$r_{j\infty} = \frac{(.8)^{j(j-1)/2}(.9)^j}{1 - (.8)^j} - \frac{2(.8)^{j(j+1)/2}(.9)^{j+1}}{1 - (.8)^{j+1}} + \frac{(.8)^{(j+1)(j+2)/2}(.9)^{j+2}}{1 - (.8)^{j+2}}. \tag{4.86}$$

If we wish to know how many runs of isolated errors our model predicts, we would set $j = 1$. If we wish to know how many errors our model would predict occurring in pairs, we would set $j = 2$. We do this in Eqs. (4.87) and (4.88).

$$r_{1\infty} = \frac{.9}{1 - .8} - \frac{2(.8)(.9)^2}{1 - (.8)^2} + \frac{(.8)^3(.9)^3}{1 - (.8)^3},$$

$$r_{1\infty} = 1.66; \tag{4.87}$$

$$r_{2\infty} = \frac{(.8)(.9)^2}{1 - (.8)^2} - \frac{2(.8)^3(.9)^3}{1 - (.8)^3} + \frac{(.8)^6(.9)^4}{1 - (.8)^4},$$

$$r_{2\infty} = .562. \tag{4.88}$$

Problems

1. Show that Eq. (4.40) is solved as Eq. (4.41), using the summation technique as given in Table 3.4.

2. Derive the variance for the experimenter–subject-controlled model, as suggested immediately following Eq. (4.63).

3. Assume that you have run 10 subjects in an experiment in which they each had to throw a penny into a cigar box from a distance of 10 feet. Assume that each subject continued until he had been successful 10 consecutive times. Further, assume that you wished to see how well the Bush and Sternberg (1959) single operator model fitted the data.

Artificial data are presented below. A 1 implies an error on that trial and a 0 implies a correct response. The last 1 shown for each subject is his last error prior to 10 consecutive successes (the 0's for these 10 consecutive successes are not shown).

	Trial										
Subject	1	2	3	4	5	6	7	8	9	10	11
1	1	0	1	1	0	1	0	0	1		
2	1	1	1	1	0	1	0	1			
3	0	1	0	1	1	0	0	0	0	0	1
4	1	1	0	0	0	1					
5	1	0	0	0	0	0	1				
6	1	0	0	1	1	0	0	1			
7	1	1	1								
8	1	0	0	0	1						
9	1	1	1	0	0	0	0	0	0	1	
10	1	1	1	0	1	0	1	1	0	1	

Obtain the parameters for the single operator model that would fit the fantasied data of this problem.

4. Using the example of Problem 3, what would be the probability distribution for errors over trials? That is, with trials on the x axis and the probability of an error on the y axis, there would be both an empirical relative frequency of errors at each trial and a theoretical probability of an error at each trial. Give that theoretical distribution over trials 1 through 5 (use numerical values). .

5. Using the example of Problem 3, what would be the expected total number of errors by each trial from trial 1 through trial 7? (Obtain numerical values, using the parameter values obtained in answer to Problem 3.)

6. Use the example of Problem 3 and the parameter values obtained in answering that problem to answer these questions.

(a) If 100 subjects were run, what number of subjects would the theory predict to have errors on all first three trials?

(b) [Check the answer to (a) before trying (b).] If 100 subjects were run, what number of subjects would be predicted to have errors on the first two trials, but a success on the third?

7. For the example in Problem 3, predict the expected number of single (isolated) errors.

8. For the example in Problem 3, predict the expected number of occurrences of precisely three consecutive errors.

Chapter Five

Matrix Algebra

This chapter presents some necessary matrix algebra. Specifically, it details matrix addition and multiplication. It then presents techniques for obtaining determinants and inverses of matrices. The chapter ends with an explication of the technique of spectral resolution, for obtaining the nth power of a matrix.

You have probably been exposed to most or all of this material in a course in linear algebra. However, the techniques for obtaining inverses and the nth power of matrices are generally forgotten through lack of use. This chapter offers both a brief introduction to, and reminder of, the techniques of matrix algebra that will be encountered in the remainder of this book.

Probabilities and random variable values are used as the cell values of the matrices throughout this chapter in order to illustrate matrix algebra as applied to psychological theory. The operations themselves, however, can be applied to any sets of values in matrix form.

Transition Matrices

It is often possible, and convenient, to place a set of data or beliefs about values, etc., into a matrix. For example, if we had the probabilities for transitions from some unconditioned state (U) to some conditioned state (C), we might wish to present them as in Table 5.1.

Note that if our matrix consists of transition probabilities, the sum of any row must equal 1. That is, the values in any ith row represent all of the possible

TABLE 5.1

Transition Probabilities between an
Unlearned State and a
Conditioned State

		Trial $n+1$	
		C	U
Trial n	C	d	$1-d$
	U	c	$1-c$

transitions, conditional on being in the ith row. The sum of the probabilities of all possible transitions from the ith state must sum to 1. Of course, transition probabilities, like all probabilities, can never be negative.

We can present a general matrix of unknown values by indexing each value in terms of its row and column placement. For example, we can restate Table 5.1 as Table 5.2.

TABLE 5.2

Transition Probabilities between
Two States[a]

		Trial $n+1$	
		C	U
Trial n	C	a_{11}	a_{12}
	U	a_{21}	a_{22}

[a] Unspecified values are indexed as to row i and column j (in that order).

When our matrix components are the probabilities of transition, we generally have a square matrix, one with the same number of rows and columns. That is, we tabulate all probabilities of going from any one state on trial n to all possible states on trial $n+1$ (all possible columns), and do this for all possible nth trial states (all possible rows). The number of rows (and columns) in a square matrix is generally called the *order* of the matrix.

When indexing a probability, or any other matrix component, we subscript the row placement first and the column placement second, as shown in Table 5.2.

Matrix Addition

Let us assume a problem where we have two alternate paths to some transition event, for example, two ways in which the subject can go from the unlearned to the conditioned state, in Table 5.2. The probability of reaching the conditioned state would then require summing the two probabilities (since we would be dealing with an " or " relationship). If each of the transitions had two probabilities, we could construct a second matrix of transition probabilities. The two matrices could then be summed as a third matrix expressing the probabilities of going from one state to another over all possible paths. It might look like

$$\begin{pmatrix} a_{11} & a_{12} \\ a_{21} & a_{22} \end{pmatrix} + \begin{pmatrix} b_{11} & b_{12} \\ b_{21} & b_{22} \end{pmatrix} = \begin{pmatrix} a_{11} + b_{11} & a_{12} + b_{12} \\ a_{21} + b_{21} & a_{22} + b_{22} \end{pmatrix}. \tag{5.1}$$

In general, we sum two matrices by adding the identically placed components in each matrix, as we did in Eq. (5.1) That is, a matrix C consisting of components $\{c_{ij}\}$, C being a sum of matrices A and B, consisting of components $\{a_{ij}\}$ and $\{b_{ij}\}$, respectively, could be symbolized as

$$\{c_{ij}\} = \{a_{ij}\} + \{b_{ij}\} = \{a_{ij} + b_{ij}\}. \tag{5.2}$$

If we wished to subtract matrix B from matrix A, we would simply subtract b_{ij} from the corresponding a_{ij}.

The null matrix, with all entries zero, is an additive identity.

Matrix Multiplication

In our discussions of expectations, we described expectations as consisting of sums of products, where each product in a sum was a probability times a random variable value. Each random variable value must be multiplied by its corresponding probability.

If we were to order a group of random variable values in the form of a row vector, we could symbolize it as

$$R_i = (r_{i1} \quad r_{i2} \quad r_{i3}).$$

We could also list each of their probabilities in the same order, but express it as a column vector, such as

$$\mathbf{P}_j = \begin{pmatrix} p_{1j} \\ p_{2j} \\ p_{3j} \end{pmatrix}.$$

To obtain the expectation of the random variable value (assuming that r_{i1} to r_{i3} constitute all of the possible values), we multiply the row vector times the column vector:

$$\mathbf{R}_i \cdot \mathbf{P}_j = (r_{i1} \quad r_{i2} \quad r_{i3}) \begin{pmatrix} p_{1j} \\ p_{2j} \\ p_{3j} \end{pmatrix} = (r_{i1}p_{1j} + r_{i2}p_{2j} + r_{i3}p_{3j}). \qquad (5.3)$$

In general, we multiply vectors times vectors by multiplying sequentially identical row components and column components and summing these products for a single row (and column), as we did in Eq. (5.3). Clearly such a procedure is only possible if we have an equal number of components in the row and column.

Note that the product of a single row and a single column (with an equal number of components in each) yields a single number. If, however, the column vector appeared to the left of the row vector, the product would be a square matrix having as many rows (and columns) as the number of components in each vector.

What would happen if we had two different sets of three random variable values, although each had the same probability set? This would yield two numbers. We express the resulting pair of expected values in Eq. (5.4), each value coming from multiplication of the appropriate row vector by the column vector.

$$\mathbf{R} \cdot \mathbf{P}_j = \begin{pmatrix} r_{11} & r_{12} & r_{13} \\ r_{21} & r_{22} & r_{23} \end{pmatrix} \cdot \begin{pmatrix} p_{1j} \\ p_{2j} \\ p_{3j} \end{pmatrix} = \begin{pmatrix} r_{11}p_{1j} + r_{12}p_{2j} + r_{13}p_{3j} \\ r_{21}p_{1j} + r_{22}p_{2j} + r_{23}p_{3j} \end{pmatrix}. \qquad (5.4)$$

We could also have three or more sets of random variable values. It is also possible that there could be two alternate possible sets of probabilities. The resulting matrix of expected values for one pair of matrices is expressed as

$$\mathbf{R} \cdot \mathbf{P} = \begin{pmatrix} r_{11} & r_{12} & r_{13} \\ r_{21} & r_{22} & r_{23} \\ r_{31} & r_{32} & r_{33} \end{pmatrix} \cdot \begin{pmatrix} p_{11} & p_{12} \\ p_{21} & p_{22} \\ p_{31} & p_{32} \end{pmatrix}, \qquad (5.5a)$$

$$\mathbf{R} \cdot \mathbf{P} = \begin{pmatrix} (r_{11}p_{11} + r_{12}p_{21} + r_{13}p_{31}) & (r_{11}p_{12} + r_{12}p_{22} + r_{13}p_{32}) \\ (r_{21}p_{11} + r_{22}p_{21} + r_{23}p_{31}) & (r_{21}p_{12} + r_{22}p_{22} + r_{23}p_{32}) \\ (r_{31}p_{11} + r_{32}p_{21} + r_{33}p_{31}) & (r_{31}p_{12} + r_{32}p_{22} + r_{33}p_{32}) \end{pmatrix}. \qquad (5.5b)$$

We see from Eqs. (5.3), (5.4), and (5.5a) that what is required for multiplication is a number of components in a row of the left-hand matrix that is equal to the number of components in a column of the right-hand matrix.

Let us identify each matrix by its number of rows times its number of columns, that is, as an $r \times c$ matrix. We can then see that in Eq. (5.4) we have multiplied a 2×3 matrix times a 3×1 matrix. The result was a 2×1 matrix. In Eq. (5.5a) we have multiplied a 3×3 matrix times a 3×2 matrix, resulting in a 3×2 matrix. In general, we can multiply an $m \times k$ matrix times a $k \times n$ matrix, which yields an $m \times n$ matrix. The number of rows of the left-hand matrix and the number of columns in the right-hand matrix determine the rows and columns (respectively) of the resulting matrix.

A matrix can also be multiplied by a single number. This multiplier is called a *scalar* and is multiplied against each element within the matrix. If we have a matrix of elements $\{a_{ij}\}$, then $c\mathbf{A}$ implies

$$c\{a_{ij}\} = \{ca_{ij}\}. \tag{5.6}$$

POWERS OF MATRICES

Sometimes it is desirable to multiply a matrix by itself. (This must be a square matrix, as implied by the necessity of having the column number of one matrix equal in number to the rows of the other.) For example, when dealing with a transition matrix, it might be desirable to have the probability over two transitions. That is, a transition matrix like Table 5.2 might offer the probabilities of going from one state to another on any one trial, and it might be desired to have the probability over two trials of going from, say, U to C. If the matrix offers the probability for one trial, the second power of that matrix will offer the probability of first going anywhere in the matrix from a specified trial n state, and then going to the state indicated in the column of the matrix two trials later. An example of this is

$$\text{trial } n \; \begin{matrix} C \\ U \end{matrix} \begin{pmatrix} a_{11} & a_{12} \\ a_{21} & a_{22} \end{pmatrix}^2 = \text{trial } n \; \begin{matrix} C \\ U \end{matrix} \begin{pmatrix} a_{11}a_{11} + a_{12}a_{21} & a_{11}a_{12} + a_{12}a_{22} \\ a_{21}a_{11} + a_{22}a_{21} & a_{21}a_{12} + a_{22}a_{22} \end{pmatrix}.$$

$$\tag{5.7}$$

The third power of the matrix is obtained by multiplying the original one-trial transition matrix against the same matrix to the second power. In this way, any power of the matrix can be obtained.

The Identity Matrix

We have a matrix to the zeroth power. This is called the *identity matrix*. It is a matrix that, when multiplied by any other matrix, yields a product that is the same matrix as the matrix that had been multiplied by the identity matrix. That is, the identity matrix acts very much like the number one does in ordinary multiplication of individual numbers, which justifies its label as the identity matrix. The analogy with the number one also holds in that just as any real number to the zeroth power equals 1, any matrix to the zeroth power equals the identity matrix.

To identify the identity matrix, we first define the main diagonal of a matrix. Any element of the matrix a_{ij} for which $i = j$ is a member of the main diagonal.

The matrix that is found to always yield an identity in multiplication is a matrix with 1's at the main diagonal and a 0 for all other elements. It can be of any size, but must always have an equal number of rows and columns. Two such matrices would be

$$\mathbf{I} = \begin{pmatrix} 1 & 0 \\ 0 & 1 \end{pmatrix} \quad \text{and} \quad \mathbf{I} = \begin{pmatrix} 1 & 0 & 0 \\ 0 & 1 & 0 \\ 0 & 0 & 1 \end{pmatrix}. \tag{5.8a}$$

Another way of identifying these two identity matrices, where each superscript zero means to raise the matrix to the zeroth power, would be

$$\mathbf{I} = \begin{pmatrix} a_{11} & a_{12} \\ a_{21} & a_{22} \end{pmatrix}^0 \quad \text{and} \quad \mathbf{I} = \begin{pmatrix} a_{11} & a_{12} & a_{13} \\ a_{21} & a_{22} & a_{23} \\ a_{31} & a_{32} & a_{33} \end{pmatrix}^0. \tag{5.8b}$$

If you are unfamiliar with matrix algebra, you should carry out the multiplication in Eq. (5.9) to see how the identity matrix preserves the original matrix in multiplication.

$$\begin{pmatrix} 1 & 0 & 0 \\ 0 & 1 & 0 \\ 0 & 0 & 1 \end{pmatrix} \times \begin{pmatrix} a_{11} & a_{12} & a_{13} \\ a_{21} & a_{22} & a_{23} \\ a_{31} & a_{32} & a_{33} \end{pmatrix} = \begin{pmatrix} a_{11} & a_{12} & a_{13} \\ a_{21} & a_{22} & a_{23} \\ a_{31} & a_{32} & a_{33} \end{pmatrix}. \tag{5.9}$$

Direction of Multiplication

If you were to reverse the left-hand side of Eq. (5.9), you would find that the identity still held. That is, if $\mathbf{A}$ is a matrix, then it is true that

$$\mathbf{I} \cdot \mathbf{A} = \mathbf{A} \cdot \mathbf{I} = \mathbf{A}.$$

We say that multiplication with the identity matrix is commutative. Multiplication between other matrices can also be commutative. However, usually this is not true of other matrices. That is, generally, we should not assume that

$$\mathbf{A} \cdot \mathbf{B} = \mathbf{B} \cdot \mathbf{A} \quad \text{(usually false)}.$$

Order of Multiplication

In multiplying several matrices against each other, the sequence in which the multiplication is carried out will not change the results, providing that it is always a more leftward matrix that is multiplied against a more right-hand matrix. That is,

$$\mathbf{A} \cdot \mathbf{B} \cdot \mathbf{C} = (\mathbf{A} \cdot \mathbf{B}) \cdot \mathbf{C} = \mathbf{A} \cdot (\mathbf{B} \cdot \mathbf{C}).$$

Summarizing, we can say that the order (or direction) of multiplication cannot be reversed (except with the identity matrix), but the sequence of multiplication can be varied, without changing the resulting product.

The Inverse of a Matrix

We have discussed the addition, subtraction, and multiplication of matrices. There is also a matrix operation that is loosely analogous to division. We define the inverse of a square matrix $\mathbf{A}$, symbolized $\mathbf{A}^{-1}$, for this purpose. A matrix that is not square cannot have an inverse.

The inverse $\mathbf{A}^{-1}$ of a matrix $\mathbf{A}$ is that matrix which, when multiplied against the matrix $\mathbf{A}$ (in any order), will yield the identity matrix. That is,

$$\mathbf{A} \cdot \mathbf{A}^{-1} = \mathbf{A}^{-1} \cdot \mathbf{A} = \mathbf{I}$$

(offering the analogy of a real number being multiplied by its reciprocal to yield the number one).

Multiplying a matrix $\mathbf{C}$ by the inverse of a matrix $\mathbf{B}$ might then be thought of as dividing $\mathbf{C}$ by the original matrix $\mathbf{B}$. For example, given an equation of square matrices such as

$$\mathbf{A} \cdot \mathbf{B} = \mathbf{C},$$

we would have the resulting equivalence

$$\mathbf{A} = \mathbf{B}^{-1} \cdot \mathbf{C}$$

if the matrix $\mathbf{B}$ had an inverse.

There are algorithms for obtaining the inverse of a matrix. Not all square matrices have an inverse. However, matrices with an inverse have only one inverse.

In order to obtain the inverse of a matrix using a very general procedure, it will be helpful to define the following three functions of a matrix $\mathbf{A}$: the transpose $\mathbf{A}'$; the determinant $|\mathbf{A}|$; and the cofactor matrix $\mathbf{A}_{cf}$.

THE TRANSPOSE OF A MATRIX

The transpose of a matrix is a matrix with the identical components of the original, but with the placement of the components changed in a specific way. The rows of $\mathbf{A}$ become the columns of the transpose $\mathbf{A}'$, and vice versa. As an example, if

$$\mathbf{A} = \begin{pmatrix} a_{11} & a_{12} & a_{13} \\ a_{21} & a_{22} & a_{23} \\ a_{31} & a_{32} & a_{33} \end{pmatrix} = \begin{pmatrix} 1 & 2 & 3 \\ 4 & 5 & 6 \\ 7 & 8 & 9 \end{pmatrix},$$

then

$$\mathbf{A}' = \begin{pmatrix} a_{11} & a_{21} & a_{31} \\ a_{12} & a_{22} & a_{32} \\ a_{13} & a_{23} & a_{33} \end{pmatrix} = \begin{pmatrix} 1 & 4 & 7 \\ 2 & 5 & 8 \\ 3 & 6 & 9 \end{pmatrix}.$$

THE DETERMINANT OF A MATRIX

For any matrix which has an inverse, there is a constant nonzero value that can be computed to represent the matrix. This value, called the *determinant* of the matrix, is invariant with certain operations on the matrix and changes predictably with other operations. We shall describe two techniques for obtaining the determinant of a matrix.

Obtaining a Determinant through Subscript Permutations

The determinant is the sum of all possible products of components in the matrix, where each product consists of one component from each row and each column (with specific products to be given a minus sign). For example, in Eq. (5.10), we can abstract the elements of the main diagonal of the matrix.

$$\mathbf{A} = \begin{pmatrix} a_{11} & a_{12} & a_{13} \\ a_{21} & a_{22} & a_{23} \\ a_{31} & a_{32} & a_{33} \end{pmatrix}. \tag{5.10}$$

This diagonal is

$$a_{11} \quad a_{22} \quad a_{33},$$

which fits the criterion of one component from each column and each row. We could obtain a new set by placing two different components into the group, for example, reversing the second subscript for the last two components. That is, we could use the set

$$a_{11} \quad a_{23} \quad a_{32},$$

again fulfilling the criterion of one component from each column and each row. We can construct all possible variations by maintaining the first subscript in each component constant, and varying the components so that we have every possible order of 1, 2, and 3 as the second subscript. Three subscripts can be permuted $3! = 6$ ways. For a 3×3 matrix, six products of three components each would need to be added (or subtracted, as discussed below) to obtain the determinant. If

$$\mathbf{A} = \begin{pmatrix} a_{11} & a_{12} & a_{13} \\ a_{21} & a_{22} & a_{23} \\ a_{31} & a_{32} & a_{33} \end{pmatrix},$$

then

$$|\mathbf{A}| = (a_{11} \cdot a_{22} \cdot a_{33}) + (a_{13} \cdot a_{21} \cdot a_{32}) + (a_{12} \cdot a_{23} \cdot a_{31})$$
$$- (a_{11} \cdot a_{23} \cdot a_{32}) - (a_{12} \cdot a_{21} \cdot a_{33}) - (a_{13} \cdot a_{22} \cdot a_{31}). \quad (5.11)$$

Note that three of the components are subtracted from the sum rather than added to it. We use the number of transpositions of subscripts to determine whether a component should be added or subtracted. When the number of transpositions is even, we add the component. When the number of transpositions is odd, we subtract the component. We use the main diagonal set as the beginning point, and then transpose the second of the two subscripts for some pair of elements. We can do this one or more times to obtain a set that we have not yet constructed. (By transposing the subscripts, we always maintain all of them, so we do not lose any columns.) When we previously went from

$$a_{11} \quad a_{22} \quad a_{33}$$

to

$$a_{11} \quad a_{23} \quad a_{32},$$

we had one transposition, an odd number, putting a minus in front of $(a_{11} \cdot a_{23} \cdot a_{32})$ in Eq. (5.11). On the other hand, for

$$a_{13} \quad a_{21} \quad a_{32}$$

we made two "switches" from the main diagonal elements, giving us a plus in front of $(a_{13} \cdot a_{21} \cdot a_{32})$.

For a 2×2 matrix, such as the one in Table 5.2, only one variation from the main diagonal would be possible. That is, if

$$\mathbf{A} = \begin{pmatrix} a_{11} & a_{12} \\ a_{21} & a_{22} \end{pmatrix},$$

then

$$|\mathbf{A}| = (a_{11} \cdot a_{22}) - (a_{12} \cdot a_{21}). \quad (5.12)$$

Equation (5.12) is the smallest possible general determinant, and offers a component for another means of obtaining determinants of larger matrices.

Obtaining a Matrix Determinant through the Determinants of Minors

To utilize this second technique for obtaining determinants, we shall need to define a minor of a matrix.

A minor m_{ij} of a matrix $\mathbf{A}$ is the submatrix formed from $\mathbf{A}$ by eliminating the row and column containing a_{ij} from $\mathbf{A}$. For example, in Eq. (5.10), the minor m_{11} would be

$$\begin{pmatrix} a_{22} & a_{23} \\ a_{32} & a_{33} \end{pmatrix}.$$

The minor m_{22} would be

$$\begin{pmatrix} a_{11} & a_{13} \\ a_{31} & a_{33} \end{pmatrix}.$$

In this second method for obtaining a determinant, we select one row or column of the matrix and use the minor of each of these components in that row (or column) for our next step in the process. Having constructed the minor for the component, we then obtain the determinant of the minor. We then multiply this determinant of a minor by the component of the row (or column) for which this is the minor. We then add (or subtract) each such product, and this is the determinant of our complete matrix. As an example, let us look once more at Eq. (5.10). We can select the top row, and obtain the minor of each component. The minors, each multiplied by its appropriate component, are listed in Figure 5.1. The determinants from these minors, each multiplied

$$a_{11} \cdot \begin{pmatrix} a_{22} & a_{23} \\ a_{32} & a_{33} \end{pmatrix} \qquad a_{12} \cdot \begin{pmatrix} a_{21} & a_{23} \\ a_{31} & a_{33} \end{pmatrix} \qquad a_{13} \cdot \begin{pmatrix} a_{21} & a_{22} \\ a_{31} & a_{32} \end{pmatrix}$$

Figure 5.1. Three minors of a 3×3 matrix, each multiplied against its appropriate component.

against its appropriate component, appear in Eq. (5.13), giving the determinant for the matrix in Eq. (5.10). We have included the appropriate signs, to be explained immediately following

$$|\mathbf{A}| = a_{11}(a_{22} \cdot a_{33} - a_{23} \cdot a_{32}) - a_{12}(a_{21} \cdot a_{33} - a_{23} \cdot a_{31})$$
$$+ a_{13}(a_{21} \cdot a_{32} - a_{22} \cdot a_{31}). \quad (5.13)$$

Each determinant of a minor $|m_{ij}|$ receives a sign, depending on the values of i and j (that is, the position in the matrix of a_{ij}).

The properly signed determinant of the minor is called a *cofactor*, symbolized c_{ij}. The exact relationship between the determinant of the minor and the cofactor is

$$c_{ij} = (-1)^{i+j}|m_{ij}|. \tag{5.14}$$

We can see from Eq. (5.14) that when i and j sum to an even number, the determinant is multiplied by $+1$, and when it sums to an odd number, it is multiplied by a -1. This would explain the signs used in Eq. (5.13). Multiplying through with the factors in Eq. (5.13) will give an identity with Eq. (5.11), which offered the determinant for the same matrix using the permutation method.

We can verbally summarize this second method for obtaining determinants as taking *the sum of the products of all of the components of a row* (or *column*) *times their respective cofactors*. We symbolize this method (and definition) as

$$|\mathbf{A}| = \sum_{j=1}^{c} a_{ij}(-1)^{i+j}|m_{ij}| = \sum_{j=1}^{c} a_{ij}(c_{ij}), \tag{5.15a}$$

taking all a_{ij} in a row i;

$$|\mathbf{A}| = \sum_{i=1}^{r} a_{ij}(-1)^{i+j}|m_{ij}| = \sum_{i=1}^{r} a_{ij}(c_{ij}), \tag{5.15b}$$

taking all a_{ij} in a column j.

For a 4×4 matrix, we would obtain our four cofactors from four minors that are themselves 3×3 matrices. We would continue breaking down each 3×3 minor to three 2×2 matrices, and obtain each determinant for a 2×2 matrix from Eq. (5.12). At each point, when forming a cofactor from a determinant $|m_{ij}|$, we would obtain its sign in terms of the position of the component a_{ij} in the last submatrix. Thus, the numbers i and j would be revalued for each new submatrix.

A 3×3 matrix that was a minor in a 4×4 matrix would itself have three 2×2 minors. The three determinants of 2×2 matrices in this 3×3 matrix would be multiplied by -1 or $+1$ in terms of component positions of the components a_{ij} for each m_{ij} used in the 3×3 matrix. However, the overall determinant of the 3×3 matrix would be signed according to the position of the component identifying that 3×3 minor in the 4×4 matrix. Thus, in a 4×4 matrix, the minor obtained for the component a_{44} would be the matrix in Eq. (5.10). Therefore, one component of the determinant of a 4×4 matrix could be a_{44} multiplied against the right-hand side of Eq. (5.13). Since for a_{44}, $i + j = 8$, an even-numbered position, it would be added in the set of four products making up the determinant of the 4×4 matrix.

The two methods for finding determinants can each be used as a check on the other. For large matrices these methods are cumbersome and errors are common, so a second method for checking is essential.

The determinants for matrices of the second, third, and fourth order are presented in Table 5.3.

TABLE 5.3

Determinants for Matrices with Components a_{ij}[a]

Matrix	Determinant
2×2	$(a_{11} \cdot a_{22}) - (a_{12} \cdot a_{21})$
3×3	$(a_{11} \cdot a_{22} \cdot a_{33}) + (a_{13} \cdot a_{21} \cdot a_{32}) + (a_{12} \cdot a_{23} \cdot a_{31})$
	$\quad - (a_{11} \cdot a_{23} \cdot a_{32}) - (a_{12} \cdot a_{21} \cdot a_{33}) - (a_{13} \cdot a_{22} \cdot a_{31})$
4×4	$(a_{11} \cdot a_{22} \cdot a_{33} \cdot a_{44}) + (a_{11} \cdot a_{23} \cdot a_{34} \cdot a_{42}) + (a_{11} \cdot a_{24} \cdot a_{32} \cdot a_{43})$
	$+ (a_{12} \cdot a_{21} \cdot a_{34} \cdot a_{43}) + (a_{13} \cdot a_{21} \cdot a_{32} \cdot a_{44}) + (a_{14} \cdot a_{21} \cdot a_{33} \cdot a_{42})$
	$+ (a_{12} \cdot a_{23} \cdot a_{31} \cdot a_{44}) + (a_{13} \cdot a_{24} \cdot a_{31} \cdot a_{42}) + (a_{14} \cdot a_{22} \cdot a_{31} \cdot a_{43})$
	$+ (a_{12} \cdot a_{24} \cdot a_{33} \cdot a_{41}) + (a_{13} \cdot a_{22} \cdot a_{34} \cdot a_{41}) + (a_{14} \cdot a_{23} \cdot a_{32} \cdot a_{41})$
	$- (a_{11} \cdot a_{22} \cdot a_{34} \cdot a_{43}) - (a_{11} \cdot a_{23} \cdot a_{32} \cdot a_{44}) - (a_{11} \cdot a_{24} \cdot a_{33} \cdot a_{42})$
	$- (a_{12} \cdot a_{21} \cdot a_{33} \cdot a_{44}) - (a_{13} \cdot a_{21} \cdot a_{34} \cdot a_{42}) - (a_{14} \cdot a_{21} \cdot a_{32} \cdot a_{43})$
	$- (a_{12} \cdot a_{24} \cdot a_{31} \cdot a_{43}) - (a_{13} \cdot a_{22} \cdot a_{31} \cdot a_{44}) - (a_{14} \cdot a_{23} \cdot a_{31} \cdot a_{42})$
	$- (a_{12} \cdot a_{23} \cdot a_{34} \cdot a_{41}) - (a_{13} \cdot a_{24} \cdot a_{32} \cdot a_{41}) - (a_{14} \cdot a_{22} \cdot a_{33} \cdot a_{41})$

[a] Where i stands for the row and j stands for the column.

Triangular Matrices

A matrix that has all zeros on one side of the main diagonal is called a *triangular matrix*. If components a_{12}, a_{13}, and a_{23} in Eq. (5.10) were all zeros, it would be a triangular matrix. If either a_{12} or a_{21} in Table 5.2 were zeros, we would have a triangular matrix. A triangular matrix offers some computational conveniences. One of them is that the determinant will simply be the product of the components on the main diagonal. Using our permutation technique for developing determinants, we would find that, in a triangular matrix, every product of components that are not all on the main diagonal would include a zero, and therefore yield a product of zero. This would leave only the components on the main diagonal as the elements of a product constituting the determinant.

THE COFACTOR MATRIX

The basic formula that we shall use for obtaining the inverse $\mathbf{A}^{-1}$ of a matrix $\mathbf{A}$ is

$$\mathbf{A}^{-1} = \frac{1}{|\mathbf{A}|} \mathbf{A}'_{cf}. \tag{5.16}$$

Equation (5.16) makes clear the necessity of a nonzero determinant for any matrix having an inverse, since the determinant appears as a denominator in the formula.

We have learned how to form a determinant and how to form the transpose of a matrix. We have also discussed the means of obtaining minors of a matrix. We then indicated how we would sign the determinants of the minors to obtain cofactors that we would require for the general determinant of the original matrix. What we have in $\mathbf{A}_{cf}$ is a full matrix of cofactors. That is, for each a_{ij} in the original matrix $\mathbf{A}$ (not just those in one row or column), we would obtain a minor; we would then obtain the determinant of that minor and sign it properly to obtain a cofactor [using Eq. (5.14)], and place the value of that cofactor at the ith row, jth column of the cofactor matrix.

Our cofactor matrix $\mathbf{A}_{cf}$ is simply the matrix of these individual cofactors $\{c_{ij}\}$, each placed at the ith row, jth column of $\mathbf{A}_{cf}$.

We can take the transpose of the cofactor matrix, as we can of any matrix, by placing the kth row as the kth column, or vice versa.

We therefore have all of the steps for obtaining the inverse $\mathbf{A}^{-1}$ of a matrix $\mathbf{A}$ according to Eq. (5.16).

As an example, let us take the triangular matrix

$$\mathbf{A} = \begin{pmatrix} 1 & 0 & 0 \\ c & 1-c & 0 \\ 0 & d & 1-d \end{pmatrix}. \tag{5.17}$$

Since the matrix of Eq. (5.17) is a triangular matrix, the determinant is simply the product of the elements of the main diagonal. That is,

$$|\mathbf{A}| = (1-c)(1-d). \tag{5.18}$$

We can form minors in the matrix of Eq. (5.17), and obtain a determinant for each minor, with Eq. (5.12). We can then substitute the determinants for the components of the matrix. This would give us a matrix of determinants of minors $\{|m_{ij}|\} = \mathbf{A}_{|m_{ij}|}$ as in

$$\mathbf{A}_{|m_{ij}|} = \begin{pmatrix} (1-c)(1-d) & c(1-d) & cd \\ 0 & 1-d & d \\ 0 & 0 & 1-c \end{pmatrix}. \tag{5.19}$$

Applying the definition implied in Eq. (5.14) to the matrix in Eq. (5.19), we obtain the matrix

$$\mathbf{A}_{cf} = \begin{pmatrix} (1-c)(1-d) & -c(1-d) & cd \\ 0 & (1-d) & -d \\ 0 & 0 & (1-c) \end{pmatrix}. \tag{5.20}$$

We now transpose the matrix in Eq. (5.20), which gives us, in Eq. (5.21), the transpose of the cofactor matrix $\mathbf{A}'_{cf}$, where $\mathbf{A}$ is the matrix in Eq. (5.17).

$$\mathbf{A}'_{cf} = \begin{pmatrix} (1-c)(1-d) & 0 & 0 \\ -c(1-d) & (1-d) & 0 \\ cd & -d & (1-c) \end{pmatrix}. \qquad (5.21)$$

For the inverse of $\mathbf{A}$, we must multiply the matrix in Eq. (5.21) by the reciprocal of the determinant as obtained in Eq. (5.18). We have, then, the inverse of $\mathbf{A}$, using the formula of Eq. (5.16):

$$\mathbf{A}^{-1} = \frac{1}{(1-c)(1-d)} \begin{pmatrix} (1-c)(1-d) & 0 & 0 \\ -c(1-d) & (1-d) & 0 \\ cd & -d & (1-c) \end{pmatrix}. \qquad (5.22)$$

We can verify that Eq. (5.22) is correct by multiplying the right-hand side of Eq. (5.22) times the matrix in Eq. (5.17) and finding that this yields the identity matrix.

Two Special Cases of an Inverse

For a 2×2 matrix the minor m_{ij} for each element a_{ij} is, in each instance, a single cell component itself. This single element would then become the determinant of the minor. Returning again to the matrix in Table 5.2 as our example of the standard 2×2 matrix, we would restate the matrix as a cofactor matrix in Eq. (5.23).

$$\mathbf{A}_{cf} = \begin{pmatrix} a_{22} & -a_{21} \\ -a_{12} & a_{11} \end{pmatrix}. \qquad (5.23)$$

We can now transpose the cofactor matrix in Eq. (5.23) and multiply it by the reciprocal of the determinant of the original matrix in Table 5.2, from Eq. (5.12), to obtain the inverse. We present this in Eqs. (5.24a) and (5.24b). If

$$\mathbf{A} = \begin{pmatrix} a_{11} & a_{12} \\ a_{21} & a_{22} \end{pmatrix}, \qquad (5.24a)$$

then

$$\mathbf{A}^{-1} = \frac{1}{(a_{11} \cdot a_{22} - a_{12} \cdot a_{21})} \begin{pmatrix} a_{22} & -a_{12} \\ -a_{21} & a_{11} \end{pmatrix}. \qquad (5.24b)$$

In general then, to obtain the inverse of a 2×2 matrix, we simply change the signs of a_{12} and a_{21}, diagonally reverse the other two elements, and finally multiply this new matrix by the reciprocal of the determinant of the original.

Another standard matrix with a very simple inverse is the diagonal matrix. If we applied the foregoing techniques to the diagonal matrix, we would find that the inverse is simply the original diagonal matrix, with each non-zero element replaced by its own reciprocal. Therefore, if

$$\mathbf{A} = \begin{pmatrix} a_{11} & 0 & 0 \\ 0 & a_{22} & 0 \\ 0 & 0 & a_{33} \end{pmatrix}, \tag{5.25a}$$

then

$$\mathbf{A}^{-1} = \begin{pmatrix} \dfrac{1}{a_{11}} & 0 & 0 \\ 0 & \dfrac{1}{a_{22}} & 0 \\ 0 & 0 & \dfrac{1}{a_{33}} \end{pmatrix}. \tag{5.25b}$$

EFFECTS ON THE DETERMINANTS OF CHANGES IN THE MATRIX

The ease with which we were able to obtain the determinant of the matrix of Eq. (5.17) clearly indicates the advantages of working with triangular matrices. We indicated previously that the determinant is either invariant, or changes predictably, given certain changes in the matrix. We use this fact to permit us to change a matrix so that a nontriangular matrix can become a triangular matrix, without changing the value of the determinant that will result. There are a number of changes possible, but we shall mention three that are particularly easy to use.

Rule 1. $|\mathbf{A}^*| = |\mathbf{A}|$, where $\mathbf{A}^*$ is $\mathbf{A}$ changed by adding a multiple of any row to any other row, or a multiple of any column to any other column.

Rule 2. $|\mathbf{A}^*| = -|\mathbf{A}|$, where $\mathbf{A}^*$ is $\mathbf{A}$ changed by interchanging two rows (or columns) of $\mathbf{A}$.

Rule 3. $|\mathbf{A}^*| = c|\mathbf{A}|$, where $\mathbf{A}^*$ is $\mathbf{A}$ changed by multiplying each element in a certain row (or column) by c.

As illustrations of Rules 1–3, we present the following examples. If

$$\mathbf{A} = \begin{pmatrix} a & b \\ c & d \end{pmatrix},$$

then

$$|\mathbf{A}| = ad - bc. \tag{5.26}$$

As an example of Rule 1, if

$$\mathbf{A}^* = \begin{pmatrix} a & b + ax \\ c & d + cx \end{pmatrix}$$

then

$$|\mathbf{A}^*| = (ad + acx) - (bc + acx),$$
$$|\mathbf{A}^*| = ad - bc. \tag{5.27}$$

As expected from Rule 1, Eq. (5.27) is equal to Eq. (5.26).

As an example of Rule 2, if

$$\mathbf{A}^* = \begin{pmatrix} b & a \\ d & c \end{pmatrix},$$

then

$$|\mathbf{A}^*| = bc - ad. \tag{5.28}$$

As expected from Rule 2, Eq. (5.28) is equal to Eq. (5.26) times -1.

As an example of Rule 3, if

$$\mathbf{A}^* = \begin{pmatrix} ax & b \\ cx & d \end{pmatrix},$$

then

$$|\mathbf{A}^*| = adx - bcx,$$
$$|\mathbf{A}^*| = x(ad - bc). \tag{5.29}$$

As expected from Rule 3, Eq. (5.29) is equal to Eq. (5.26) times x.

To convert a nontriangular matrix into a triangular matrix, we use rules such as Rules 1–3 to alter the matrix without altering the determinant, or at most, altering the determinant in a known way, so that we can reconstruct the original determinant. With a stochastic matrix, it is always possible to add all of the columns except one to the remaining column. In this way, we would have a column of 1's. By then subtracting, say, the top (or any other) row from all of the others in turn, we would have a column of all 0's, with the exception of the top, which would have a 1. We use all of the rules as needed until we have a triangular matrix. As an example, let us take the matrix of Table 5.2, and assume it is a stochastic matrix. We would add the second column to the first (Rule 1), which would give us

$$\mathbf{A}^* = \begin{pmatrix} 1 & a_{12} \\ 1 & a_{22} \end{pmatrix}.$$

We could then subtract the first row from the second (Rule 1 again), which would give us the triangular matrix

$$\mathbf{A}^* = \begin{pmatrix} 1 & a_{12} \\ 0 & a_{22} - a_{12} \end{pmatrix}. \tag{5.30}$$

Our determinant would then be

$$|\mathbf{A}^*| = a_{22} - a_{12}. \tag{5.31}$$

The equivalence of Eq. (5.31) to Eq. (5.12) is found by recognizing that

$$a_{11}a_{22} - a_{12}a_{21} = (1 - a_{12})a_{22} - a_{12}(1 - a_{22}),$$

since row sums equal 1. The right-hand side then reduces to

$$a_{22} - a_{12}$$

as the determinant for a 2×2 stochastic matrix.

Obtaining the nth Power of a Matrix

We shall frequently require a means of determining the nth power of a matrix $\mathbf{A}$. That is, we shall want to know what the values in the resulting matrix would be when we have multiplied $\mathbf{A} \cdot \mathbf{A} \cdot \mathbf{A} \cdots \mathbf{A}$ where $\mathbf{A}$ appears n times. The burden of actually repeating the multiplication of even a 3×3 matrix some 10 or 15 times makes the possession of some general solution to the nth value of a matrix important. The general solution that we shall use involves the isolation first of the "latent roots" of the matrix whose nth power we seek. These latent roots then play the role of scalar values [Eq. (5.6)] being multiplied by some derived matrix that does not itself have to be raised to any power. This process is analogous to our difference equation solutions, where we obtained some root which we raised to some nth power and then multiplied against some constant. In the nth-power solution of matrices, by using a constant matrix that does not have to be raised to the nth power, but requiring only that some number (the root) be raised to the nth power, we obtain a useful general solution (though it is cumbersome to obtain). We call the technique to be discussed in this section *spectral resolution* of a matrix. We summarize the procedure in Eq. (5.32).

$$\mathbf{P}^n = \sum_{j=1}^{k} \mathbf{A}_j \lambda_j^{\,n}, \tag{5.32}$$

where k is the number of latent roots, λ_j is the jth root, and each $\mathbf{A}_j$ is one of k matrices to be determined by the process of spectral resolution described later.

The latent roots are a set of scalar values $\{\lambda_1, \lambda_2, \ldots, \lambda_j, \ldots, \lambda_k\}$ equal in number to the order of the matrix. The latent roots are obtained from the determinant of a matrix $\mathbf{L}$, where

$$\mathbf{L} = \mathbf{P} - \lambda\mathbf{I}. \tag{5.33}$$

The values of λ that would satisfy the equality

$$|\mathbf{L}| = 0 \tag{5.34}$$

are the latent roots that we seek.

For example, in the case of a 2×2 stochastic matrix $\mathbf{P}$, where

$$\mathbf{P} = \begin{pmatrix} a_{11} & a_{12} \\ a_{21} & a_{22} \end{pmatrix},$$

we have, from Eq. (5.33),

$$\mathbf{L} = \begin{pmatrix} a_{11} & a_{12} \\ a_{21} & a_{22} \end{pmatrix} - \begin{pmatrix} \lambda & 0 \\ 0 & \lambda \end{pmatrix},$$

$$\mathbf{L} = \begin{pmatrix} a_{11} - \lambda & a_{12} \\ a_{21} & a_{22} - \lambda \end{pmatrix}, \tag{5.35}$$

so that

$$|\mathbf{L}| = (a_{11} - \lambda)(a_{22} - \lambda) - (a_{21})(a_{12}). \tag{5.36}$$

With the determinant in the form of Eq. (5.36), it is not clear what values of λ would satisfy Eq. (5.34). We therefore return to the matrix $\mathbf{L}$ [Eq. (5.35)] and alter its form to alter the form of the determinant without altering its value. We attempt to form a triangular matrix, if possible, since the main diagonal will then give the determinant of the matrix in Eq. (5.35) as a factor of components equal in number to the order of the matrix. In this example, for the matrix in Eq. (5.35), we add the second column to the first, which gives us the altered matrix

$$\mathbf{L}^* = \begin{pmatrix} 1 - \lambda & a_{12} \\ 1 - \lambda & a_{22} - \lambda \end{pmatrix}.$$

We then subtract the top row from the bottom row, which yields

$$\mathbf{L}^{**} = \begin{pmatrix} 1 - \lambda & a_{12} \\ 0 & a_{22} - a_{12} - \lambda \end{pmatrix}.$$

The determinant, still unaltered in value, but altered in form, is now

$$|\mathbf{L}| = (1 - \lambda)(a_{22} - a_{12} - \lambda).$$

Setting this equal to 0, and recognizing the values of λ that would satisfy that equality, we would have

$$\lambda_1 = 1 \tag{5.37a}$$

and

$$\lambda_2 = a_{22} - a_{12}. \tag{5.37b}$$

Returning to Eq. (5.32) with our example of a 2×2 stochastic matrix, we can restate it as

$$\mathbf{P}^n = \mathbf{A}_1 1^n + \mathbf{A}_2 (a_{22} - a_{12})^n$$

$$= \begin{pmatrix} a_{11} & a_{12} \\ a_{21} & a_{22} \end{pmatrix}^n . \tag{5.38}$$

We now show the technique of obtaining $\mathbf{A}_j$ for Eq. (5.38).

SPECTRAL RESOLUTION

Each $\mathbf{A}_j$ is obtained as the product of a column matrix $\mathbf{C}_j$ times a row matrix $\mathbf{R}_j$.

$$\mathbf{A}_j = \mathbf{C}_j \mathbf{R}_j . \tag{5.39}$$

Both $\mathbf{C}_j$ and $\mathbf{R}_j$ are transforming matrices which can be multiplied against the original matrix $\mathbf{P}$, so that

$$\mathbf{R}_j \mathbf{P} = \lambda_j \mathbf{R}_j \tag{5.40}$$

and

$$\mathbf{P} \mathbf{C}_j = \lambda_j \mathbf{C}_j . \tag{5.41}$$

We shall begin with a knowledge of our original matrix $\mathbf{P}$ and our derived λ_j values. We shall find that we can use the equalities of Eqs. (5.40) and (5.41) to obtain the values of $\mathbf{R}_j$ and $\mathbf{C}_j$, and then from these two we shall obtain $\mathbf{A}_j$ in accord with Eq. (5.39).

Let us begin with $\mathbf{R}_j$. We must have the form

$$\mathbf{R}_j = [x_j \cdots z_j].$$

For a 2×2 matrix, and a particular row, say row one, we would have

$$\mathbf{R}_1 = [x_1 \quad y_1]. \tag{5.42}$$

Then, following Eq. (5.40), using Eq. (5.42) and $\lambda_1 = 1$ [from Eq. (5.37a)], we would have

$$[x_1 \quad y_1] \begin{pmatrix} a_{11} & a_{12} \\ a_{21} & a_{22} \end{pmatrix} = [x_1 \quad y_1],$$

from which

$$[(a_{11}x_1 + a_{21}y_1) \quad (a_{12}x_1 + a_{22}y_1)] = [x_1 \quad y_1]. \tag{5.43}$$

We now have two equations in x_1 and y_1, which we can solve for relative values. That is, we attempt to solve for y_1 in terms of its values relative to x_1. From Eq. (5.43), we have

$$x_1 = a_{11}x_1 + a_{21}y_1, \qquad y_1 = a_{12}x_1 + a_{22}y_1,$$

from which we have

$$(a_{11} - 1)x_1 + a_{21}y_1 = 0,$$
$$a_{12}x_1 + (a_{22} - 1)y_1 = 0,$$

Noting that $a_{11} - 1 = -a_{12}$ and $a_{22} - 1 = -a_{21}$, both equations become

$$a_{12}x_1 - a_{21}y_1 = 0,$$

which means that

$$y_1 = \frac{a_{12}}{a_{21}} x_1. \tag{5.44}$$

Then, any values of y_1 and x_1 in Eq. (5.42) that maintain the proportionality in Eq. (5.44) are acceptable. For example, if we substitute the values a_{12} for y_1 and a_{21} for x_1 in Eq. (5.44) we would maintain the equality. Any other values maintaining the equality would be acceptable for x_1 and y_1 in Eq. (5.42). Thus we can express $\mathbf{R}_1$ as

$$\mathbf{R}_1 = k_1[a_{21} \quad a_{12}], \tag{5.45}$$

or

$$\mathbf{R}_1 = k_1\left[1 \quad \frac{a_{12}}{a_{21}}\right], \quad \text{or} \quad \mathbf{R}_1 = k_1\left[\frac{a_{21}}{a_{12}} \quad 1\right].$$

where k_1 is a constant which we are free to evaluate in any way we wish.

The fact that the two equations reduce to a single one is important. When, in your past studies, you have had two equations in two unknowns, you have usually been able to solve for unique values of the unknowns. In the present case the two equations duplicate information, that is, they are both equivalent to a single equation. This means that we can obtain only a relational solution, a solution up to a constant of proportionality.

We can follow the same procedure for $\mathbf{R}_2$.

$$\mathbf{R}_2 = [x_2 \quad y_2] \tag{5.46}$$

Following Eqs. (5.40), (5.46), and (5.37b), we have

$$[x_2 \quad y_2]\begin{pmatrix} a_{11} & a_{12} \\ a_{21} & a_{22} \end{pmatrix} = (a_{22} - a_{12})[x_2 \quad y_2]. \tag{5.47}$$

We carry out the multiplication on both sides of Eq. (5.47), and then have an equality between two vectors:

$$[(a_{11}x_2 + a_{21}y_2) \quad (a_{12}x_2 + a_{22}y_2)] = [(a_{22} - a_{12})x_2 \quad (a_{22} - a_{12})y_2]. \tag{5.48}$$

This reduces to the two equalities

$$(a_{22} - a_{12})x_2 = a_{11}x_2 + a_{21}y_2,$$
$$(a_{22} - a_{12})y_2 = a_{12}x_2 + a_{22}y_2,$$

which can be restated as

$$-a_{21}y_2 = (a_{11} + a_{12} - a_{22})x_2,$$
$$(a_{22} - a_{22} - a_{12})y_2 = a_{12}x_2.$$

If we note that

$$a_{11} + a_{12} - a_{22} = 1 - a_{22} = a_{21}$$

and

$$a_{22} - a_{22} - a_{12} = -a_{12},$$

then the equations become

$$-a_{21}y_2 = a_{21}x_2$$

and

$$-a_{12}y_2 = a_{12}x_2,$$

which are both satisfied by the single equation

$$x_2 = -y_2. \tag{5.49}$$

Equation (5.49) indicates the relative values of x_2 and y_2, so that for any constant k_2, we could state

$$\mathbf{R}_2 = k_2[1 \quad -1]. \tag{5.50}$$

We shall now follow an analogous procedure to obtain $\mathbf{C}_1$ and $\mathbf{C}_2$. Each $\mathbf{C}_j$ is a single column matrix (for the jth column), so it must have the form

$$\begin{matrix} d_j \\ \vdots \\ f_j. \end{matrix}$$

For a 2×2 matrix, we would have

$$\mathbf{C}_1 = \begin{pmatrix} d_1 \\ e_1 \end{pmatrix}.$$

From Eq. (5.41) we have

$$\mathbf{PC}_j = \lambda_j \mathbf{C}_j.$$

For a 2×2 stochastic matrix we saw that

$$\lambda_1 = 1.$$

We therefore have, for Eq. (5.41),

$$\begin{pmatrix} a_{11} & a_{12} \\ a_{21} & a_{22} \end{pmatrix}\begin{pmatrix} d_1 \\ e_1 \end{pmatrix} = \begin{pmatrix} d_1 \\ e_1 \end{pmatrix}.$$

We multiply the left-hand side and obtain the equality of two column vectors

$$\begin{pmatrix} a_{11}d_1 + a_{12}e_1 \\ a_{21}d_1 + a_{22}e_1 \end{pmatrix} = \begin{pmatrix} d_1 \\ e_1 \end{pmatrix}.$$

We now solve for e_1 in terms of d_1, again looking for relative values.

$$(a_{11} - 1)d_1 + a_{12}e_1 = 0,$$
$$a_{21}d_1 + (a_{22} - 1)e_1 = 0,$$

Since $a_{11} - 1 = -a_{12}$ and $a_{22} - 1 = -a_{21}$, the equations become

$$-a_{12}d_1 = -a_{12}e_1 \qquad \text{and} \qquad a_{21}d_1 = a_{21}e_1.$$

Both equations then give the same equality

$$e_1 = d_1. \tag{5.51}$$

Equation (5.51) leads to

$$\mathbf{C}_1 = h_1\begin{pmatrix} 1 \\ 1 \end{pmatrix}. \tag{5.52}$$

We now proceed similarly with $\mathbf{C}_2$. We symbolize

$$\mathbf{C}_2 = \begin{pmatrix} d_2 \\ e_2 \end{pmatrix}.$$

Again proceeding with Eq. (5.41), but this time with $\lambda_2 = (a_{22} - a_{12})$ from Eq. (5.37b), we obtain, for

$$\mathbf{P}\mathbf{C}_2 = \lambda_2\,\mathbf{C}_2,$$

the equality

$$\begin{pmatrix} a_{11} & a_{12} \\ a_{21} & a_{22} \end{pmatrix}\begin{pmatrix} d_2 \\ e_2 \end{pmatrix} = \begin{pmatrix} (a_{22} - a_{12})d_2 \\ (a_{22} - a_{12})e_2 \end{pmatrix},$$

which yields the column vector equality

$$\begin{pmatrix} (a_{11}d_2 + a_{12}e_2) \\ (a_{21}d_2 + a_{22}e_2) \end{pmatrix} = \begin{pmatrix} (a_{22} - a_{12})d_2 \\ (a_{22} - a_{12})e_2 \end{pmatrix}.$$

We can arrange our equations as equalities with zero, giving us

$$(a_{11} + a_{12} - a_{22})d_2 + a_{12}e_2 = 0,$$
$$(a_{22} - a_{22} + a_{12})e_2 + a_2 d_{12} = 0.$$

Noting that

$$a_{12} = 1 - a_{11}, \quad \text{and} \quad a_{21} = 1 - a_{22},$$

we have

$$a_{21}d_2 + a_{12}e_2 = 0$$

for both equalities. This is then equivalent to

$$a_{12}e_2 = -a_{21}d_2$$

and, therefore

$$e_2 = -\frac{a_{21}}{a_{12}} d_2 ; \tag{5.53}$$

$$\mathbf{C}_2 = h_2 \begin{pmatrix} a_{12} \\ -a_{21} \end{pmatrix}. \tag{5.54}$$

We can check on our work to this point by seeing if we obtain the following equalities with zero. From Eqs. (5.45) and (5.54)

$$\mathbf{R}_1\mathbf{C}_2 = k_1[a_{21} \quad a_{12}]h_2 \begin{pmatrix} a_{12} \\ -a_{21} \end{pmatrix}$$

$$= k_1 h_2(a_{12}a_{21} - a_{12}a_{21}) = 0, \tag{5.55}$$

and from Eqs. (5.50) and (5.52)

$$\mathbf{R}_2\mathbf{C}_1 = k_2[1 \quad -1]h_1 \begin{pmatrix} 1 \\ 1 \end{pmatrix}$$

$$= k_2 h_1(1 - 1) = 0. \tag{5.56}$$

Next we shall choose values for the constants k_1, k_2, h_1, and h_2 so as to make

$$\mathbf{R}_1\mathbf{C}_1 = \mathbf{R}_2\mathbf{C}_2 = 1. \tag{5.57}$$

From Eqs. (5.45) and (5.52) we have

$$\mathbf{R}_1\mathbf{C}_1 = k_1[a_{21} \quad a_{12}]h_1 \begin{pmatrix} 1 \\ 1 \end{pmatrix} = k_1 h_1(a_{21} + a_{12}).$$

If Eq. (5.57) is satisfied we have

$$k_1 h_1(a_{21} + a_{12}) = 1,$$

or

$$k_1 h_1 = \frac{1}{a_{12} + a_{21}}. \tag{5.58}$$

This indicates that any two values which give a product equal to the right side of Eq. (5.58) will do. A simple choice is

$$k_1 = 1, \tag{5.59}$$

$$h_1 = \frac{1}{a_{12} + a_{21}}. \tag{5.60}$$

Proceeding similarly for h_2 and k_2, using Eqs. (5.50) and (5.54),

$$\mathbf{R}_2\mathbf{C}_2 = k_2[1 \quad -1]h_2\begin{pmatrix} a_{12} \\ -a_{21} \end{pmatrix} = k_2 h_2(a_{12} + a_{21}).$$

We now set this equal to 1, which yields

$$k_2 h_2 = \frac{1}{a_{12} + a_{21}}. \tag{5.61}$$

Again, we make a simple choice, taking

$$k_2 = 1, \tag{5.62}$$

$$h_2 = \frac{1}{a_{12} + a_{21}}. \tag{5.63}$$

We are now ready to form the $\mathbf{A}_j$ matrices. Recalling Eq. (5.39) we have

$$\mathbf{A}_1 = \mathbf{C}_1\mathbf{R}_1,$$

where from Eqs. (5.52) and (5.60)

$$\mathbf{C}_1 = \frac{1}{a_{12} + a_{21}}\begin{pmatrix} 1 \\ 1 \end{pmatrix}$$

and from Eqs. (5.45) and (5.59)

$$\mathbf{R}_1 = [a_{21} \quad a_{12}].$$

Therefore we obtain

$$\mathbf{A}_1 = \frac{1}{a_{12} + a_{21}}\begin{pmatrix} a_{21} & a_{12} \\ a_{21} & a_{12} \end{pmatrix}. \tag{5.64}$$

From Eqs. (5.54) and (5.63) we have

$$\mathbf{C}_2 = \frac{1}{a_{12} + a_{21}}\begin{pmatrix} a_{12} \\ -a_{21} \end{pmatrix}. \tag{5.65}$$

From Eqs. (5.50) and (5.62) we have

$$\mathbf{R}_2 = [1 \quad -1], \tag{5.66}$$

so that, from Eqs. (5.39), (5.65), and (5.66)

$$\mathbf{A}_2 = \frac{1}{a_{12} + a_{21}} \begin{pmatrix} a_{12} \\ -a_{21} \end{pmatrix} [1 \quad -1] = \frac{1}{a_{12} + a_{21}} \begin{pmatrix} a_{12} & -a_{12} \\ -a_{21} & a_{21} \end{pmatrix}. \quad (5.67)$$

We now return to Eq. (5.38) with $\mathbf{A}_1$ from Eq. (5.64), $\mathbf{A}_2$ from Eq. (5.67), and λ_1 and λ_2 from Eqs. (5.37a) and (5.37b), respectively. This gives us

$$\mathbf{P}^n = \frac{1}{a_{12} + a_{21}} \left[\begin{pmatrix} a_{21} & a_{12} \\ a_{21} & a_{12} \end{pmatrix} + \begin{pmatrix} a_{12} & -a_{12} \\ -a_{21} & a_{12} \end{pmatrix} \cdot (a_{22} - a_{12})^n \right]. \quad (5.68)$$

In particular, we can show by substitution that, for $n = 0$

$$\mathbf{P}^0 = \mathbf{A}_1 + \mathbf{A}_2 = \mathbf{I} \quad (5.69)$$

and, for $n = 1$, that

$$\mathbf{P}^1 = \mathbf{A}_1 + \mathbf{A}_2(a_{22} - a_{12}) = \mathbf{P} \quad (5.70)$$

We can check our work by seeing if we obtain the following equality with the additive identity matrix.

$$\mathbf{A}_1\mathbf{A}_2 = \mathbf{A}_2\mathbf{A}_1 = \begin{pmatrix} 0 & 0 \\ 0 & 0 \end{pmatrix} \quad (5.71)$$

The proof of this is found by noting from Eq. (5.39) that

$$\mathbf{A}_1\mathbf{A}_2 = \mathbf{C}_1\mathbf{R}_1\mathbf{C}_2\mathbf{R}_2$$

and recognizing, from Eq. (5.55), that the middle two factors are equal to zero. Another helpful identity is

$$\mathbf{A}_1^2 = \mathbf{A}_1, \qquad \mathbf{A}_2^2 = \mathbf{A}_2. \quad (5.72)$$

The proof of Eq. (5.72) is found by noting from Eq. (5.39) that

$$\mathbf{A}_j\mathbf{A}_j = \mathbf{C}_j\mathbf{R}_j\mathbf{C}_j\mathbf{R}_j$$

and recognizing from Eq. (5.57) that the middle two factors yield the scalar value 1, so that

$$\mathbf{A}_j\mathbf{A}_j = \mathbf{C}_j \cdot 1 \cdot \mathbf{R}_j = \mathbf{C}_j\mathbf{R}_j = \mathbf{A}_j.$$

Equations (5.71) and (5.72) can be helpful in checking your nth power solution, through mathematical induction (see Problem 7).

In Chapter Six we shall have occasion to examine the stochastic matrix in Eq. (5.73).

$$\mathbf{P} = \begin{pmatrix} 1 & 0 \\ c & 1 - c \end{pmatrix}. \quad (5.73)$$

We can list the corresponding values for the matrix of Eq. (5.73) and the general 2×2 matrix solved in Eq. (5.68) as

$$a_{11} = 1, \qquad a_{12} = 0, \qquad a_{21} = c, \qquad a_{22} = (1 - c).$$

The resulting solution for the nth power of the matrix in Eq. (5.73) would be

$$\mathbf{P}^n = \frac{1}{c}\left[\begin{pmatrix} c & 0 \\ c & 0 \end{pmatrix} + \begin{pmatrix} 0 & 0 \\ -c & c \end{pmatrix} \cdot (1 - c)^n\right]$$

$$= \begin{pmatrix} 1 & 0 \\ 1 & 0 \end{pmatrix} + \begin{pmatrix} 0 & 0 \\ -1 & 1 \end{pmatrix} \cdot (1 - c)^n.$$

The third power of the matrix in Eq. (5.73), for example, would then be

$$\mathbf{P}^3 = \begin{pmatrix} 1 & 0 \\ 1 - (1 - c)^3 & (1 - c)^3 \end{pmatrix},$$

and, in general, for this matrix,

$$\mathbf{P}^n = \begin{pmatrix} 1 & 0 \\ 1 - (1 - c)^n & (1 - c)^n \end{pmatrix}. \tag{5.74}$$

Problems

1. Do the indicated summation.

$$\begin{pmatrix} k & k + e \\ c & c + e \end{pmatrix} + \begin{pmatrix} e & 1 - e \\ d & 1 - c \end{pmatrix} = ?$$

2. If $\mathbf{A}$ is a stochastic matrix of probabilities, and we want a matrix $\mathbf{B}$ consisting of the complements of the probabilities in $\mathbf{A}$, how would we obtain this new matrix of complements of $\mathbf{A}$?

3. Do the indicated multiplication.

$$d \cdot \begin{pmatrix} q & x \\ y & z \end{pmatrix} = ?$$

4. Do the indicated multiplication.

$$\begin{pmatrix} 1 & 0 & 0 \\ s & 1 - s & 0 \\ e & (1 - e)p & (1 - e)(1 - p) \end{pmatrix} \cdot \begin{pmatrix} c & 0 & 1 - c \\ s & 1 - s & 0 \\ e & 0 & 1 - e \end{pmatrix} = ?$$

5. (a) Obtain the determinant of the following matrix by changing it to a triangular matrix.

$$\begin{pmatrix} 1 & 0 & 0 \\ c & (1 - c)p & (1 - c)(1 - p) \\ c & d & 1 - c - d \end{pmatrix}$$

(b) Show that your answer to part (a) is correct by obtaining the determinant through the use of minors of the matrix.

6. What is $\mathbf{B}^{-1}$ if

$$\mathbf{B} = \begin{pmatrix} c & 1 - c \\ 1 - b & b \end{pmatrix}?$$

7. The validity of Eq. (5.68) can be established by mathematical induction. Equation (5.70) establishes (5.68) for $n = 1$. Assume the validity for $n = k$, and calculate

$$\mathbf{P}^{k+1} = \mathbf{P} \cdot \mathbf{P}^k = [\mathbf{A}_1 + \mathbf{A}_2(a_{22} - a_{12})] \cdot [\mathbf{A}_1 + \mathbf{A}_2(a_{22} - a_{12})^k].$$

Use Eqs. (5.71) and (5.72) to carry out the induction.

Chapter Six

Markov Chains

A frequent definition of learning is that of a change in the probability of a particular response. The response can be the arbitrarily defined "correct" response when mapping an increasing probability, or conversely, the arbitrarily defined "error" when mapping a decreasing probability. This is a convenient conception of learning when learning is assumed to be a gradual process, as in the linear operator model discussed in Chapter Four, or in the older, more encompassing Hullian model.

A more stringent definition might include no further occurrence of errors. For example, in a paired-associate learning task, "being conditioned" or "learning," might both be equated with the cessation of all errors to a particular stimulus word. This would be appropriate for some all-or-none learning models, such as the Bower model discussed in Chapter Two. However, since a subject might sometimes guess correctly the last few times before learning has occurred, we would have to recognize that we would not have unambiguous behavioral criteria for the point at which learning had taken place. An error would establish that the subject is not currently "conditioned," but a correct response would not by itself indicate that the subject was conditioned. An infinite sequence of correct responses would be needed to ascertain that "learning" had occurred. Even establishing some criterion at which we safely assume that learning has occurred (some arbitrary number of errorless trials), we still could not establish precisely at which trial learning took place (assuming that it took place on some one trial).

We can see then that "having learned" or "having been conditioned," although tied eventually to behavior, is not so directly tied as we might wish. "Learning" can then be considered to be a construct, an indication that a new state has been reached. Even in the conceptions of learning as a gradual process, the occurrence of a new probability of correct responding has to be indirectly inferred from many responses, with variance confusing the exact value of the probability. The change to a new probability of a correct response would also have to be an inferred disposition, a notion of an inner state, with the same construct status as in the all-or-none models. In a gradual learning conception, however, the infinite number of possible probabilities of correct responding would imply an infinity of states, which would not appear to contribute functionally to an analytic scheme. However, in the all-or-none models, conceiving of learning as the entry into a new state can be an aid in the development of theories. It does not have to be restricted to the notion of two states, learned or not learned. The number of states can be increased, allowing for such notions as short-term and long-term commitments to memory or duo-process theories of learning; or, if large increases in the number of states are acceptable, more involved conceptions of the learning process can be described in terms of state changes. Using the language of state change is of interest because this facilitates the direct translation from verbal theory to mathematical theory.

A mathematical analogy for the probabilities of changing states is found in Markov processes. When it is possibly useful to conceptualize learning as involving changes in states, Markov processes should be considered as an aid in the analyses. The next section defines Markov processes.

Independence of Previous Sequence of States in Markov Processes

In a conditioned versus not-conditioned dichotomy of states (a two-state model) the probability of going to the conditioned state from the conditioned state (that is, the probability of remaining in the conditioned state) might well be different from the probability of going to the conditioned state from the not-conditioned state (the probability of being conditioned on some particular trial).

In general, for any finite number of states, it is reasonable that the particular current state of the organism may be relevant to which state is next entered. Given presence in one state on some trial n, each of the other states would have a particular probability of being entered on the next trial, trial $n + 1$. Each different state would have a different set of such transition probabilities when it serves as the state on trial n. If we were to consider the trial n state as the only determiner of the probability of entry into a particular state on trial $n + 1$, we would have an almost ahistorical conception of the learning process. States of the system on trials previous to trial n would not be relevant to the probability of state entrance on trial $n + 1$. We would have only a one-trial dependence on the past.

Such a sequence of probabilistic events, where there is only a one-trial dependence, is what is meant by a Markov process, named after the Russian mathematician who first extensively explored the mathematical implications of such a probabilistic sequence. It takes its simplest form under the assumption that the probabilities of going from one state to another, although dependent on the immediately preceding state, are independent of the number of previous transitions. The conditional probability $P(S_{jn+1} | S_{in})$ is then independent of the integer value of n (where S_{in} is the occupation of the ith state on the nth trial). Given this independence of n, we meet the assumptions of a Markov chain, distinguished from the more general Markov process only by its independence of trial number. This constancy over n has simplified the explorations of Markov chains, resulting in more theorems and computational aids for this type of Markov process. To take full advantage of these mathematical developments, finite-state models of learning have tended to restrict themselves to circumstances where they could assume a Markov chain process.

MARKOV CHAINS GRAPHICALLY PRESENTED AS A BRANCHING TREE

The Bower model of paired-associate learning offers a convenient illustration of a Markov model. We can draw a tree diagram for the transition probabilities of the guessing and the conditioned states. (You might find it helpful, at this point to return to Chapter Two and reread the brief section presenting the axioms of Bower's theory.) We can see in Figure 6.1 that any one branch (continuous route) of this tree presents the sequence of joint events necessary to reach a particular state on a particular trial by a particular route. The probability of a particular route is simply the product of the transition probabilities joining the states in that branch (the route being an "and" relation). The probability of being in a particular state on a particular trial is the sum of all of the different branch probabilities that lead to that state on that trial. For example, to be in the conditioned state on trial 3, there are two branches that could be taken (according to Figure 6.1). Our probability axioms suggest that we therefore sum the probability of each of the probabilities of being in state C on trial 3 (this being an "or" relation). To get each of these probabilities, we must first multiply the transitions in each branch.

The complete partition of the sample space of ways of being in state C on trial 3 is, in the form of Eq. (2.21),

$$P(C_3) = P(C_3 C_2 G_1) + P(C_3 G_2 G_1). \tag{6.1}$$

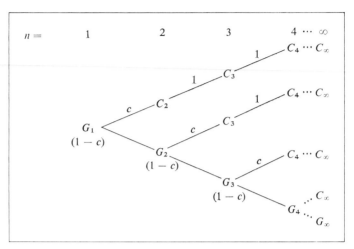

Figure 6.1. A tree of state transitions in the Bower model of paired associate learning. The values c, 1, and $(1 - c)$ represent the probabilities of each of the implied transitions. The n values at the top represent trials.

We can restate Eq. (6.1) as

$$P(C_3) = P(C_3 | C_2 G_1)P(C_2 | G_1)P(G_1) + P(C_3 | G_2 G_1)P(G_2 | G_1)P(G_1), \quad (6.2)$$

once again using Eq. (2.16). Since the probabilities are independent of the steps prior to the immediately preceding one (one-trial dependence only), we can restate the conditional probabilities in Eq. (6.2) as

$$P(C_3) = P(C_3 | C_2)P(C_2 | G_1)P(G_1) + P(C_3 | G_2)P(G_2 | G_1)P(G_1). \quad (6.3)$$

From Figure 6.1 we can restate Eq. (6.3) as

$$P(C_3) = [1 \cdot c \cdot 1] + [c \cdot (1 - c) \cdot 1]$$
$$= c + c - c^2$$
$$= 1 - (1 - c)^2.$$

For the probability of being in the conditioned state on the fourth trial we would have

$$P(C_4) = P(C_4 C_3 C_2 G_1) + P(C_4 C_3 G_2 G_1) + P(C_4 G_3 G_2 G_1)$$
$$= P(C_4 | C_3 C_2 G_1)P(C_3 | C_2 G_1)P(C_2 | G_1)P(G_1)$$
$$+ P(C_4 | C_3 G_2 G_1)P(C_3 | G_2 G_1)P(G_2 | G_1)P(G_1)$$
$$+ P(C_4 | G_3 G_2 G_1)P(G_3 | G_2 G_1)P(G_2 | G_1)P(G_1), \quad (6.4)$$

from Eqs. (6.4) and (2.17). Again, we can omit all steps more than one trial back in considering the conditional probabilities. Again, if we follow the tree, as we did in determining $P(C_3)$, we find that we have

$$P(C_4) = c + c(1 - c) + c(1 - c)^2$$
$$= 3c + 3c^2 + c^3$$
$$= 1 - (1 - c)^3.$$

We might begin to speculate on the possibility that the probability of being in the conditioned state on some trial n is, in general,

$$P(C_n) = 1 - (1 - c)^{n-1}.$$

This is indeed the case, as we found in Chapter Two [see Eq. (2.42)]. We can also see from the tree diagram, where there is only one branch leading to a continuous return to the guessing state, that the probability of being in the guessing state on any trial is simply

$$P(G_n) = (1 - c)^{n-1},$$

which we also found to be true in Chapter Two [see Eq. (2.32)].

A Single Matrix Represents All Information in a Markov Chain

The fact that we only have one-trial dependence in a Markov chain, with probabilities constant over all values of n, permits us to summarize the chain of transition probabilities in a single trial n to trial $n + 1$ matrix, such as that shown in Table 6.1. For clarity in a later discussion of submatrices, we outline the separate cells of the matrix, which gives a somewhat different appearance than for the identical matrices in Chapter Five.

TABLE 6.1

A 2 × 2 Transition Matrix Stated in Terms of the Conditional
Probabilities Such a Matrix Implies

		Trial $n + 1$	
		State 1	State 2
Trial n	State 1	$P(S_{1n+1} \mid S_{1n})$	$P(S_{2n+1} \mid S_{1n})$
	State 2	$P(S_{1n+1} \mid S_{2n})$	$P(S_{2n+1} \mid S_{2n})$

THE MATRIX ALGEBRA OF SOLUTIONS

We can see that setting $n = 1$ and using the matrix to get the conditional probabilities of trial 2 states, then moving to $n = 2$ and again using the original transition matrix to get the conditional probabilities of trial 3 states (conditional now on trial 2 status), etc., we can inductively move to the probability of any state occupancy on any trial conditional upon the state originally occupied. If we wish to know the probability of transition over a pair of trials, say trial n to trial $n + 1$ to trial $n + 2$, we would have an "and" relation, suggesting multiplication. That is, the square of the matrix would give us the transition probabilities on trial $n + 2$, conditional on trial n status. To obtain the trial $n + 3$ probabilities, conditional on trial n status, we would use the third power of the original trial n to trial $n + 1$ matrix.

The process abstractly described in the preceding paragraph is precisely the process mapped in our branching tree (Figure 6.1).

The transition matrix does not contain the probabilities of being in each of the states on trial n, only the transition probabilities, conditional on some trial n status. To obtain unconditional probabilities, we construct a row vector giving the probability of being in each state on trial n, and when this is multiplied against the transition matrix, we obtain a row vector giving us the unconditional probabilities of being in each state on trial $n + 1$. If we take some mth power of the original transition matrix, and multiply this trial n to trial $n + m$ matrix by a row vector of initial (trial n) probabilities, we have each unconditional probability of being in a specific state on trial $n + m$.

We can illustrate the construction of a transition matrix by again using the Bower model. Our matrix should be precisely analogous to the matrix in Table 6.1, with theoretical values obtained from either the branching tree in Figure 6.1 or the axioms of Bower's theory presented in Chapter Two. We illustrate the matrix in Table 6.2.

In Eqs. (6.5) and (6.6), we illustrate the multiplication of the Bower transition matrix by an appropriate row vector, $[P(C_n)\ \ P(G_n)]$, the probability of being in the conditioned or guessing state on trial n.

$$[P(C_{n+1})\ \ P(G_{n+1})] = [P(C_n)\ \ P(G_n)] \times \begin{array}{|c|c|} \hline 1 & 0 \\ \hline c & 1-c \\ \hline \end{array} \qquad (6.5)$$

$$[P(C_{n+1})\ \ P(G_{n+1})] = [\{P(C_n) + P(G_n)c\}\ \ \{P(G_n)(1-c)\}]. \qquad (6.6)$$

Note that in Eq. (6.6), the equivalence for $P(G_{n+1})$ is the familiar $P(G_n) \times (1 - c)$ [Eq. (3.2)], which suggests the recursive form of a difference equa-

TABLE 6.2

Transition Matrix for the
Bower Model[a]

	C_{n+1}	G_{n+1}
C_n	1	0
G_n	c	$1-c$

[a] The cell values are the probabilities of the transitions given in the Bower axioms.

tion from the Bower model. We shall see below that in working with powers of transition matrices and their products with initial trial probability vectors, we obtain Markov chain solutions that are identical to our difference equation solutions of recursive equations.

To illustrate the Markov chain solutions, we shall require the general equation for the power of the matrix in which we are interested. We can apply the technique of spectral resolution to the Bower transition matrix. This was already done in Chapter Five, and the solution was, from Eq. (5.74),

$$\mathbf{P}^n = \begin{array}{c|c|c} & C_{n+1} & G_{n+1} \\ \hline C_1 & 1 & 0 \\ \hline G_1 & 1-(1-c)^n & (1-c)^n \end{array}.$$

This states that the nth power of the matrix would offer these values. Since our matrix is a transition matrix, the nth power would imply n transitions, so the probabilities implied in the cells would refer to states of the system at the $(n+1)$st trial. For states of the system at the nth trial, we would want the $(n-1)$st power of the matrix. However, this would still be a conditional matrix, so we then multiply the $(n-1)$st power of the matrix by the vector of initial probabilities. We find this vector to be

$$[P(C_1) \quad P(G_1)] = [0 \quad 1], \tag{6.7}$$

since the subject must begin in the guessing state. We then multiply $\mathbf{P}^{n-1}$ by Eq. (6.7), which yields

$$[0 \quad 1] \begin{array}{|c|c|} \hline 1 & 0 \\ \hline 1-(1-c)^{n-1} & (1-c)^{n-1} \\ \hline \end{array} = [1-(1-c)^{n-1} \quad (1-c)^{n-1}].$$

(6.8)

Equation (6.8) gives us a row matrix that contains the same probabilities of being in each of the states on trial n for Bower's model as we found in Chapter Two with our familiar Eqs. (2.42) and (2.32).

The Canonical Matrix

The canonical matrix offers a useful schema for stochastic transition matrices. We shall designate four submatrices within a matrix $\mathbf{P}$. One submatrix will consist of ergodic states. A set of ergodic states is a set of states that are reachable from all other states. That is, given any state in the matrix that is not in the ergodic set, the system can go from that state to any of the states in the ergodic set. A trivial example would be the Bower matrix Table 6.2, where the conditioned state would be reachable from the guessing state, and the conditioned state would constitute the one state in the ergodic set of states. We shall frequently be interested in instances where the ergodic states are absorbing states. An absorbing state is one that, once entered, cannot be left. Again, the conditioned state in the Bower matrix would qualify. Table 6.3 offers an example of a four-state transition matrix with two absorbing states S_1 and S_2. It is convenient to juxtapose the absorbing states in the leftmost cells.

We can also identify a transient state submatrix, which we shall symbolize as $\mathbf{Q}$. The term "transient state" designates a set of states that must eventually be left, without any possibility of returning. An example would be the guessing state in the Bower matrix, Table 6.2.

In Table 6.3 states S_3 and S_4 are transient states from which the absorbing states S_1 and S_2 will eventually be reached. (Note, however, that it is not necessary that every absorbing state be directly reachable from every transient state. One or more r_k values can be equal to 0.) Once S_1 or S_2 is reached, the transient states can no longer be reentered. This is because S_1 and S_2 each has a probability of 1 of returning to itself.

The necessity of eventually leaving the transient set is more clearly

TABLE 6.3

A 4×4 Matrix of an Absorbing Markov Chain[a]

	S_1	S_2	S_3	S_4
S_1	1	0	0	0
S_2	0	1	0	0
S_3	r_1	r_2	q_1	q_2
S_4	r_3	r_4	q_3	q_4

[a] In this case, $0 \leq r_j < 1, 0 \leq q_j < 1$ with some $r_j > 0$.

expressed with the aid of a three-state matrix having only one ergodic state, such as that in Table 6.4.

If the system is in state S_2, with probability a it remains in S_2, with probability b it moves to S_3. We assume a stochastic matrix with the probabilities of a and b each less than 1, and with some remaining nonzero probability $1 - a - b$ of going to the absorbing state S_1 on any trial from S_2. Similarly for S_3, we assume a probability $1 - c - d$ of going to an absorbing state on any one trial. Thus, in the set of transient states $\mathbf{Q}$, there is a probability on any trial of going to an absorbing state of either $1 - a - b$ or $1 - c - d$, depending on whether the system is currently in S_2 or S_3. If each

TABLE 6.4

A 3×3 Matrix of an Absorbing Markov Chain[a]

	S_1	S_2	S_3
S_1	1	0	0
S_2	$1 - a - b$	a	b
S_3	$1 - c - d$	c	d

[a] Note that in a stochastic matrix, row sums are equal to 1. $a < 1, d < 1$.

of these values is less than 1 but greater than 0, let us take the smaller of these, which is then the smallest probability on any one trial of going to an absorbing state. Whichever one this is, let us designate it as p. The greatest probability of remaining in the transient state on any trial would then have to be $1 - p$. (That is, the complement of the smaller of two probability values would be the larger complement.) Therefore, the probability of remaining in the transient state over n trials can be no greater than $(1 - p)^n$. Since $1 - p$ is a value between 0 and 1, the value $(1 - p)^n$ approaches 0 with increasing n. Therefore, the probability of remaining in the transient set approaches 0 with increasing trials.

(This is also true when one of the values $1 - a - b$ or $1 - c - d$ equals 1, but the proof is not quite so simple. Moreover, there are cases of *cyclic* matrices in which transitions occur on trials that are multiples of an integer k, $k > 1$, but we shall ignore these.)

The matrices of interest can be written canonically in the form

$$\mathbf{P} = \begin{pmatrix} 1 & 0 \\ \mathbf{R} & \mathbf{Q} \end{pmatrix},$$

where $\mathbf{Q}$ is the submatrix of one-step transitions within the transient states and $\mathbf{R}$ is the submatrix giving the probabilities of entering the absorbing state on any trial. The zero represents a matrix of only zeros.

When the class of ergodic states consists of a single absorbing state, the main questions of interest focus on the occupancies of the transient states. When there is more than one state in the class there is further interest in the probability of entry into each ergodic state from each transient state.

THE FUNDAMENTAL MATRIX

We have argued that there is a probability of 0 [less than the ultimate limit of $(1 - p)^n$] that the transient states are occupied for infinitely many trials. The number of trials that the system is in the set of transient states is a random variable of some importance. The reason for this is that psychologically meaningful events, such as conditioning or choice after vicarious trial and error, are examples of the kinds of things that can be represented mathematically as exits from a transient set of states into an absorbing state.

It is possible to construct a matrix of the expected number of times in each of the transient states. Such a matrix not only offers us answers to questions about mean values, but also happens to be useful in the construction of further matrices of interest to us. This matrix of expected times in the transient states is called *the fundamental matrix* and is derived from the transient state matrix $\mathbf{Q}$.

The Fundamental Matrix Obtained as a Sum of All Powers of the Transient State Matrix

We have previously defined as expected values, sums of products, where each product consists of a random variable value times a probability of that value. In the construction of the fundamental matrix, the expected values of interest to us are the number of times the system is expected to go to each particular state S_{jn+1} from each specified state S_{in} over all trials. On any one trial, there are only two possible events for each possible nth-trial starting state S_{in} and a specified new state S_{jn+1}. The system either does or does not enter S_{jn+1} (from S_{in}). We can then deal with our random variables dichotomized into two values, 0 or 1, with 1 being the value for the occurrence of the transition in question. As we did in Chapter Two, we can simply add the probabilities of the random variable value 1 over all trials, in order to obtain the number of trials on which the event given random variable value 1 will be expected to occur.

Any one cell of the $\mathbf{Q}$ matrix indicates the probability of having made a transition to a particular state on a trial $n + 1$ (conditional on some state during trial n). If we take the square of the $\mathbf{Q}$ matrix, we have the probability of being in a particular state on trial $n + 2$, and in general, the mth power of the matrix gives the probability of being in a particular state on the $(m + 1)$st trial, given a particular origin on the first trial. Therefore, if we wished to have the sum of all probabilities, over all trials, of being in each particular state (given each state as an initial state), we would sum all powers of the transient state. That is, the fundamental matrix would be

$$\mathbf{N} = \mathbf{I} + \mathbf{Q} + \mathbf{Q}^2 + \mathbf{Q}^3 + \cdots, \tag{6.9}$$

where the ellipses ($\cdots$) are used to imply an unending series of terms $\mathbf{Q}^n$, with n increasing by 1 for each successive term.

The matrix $\mathbf{Q}$ to the first power represents the various probabilities of going to all states on the second trial from all first-trial states. Were we to begin the summation with $\mathbf{Q}^1$ rather than $\mathbf{Q}^0$, we would be starting with the second trial in our summing.

We begin the sum equaling $\mathbf{N}$ with the identity matrix ($\mathbf{Q}^0 = \mathbf{I}$) [in Eq. (6.9)] because the fundamental matrix, like the transient state matrix from which it is derived, is a conditional matrix. Each cell of the $\mathbf{N}$ matrix indicates the expected number of times for a particular transition, assuming that the system begins in the state of a particular row (say the ith row). This presumes an expected value of at least 1 for each of the elements of the main diagonal of $\mathbf{N}$ (so that the ith row has a 1 at the ith column). The identity matrix adds that necessary value of 1 to each diagonal cell. Then we add the number of future times in that state, which depends on the sum of the probabilities of transitions *to* that state. For the nondiagonal states in that row, there is no need to add a 1 for conditionally beginning in that row, but rather the sum of probabilities of future transitions to each of those states offers the expected number of times in those states.

We can illustrate the development of the fundamental matrix from a set of axioms of a theory by again turning to the Bower theory and model. To incorporate response probabilities, along with state probabilities, we expand the Bower matrix of Table 6.2 so that it now has three states. That is, we take the single guessing state G and convert it into two states, a guessing-with-error state $(E \cap G)$, and a guessing correctly state $(\bar{E} \cap G)$. During the conditioned state, only one class of response is possible, a correct response, so that state and its implied response remain symbolized as C. During the guessing state, two classes of response are possible, a correct response or an incorrect response. We therefore define two states where previously there was only one. We shall therefore have the probabilities of correct and incorrect responses overtly stated in the matrix. In the 2×2 matrix, only the probability of a state is indicated, and the probability of a correct response is inferred from the axioms. The two guessing states are transient states, since the subject can go from one to the other, but once having left this set of transient states for the conditioned state, which is an absorbing state, there can be no return to the transient states (no more guessing). This new matrix, with its probabilities of transition, are presented in Table 6.5. Note the addition of p and q, which did not appear in Table 6.2. The probability of a correct response in the guessing state is p; therefore, given that the subject is in the guessing state on trial n, the probability of remaining in the guessing state on trial $n + 1$ and guessing

TABLE 6.5

The Matrix of Transition Probabilities for Bower's Model[a]

	C_{n+1}	$(\bar{E}_{n+1} \cap G_{n+1})$	$(E_{n+1} \cap G_{n+1})$
C_n	1	0	0
$(\bar{E}_n \cap G_n)$	c	$p(1 - c)$	$q(1 - c)$
$(E_n \cap G_n)$	c	$p(1 - c)$	$q(1 - c)$

[a] The matrix is expanded so as to include guessing with error $(E_n \cap G_n)$ and guessing with the correct response $(\bar{E}_n \cap G_n)$. Note that $p + q = 1$, so that $c + p(1 - c) + q(1 - c) = 1$. The transient state matrix $\mathbf{Q}$ has been enclosed in a double line for clarity in this instance.

correctly is the probability of the joint event (an "and" relation) requiring the product of the two probabilities, which yields $p(1 - c)$. The probability of an error in the guessing state is q, which leads to $q(1 - c)$ as the probability of remaining in the guessing state and making an error, with similar logic.

We will be interested in knowing the expected number of times in the transient states, which we know can be obtained from the fundamental matrix. In this instance, the expected number of times in the guessing state with error would give us the average number of errors that we should expect from our individual subjects.

To obtain the fundamental matrix, we shall need the infinite summation of the matrix $\mathbf{Q}^n$ over all values of n, as indicated in Eq. (6.9) and again in (6.10).

$$\mathbf{N} = \sum_{n=0}^{\infty} \mathbf{Q}^n = \sum_{n=0}^{\infty} \begin{array}{|c|c|} \hline p(1-c) & q(1-c) \\ \hline p(1-c) & q(1-c) \\ \hline \end{array}^{\,n}. \qquad (6.10)$$

When we sum the $\mathbf{Q}^n$ matrices of this model over all n, we find that the individual cells inductively imply some sequence, which we can then check by mathematical induction. We illustrate this procedure as follows.

$$\sum_{n=0}^{\infty} \begin{array}{|c|c|} \hline p(1-c) & q(1-c) \\ \hline p(1-c) & q(1-c) \\ \hline \end{array}^{\,n} = \begin{array}{|c|c|} \hline 1 & 0 \\ \hline 0 & 1 \\ \hline \end{array} + \begin{array}{|c|c|} \hline p(1-c) & q(1-c) \\ \hline p(1-c) & q(1-c) \\ \hline \end{array}$$

$$+ \begin{array}{|c|c|} \hline [(p^2 + pq)(1-c)^2] & [(q^2 + pq)(1-c)^2] \\ \hline [(p^2 + pq)(1-c)^2] & [(q^2 + pq)(1-c)^2] \\ \hline \end{array} + \cdots. \qquad (6.11)$$

In $\mathbf{Q}^2$ [the third matrix in the right-hand equality of Eq. (6.11)] we have a term $(p^2 + pq)$ in the upper left-hand cell. Since $p + q = 1$, this can be simplified in the following way.

$$p^2 + pq = p(p + q) = p. \qquad (6.12)$$

Similarly, in the lower right-hand cell, we would find that

$$q^2 + pq = q. \qquad (6.13)$$

Summarizing, for $\mathbf{Q}^2$, from Eqs. (6.11), (6.12), and (6.13), we would have

$$\mathbf{Q}^2 = \begin{array}{|c|c|} \hline p(1-c)^2 & q(1-c)^2 \\ \hline p(1-c)^2 & q(1-c)^2 \\ \hline \end{array} \qquad (6.14)$$

and

$$\mathbf{Q}^3 = \mathbf{Q} \cdot \mathbf{Q}^2 = \begin{array}{|c|c|} \hline [(p^2 + pq)(1 - c)^3] & [(q^2 + pq)(1 - c)^3] \\ \hline [(p^2 + pq)(1 - c)^3] & [(q^2 + pq)(1 - c)^3] \\ \hline \end{array}$$

$$= \begin{array}{|c|c|} \hline p(1 - c)^3 & q(1 - c)^3 \\ \hline p(1 - c)^3 & q(1 - c)^3 \\ \hline \end{array},$$

(6.15)

from Eqs. (6.10), (6.12), (6.13), and (6.14). Consequently,

$$\sum_{n=0}^{\infty} \mathbf{Q}^n = \begin{array}{|c|c|} \hline 1 & 0 \\ \hline 0 & 1 \\ \hline \end{array} + \begin{array}{|c|c|} \hline p(1 - c) & q(1 - c) \\ \hline p(1 - c) & q(1 - c) \\ \hline \end{array} + \begin{array}{|c|c|} \hline p(1 - c)^2 & q(1 - c)^2 \\ \hline p(1 - c)^2 & q(1 - c)^2 \\ \hline \end{array}$$

$$+ \begin{array}{|c|c|} \hline p(1 - c)^3 & q(1 - c)^3 \\ \hline p(1 - c)^3 & q(1 - c)^3 \\ \hline \end{array} + \cdots + \begin{array}{|c|c|} \hline p(1 - c)^n & q(1 - c)^n \\ \hline p(1 - c)^n & q(1 - c)^n \\ \hline \end{array} + \cdots .$$

(6.16)

To obtain the value of $\mathbf{N}$, we now merely sum each cell of the matrix, through all powers of n, as implied in Eq. (6.16).

For example, if we sum the lower left-hand cell of Eq. (6.16), we find that we have

$$0 + p(1 - c) + p(1 - c)^2 + p(1 - c^3) + \cdots + p(1 - c)^n + \cdots$$

$$= p(1 - c) \sum_{n=1}^{\infty} (1 - c)^{n-1} = \frac{p(1 - c)}{c} .$$

Summing the upper left-hand cell, we find that we have

$$1 + p(1 - c) + p(1 - c)^2 + p(1 - c)^3 + \cdots + p(1 - c)^n + \cdots$$

$$= 1 + p(1 - c) \sum_{n=1}^{\infty} (1 - c)^{n-1} = 1 + \frac{p(1 - c)}{c}$$

$$= \frac{c + p(1 - c)}{c} = \frac{p + c(1 - p)}{c}$$

$$= \frac{p + cq}{c} .$$

Therefore, we have as the matrix of expected number of times in each transition state in Bower's model,

$$
\mathbf{N} = \begin{array}{|c|c|}
\hline
\dfrac{p + cq}{c} & \dfrac{q(1 - c)}{c} \\
\hline
\dfrac{p(1 - c)}{c} & \dfrac{q + cp}{c} \\
\hline
\end{array}.
\tag{6.17}
$$

The terms that we summed in Eq. (6.11) and its simplified form in Eq. (6.16), were actually calculated for only a few values of $\mathbf{Q}^n$. We then guessed at the general form. Although in this instance our guess would appear to be a safe one, in that the matrix multiplication appeared to offer a stable patterned outcome, it is instructive to see that we can check this guess by mathematical induction. We therefore use the technique of mathematical induction here, as we did in Chapter Three, to prove the validity of our guess. You might, at some future time, wish to obtain the fundamental matrix for some set of axioms implying a Markov chain sequence. Summing the transient state matrix may be the method you select for this purpose, and you might want to use the check of mathematical induction.

We shall designate the nth-trial cell entry of either of the two left-hand cells in the transient state matrix $\mathbf{Q}^n$ to be X_n. We shall wish to prove that on the nth trial the value in that cell is

$$
X_n = p(1 - c)^n. \quad \text{[To be proven.]}
\tag{6.18}
$$

We now need a defining equation, which is in fact the multiplication operation that takes the process from an nth-trial value to an $(n + 1)$st-trial value

$$
X_{n+1} = p(1 - c)[p(1 - c)^n] + q(1 - c)[p(1 - c)^n]
\tag{6.19}
$$

(defining equation, obtained from the multiplications implied in deriving $\mathbf{Q}^n$).

STEP 1. *We verify the following:*
For $n = 1$, $X_n = p(1 - c)^n$, from Table 6.5.
For $n = 2$, $X_n = p(1 - c)^n$, from Eq. (6.14).

Having now accounted for X_1 and X_2, and having thus established that for $n = $ some k ($k = 1$ or 2), the general statement of Eq. (6.18) can be true, we now attempt to prove that if it is true for any $n = k$, it is also true for $n = k + 1$, and then by step-by-step induction, true for all n.

STEP 2. *Assume that for $n = k$*
$$
X_k = p(1 - c)^k.
$$

STEP 3a.   *Operate on the kth term in the series* according to the defining equation (6.19) to produce the $(k + 1)$st term in the series, applying the operation to the equation in Step 2.

$$X_{k+1} = p(1 - c)[p(1 - c)^k] + q(1 - c)[p(1 - c)^k].$$

(Note that matrix multiplication requires that both cells in a column be properly multiplied and added, to obtain the value in any one cell in a column.)

STEP 3b.   *Algebraically manipulate the results of the previous step.* We therefore have

$$X_{k+1} = (p^2 + pq)(1 - c)^{k+1}.$$

But we saw, in deriving Eq. (6.12), that this is equal to

$$X_{k+1} = p(1 - c)^{k+1}.$$

STEP 4.   *Conclusion.* If any

$$X_k = p(1 - c)^k,$$

then

$$X_{k+1} = p(1 - c)^{k+1}.$$

But some X_k does equal $p(1 - c)^k$ (as seen in Step 1), so the general statement is true for $n =$ any k, and we have proven the validity of Eq. (6.18).

We could also proceed in identical fashion for the right-hand column of the transition matrix.

The Fundamental Matrix Obtained as the Inverse of $(\mathbf{I} - \mathbf{Q})$

There is another method that we can use to obtain $\mathbf{N}$. This method requires that we theoretically sum a power series of matrices the way that we did in Chapter Two when we summed a power series with the common factor a number C, with $-1 < C < 1$. For example, we had

$$\sum_{0}^{\infty} C^n = \frac{1}{1 - C}$$
$$= (1 - C)^{-1}.$$

Analogously,

$$\mathbf{N} = \mathbf{Q}^0 + \mathbf{Q}^1 + \mathbf{Q}^2 + \mathbf{Q}^3 + \cdots + \mathbf{Q}^n + \cdots,$$
$$\mathbf{QN} = \mathbf{Q}^1 + \mathbf{Q}^2 + \mathbf{Q}^3 + \qquad \cdots + \mathbf{Q}^n + \cdots,$$

$$\mathbf{N} - \mathbf{QN} = \mathbf{Q}^0,$$
$$\mathbf{N}(\mathbf{I} - \mathbf{Q}) = \mathbf{I}. \tag{6.20}$$

We can multiply both sides of Eq. (6.20) by the inverse of $(\mathbf{I} - \mathbf{Q})$. A matrix multiplied by its inverse yields the identity matrix. We then have

$$\mathbf{N}(\mathbf{I} - \mathbf{Q})(\mathbf{I} - \mathbf{Q})^{-1} = (\mathbf{I} - \mathbf{Q})^{-1},$$
$$\mathbf{N} = (\mathbf{I} - \mathbf{Q})^{-1}. \tag{6.21}$$

Equation (6.21) now gives us another way to obtain the fundamental matrix $\mathbf{N}$. We simply subtract the transient state matrix $\mathbf{Q}$ from the standard identity matrix $\mathbf{I}$ and then take the inverse of this new matrix, as indicated in Chapter Five (providing the matrix $\mathbf{I} - \mathbf{Q}$ does have an inverse).

In the case of the Bower model with the expanded matrix, the transient state matrix is a 2×2 matrix, which permits us to use the rule implied in Eqs. (5.18a) and (5.18b). Applying that technique from Chapter Five, we find that the fundamental matrix is precisely the matrix that we obtained in Eq. (6.17).

Obtaining the Expected Number of Errors with the Fundamental Matrix

Since the fundamental matrix gives us information that is conditional upon presence in a particular state on an initial trial, we need to weight these numbers (in the cells of $\mathbf{N}$) by the initial probability vector, which we can designate as π_0. For the expanded Bower matrix, this would be

$$\pi_0 = [0 \quad p \quad q].$$

However, we wish the initial probability vector for multiplication against the 2×2 matrix $\mathbf{N}$. We therefore define a truncated initial probability vector

$$\pi_0' = [p \quad q].$$

From Eq. (6.17) and the truncated probability vector, we have (note that we have stopped drawing lines demarcating the cells of the matrix, and have returned to the correct form used in Chapter Five)

$$\pi_0'\mathbf{N} = [p \quad q] \begin{pmatrix} \dfrac{p + cq}{c} & \dfrac{q(1 - c)}{c} \\ \dfrac{p(1 - c)}{c} & \dfrac{q + cp}{c} \end{pmatrix}$$

$$= \left[\frac{p^2 + pqc + pq(1 - c)}{c} \quad \frac{q^2 + pqc + pq(1 - c)}{c} \right]$$

$$= \left[\frac{p^2 + pq}{c} \quad \frac{q^2 + pq}{c} \right],$$

$$\pi_0'\mathbf{N} = \left[\frac{p}{c} \quad \frac{q}{c} \right]. \tag{6.22}$$

The two resulting terms in the vector of Eq. (6.22) are the unconditional expected number of times in the guessing state with correct guessing, and the unconditional expected number of times in the guessing state with error, reading from left to right. The number of times in the guessing state with correct guessing overlaps with the conditioned state, behaviorally, but the guessing with error does not overlap with any other state, hence is clearly definable behaviorally. We take advantage of this fact to equate the theoretical value with the empirical number of average errors (for each subject). We did this earlier, in Chapter Two, for the same model; there we obtained the expected number of errors, in Eq. (2.51), as

$$\text{expectation (mean number of errors)} = \frac{(1 - 1/N)}{c}.$$

Axiom 4 of Bower's theory, as numbered in Chapter Two, defines the probability of an error in the guessing state as $1 - 1/N$. But we have also defined q as the probability of an error (when expanding the matrix in Table 6.2 to Table 6.5). We therefore have, for the rightmost element in Eq. (6.22),

$$\frac{q}{c} = \frac{(1 - 1/N)}{c} ;$$

thus the two theoretical estimates of the value of the expected number of errors per subject is found to be the same when obtained with the methods of Chapter Two and with the Markov chain methods of this chapter.

The Variance for the Fundamental Matrix

A formula has also been derived for the variance of the average number of times that the system is in the individual transient states before absorption. We can symbolize this as N_2. Noting that

$$N_{dg} = \text{diagonal cell values of } N,$$

with all other cells equal to zero, we have

$$N_2 = N(2 \cdot N_{dg} - I). \tag{6.23}$$

We shall find the fundamental matrix to be a component in the derivation of other helpful matrices, which answer additional questions for us on Markov chain processes.

THE H MATRIX OF PROBABILITIES OF GOING TO A STATE AT LEAST ONCE

At the end of Chapter Two, we derived a complex equation for the probability of no more errors after the first success, in Bower's theory. We shall now ask a similar but slightly simpler question. What is the probability that a subject has 0 errors on some item in a paired-associate task? We shall find that this probability can be obtained with the aid of two matrices: the **H** matrix, which is a matrix of probabilities of ever going to each particular state, and will be described in the immediately following section; and the square matrix of ones $\mathbf{E}$ (of the same order as $\mathbf{H}$). These two define a third matrix

$$\mathbf{K}[0] = \mathbf{E} - \mathbf{H}. \tag{6.24}$$

This is the complement of $\mathbf{H}$, and whereas $\mathbf{H}$ offers the set of probabilities of ever going to particular states, its complement offers the set of probabilities of never going to particular states. If one of these states is the error state, then $\mathbf{K}[0]$ would give the probability of no error. We have offered a reason for obtaining a matrix with the characteristics ascribed to $\mathbf{H}$, and we shall now derive such a matrix.

Obtaining the $\mathbf{H}$ Matrix

We already know the characteristics of $\mathbf{N}$, and have defined it in two different but equivalent ways [Eqs. (6.9) and (6.21)]. We can define it in a third way, which will allow us to analyze out a component which is our $\mathbf{H}$ matrix.

Let us reduce $\mathbf{N}$, which offers the expected number of times in a state S_j when beginning in some specified state S_i (which we can symbolize as n_{ij}), to $\mathbf{N}_{dg}$, which offers the expected number of times in a state S_j when beginning in that same state (which we can symbolize as n_{jj}).

(It may be helpful, in what follows, to keep in mind that the transition matrix from which $\mathbf{N}$ is derived is independent of the trial number. Therefore, numerical expectations are valid at any point in time. That is, "beginning" in a particular state does not imply some true first trial, but rather the trial number from which you wish to begin making your predictions. Being in a transient state always "resets" the system, so that as long as the system has not gone to an absorption state, expected values from that point on are identical for all trials.)

The new matrix that we wish to derive, $\mathbf{H}$, offers the probabilities of ever going to particular states. But it too would be conditional prior to multiplication by initial-trial probabilities. Therefore, we can restate the elements of $\mathbf{H}$ as the probabilities of ever going to particular states S_j, each conditional on beginning in some particular state S_i, symbolizing these elements as h_{ij}. If this hypothetical $\mathbf{H}$ matrix $\{h_{ij}\}$ were multiplied against $\mathbf{N}_{dg}$, $\{n_{jj}\}$, we would have in $\mathbf{H}\mathbf{N}_{dg}$ a matrix of probabilities, each multiplied by a random variable value, giving us a matrix of elements $\{h_{ij}n_{jj}\}$. The probabilities, the h_{ij} values, would be precisely those in $\mathbf{H}$, in the same positions as in $\mathbf{H}$, but the values from $\mathbf{N}_{dg}$, the n_{jj} values, would each repeatedly recur in each jth column. For example,

$$\begin{pmatrix} h_{11} & h_{12} \\ h_{21} & h_{22} \end{pmatrix} \cdot \begin{pmatrix} n_{11} & 0 \\ 0 & n_{22} \end{pmatrix} = \begin{pmatrix} h_{11}n_{11} & h_{12}n_{22} \\ h_{21}n_{11} & h_{22}n_{22} \end{pmatrix}.$$

The new matrix $\mathbf{HN}_{dg}$ would give us a matrix consisting of the probabilities of ever going to each S_j from each S_i, in each case times the number of times expected in S_j, when beginning in S_j. For the terms off the diagonal (when $i \neq j$) we have $\{h_{ij}n_{jj}\}$. This is a set of expectations that are equivalent to the identically placed $\{n_{ij}\}$ values in $\mathbf{N}$. The terms off the diagonal in $\mathbf{N}$ assume initial trials not in S_j. Their n_{ij} values must include the probability of ever going to S_j from their initial S_i, and then the expected number of times in S_j if and when the system were to go to S_j. This is precisely our general term for the set of elements in the matrix $\{h_{ij}n_{jj}\}$. [The sample space of possibilities can be completely partitioned into two events. Either the system goes to S_j or it does not. If it goes to S_j (with probability h_{ij}), then we expect the random variable value n_{jj} as the number of times in S_j. If it does not go to S_j (with probability $1 - h_{ij}$), then we expect the random variable of 0 as the number of times in S_j. These exhaust the possible random variable values in this partitioning. Therefore, the sum of all of the products of all random variable values times their probabilities yields the value $h_{ij}n_{jj}$ as the expected value for the number of times in S_j.]

The terms on the diagonal of $\mathbf{HN}_{dg}$ are not identical to the diagonal terms in $\mathbf{N}$. The diagonal terms in $\mathbf{HN}_{dg}$ are $\{h_{jj}n_{jj}\}$, each of which consists of the probability of ever going to state S_j once in it (restatable as ever *returning* to S_j) times the expected number of times in S_j starting with being there. But we have assumed a *return* as the beginning for our count of times in S_j. This constitutes a loss of 1 in the count of times expected in S_j if it is assumed that the system begins in S_j. Therefore, to equate the diagonals in $\mathbf{HN}_{dg}$ with the diagonals in $\mathbf{N}$, we add a 1 to the diagonal expectations $\{h_{jj}n_{jj}\}$. The result of the foregoing logic is

$$\mathbf{N} = \mathbf{I} + \mathbf{HN}_{dg}. \qquad (6.25)$$

Now all that we have to do is isolate $\mathbf{H}$ in Eq. (6.25), and we shall have defined this new matrix out of some functions of the fundamental matrix. We restate Eq. (6.25) as

$$\mathbf{HN}_{dg} = \mathbf{N} - \mathbf{I},$$
$$\mathbf{H} = (\mathbf{N} - \mathbf{I})\mathbf{N}_{dg}^{-1}. \qquad (6.26)$$

To obtain $\mathbf{N}_{dg}^{-1}$ we simply take the inverse of $\mathbf{N}_{dg}$ according to the technique for obtaining inverses of diagonal matrices in Chapter Five.

Note that $\mathbf{H}$ is the probability of ever going to a particular state conditional upon a specified starting state. Therefore, the diagonal values in $\mathbf{H}$ are probabilities of ever returning to a particular state, and those off the diagonal are the values of ever going to a particular state from some other initial state.

Note also, however, that there is no implied limitation to the number of times for going to a particular state, so that $\{h_{ij}\}$ are all probabilities of going (or returning) *at least once* to S_j.

As an example of the computation of **H** from Eqs. (6.26) and (6.17), let us obtain **H** in the Bower theory.

$$\mathbf{H} = (\mathbf{N} - \mathbf{I})\mathbf{N}_{dg}^{-1}$$

$$= \left(\left[\begin{pmatrix} \dfrac{p+cq}{c} & \dfrac{q(1-c)}{c} \\[2ex] \dfrac{p(1-c)}{c} & \dfrac{q+cp}{c} \end{pmatrix} - \begin{pmatrix} 1 & 0 \\ 0 & 1 \end{pmatrix}\right]\begin{pmatrix} \dfrac{p+cq}{c} & 0 \\[2ex] 0 & \dfrac{q+cp}{c} \end{pmatrix}\right)^{-1}$$

$$= \begin{pmatrix} \dfrac{p+cq}{c} - 1 & \dfrac{q(1-c)}{c} \\[2ex] \dfrac{p(1-c)}{c} & \dfrac{q+cp}{c} - 1 \end{pmatrix}\begin{pmatrix} \dfrac{c}{p+cq} & 0 \\[2ex] 0 & \dfrac{c}{q+cp} \end{pmatrix},$$

$$\mathbf{H} = \begin{pmatrix} 1 - \dfrac{c}{p+cq} & \dfrac{q(1-c)}{q+cp} \\[2ex] \dfrac{p(1-c)}{p+cq} & 1 - \dfrac{c}{q+cp} \end{pmatrix}. \tag{6.27}$$

Obtaining the **K**[0] *Matrix*

From Eqs. (6.24) and (6.27),

$$\begin{pmatrix} \mathbf{K}_{11}[0] & \mathbf{K}_{12}[0] \\ \mathbf{K}_{21}[0] & \mathbf{K}_{22}[0] \end{pmatrix} = \mathbf{K}[0] = \mathbf{E} - \mathbf{H}$$

$$= \begin{pmatrix} 1 & 1 \\ 1 & 1 \end{pmatrix} - \begin{pmatrix} 1 - \dfrac{c}{p+cq} & \dfrac{q(1-c)}{q+cp} \\[2ex] \dfrac{p(1-c)}{p+cq} & 1 - \dfrac{c}{q+cp} \end{pmatrix}. \tag{6.28a}$$

$$\mathbf{K}[0] = \begin{pmatrix} \dfrac{c}{p+cq} & \dfrac{c}{q+cp} \\[2ex] \dfrac{c}{p+cq} & \dfrac{c}{q+cp} \end{pmatrix}. \tag{6.28b}$$

The values in Eq. (6.28) are again conditional values.

Each $\mathbf{K}_{ij}[0]$ value of never going to a jth guessing state after trial 1 is represented by parameters in Eq. (6.28b). However, each probability $\mathbf{K}_{ij}[0]$ is conditional on having started in the ith state. For the unconditional probability we would multiply Eq. (6.28b) by $\pi' = [p \quad q]$, giving us

$$[p \quad q]\mathbf{K}[0] = \begin{bmatrix} \dfrac{pc + qc}{p + cq} & \dfrac{pc + qc}{q + cp} \end{bmatrix}$$

$$= \begin{bmatrix} \dfrac{c}{p + cq} & \dfrac{c}{q + cp} \end{bmatrix}. \qquad (6.28c)$$

Equation (6.28c) offers the unconditional probability of never going to the jth state after trial 1. (Remember that it is a matrix of nonreturns.) For the probability of no errors, we would take the unconditional probability of never going to S_2 from Eq. (6.28c), and multiply it by the probability of not making an error on the first trial, p. This would yield the desired probability in Eq. (6.29).

$$\text{Probability of no errors} = \frac{cp}{q + cp} \qquad (6.29)$$

Remembering that

$$p = 1/N \qquad \text{and} \qquad q = 1 - 1/N,$$

we restate Eq. (6.29) as

$$\text{Probability of no errors} = \frac{c/N}{1 - 1/N + c/N} = \frac{c}{N - 1 + c}. \qquad (6.30)$$

We shall check the results, as expressed in Eqs. (6.29) and (6.30), by use of the direct method that we had used in Chapter Two. As we did then, we proceed by examining the verbal implications of the axioms of the theory, and then translating these into mathematical equations by the use of the probability calculus.

The subject could have 0 errors (on an individual paired-associate item) by being conditioned in the course of the first trial (so that he is in the conditioned state beginning with trial 2) and by guessing correctly on the first trial. This would represent a joint event, one with probability c and the other with probability p. The probability of this eventuality is then cp. However, there are many other ways that 0 errors could occur. The subject could guess correctly while in the guessing state on both the first and second trials, and then be in the conditioned state on the third. This would occur with probability $c(1 - c)p^2$, since it would require not only being conditioned on the second trial (probability c) but also not being conditioned on the first trial (probability $1 - c$), along with two correct guesses (probability p^2). If we were to add all of the alternate ways in which zero errors could occur (since alternate ways of an event constitute an "or" relation, to be summed), we would have a sum looking like

$$\text{Probability of no errors} = cp + c(1 - c)p^2 + c(1 - c)^2 p^3$$
$$+ \cdots + c(1 - c)^n p^{n+1} + \cdots$$

$$= cp \sum_{n=0}^{\infty} [(1 - c)p]^n$$

$$= \frac{cp}{1 - (1 - c)p}$$

$$= \frac{cp}{1 - p + cp}$$

$$= \frac{cp}{q + cp},$$

which is identical to Eq. (6.29). We therefore have derived a single equation in two different ways, each technique offering a check on the results of the other.

Obtaining the K[k] *Matrix*

Just as we have obtained the probability of going to a particular state 0 times, we can also ask for the probability of going to a particular state k times, where k is any number greater than 0. We had specified the error state as the state of interest to obtain the probability of 0 errors. If we did this for all possible values of numbers of errors, we could graph a probability distribution with the number of errors on the axis of the abscissa and the probability of each such occurrence on the axis of the ordinate. If our theory is a good one, we should be able to find that the relative occurrence of k errors for a paired-associate item is distributed as the theoretical distribution from our equation.

That is, we would record the errors for some one subject, count how many subjects have that many errors, and enter the proportion of such subjects on a graph. We would then do this for each number of errors k. We would then have an empirical distribution, which we hope would look like the theoretical distribution. (Or we could compare empirical and theoretical frequencies. The latter would be obtained as a product of probabilities and number of subjects.)

We now derive the formula for the equation from which we shall obtain this theoretical distribution. We use the symbol

K[k] = probability of going to a state k times

We again use the matrix $\mathbf{H}$ in our derivation of $\mathbf{K}[k]$. However, our logic will be a bit more complex than in our derivation of $\mathbf{K}[0]$.

To go to a given state k times, a subject must go there at least one time and then must return an additional $k - 1$ times but not return again. These are joint events, so we must multiply the probabilities of each of these events. The three events occur with probabilities obtained from the matrices $\mathbf{H}$, $\mathbf{H}_{dg}^{k-1}$, and $(\mathbf{I} - \mathbf{H}_{dg})$, respectively, as explained below.

$$\mathbf{K}[k] = \mathbf{H} \cdot \mathbf{H}_{dg}^{k-1} \cdot (\mathbf{I} - \mathbf{H}_{dg}). \tag{6.31}$$

The first term in this product, Eq. (6.31), is simply the previously derived formula for $\mathbf{H}$, from Eq. (6.26), offering the probability of going to a state at least once. The second term $\mathbf{H}_{dg}^{k-1}$ is the set of joint events of going to the same state $k - 1$ times (where using only the diagonals analogizes returns to the same states). The product of a diagonal matrix with itself $k - 1$ times is simply that matrix with each of its elements raised to the $(k - 1)$st power. The third term $(\mathbf{I} - \mathbf{H}_{dg})$ is necessary because we need to signify no further returns after the $k - 1$ returns. The $\mathbf{H}$ matrix always signifies going to a state at least once. Therefore, $\mathbf{H}_{dg}^{k-1}$ signifies returning at least $k - 1$ times, and $(\mathbf{I} - \mathbf{H}_{dg})$ represents not returning to the same state at least one time (and therefore, not returning again). Therefore, we have the justification for Eq. (6.31).

We can restate Eq. (6.31) as

$$\mathbf{K}[k] = (\mathbf{N} - \mathbf{I})\mathbf{N}_{dg}^{-1} \cdot (\mathbf{I} - \mathbf{N}_{dg}^{-1})^{k-1} \cdot \mathbf{N}_{dg}^{-1}. \tag{6.32}$$

The first term in Eq. (6.32) is simply $\mathbf{H}$ as defined by Eq. (6.26). The second term is just a restatement of Eq. (6.26) as a diagonal matrix; that is,

$$\mathbf{H}_{dg} = (\mathbf{N}_{dg} - \mathbf{I})\mathbf{N}_{dg}^{-1}. \tag{6.33}$$

If we carry out the multiplication of the term in the parentheses in Eq. (6.33) by $\mathbf{N}^{-1}$, we obtain

$$\mathbf{H}_{dg} = (\mathbf{I} - \mathbf{N}_{dg}^{-1}). \tag{6.34}$$

For the third term in the product of Eq. (6.31), we note that, from Eq. (6.34),

$$(\mathbf{I} - \mathbf{H}_{dg}) = \mathbf{I} - (\mathbf{I} - \mathbf{N}_{dg}^{-1}),$$
$$(\mathbf{I} - \mathbf{H}_{dg}) = \mathbf{N}_{dg}^{-1}. \tag{6.35}$$

We then combine Eqs. (6.26), (6.34), and (6.35) to restate Eq. (6.31) as Eq. (6.32).

When we know how to obtain $\mathbf{N}$ for some model, we can then obtain $\mathbf{K}[k]$ from Eq. (6.32).

Let us apply Eq. (6.32) to the expanded Bower matrix given in Table 6.5. We again use N, from Eq. (6.17).

$$\mathbf{K}[k] = (\mathbf{N} - \mathbf{I}) \cdot \mathbf{N}_{\mathrm{dg}}^{-1} \cdot (\mathbf{I} - \mathbf{N}_{\mathrm{dg}}^{-1})^{k-1} \cdot \mathbf{N}_{\mathrm{dg}}^{-1}$$

$$= (\mathbf{N} - \mathbf{I}) \cdot \mathbf{N}_{\mathrm{dg}}^{-2} \cdot (\mathbf{I} - \mathbf{N}_{\mathrm{dg}}^{-1})^{k-1},$$

$$\mathbf{K}[k] = \left[\begin{pmatrix} \dfrac{p+cq}{c} & \dfrac{q(1-c)}{c} \\ \dfrac{p(1-c)}{c} & \dfrac{q+cp}{c} \end{pmatrix} - \begin{pmatrix} 1 & 0 \\ 0 & 1 \end{pmatrix} \right]$$

$$\cdot \begin{pmatrix} \dfrac{p+cq}{c} & 0 \\ 0 & \dfrac{q+cp}{c} \end{pmatrix}^{-2} \left[\begin{pmatrix} 1 & 0 \\ 0 & 1 \end{pmatrix} - \begin{pmatrix} \dfrac{p+cq}{c} & 0 \\ 0 & \dfrac{q+cp}{c} \end{pmatrix}^{-1} \right]^{k-1}. \quad (6.36)$$

Remembering from Chapter Five that

$$\begin{pmatrix} a & 0 \\ 0 & b \end{pmatrix}^{-2} = \begin{pmatrix} \left(\dfrac{1}{a}\right)^2 & 0 \\ 0 & \left(\dfrac{1}{b}\right)^2 \end{pmatrix},$$

we have

$$\mathbf{K}[k] = \begin{pmatrix} \dfrac{cp+c^2q-c^2}{(p+cq)^2} & \dfrac{cq(1-c)}{(q+cp)^2} \\ \dfrac{cp(1-c)}{(p+cq)^2} & \dfrac{cq+c^2p-c^2}{(q+cp)^2} \end{pmatrix} \cdot \begin{pmatrix} \dfrac{p+cq-c}{p+cq} & 0 \\ 0 & \dfrac{q+cp-c}{q+cp} \end{pmatrix}^{k-1}.$$

$$(6.37)$$

Noting that

$$cp + c^2q - c^2 = cp + c^2(1-p) - c^2$$
$$= cp - c^2p$$
$$= cp(1-c),$$

and similarly,

$$p + cq - c = p(1-c),$$
$$cq + c^2p - c^2 = cq(1-c),$$
$$q + cp - c = q(1-c),$$

Eq. (6.37) becomes

$$
\mathbf{K}[k] = \begin{pmatrix} \dfrac{cp(1-c)}{(p+cq)^2} & \dfrac{cq(1-c)}{(q+cp)^2} \\[2mm] \dfrac{cp(1-c)}{(p+cq)^2} & \dfrac{cq(1-c)}{(q+cp)^2} \end{pmatrix} \cdot \begin{pmatrix} \dfrac{p(1-c)}{p+cq} & 0 \\[2mm] 0 & \dfrac{q(1-c)}{q+cp} \end{pmatrix}^{k-1}. \tag{6.38}
$$

We can see that our matrix, as represented in Eq. (6.36) or its simplified form in Eq. (6.38), is a matrix of conditional probabilities. To transform this to unconditional probabilities, we need the initial probability vector

$$
\pi_0' = [p \quad q], \tag{6.39}
$$

which follows from the initial-trial probabilities of being in either of the two states in the transient state matrix. We first need to multiply Eq. (6.39) by one term of the product constituting Eq. (6.38).

$$
[p \quad q] \begin{pmatrix} \dfrac{cp(1-c)}{(p+cq)^2} & \dfrac{cq(1-c)}{(q+cp)^2} \\[2mm] \dfrac{cp(1-c)}{(p+cq)^2} & \dfrac{cq(1-c)}{(q+cp)^2} \end{pmatrix}
$$

$$
= \left[\dfrac{cp^2(1-c)+cpq(1-c)}{(p+cq)^2} \quad \dfrac{cpq(1-c)+cq^2(1-c)}{(q+cp)^2} \right]
$$

$$
= \left[\dfrac{cp(1-c)(p+q)}{(p+cq)^2} \quad \dfrac{cq(1-c)(p+q)}{(q+cp)^2} \right]
$$

$$
= \left[\dfrac{cp(1-c)}{(p+cq)^2} \quad \dfrac{cq(1-c)}{(q+cp)^2} \right]. \tag{6.40}
$$

We now multiply Eq. (6.40) by the second factor in Eq. (6.38) to obtain the unconditional probability of being in a particular state k times, assuming $k > 0$.

$$
[p \quad q] \cdot \mathbf{K}[k] = \left[\dfrac{cp(1-c)}{(p+cq)^2} \quad \dfrac{cq(1-c)}{(q+cp)^2} \right] \cdot \begin{pmatrix} \dfrac{p(1-c)}{p+cq} & 0 \\[2mm] 0 & \dfrac{q(1-c)}{q+cp} \end{pmatrix}^{k-1},
$$

$$
[p \quad q] \cdot \mathbf{K}[k] = \left[\dfrac{cp(1-c)}{(p+cq)^2} \cdot \left(\dfrac{p(1-c)}{p+cq}\right)^{k+1} \quad \dfrac{cq(1-c)}{(q+cp)^2} \cdot \left(\dfrac{q(1-c)}{q+cp}\right)^{k-1} \right]. \tag{6.41}
$$

The ways of making k errors are (1) to start with a correct response and subsequently enter the error state k times and; (2) to start with an error and subsequently return to the error state $k - 1$ times. The probability of k errors is therefore

$$p\mathbf{K}_{12}[k] + q\mathbf{K}_{22}[k - 1] = \left[\frac{cpq(1 - c)}{(q + cp)^2}\right] \cdot \left[\frac{q(1 - c)}{q + cp}\right]^{k-1}$$
$$+ \left[\frac{cpq(1 - c)}{(q + cp)^2}\right] \cdot \left[\frac{q(1 - c)}{(q + cp)}\right]^{k-2}.$$

After algebraic simplification this becomes

$$\text{Probability of } k \text{ errors} = \left[\frac{cq}{(q + cp)^2}\right] \cdot \left[\frac{q(1 - c)}{q + cp}\right]^{k-1}. \qquad (6.42)$$

Substituting for p and q from Bower's theory we have, after simplification,

$$\text{Probability of } k \text{ errors} = \left[\frac{N(N - 1)c}{(N - 1 + c)^2}\right] \cdot \left[\frac{(N - 1)(1 - c)}{N - 1 + c}\right]^{k-1}, \qquad (6.43)$$

which probability refers to a single paired-associate item prior to perfect learning of it in the Bower model, for $k > 0$.

THE PROBABILITY OF ABSORPTION IN A PARTICULAR STATE

We have been discussing the transient states and the expected number of times in these states. The finite expectations are made possible by the assumption that the system must at some point leave the transient states, to which it cannot return. We have further assumed that when it leaves the transient states, it enters a particular individual state and remains there. Thus the name "absorbing state." Sometimes the term "absorbing chain" is applied to a Markov chain, if the matrix contains at least one absorbing state.

If there is only one absorbing state in the chain, interest centers on times spent in the transient states. But if there is more than one absorbing state, it is frequently important to know to which of the absorbing states the system goes when it finally leaves the set of transient states. We shall illustrate this with a specific model. This model is also the creation of Bower (1959), though it is a very different model from his previously discussed model, particularly in the aspects that we shall consider.

Assume a system that consists of a single experimental trial. A subject confronts a binary choice, such as the left and right arms of a T maze. Prior to his making a choice, we might assume that there is some vacillation, some-times described as vicarious trial and error. The subject might physically orient himself to the left, then right, then left again, etc., until he actually makes a gross move and runs in the direction of one of the goal boxes. We can consider the organism's attainment of a goal box as the end of the trial. The particular goal box will represent a particular absorbing state, so that a T maze would have two possible absorbing states in its Markov chain represen-tation. The transient states would be the left and right orientations preceding the actual running, since these two states would each be reachable from the other, but not reachable once having chosen an alley. We can categorize the orientation responses as we had the goal box placements. We thus have a left and right orientation possible, and a left or right run to a goal box. There being four events possible, we can equate each with a state of the system, which includes the reacting organism and his environment. We can then use a Markov chain analysis with four states. We can consider this to be a Markov chain rather than a more general Markov process, because the analysis covers a relatively small period of time, just one trial. During one trial the prob-abilities of transition from one of these states to another might reasonably be expected, or assumed, to remain constant, which is the criterion for calling a Markov process a Markov chain. During a particular trial, then, this model assumes that the probability of the organism moving its head from right to left will not change, nor will its probability of running to the right (or left), given that it is oriented to the right (or left) change during this brief interval. A matrix of transition probabilities can therefore be constructed, which shows transition probabilities between four mutually exclusive behaviors of the organism during a single trial. The transitions then are between successive responses within a trial, rather than between trials, The n to $n + 1$ transition refers to the n to $n + 1$ response in a sequence of responses, all categorized as one of the four possible. The n to $(n + 2)$nd transition would refer to a re-sponse probability conditional on a response emitted the response before the last, etc.

We shall now symbolize the states and their respective probabilities.

G_1 = running to the left-hand goal box.
G_2 = running to the right-hand goal box.
O_1 = orienting toward the left-hand goal box.
O_2 = orienting toward the right-hand goal box.

We can now present, in Table 6.6, the canonical matrix from Table 6.3 with new state labels.

Our reason for looking at this model is that we wish to find general equa-tions for the probabilities of absorption in the different possible absorption

TABLE 6.6

The Canonical Matrix Identified with States in a
T-Maze Choice Paradigm

	G_1	G_2	O_1	O_2
G_1	1	0	0	0
G_2	0	1	0	0
O_1	r_1	r_2	q_1	q_2
O_2	r_3	r_4	q_3	q_4

states. In our model, absorption would correspond to overt choice of a maze arm. There would only be two choices possible, and transitions during the period in the transient state matrix would have to be between only two states. However, we shall analyze the paradigm in a more general way mathematically, so that our results could be applied to a finite matrix of any size, with any number of absorption or transition states.

Obtaining the **B** *Matrix*

We wish to find a matrix offering us the probabilities of being absorbed in each of the ergodic states, conditional upon beginning in a particular transient state. We shall identify this matrix as the **B** matrix and identify its component elements as b_{ij}. The **B** matrix would have the same state identification as the **R** matrix (r_k elements at the lower left in Table 6.6), but different probabilities. The **R** matrix is a one-trial probability matrix. The **B** matrix contains the probabilities of eventual absorption in each particular ergodic state, from each particular transient state. We shall now examine an individual component member of the **B** matrix.

We can divide the probability b_{ij} into two components, which represent an arbitrary but complete partitioning of the sample space of probabilities. One component is first-trial absorption. The second component is absorption subsequent to the first trial. We take the probability of being absorbed on the very first trial from the **R** matrix. In Table 6.6, this p_{ij} would have to equal one of the r values. We now wish to represent all other possible ways in which, having begun in transition state O_i, the system is eventually absorbed in ergodic state G_j. This would require going from O_i on the first trial to some other transient state O_k, where in the most general case, i may or may not be equal to k. However, from state O_k the system is eventually absorbed in state G_j, although we are not specific about how (or in how many steps) this occurs. Going from state O_i to O_k is easily symbolized as p_{ik}. Going from O_k to G_j in some unspecified number of steps with some unspecified probability would return us to our original symbol for absorption in an ergodic state G_j from a transient state O_k, now using b_{kj} rather than b_{ij}. We can multiply the joint events necessary for this alternative route, to be taken barring a first-trial absorption, and requiring, as indicated, the probability events $p_{ik}b_{kj}$. For the general case, k can have any value in the set of transient states, so the alternative path of postfirst-trial absorption is a sum of probabilities $\sum_{O_k} p_{ik}b_{kj}$ over all possible transient states. If we add this to the probability of a first-trial absorption p_{ij}, we have a symbolization of b_{ij}, as in Eq. (6.44).

$$b_{ij} = p_{ij} + \sum_{O_k} p_{ik} b_{kj}. \qquad (6.44)$$

Equation (6.44) is simply a restatement of an individual entry in the **B** matrix. It indicates that absorption can occur on the first response of a trial, with the subject beginning in some transient state O_i, and for the second response emitting a choice, the choice being symbolized as the state G_j. Or the second response can again be an orienting response, state O_k from the set of transient states, and at some point subsequent to that response an eventual alley choice is made, and it is the choice represented by state G_j. This apparently arbitrary partitioning will be found to be quite functional if we now reconstruct the complete matrix **B** from the components b_{ij} as defined by Eq. (6.44). We now rationalize this construction.

The probability p_{ij} we indicated was from the **R** matrix of probabilities of going, on any one trial, from a transient state to an ergodic state. We can therefore replace p_{ij} in Eq. (6.44) with **R**, in the matrix equivalent. The value p_{ik} in Eq. (6.44) refers only to transitions within the transient state matrix. A matrix of such transitions is simply the transition matrix **Q**. In (6.44) it is multiplied against the probability b_{kj}, where k is any transient state and j is any absorption state, so b_{kj} as a matrix is simply **B**, as defined earlier. We now restate Eq. (6.44) as a matrix, using the matrix equivalents that we have just rationalized.

$$\mathbf{B} = \mathbf{R} + \mathbf{QB}. \qquad (6.45)$$

[The $\sum_{O_k}$ in Eq. (6.44) is implied in the product of **QB**, which necessitates the summing of products from rows of **Q** and columns of **B** in precisely the pairing implied in each $p_{ik}b_{jk}$ product in the sum $\sum_{O_k}$.] We now isolate the matrix **R** in Eq. (6.45).

$$\mathbf{R} = \mathbf{B} - \mathbf{QB},$$
$$\mathbf{R} = (\mathbf{I} - \mathbf{Q})\mathbf{B}. \qquad (6.46)$$

We now multiply both sides of (6.46) by $(\mathbf{I} - \mathbf{Q})^{-1}$ with the goal of thereby isolating **B** again.

$$(\mathbf{I} - \mathbf{Q})^{-1}\mathbf{R} = (\mathbf{I} - \mathbf{Q})^{-1}(\mathbf{I} - \mathbf{Q})\mathbf{B} = \mathbf{B}. \qquad (6.47)$$

From Eq. (6.21), which is one of our defining equations for the fundamental matrix, we have Eq. (6.47) as equivalent to

$$\mathbf{B} = \mathbf{NR}. \tag{6.48}$$

We have now succeeded in defining a matrix of conditional probabilities of absorption in particular ergodic states in terms of two familiar matrices. We know how to obtain the fundamental matrix $\mathbf{N}$ from the $\mathbf{Q}$ matrix, and the $\mathbf{Q}$ matrix and $\mathbf{R}$ matrix are generally given in the transition matrix developed from the axioms of the theory assumed to allow a Markov chain analysis.

Let us now express the transition matrix from this second Bower model.

We must first state the special assumptions of this theory. We make the assumption that a right-goal response can only follow a right-arm orientation, and a left-goal response can only follow a left-arm orientation. We shall further assume that a right-goal orientation cannot be followed by another right-goal orientation, for by the very nature of these responses, we cannot define another response unless there is change in behavior. We therefore have right-goal orientations followed by either a left-goal orientation or absorption in a right-goal response. Similarly, a left-goal orientation can only be followed by either a right-goal orientation or a left-goal response. These assumptions give us helpful zeros in our transition matrix, shown in Table 6.7.

TABLE 6.7

Transition Matrix for Bower's Choice Model (1959)[a]

	G_1	G_2	O_1	O_2
G_1	1	0	0	0
G_2	0	1	0	0
O_1	g_1	0	0	$1 - g_1$
O_2	0	g_2	$1 - g_2$	0

[a] Subscript 1 refers to the left and subscript 2 refers to the right.

We can see that Table 6.7 has a relatively simple transient state matrix. From Table 6.7

$$\mathbf{Q} = \begin{pmatrix} 0 & 1 - g_1 \\ 1 - g_2 & 0 \end{pmatrix},$$

$$\mathbf{I} - \mathbf{Q} = \begin{pmatrix} 1 & g_1 - 1 \\ g_2 - 1 & 1 \end{pmatrix}$$

[note that the determinant of this matrix is $1 - (g_2 - 1)(g_1 - 1)$, which is equal to $1 - (1 - g_2)(1 - g_1)$];

$$\mathbf{N} = (\mathbf{I} - \mathbf{Q})^{-1} = \frac{1}{1 - (1 - g_2)(1 - g_1)} \begin{pmatrix} 1 & 1 - g_1 \\ 1 - g_2 & 1 \end{pmatrix}. \quad (6.49)$$

Equation (6.49) then gives us the fundamental matrix.

We need $\mathbf{R}$, along with $\mathbf{N}$, to obtain $\mathbf{B}$ [from Eq. (6.48)]. We find that the matrix $\mathbf{R}$, from Table 6.7, is

$$\mathbf{R} = \begin{pmatrix} g_1 & 0 \\ 0 & g_2 \end{pmatrix}. \quad (6.50)$$

From Eqs. (6.48)–(6.50), we have

$$\mathbf{B} = \frac{1}{1 - (1 - g_2)(1 - g_1)} \begin{pmatrix} 1 & 1 - g_1 \\ 1 - g_2 & 1 \end{pmatrix} \cdot \begin{pmatrix} g_1 & 0 \\ 0 & g_2 \end{pmatrix},$$

$$\mathbf{B} = \frac{1}{1 - (1 - g_2)(1 - g_1)} \begin{pmatrix} g_1 & g_2(1 - g_1) \\ g_1(1 - g_2) & g_2 \end{pmatrix}, \quad (6.51)$$

which gives us the specific solution of conditional probabilities of absorption in either of the T-maze arms. As usual, for the unconditional probabilities, we would have to multiply the right-hand side of Eq. (6.51) by the initial probability vector π_0'. Let us symbolize this vector as

$$\pi_0' = [P(O_{10}) \quad p(O_{20})]. \quad (6.52)$$

The product of Eqs. (6.51) and (6.52) is then

$$\pi_0'\mathbf{B} = \left[\frac{P(O_{10})g_1 + P(O_{20})g_1(1 - g_2)}{1 - (1 - g_2)(1 - g_1)} \quad \frac{P(O_{10})g_2(1 - g_1) + P(O_{20})g_2}{1 - (1 - g_2)(1 - g_1)} \right].$$

$$(6.53)$$

Equation (6.53) offers us the unconditional probabilities of absorption in the left and right arms of the T maze, reading from left to right.

We can check our results in Eq. (6.53) by the direct method. It will be helpful if we add a second subscript to our transition events to indicate the trial on which they occurred.

Thus, just as O_{10} refers to an initial left orientation, O_{21} would follow the first transition, going from the initial orientation to a right orientation; and we might then have a sequence such as O_{12}, O_{23}, G_{24}, which would mean that during the fifth response on that trial, which would constitute the fourth transition, the subject ran down the right arm of the T maze. Let us begin by specifying one absorption state of interest, say G_1. For absorption in that state, the last orientation must be in the same direction, that is, G_{1j}

implies O_{1j-1}. To further simplify matters, let us specify the initial response orientation. It can be either right or left, but let us have it as O_{10}. The first and last orientations must then be to the left. The probability of running down the left maze must then include all possible ways that this can happen, which simply means in all of the possible different number of responses before absorption. Since an orientation can never follow itself directionally, but always implies another direction, we must assume that the alternative number of responses must always involve pairs of orientations. If we are focusing on the probability of a particular outcome, such as G_1, given O_{10}, we would sum all of the probabilities of all of the different numbers of responses that could intervene before the outcome in focus, as in Eq. (6.54).

$$
\begin{aligned}
P(G_1, O_{10}) = {} & P(G_{11}|O_{10})P(O_{10}) + P(G_{13}|O_{12}O_{21}O_{10})P(O_{12}|O_{21}O_{10}) \\
& \times P(O_{21}|O_{10})P(O_{10}) + P(G_{15}|O_{14}O_{23}O_{12}O_{21}O_{10}) \\
& \times P(O_{14}|O_{23}O_{12}O_{21}O_{10})P(O_{23}|O_{12}O_{21}O_{10}) \\
& \times P(O_{12}|O_{21}O_{10})P(O_{21}|O_{10})P(O_{10}) + \cdots \\
& + P(G_{1m}|O_{1,m-1}O_{2,m-2}\cdots O_{10}) \\
& \times P(O_{1,m-1}|O_{2,m-2}\cdots O_{10})\cdots P(O_{21}|O_{10})P(O_{10}) + \cdots.
\end{aligned}
$$

$$(6.54)$$

Equation (6.54) sums the probabilities of the alternative ways the system can be absorbed in G_1 with O_{10}. We can restate Eq. (6.54) with the probabilities given in Table 6.7. This would give us

$$
\begin{aligned}
P(G_1, O_{10}) = {} & g_1 + g_1(1-g_2)(1-g_1) + g_1[(1-g_2)(1-g_1)]^2 \\
& + g_1[(1-g_2)(1-g_1)]^3 + \cdots + g_1[(1-g_2)(1-g_1)]^m + \cdots.
\end{aligned}
$$

$$(6.55)$$

We can restate Eq. (6.55) as

$$
P(G_1, O_{10}) = g_1 \sum_{m=0}^{\infty} [(1-g_2)(1-g_1)]^m,
$$

$$
P(G_1, O_{10}) = \frac{g_1}{1 - (1-g_2)(1-g_1)}.
$$

$$(6.56)$$

If we wished to obtain $P(G_1, O_{20})$, we would merely require an additional orientation change from right to left after the initial response, since after that point we would again require the double responses, under the assumption that the process would end in G_1 on some trial m. Following the same process as above, we would find

$$
P(G_1, O_{20}) = \frac{g_1(1-g_2)}{1 - (1-g_2)(1-g_1)}.
$$

$$(6.57)$$

To obtain the unconditional probability of $P(G_1)$ we would use the probability theorem implied in Eq. (2.21).

$$P(G_1) = P(G_1, O_{10}) + P(G_1, O_{20}).$$ (6.58)

Using Eqs. (6.56) and (6.57), we would restate Eq. (6.58) as

$$P(G_1) = \frac{P(O_{10})g_1 + P(O_{20})g_1(1 - g_2)}{1 - (1 - g_2)(1 - g_1)}.$$ (6.59)

Equation (6.59) yields precisely the same answer that we obtained for the unconditional probability of absorption in the left arm in Eq. (6.53), which we had obtained with our Markov chain analysis, confirming that equation. We would find similar confirmation, proceeding in the same way with the direct method to obtain the unconditional probability of absorption in the right arm of the T maze.

In this particular use of the **B** matrix, we are peculiarly restricted to a set of responses within a single trial of an experiment. Since most learning experiments work for change in response probabilities over trials, we would expect that the probability of entering a particular maze arm would not be a constant over trials. In this way the values of g_1 and g_2 would be expected to change over trials. In Bower's (1959) original presentation of this model, he went on to analyze the change in choice probabilities over trials with a linear operator analysis, combining the within-trial analysis using Markov chain assumptions with the trial-to-trial analysis using linear operator assumptions.

Summary

We have presented techniques from Markov chain theory to help in the analysis of data where we can conceptualize the experimental paradigm as involving state changes with constant probabilities of transition.

We have described a method for generating equations for the probability of being in each transient state k times, where k can be 0 (Eq. (6.24) for **K**[0]); or k can be any value greater than 0 (Eq. (6.32) for **K**[k]).

We have described two different methods for obtaining the mean number of times that the system will be in each of the transient states [Eq. (6.9) and (6.21) for **N**] as well as the variance for these expectations [Eq. (6.23)].

We have developed a matrix offering the probabilities of going to any particular transient state at least once [Eq. (6.26) for **H**].

Finally, we left the transient state matrix and confronted the necessity of obtaining a matrix giving us the probabilities of absorption in particular ergodic states, once having left the transient state matrix [Eq. (6.48) for **B**].

In the following chapter we shall apply these and related techniques to paradigms examining avoidance conditioning.

Problems

We can conceive of a matrix of probabilities of transitions between states. For example, in the Bower model of paired-associate learning with two states, we had a conditioned state and a guessing state. Let us assume three states (as we did with the expanded matrix for the Bower model), and look at progressively more probabilities of transitions between states, with the number of states remaining constant. For example, a relatively small number of transition possibilities are represented in Matrix 1.

Matrix 1

	S_1	S_2	S_3
S_1	1	0	0
S_2	c	$1-c$	0
S_3	0	a	$1-a$

In Matrix 1, if the system begins in S_3, it can go to S_2 or remain in S_3. It cannot go directly to S_1. If it goes to S_2, it can go to S_1 or remain in S_2. It cannot return to S_3. Once it leaves S_2 and goes to S_1, it can only stay in S_1.

We can increase the number of transitions in the system, as in Matrix 2 or Matrix 3.

Matrix 2

	S_1	S_2	S_3
S_1	1	0	0
S_2	c	$1-c$	0
S_3	b	$a(1-b)$	$(1-a)(1-b)$

Matrix 3

	S_1	S_2	S_3
S_1	1	0	0
S_2	$c(1-d)$	$(1-c)(1-d)$	d
S_3	0	a	$1-a$

Matrix 2 expands the possibilities for transition by permitting a direct transition from S_3 to S_1, although it still does not permit a return to S_3 from S_2. Matrix 3 permits a return to S_3 from S_2 but does not permit direct transition from S_3 to S_1.

Matrix 4 permits direct transition from S_3 to any other state and direct transition from S_2 to any other state.

Matrix 4

	S_1	S_2	S_3
S_1	1	0	0
S_2	$c(1-d)$	$(1-c)(1-d)$	d
S_3	b	$a(1-b)$	$(1-a)(1-b)$

1. Find the inverse of Matrix 2. (When you get the answer, multiply Matrix 2 times your answer to check that the product is equal to the identity matrix.)
2. Find the inverse of Matrix 3.
3. Find the **N** matrix (the fundamental matrix) for Matrix 3.
4. Find the **H** matrix for Matrix 3.
5. Assume Matrix 3 is the matrix of one-trial transition probabilities. Find the matrix offering the distribution of conditional probabilities for k times in each transition state $\mathbf{K}[k]$.
6. Given Matrix 5 as the matrix of one-trial transition probabilities:
   (a) Find **N**.
   (b) Find **H**.
   (c) Find **B**.

Matrix 5

	S_1	S_2	S_3	S_4	S_5
S_1	1	0	0	0	0
S_2	0	1	0	0	0
S_3	d	c	$1-c-d$	0	0
S_4	c	$d(1-c)$	0	$(1-c)(1-d)$	0
S_5	a	b	0	0	$1-a-b$

7. Assume a concept learning paradigm, such as that described in Bower and Trabasso (1964). Subjects were exposed to five-letter nonsensewords, with each of two letters possible in any given position. The particular letters in the first, second, third, and fifth positions were irrelevant (although this was not told to the subjects). The fourth letter was considered the relevant letter (akin to the relevant dimension when using geometric figures in similar concept learning problems). Two responses were possible, with the subject being reinforced for answering either "one" or "two," depending on which letter was in the fourth position. For example, the correct response to JVKRZ was "one" and the correct response to JVKQZ was "two."

Construct two stochastic transition matrices, each a 3×3 matrix, for two different interpretations of the process underlying learning within such an experimental paradigm. There are many interpretations possible, and two of them follow. Construct your third-order matrices for these two interpretations.

(a) One all-or-none learning interpretation is that on every trial the subject has an opportunity for having the reinforced response connected to the stimulus nonsense word, with some probability c. Once the connection occurs, it is permanent. Before the connection is made, the subject responds correctly on any trial with a guessing probability p, and incorrectly with a guessing probability $q = (1 - p)$.

(b) One "hypothesis testing" interpretation (Restle, 1962) is that a subject forms some strategy for the situation, such as "say 'one' if the fourth letter is an R," or "say 'two' if the fourth letter is a Q." If the response of saying "one" or "two" is reinforced, the subject maintains that strategy. If the response given under a strategy is not reinforced on a particular trial, the subject changes his strategy for the next trial, randomly selecting a new strategy from among all possible strategies. The probability of selecting the correct strategy on any one trial when a new strategy is selected is a constant value c. Prior to his selecting the correct strategy, he is correct with a guessing probability p and incorrect with a guessing probability $q = (1 - p)$. When he has selected the correct strategy, he is then always correct, and never changes his strategy, so never again has an error.

Chapter Seven

A Markov Chain Analysis of
Avoidance Conditioning

In this chapter we shall use the avoidance conditioning paradigm to explicate the material of Chapter Six. We shall begin by describing alternative theoretical speculations about the process of learning in avoidance conditioning, restricting our discussion to theories that are concordant with finite Markov chain analyses. There are other analyses possible, such as the linear operator analysis discussed in Chapter Four. However, our major purpose in this chapter is to use the material to become more familiar with Markov chain applications.

Some Theories for an Avoidance Conditioning Paradigm

We can begin with a pair of stimulus sampling interpretations. The first one is due to Theios (1963). He suggested that it might be possible to construct an avoidance conditioning paradigm in which one could conceptualize the task as the learning of two-component stimulus patterns. For example, the rats could be placed in a box containing two compartments, one black and one white, separated by a guillotine door. They would be consistently shocked, at the end of some constant time period following a constant warning stimulus situation. The warning stimuli that he used were the onset of a buzzer and a light 3 seconds prior to electrifying the grid of the Miller–Mowrer shock box. The subject (a rat) was always placed in the side of the box with the same color at the beginning of every trial. The guillotine door was then raised simultaneously with the onset of the two stimuli, the buzzer and light. If the animal left the box (say the black box) for the other box (say the white box) within 3 seconds, then he was able to avoid shock (and the warning stimuli would cease). Otherwise, he was shocked until he escaped into the other compartment. The use of two stimuli as cues, plus the use of strong shock to minimize other possible concerns or distractions for the animals, suggested that learning might possibly take place in two discrete stages: the learning to respond to one stimulus component (we can speculate that this might be either the buzzer or the light) and then the learning of the other component, as the two cues for avoidance responding. One could speculate that all of the stimuli in the environment are not always impinging. The sound of a buzzer could be treated as one stimulus, which the organism does or does not notice, and a light onset could be treated as another stimulus, being noticed or not noticed. However, such specificity is not necessary for this very simple theory. All that is required is an assumption of two components to be learned, with only one being learned on any one trial. Another axiom of Theios' model is that initially neither stimulus component is conditioned to the avoidance response. Furthermore, a stimulus pattern that does impinge is conditioned on any trial with a probability of c, and if already conditioned, it remains so. A constant transition matrix, independent of trial number, is also assumed, to permit the Markov chain analysis. Only one stimulus pattern is assumed to impinge on any one trial. Theios makes the further assumption, constraining one parameter, that the two patterns have an equal probability of being sampled on any one trial.

We can see that we have only one parameter to be estimated from data in this set of axioms. That is the parameter c, which is the probability of the avoidance response becoming conditioned to a component stimulus pattern on any one trial, given that it is impinging on the subject at that time, and is not already conditioned. We can state the gist of the foregoing axioms in a transition matrix. We shall recognize three states: the initial unlearned state, where neither component stimulus pattern has become conditioned (S_0); the second state, where one, and only one, stimulus component pattern has been conditioned (S_1); and the third and final absorbing state, where both component stimulus patterns have been conditioned, and the subject correctly avoids shock on every trial (S_2). We present this transition matrix in Eq. (7.1).

$$\mathbf{S} = \begin{array}{c} \\ S_2 \\ S_1 \\ S_0 \end{array} \begin{array}{ccc} S_2 & S_1 & S_0 \\ 1 & 0 & 0 \\ \dfrac{c}{2} & 1 - \dfrac{c}{2} & 0 \\ 0 & c & 1 - c \end{array} \qquad (7.1)$$

During the first trial, the axioms assume that neither pattern is conditioned; therefore, it does not matter which pattern is impinging. Either one can be conditioned, with probability c, or not conditioned, with probability $(1 - c)$, as indicated in Eq. (7.1). This will continue until one pattern is indeed conditioned, taking the system into the second state, state S_1. From that point on, the stimulus pattern that does impinge is important for the predictions. On any trial after state S_1 is reached, if the already conditioned stimulus pattern is sampled, then the subject responds correctly (avoids shock), but no learning takes place on that trial. If, on the other hand, the nonconditioned stimulus component impinges, then again, with probability c, it is also conditioned. On any trial, however, there is a probability of $\frac{1}{2}$ that the nonconditioned stimulus component will be the one to impinge (in state S_1). Therefore, we have a joint event. With probability $\frac{1}{2}$ the nonconditioned stimulus component impinges, and if it does, with probability c it is conditioned. This is the only way that the system can move from S_1 to S_2, so we multiply these two probabilities together to obtain the probability of moving to S_2 from S_1, giving us $c/2$ in Eq. (7.1). The system does not have any axioms permitting forgetting, so the system cannot move backward, from S_1 to S_0. Therefore, such a transition has a 0 probability, leaving only one cell still unaccounted for in row two (for S_1) in the matrix of Eq. (7.1). This is a stochastic matrix, so we have the middle cell as $1 - (c/2)$, which is the complement of the only other possible event in the row for S_1. Finally, when both stimulus patterns are conditioned, only avoidance responses can occur. Therefore, with no forgetting written into the axioms, we have an absorbing state in S_2.

A second, and related, stimulus sampling theory was suggested by Estes to Bower and Theios (1964). Assuming the experimental situation described by Theios, but a different analysis, we can describe two different sets of stimuli. One would be the complete pattern of all stimuli signaling impending shock (in the Theios case, then including both buzzer and light as one component set of stimuli), and the other would be the warning stimulus plus the shock. [In classical conditioning terminology, conditioned stimulus and conditioned stimulus plus unconditioned stimulus (CS and CS + UCS) would be the two sets of stimuli.] When the rat is shocked in the early trials (as he always is), he can be classically conditioned to run (jumping and running assumed to be a pair of reflex responses to certain levels of shock). Let us assume that this conditioning occurs on any trial with some probability c. However, there would be some overlap between the stimuli of the warning stimuli plus shock, and the warning stimuli by themselves. Thus, given classical conditioning of CS + UCS to running, when CS is presented alone, there is some proportion p of all impinging stimuli that are conditioned to the running response. If we then assume, as in most stimulus sampling models, that the probability of a response is the proportion of all impinging stimuli that are conditioned to a particular response, then on any trial after the classical conditioning has taken place, we can anticipate an avoidance response to warning stimuli alone with probability p. Once the avoidance response occurs, we can have conditioning by contiguity of the running response to CS. This event we can symbolize as having a probability of s. With these assumptions, we can construct a transition matrix like the following.

$$\mathbf{T} = \begin{array}{c} \\ S_2 \\ S_1 \\ S_0 \end{array} \begin{array}{ccc} S_2 & S_1 & S_0 \\ 1 & 0 & 0 \\ s & 1-s & 0 \\ 0 & c & 1-c \end{array} . \tag{7.2}$$

Note that in Eq. (7.2), as in Eq. (7.1), the middle state must first be entered in order to reach the third and final state. In the case of Eq. (7.2) this is because the conditioning of the running response by contiguity is assumed not to be possible until after the classical conditioning of the running response. Note that if $s = c/2$, then Eqs. (7.1) and (7.2) are identical. This would imply that the two theories can both generate the same mathematical model. When this happens, and we wish to compare the two theories, the axioms are reexamined for theorems that would generate different predictions for the two theories (most generally, given changes in the experimental paradigms).

Another interpretation is possible following a duo-process theory of learning, and was presented by Theios (1963) as an alternative explanation of his avoidance conditioning data. The animal is shocked, and this causes a series of emotional responses. The visceral upset of the emotional response becomes classically conditioned to the CS preceding the shock with some probability c on any trial. Then the animal, given the visceral upset, may exhibit a running response that takes him out of the shock side of the box with some probability p, and with probability $1 - p$, he may crouch, freeze, etc., preventing an avoidance. Given that classical conditioning of an emotional response has taken place, it is possible that in this new state the animal may be instrumentally conditioned to leave the shock section. If the classical conditioning has taken place, we can always assume the visceral upset in the presence of the CS. We can then assume that the CS is an aversive stimulus because of its aversive consequences or correlates. Therefore, if the animal avoided the new aversive CS by leaving the shock side of the box (causing the CS to be turned off and the visceral upset to be reduced), it would then be possible for an instrumental conditioning effect to be obtained through his leaving the shock box. Note that connection of the actual running response to the warning stimuli, in this theory, is only possible after the classical conditioning of an emotional reaction to the warning stimuli. This again is a theory in which a final state cannot be reached until the subject goes through an intermediate state. In a three-state transition matrix this would be reflected in a 0 probability for the transition from state S_0 to state S_2. The matrix for this theory is identical to the matrix in Eq. (7.2).

The matrix in Eq. (7.2) contains no indication of the probability of a successful avoidance during the intermediate state S_1. Consequently, more information can be presented in the transition matrix by expanding it, in a way analogous to the expansion of Bower's paired-associate transition matrix. That is, the intermediate state can be expanded into two states, an intermediate state with a correct response (shock avoidance), and an intermediate state with an error. This new matrix is presented in Eq. (7.3). Note that $p + q = 1$, with p the probability of a successful avoidance and q the probability of obtaining shock, given that the classical conditioning has taken place but the instrumental conditioning has not yet taken place. The new state designations are now different for S_1 and S_2. State S_0 is still the initial preconditioning state, and S_3 is now the final absorbing state.

$$
\mathbf{U} = \begin{array}{c@{\quad}cccc}
 & S_3 & S_2 & S_1 & S_0 \\
S_3 & 1 & 0 & 0 & 0 \\
S_2 & s & (1-s)p & (1-s)q & 0 \\
S_1 & s & (1-s)p & (1-s)q & 0 \\
S_0 & 0 & cp & cq & 1-c
\end{array}
\tag{7.3}
$$

However, state S_1 is now the state in which classical conditioning has taken place, instrumental conditioning has not, and the subject has not avoided shock. State S_2 is the same state but with a successful avoidance. The expansion of the matrix in Eq. (7.2) will fit the model described by Bower and Theios (1964) as well as the model described by Theios (1963). That is, their model also had a probability of a correct response that could be designated p, during their intermediate state, so again the state can be divided into two states, one representing error and the other representing a correct response.

Equation (7.3) offers the first four-state matrix that we have rationalized in this book. There really are only three stages in the learning process as conceptualized for our construction of the matrix in Eq. (7.3). However, it is possible to develop a rationale for this four-state matrix that does involve a conceptualization of four states of learning. Theios and Brelsford (1966) offer such a rationalization. Theirs is a short-term and long-term memory model. The middle two states are both temporary memory states, but one is the state involving forgetting of the temporarily stored material and the other is the state in which the temporarily stored material is remembered.

The first state is the initial naive state and the fourth state is the state in which the material to be remembered is now permanently stored. The particular aspect of the material that we wish to assume is being learned, and transferred from temporary to permanent storage, is also something that different theorists might select differently for the very same experimental paradigm.

We pointed out earlier that the first two theories described in this chapter could both generate the same transition matrix and the same mathematical model. The particular matrix in Eq. (7.3) could also be generated by a multitude of theories. When we test a theory, and test it through the relative accuracy of the predictions of a mathematical model generated by the theory, we really test the class of all theories that would generate that mathematical model. The further test of the different predictive advantages of the different theories all generating the same transition matrix (and therefore that same finite Markov chain model) would focus on such things as the particular parameters that are anticipated to change in the model with different experimental manipulations. For example, we might lock the rats in one side of the box during the shock on early trials, preventing escape [Theios and Brelsford (1966)]. Comparing the results of this paradigm to the original paradigm of permitting escape at all trials, we might find that the results suggest a change in the value of one or another parameter of the equations. A theory involving classical conditioning of emotional responses as a first state transition might not predict any change in the parameter showing transition out of the first state when animals are prevented from escaping for some of the trials. But a theory with the same transition matrix, which saw the first state transition as involving instrumental conditioning, might anticipate that the parameter of the first state transition might indeed be expected to change under such changed conditions, despite an identity in the form of the transition matrices for the two theories. This would allow a comparative test of such theories, although they would make the same mathematical predictions in the original paradigm generating the two theories [see Theios and Brelsford (1966)].

In this book, we are attempting to explicate the techniques for generating and testing a theory's mathematical model. Our primary interest, then, is in the classes of models generated by theories (as, for example, Markov chain models) and in the general solutions needed for predictions. When dealing with theories that can be modeled as finite Markov chains, we shall find that we simply require solutions to the implications of transition matrices, which will only differ from theory to theory (from the point of view of mathematical solutions) in the size of the matrices (3×3, 4×4, or even larger) or in the number and position of zero elements in the matrices. The actual values in each matrix element are unimportant for general solutions and only impinge as arithmetic differences or algebraic problems at some point.

We have presented a particular transition matrix in Eq. (7.3) from the

point of view of size and zero elements. The matrix is part of the class of all
4×4 transition matrices. Let us look at a more general 4×4 matrix:

$$
\mathbf{V} = \begin{array}{c} \\ S_3 \\ S_2 \\ S_1 \\ S_0 \end{array}
\begin{array}{cccc}
S_3 & S_2 & S_1 & S_0 \\
1 & 0 & 0 & 0 \\
s & (1-s)p & (1-s)q & 0 \\
e & (1-e)p' & (1-e)q' & 0 \\
cd & (1-d)cp'' & (1-d)cq'' & (1-c)
\end{array}
\tag{7.4}
$$

The matrix in Eq. (7.4) is a stochastic matrix, as are most of the others
that we have presented. Since elements in each row must sum to 1 in a stochastic matrix, symbols are used that make it easy to compute the sums. A still
more general transition matrix, without the nonreturn to the first state, could
be developed. However, we can see from Eq. (7.4) that we are already over-
burdened with parameters to be estimated, in a matrix as general as the one
that we have presented. That is, a model expressed with the matrix of Eq.
(7.4) would have as parameters the values c, d, e, s, p, p', and p'', totaling
seven parameters. We would be hard pressed to independently estimate that
many parameters, given the limited number of equations that we are capable
of constructing with some semblance of independence. In fact, it can be
shown that these seven parameters could not be uniquely determined by
estimation from data (Greeno, 1968). Limitations on empirical estimation of
parameters are discussed in Chapter Eight.

Understanding the relationships of seven relevant parameters in the
construction of a model of any theory would normally represent a very
advanced stage of understanding. We are probably not yet at that stage in the
development of the science of psychology. If we work with a model containing
four parameters and find general solutions for such a model, and if we can
then further assume some of the values for one or two of these four parameters, we would be more likely to be working with a model that would be
within the reach of contemporary psychology. However, not all theorists
would agree with this conservative position.

What kinds of general assumptions might we begin with to reduce the
number of parameters in Eq. (7.4)? We constructed the matrix of equation
(7.4) by assuming that the system could not return to the first state, once
that state has been left. This is reasonable if the first state is considered a
kind of naive state, which is passed for all time at some point in the experiment. A further assumption might be that the intervening states cannot be
completely bypassed in going from the naive state to the final absorbing
state. That is, all subjects might be assumed to have to go through all of the
stages of learning described in the theory. Such an assumption would reduce
d in Eq. (7.4) to 0. (There are many situations where we can imagine such an

assumption to be unjustified. However, since we are looking for a reduction of parameters, we would try to construct our experimental situation so as to fit our reduced parameter assumptions.)

It is general to use the letters p and q to represent success and error, respectively. If we can consider that the probability of success and error is the same during all intermediate states (being 0 and 1, respectively, during S_0, and 1 and 0, respectively, during S_3), then we can assume that $p = p' = p''$ in Eq. (7.4). This further reduces the parameters to be estimated, and gives us the matrix presented in Eq. (7.5).

$$
\mathbf{W} = \begin{array}{c c c c c} & S_3 & S_2 & S_1 & S_0 \\ S_3 & 1 & 0 & 0 & 0 \\ S_2 & s & (1-s)p & (1-s)q & 0 \\ S_1 & e & (1-e)p & (1-e)q & 0 \\ S_0 & 0 & cp & cq & (1-c) \end{array}
\qquad (7.5)
$$

There are many different ways in which the number of parameters can be reduced, and a variety of possible resulting matrices. The exact forms would depend on the theory being modeled. Let us assume, however, that the transition matrix of Eq. (7.5) was the resulting matrix of such a process, for some theory developed for an avoidance conditioning paradigm. We shall now detail the way in which the general solutions for such a model would be generated from the transition matrix.

General Solutions for a General Transition Matrix

It is common to maximize the number of predictive equations in a model to give as complete a test of the theory as is possible. There are three distributions whose equations are almost always represented. One is the probability distribution for all numbers of total errors. A second is the probability distribution for the number of errors (trials) before the first success. The third is the probability distribution for each trial number as the trial of the last error. The expectation for each of these distributions is also generally obtained. When we add to this information the prediction of sequential statistics (such as runs of errors of various lengths, or expected success–error pairs), we have a relatively full picture of the theory's predictions, and therefore a relatively complete model.

With finite Markov models it is generally useful to begin by solving for the $\mathbf{N}$ matrix, the $\mathbf{H}$ matrix, and the probability of being in any state on any trial, all of which can be useful in deriving many of the equations.

THE N MATRIX

From Eq. (7.5) we can abstract the transient state matrix.

$$\mathbf{Q} = \begin{pmatrix} (1-s)p & (1-s)q & 0 \\ (1-e)p & (1-e)q & 0 \\ cp & cq & (1-c) \end{pmatrix},$$

$$\mathbf{I} - \mathbf{Q} = \begin{pmatrix} q+ps & -q+qs & 0 \\ -p+pe & p+qe & 0 \\ -cp & -cq & c \end{pmatrix} \tag{7.6}$$

[note that $1 - p(1 - s) = 1 - p + ps = q + ps$, etc.]. Now consider the determinant $|\mathbf{I} - \mathbf{Q}|$. Using the technique described in Chapter Five, we have

$$\begin{aligned}
|\mathbf{I} - \mathbf{Q}| &= O[(-p+pe)(-cq) - (-cp)(p+qe)] \\
&\quad - O[(q+ps)(-cq) - (-q+qs)(-cp)] \\
&\quad + c[(q+ps)(p+qe) - (-q+qs)(-p+pe)] \\
&= c[pq + p^2s + q^2e + pqes - pqes + pqs + pqe - pq] \\
&= c(p^2s + pqs + q^2e + pqe) \\
&= c[p(ps+qs) + q(qe+pe)] \\
&= c\{p[s(p+q)] + q[e(q+p)]\}, \\
|\mathbf{I} - \mathbf{Q}| &= c(ps + qe). \tag{7.7}
\end{aligned}$$

Let the cofactor matrix of $(\mathbf{I} - \mathbf{Q})$ be called $\mathbf{C}$.

$$\mathbf{C} = $$

$$\begin{pmatrix} c(p+qe) & -c(-p+pe) & (cp)(p+qe) - (cq)(-p+qe) \\ -c(-q+qs) & c(q+ps) & -(-cq)(q+ps) + (cp)(-q+qs) \\ 0 & 0 & (q+ps)(p+qe) - (-q-qs)(-p+pe) \end{pmatrix}.$$

Simplifying, we have

$$\mathbf{C} = \begin{pmatrix} c(p+qe) & c(p-pe) & cp \\ c(q-qs) & c(q+ps) & cq \\ 0 & 0 & ps+qe \end{pmatrix}.$$

We symbolize the transpose of $\mathbf{C}$ as $\mathbf{C}'$.

$$\mathbf{C}' = \begin{pmatrix} c(p+qe) & c(q-qs) & 0 \\ c(p-pe) & c(q+ps) & 0 \\ cp & cq & ps+qe \end{pmatrix}. \tag{7.8}$$

From Chapter Five, we know that

$$(\mathbf{I} - \mathbf{Q})^{-1} = \frac{1}{|\mathbf{I} - \mathbf{Q}|} \, \mathbf{C}'.$$

We therefore have, from Eqs. (7.7) and (7.8), the fundamental matrix $\mathbf{N}$, equal to

$$\frac{1}{\mathbf{I} - \mathbf{Q}} = \frac{1}{c(ps + qe)} \begin{pmatrix} c(p + qe) & c(q - qs) & 0 \\ c(p - pe) & c(q + ps) & 0 \\ cp & cq & ps + qe \end{pmatrix}. \tag{7.9}$$

To check on the validity of Eq. (7.9) we would multiply Eqs. (7.6) and (7.9) to see if the product was equal to the identity matrix.

For simplicity in writing equations, let us use the symbol γ as follows.

$$\gamma = ps + qe. \tag{7.10}$$

We can now restate Eq. (7.9) as

$$\mathbf{N} = \begin{pmatrix} \dfrac{p + qe}{\gamma} & \dfrac{q - qs}{\gamma} & 0 \\[2mm] \dfrac{p - pe}{\gamma} & \dfrac{q + ps}{\gamma} & 0 \\[2mm] \dfrac{p}{\gamma} & \dfrac{q}{\gamma} & \dfrac{1}{c} \end{pmatrix}. \tag{7.11}$$

Since in the avoidance conditioning paradigm the system always begins in the first state (making an error), we can present the truncated initial state vector as

$$\pi_0' = [0 \quad 0 \quad 1]. \tag{7.12}$$

We then have, as the expected times in each state, from Eqs. (7.11) and (7.12),

$$\pi_0' \mathbf{N} = \begin{bmatrix} \dfrac{p}{\gamma} & \dfrac{q}{\gamma} & \dfrac{1}{c} \end{bmatrix}. \tag{7.13}$$

THE H MATRIX

We recall Eq. (6.26) as

$$\mathbf{H} = (\mathbf{N} - \mathbf{I})\mathbf{N}_{\mathrm{dg}}^{-1},$$

so that we can combine Eqs. (6.26) and (7.11) to obtain

$$
\mathbf{H} = \begin{pmatrix} \dfrac{p+qe}{\gamma} - 1 & \dfrac{q-qs}{\gamma} & 0 \\[2ex] \dfrac{p-pe}{\gamma} & \dfrac{q+ps}{\gamma} - 1 & 0 \\[2ex] \dfrac{p}{\gamma} & \dfrac{q}{\gamma} & \dfrac{1}{c} - 1 \end{pmatrix} \begin{pmatrix} \dfrac{\gamma}{p+qe} & 0 & 0 \\[2ex] 0 & \dfrac{\gamma}{q+ps} & 0 \\[2ex] 0 & 0 & c \end{pmatrix},
$$

$$
\mathbf{H} = \begin{pmatrix} 1 - \dfrac{\gamma}{p+qe} & \dfrac{q-qs}{q+ps} & 0 \\[2ex] \dfrac{p-pe}{p+qe} & 1 - \dfrac{\gamma}{q+ps} & 0 \\[2ex] \dfrac{p}{p+qe} & \dfrac{q}{q+ps} & 1-c \end{pmatrix}. \tag{7.14}
$$

THE PROBABILITY OF BEING IN ANY STATE ON TRIAL n

The logically simplest method for obtaining the probability of being in any state on trial n is to obtain $\mathbf{P}^n$ and multiply it by the initial vector. However, in order to use the method of spectral resolution presented in Chapter Five, we would need the latent roots of $(\mathbf{P} - \lambda\mathbf{I})$. For our illustration in Chapter Five, we obtained the roots by converting the matrix $(\mathbf{P} - \lambda\mathbf{I})$ to a triangular matrix. In the case of our current matrix $\mathbf{W}$ in Eq. (7.5) we would find that we could not convert the matrix $(\mathbf{W} - \lambda\mathbf{I})$ to a triangular matrix. We shall therefore use a different approach for obtaining $P(S_{jn})$. We shall translate our probabilistic assumptions into equations (the "direct method," Chapter Two), and combine this with some difference equation solutions. This will lead us to the desired equations for the probabilities of being in particular states on particular trials.

We first look at $P(S_{0n})$, the probability of being in state S_0 on trial n in Eq. (7.5). The subject begins in that state and is there on subsequent trials by being there continuously. That is, it requires the joint event of returns there $n - 1$ times for being there on the nth trial. This is an "and" relation, and each event occurs with probability $(1 - c)$, yielding

$$
P(S_{0n}) = (1 - c)^{n-1}. \tag{7.15}
$$

Equation (7.15) could also have been obtained as the solution to the recursive equation

$$
P(S_{0n+1}) = P(S_{0n})(1 - c),
$$

as implied by Eq. (7.5).

The probability of being in S_2 or S_1 on any trial can be stated in terms of the sum of the various probabilities with which the state of interest can be reached from all other states from which it is reachable. Therefore, from Eq. (7.5),

$$P(S_{1n+1}) = P(S_{1n})(1 - e)q + P(S_{2n})(1 - s)q + P(S_{0n})cq. \qquad (7.16)$$

The last term in Eq. (7.16) can be restated with the aid of Eq. (7.15). This yields

$$P(S_{1n+1}) = P(S_{1n})(1 - e)q + P(S_{2n})(1 - s)q + cq(1 - c)^{n-1}. \qquad (7.17)$$

We form a similar equation for state S_2, again using Eq. (7.5).

$$P(S_{2n+1}) = P(S_{1n})(1 - e)p + P(S_{2n})(1 - s)p + P(S_{0n})cp. \qquad (7.18)$$

Restating Eq. (7.18) yields

$$P(S_{2n+1}) = P(S_{1n})(1 - e)p + P(S_{2n})(1 - s)p + cp(1 - c)^{n-1}. \qquad (7.19)$$

Comparing Eqs. (7.17) and (7.19), we find that they are identical except for the common factor of q or p as coefficients for the terms being summed. Multiplying both sides of Eq. (7.17) by p and both sides of Eq. (7.19) by q, we find that

$$p[P(S_{1n+1})] = q[P(S_{2n+1})]. \qquad (7.20)$$

Since n is an arbitrary number, Eq. (7.20) is as true for n as it is for $n + 1$. We therefore can equate $P(S_{1n})$ and $P(S_{2n})$ in the following way.

$$P(S_{1n}) = \frac{q[P(S_{2n})]}{p}, \qquad (7.21)$$

$$P(S_{2n}) = \frac{p[P(S_{1n})]}{q}, \qquad (7.22)$$

We can now replace $P(S_{2n})$ and $P(S_{1n})$ in Eqs. (7.17) and (7.19), respectively. This would yield, for Eq. (7.17).

$$P(S_{1n+1}) = P(S_{1n})(1 - e)q + \frac{p}{q[P(S_{1n})]}(1 - s)q + cq(1 - c)^{n-1},$$

which is reducible to a recursive equation through the following steps.

$$P(S_{1n+1}) = P(S_{1n})[(1 - e)q + (1 - s)p] + cq(1 - c)^{n-1},$$
$$P(S_{1n+1}) = P(S_{1n})[1 - (ps + qe)] + cq(1 - c)^{n-1}$$
$$P(S_{1n+1}) = P(S_{1n})(1 - \gamma) + cq(1 - c)^{n-1} \qquad (7.23)$$

[from Eq. (7.10)]. For Eq. (7.19) we would have

$$P(S_{2n+1}) = \frac{q[P(S_{2n})]}{p}(1 - e)p + P(S_{2n})(1 - s)p + cp(1 - c)^{n-1},$$

which is reducible to a recursive equation through the following steps.

$$P(S_{2n+1}) = P(S_{2n})[(1 - e)q + (1 - s)p] + cp(1 - c)^{n-1},$$
$$P(S_{2n+1}) = P(S_{2n})[1 - (ps + qe)] + cp(1 - c)^{n-1},$$
$$P(S_{2n+1}) = P(S_{2n})(1 - \gamma) + cp(1 - c)^{n-1}. \qquad (7.24)$$

Both Eq. (7.23) and Eq. (7.24) are recursive equations of the form of Eq. (3.41), with the solution worked through in Table 3.3. Applying that solution to both Eq. (7.23) and Eq. (7.24), remembering that $P(S_{11})$ and $P(S_{21})$ both equal zero, we would have

$$P(S_{1n}) = \frac{cq}{c - \gamma}[(1 - \gamma)^{n-1} - (1 - c)^{n-1}] \qquad (7.25)$$

and

$$P(S_{2n}) = \frac{cp}{c - \gamma}[(1 - \gamma)^{n-1} - (1 - c)^{n-1}]. \qquad (7.26)$$

To obtain $P(S_{3n})$, we would use Eqs. (7.15), (7.25), and (7.26) in Eq. (7.27).

$$P(S_{3n}) = 1 - [P(S_{2n}) + P(S_{1n}) + P(S_{0n})]. \qquad (7.27)$$

THE DISTRIBUTION OF ERRORS BEFORE THE FIRST SUCCESS

We see in Eq. (7.5) that there are only two states in which errors can occur; they are state S_0 and state S_1. As long as the subject stays in state S_0, he will make errors. Once he leaves state S_0 he cannot return, so errors in S_0 have to be both initial and consecutive. Subsequent to his leaving S_0, he can only make errors in S_1, prior to the first success. These also have to be consecutive, since once he leaves S_1, it can only be for S_2 or S_3, both of which imply that the subject's first success has occurred.

We shall let J_0 be the random variable for the number of errors before the first success, following the notation of Bower and Theios (1964). For $J_0 = k$, we shall have to sum all of the probabilities for each number of errors in S_0 and each number of errors in S_1 that will give a total of k. For example, all of the errors before the first success can occur in S_0 if the system left S_0 for S_2. Or there could be $k - 1$ errors in S_0 and just one in S_1 before moving to either S_2 or S_3. There must be at least one error in S_0, however, since the avoidance conditioning paradigm assumes an error on the first trial. The probability, then, of any number k of errors before the first success is the sum of all of the alternate possible ways in which k errors can occur, with any number from 1 to k of them occurring in S_0 and the remainder occurring in S_1, the sum from both states summing to k.

For k errors in S_0, we simply need the probability of the subject being in S_0 on the kth trial. We know from Eq. (7.15) that this is

$$S_{0k} = (1 - c)^{k-1}.$$

For there to be only k errors, however, we require that the system then move from S_0 to S_2. From Eq. (7.5) we see that this occurs with probability cp. We therefore have as the probability of k errors, all in S_0,

$$P(J_0 = k, \text{ all in } S_0) = cp(1 - c)^{k-1}. \tag{7.28}$$

We shall need the probability of the subject making some number j errors in S_0, and the remaining $k - j$ errors in S_1, followed by a move to either S_2 or S_3 for the first success. We shall then add each probability, for $(1 \leq j \leq k - 1)$, to Eq. (7.28), and then have a sum of all of the alternate ways in which k errors can occur before the first success.

We begin with the alternate possibility of that which is implied in Eq. (7.28); that is, we assume that after leaving S_0, the subject goes to S_1. This occurs with a probability of cq, from Eq. (7.5). We would then have as the probability of j errors in S_0 followed by a move to S_1,

probability of j errors in S_0 followed by a move to $S_1 = cq(1 - c)^{j-1}$. (7.29)

We would then need some number of repeats in S_1, totaling $k - j - 1$, so that the total of times in S_1 would be $k - j$ (including the entrance into S_1). From Eq. (7.5) we see that once in S_1, the subject remains in S_1 with a probability of $(1 - e)q$ on each subsequent trial. The probability of $k - j - 1$ repeats is then

$$[(1 - e)q]^{k-j-1}. \tag{7.30}$$

For symbolic simplicity, let us use

$$\alpha = (1 - e)q. \tag{7.31}$$

We can then restate (7.30) as

probability of $k - j - 1$ repetitions in $S_1 = \alpha^{k-j-1}$. (7.32)

To complete our equation, we need the probability of moving to either S_3 or S_2 from S_1 after the $k - j - 1$ repetitions in S_1. Since moving to either of these two correct response states is the only possible event if the subject does not remain in state S_1 for an additional trial, we can use the complement of

$(1 - e)q$ as the probability of moving to either S_2 or S_3. In keeping with the symbolism introduced in Eq. (7.31), we represent this latter probability as $1 - \alpha$:

$$\text{probability of going to either } S_2 \text{ or } S_3 \text{ from } S_1 = (1 - \alpha). \quad (7.33)$$

We can now combine Eqs. (7.28), (7.29), (7.32), and (7.33) to obtain the desired equation for the probability of k errors before the first success,

$$P(J_0 = k) = cp(1 - c)^{k-1} + \sum_{j=1}^{k-1} cq(1 - c)^{j-1}\alpha^{k-j-1}(1 - \alpha)$$

or

$$P(J_0 = k) = cp(1 - c)^{k-1} + cq(1 - \alpha) \sum_{j=1}^{k-1} (1 - c)^{j-1}\alpha^{k-j-1}. \quad (7.34)$$

Equation (7.34) offers a form of summation that we have not previously encountered in this book. It requires adding a series of products of paired factors, such as $\sum_{j=1}^{k} x^j y^{k-j}$, where the paired factors each have an exponent such that the pair of exponents sum to a constant (in this case k). The required technique is called *convolution of a sum* and is presented in the next section.

Convoluting a Sum

A convolution of a sum of probabilities is similar to the less complex summation of probabilities of one random variable over many values of that random variable. However, in the convolution of a sum of probabilities we sum the products of two (or more) probabilities of two (or more) random variables over a set of related values for the two random variables (such as k and $k - j$ in $\sum_{j=1}^{k} x^j y^{k-j}$). There are alternative ways of obtaining such sums of products of probabilities. The procedure that we shall describe here allows a use of summation techniques that are familiar from Chapter Two. The familiar summation technique is applied after the differing exponents are all converted to a single identical exponent with the aid of the proper choice of additional factors for the sum.

In order to sum an exponential series such as $\sum_{j=1}^{k-1} (1 - c)^{j-1}\alpha^{k-j-1}$ in Eq. (7.34), we need to have all factors on the right-hand side of the summation sign raised to the same power. Since the number k is a constant, we can place α^k to the left of the summation sign to obtain

$$\sum_{j=1}^{k-1} (1 - c)^{j-1}\alpha^{k-j-1} = \alpha^k \sum_{j=1}^{k-1} (1 - c)^{j-1}\alpha^{-j-1}. \quad (7.35)$$

The two factors in the sum on the right-hand side of Eq. (7.35) are still not raised to the same powers, but we can see a greater similarity. In this technique for convoluting, we generally take advantage of the fact that by placing a term in a denominator, we reverse the sign of its exponent. We adjust the expression so that the reversed signs will give us a desired identity of numerator and denominator exponents. For example,

$$\alpha^k \sum_{j=1}^{k-1} (1 - c)^{j-1} \alpha^{-j-1} = \alpha^{k-2} \sum_{j=1}^{k-1} (1 - c)^{j-1} \alpha^{-j+1},$$

after which, placement of the α term in the denominator transforms (7.35) to

$$\sum_{j=1}^{k-1} (1 - c)^{j-1} \alpha^{k-j-1} = \alpha^{k-2} \sum_{j=1}^{k-1} \frac{(1 - c)^{j-1}}{\alpha^{j-1}}. \tag{7.36}$$

We can now use Eq. (7.36) to replace the relevant section of Eq. (7.34), which will enable us to carry out the summation in

$$P(J_0 = k) = cp(1 - c)^{k-1} + cq(1 - \alpha)\alpha^{k-2} \sum_{j=1}^{k-1} \left[\frac{(1 - c)}{\alpha} \right]^{j-1}. \tag{7.37}$$

We use the summation technique presented in Chapter Two, with which we find that

$$\sum_{j=1}^{k-1} X^{j-1} = \frac{1 - X^{k-1}}{1 - X}.$$

Equation (7.37) then becomes

$$P(J_0 = k) = cp(1 - c)^{k-1} + cq(1 - \alpha)\alpha^{k-2} \left\{ \frac{1 - [(1 - c)/\alpha]^{k-1}}{1 - [(1 - c)/\alpha]} \right\}$$

$$= cp(1 - c)^{k-1} + cq(1 - \alpha)\alpha^{k-2} \left\{ \frac{[\alpha^{k-1} - (1 - c)^{k-1}/\alpha^{k-1}]}{[\alpha - (1 - c)]/\alpha} \right\}$$

$$= cp(1 - c)^{k-1} + cq(1 - \alpha)\alpha^{k-2} \left\{ \frac{[\alpha^{k-1} - (1 - c)^{k-1}]/\alpha^{k-2}}{\alpha - (1 - c)} \right\},$$

$$P(J_0 = k) = cp(1 - c)^{k-1} + \frac{cq(1 - \alpha)}{\alpha - (1 - c)} [\alpha^{k-1} - (1 - c)^{k-1}], \tag{7.38}$$

which gives us, in Eq. (7.38), the probability distribution for the number of errors before the first success.

Expected Number of Errors before the First Success

The expected number of errors before the first success should consist of the expected number of times in states S_0 and S_1 prior to entering either S_2 or S_3. Since all times in state S_0 are prior to times in other states, we simply require the expected total number of times in S_0, from **N**, for part of our answer.

From Eq. (7.13) we see this to be

$$E(S_0) = \frac{1}{c}. \tag{7.39}$$

The second part of the answer requires the expected number of times in S_1 before a success. We again use the technique of summing the probabilities of the event in question (presence in state S_1 prior to a success) over all possible trials, since on any trial the event either does or does not occur. We sum the probabilities of reentering S_1 repetitively, some j times, symbolized as

$$\sum_{j=1}^{\infty} [(1 - e)q]^{j-1}$$

[from Eq. (7.5)]. The probability of going to S_1, *given that an intermediate state is entered*, is simply q. (With probability p the entrance into S_1 prior to success would not occur.) The expected number of times in S_1, then, assuming that S_0 has been left, is

$$q \sum_{j=1}^{\infty} [(1 - e)q]^{j-1} = \frac{q}{1 - [(1 - e)q]},$$

$$E(S_1 \mid \text{having left } S_0) = \frac{q}{p + qe}. \tag{7.40}$$

To obtain the expected number of errors before the first success, we sum Eqs. (7.39) and (7.40):

$$E(J_0) = \frac{1}{c} + \frac{q}{p + qe}. \tag{7.41}$$

[You may wonder why we did not use cq as the transition probability to state S_1 from S_0, rather than q. The reason is that Eq. (7.41) achieves its expectation in two parts. The first is the expected number of times in S_0, and the second denotes times in S_1, assuming that S_0 has been left.]

THE PROBABILITY OF NO MORE ERRORS IN A PARTICULAR INTERMEDIATE STATE

In order to obtain the distributions for the trial of the last error and for the total number of errors, we shall find it convenient to use two other equations. One of these equations is the probability of there being no more errors made once in state S_2, which we shall symbolize as $(ne)_2$. The other is the probability of making no more errors once in state S_1, which we shall symbolize as $(ne)_1$.

Once in state S_2, the subject can make no more errors by being conditioned on that trial [with probability s, from Eq. (7.5)]; or he can stay in S_2 for one trial and then be conditioned with probability $[(1-s)p]s$; or stay there twice, and then be conditioned, with probability $[(1-s)p]^2s$; etc. To obtain $(ne)_2$, we simply sum all of the probabilities of all of these alternate ways of obtaining no more errors. This gives us Eq. (7.42).

$$(n)_2 = s + (1-s)ps + [(1-s)p]^2s + \cdots + [(1-s)p]^{\infty}s$$

$$= s \sum_{i=1}^{\infty} [(1-s)p]^{i-1}$$

$$= \frac{s}{1-(1-s)p}$$

$$(ne)_2 = \frac{s}{q+ps}. \tag{7.42}$$

Once in state S_1, the subject can make no more errors either by going to S_3 (that is, being conditioned) or by going first to state S_2 for some number of trials before going to S_3. The first of these alternatives occurs with probability e, from Eq. (7.5). The second of these occurs through a joint event. First the system moves to S_2 from S_1 [with probability $(1-e)p$, from Eq. (7.5)], and then from that state makes no more errors, as we just saw in Eq. (7.42), with probability $(ne)_2$. We therefore have as the probability of no more errors once in state S_1

$$(ne)_1 = e + (1-e)p(ne)_2$$

$$= e + \frac{(1-e)ps}{q+ps}$$

$$= \frac{qe + pes + ps - pes}{q+ps}$$

$$= \frac{ps + qe}{q+ps},$$

which, from Eq. (7.10) can be expressed as

$$(ne)_1 = \frac{\gamma}{q+ps}. \tag{7.43}$$

It is possible to obtain $(ne)_1$ and $(ne)_2$ in another way. The probability of no more errors once in a particular state can be obtained from the use of the proper entry in the matrix $\mathbf{E} - \mathbf{H}$, which is simply the matrix consisting of one in every cell minus the $\mathbf{H}$ matrix, with $\mathbf{E}$ of the same order as $\mathbf{H}$.

Since **H** gives the probabilities of returning at least once to a particular state, given that the system is already in a particular state, the matrix $\mathbf{E} - \mathbf{H}$ would give the probability of not returning to a state from a particular state. We can form the matrix $\mathbf{E} - \mathbf{H}$ with the aid of Eq. (7.14). This gives us

$$
\mathbf{E} - \mathbf{H} = \begin{pmatrix} \dfrac{\gamma}{p+qe} & \dfrac{s}{q+ps} & 1 \\[2ex] \dfrac{e}{p+qe} & \dfrac{\gamma}{q+ps} & 1 \\[2ex] \dfrac{qe}{p+qe} & \dfrac{ps}{q+ps} & c \end{pmatrix}.
\tag{7.44}
$$

The cell that is in the second row and second column, for example, can then be verbalized as "the probability of not returning to S_1, once in S_1." This statement is equivalent to having no more errors after an error. But this is our definition of $(ne)_1$. In general, for Eq. (7.44) we can note that the columns contain the probabilities of never again going to S_0, S_1, and S_2, reading from right to left. The matrix on the right-hand side of Eq. (7.44) contains an identity with $(ne)_1$ in the entry in the second column, second row, and an identity with $(ne)_2$ in the entry in the second column, top row. We thus have confirmed Eqs. (7.42) and (7.43) for $(ne)_2$ and $(ne)_1$ with the Markov chain technique, having first obtained them with the direct method.

THE DISTRIBUTION OF THE TRIAL OF THE LAST ERROR

With the aid of Eqs. (7.42) and (7.43), coupled with Eqs. (7.15) and (7.25), we can now find the probability distribution for the trial of the last error.

The last error can occur in only two states. If it occurs in state S_0, then state S_1 has to be bypassed for S_2, and no errors can occur once in state S_2 (for the last error to have occurred in state S_0). Pursuing that path of last error, we must first have the probability of an error occurring in state S_0 on some trial j, which we can obtain from the probability of being in state S_0 on trial j from Eq. (7.15). Then this last error in state S_0 occurs jointly with passage to S_2 on that trial [which Eq. (7.5) indicates occurs with probability cp], and no more errors occur, which occurs with probability $(ne)_2$, presented in Eq. (7.42). Multiplying all of the probabilities along this path for no more errors after an error on trial j would give us

$$
S_{0j}\, cp(ne)_2 = \frac{(1-c)^{j-1} cps}{(q+ps)}.
\tag{7.45}
$$

The other path would be for the last error on trial j to occur in state S_1. This requires that the subject be in S_1 on trial j, the probability of which is given in Eq. (7.25), and then that there be no more errors from this presence in state S_1, which we have obtained as $(ne)_1$ in Eq. (7.43). This would give the product

$$S_{ij}(ne)_1 = \frac{cq\gamma}{(q + ps)(c - \gamma)} [(1 - \gamma)^{j-1} - (1 - c)^{j-1}]. \qquad (7.46)$$

The answer, then, to what the equation for the probability distribution of the trial of the last error would look like is obtained from the sum of either side of Eqs. (7.45) and (7.46), as seen in Eqs. (7.47) and (7.48).

$$P(L = k) = S_{0k}\, cp(ne)_2 + S_{1k}(ne)_1. \qquad (7.47)$$

$$P(L = k) = \left[\frac{cps}{q + ps} - \frac{cq\gamma}{(q + ps)(c - \gamma)}\right](1 - c)^{k-1}$$

$$+ \frac{cq\gamma}{(q + ps)(c - \gamma)}(1 - \gamma)^{k-1}. \qquad (7.48)$$

Expected Trial of the Last Error

To obtain the expected trial of the last error, we sum the probabilities of Eq. (7.48) over all values of k, multiplying each such probability by the value of k to obtain the expectation resulting from the sum of the products of all possible random variable values, each times its probability (as suggested earlier in Chapter Two for such problems). Table 2.3 offers us the appropriate summation, which is

$$\sum_{k=1}^{\infty} k(1 - c)^{k-1} = \frac{1}{c^2}.$$

Applying this to Eq. (7.48) gives

$$\left[\frac{cps}{q + ps} - \frac{cq\gamma}{(q + ps)(c - \gamma)}\right] \sum_{k=1}^{\infty} k(1 - c)^{k-1} + \frac{cq\gamma}{(q + ps)(c - \gamma)} \sum_{k=1}^{\infty} k(1 - \gamma)^{k-1}$$

$$= \frac{ps}{c(q + ps)} - \frac{q\gamma}{c(q + ps)(c - \gamma)} + \frac{cq}{\gamma(q + ps)(c - \gamma)}$$

$$= \frac{ps}{c(q + ps)} - \frac{q\gamma^2}{c\gamma(q + ps)(c - \gamma)} + \frac{c^2 q}{c\gamma(q + ps)(c - \gamma)}$$

$$= \frac{ps}{c(q + ps)} + \frac{c^2 q - q\gamma^2}{c\gamma(q + ps)(c - \gamma)}$$

$$= \frac{ps}{c(q + ps)} + \frac{q(c^2 - \gamma^2)}{c\gamma(q + ps)(c - \gamma)}.$$

Recalling the algebraic equality $(c^2 - \gamma^2) = (c + \gamma)(c - \gamma)$, we have

$$\frac{ps}{c(q + ps)} + \frac{q(c + \gamma)}{c\gamma(q + ps)} = \frac{\gamma ps + qc + q\gamma}{c\gamma(q + ps)}$$

$$= \frac{\gamma(q + ps) + qc}{c\gamma(q + ps)}$$

which yields

$$E(L) = \frac{1}{c} + \frac{q}{\gamma(q + ps)} \tag{7.49}$$

which gives us Eq. (7.49) as the expected trial of the last error.

THE DISTRIBUTION OF TOTAL ERRORS

We shall again have to use convolutions of sums for the distribution of total errors. That is, each number of errors in the distribution can occur in all of the ways that a particular total k can be divided up between two states (S_0 and S_1). In addition, it will again be convenient to use the probabilities of no more errors, once in state S_1 [Eq. (7.43) for $(ne)_1$] and once in state S_2 [Eq. (7.42) for $(ne)_2$]. The logic is similar to that which we used for the previous two distributions discussed in this chapter. We have a first component in the sum of probabilities which indicates the probability of all of the errors occurring in state S_0. This requires being in state S_0 on some trial k, and then no more errors occurring. Equation (7.15) gives the probability of being in state S_0 on trial k. The subject then moves to an intermediate state with probability c. Once in the intermediate state, he makes a correct response with probability p, and with probability $(ne)_2$ makes no errors from that point on. These three events jointly occur with probability

$$P(T = k \mid \text{all in } S_0) = (1 - c)^{k-1} cp(ne)_2. \tag{7.50}$$

The sharing of the total of k errors in two states requires some j errors in S_0 with probability $(1 - c)^{j-1}$, followed by the subject moving to an intermediate state with probability c. The next bit of logic is slightly more complex. In the intermediate state, the probability of his moving to an errorless state and making no more errors from that point on (the case if all errors occurred in S_0) is $p(ne)_2$. If we wished the probability of this event not occurring, we would use the complement, $[1 - p(ne)_2]$. This would include all alternatives, such as going to S_1; or going to S_2 and then going to S_1; or going to S_2 several times in a row, and then going to S_1. That is, this expression would include all of the events that would be ways of additional errors occurring. We would then have three components of a complex joint event. We would have the probability of j errors in S_0, with probability $(1 - c)^{j-1}$; moving to an intermediate state, with probability c; and moving to S_1, at some point, with probability $[1 - p(ne)_2]$. That would give this joint event the probability

$$c[1 - p(ne)_2](1 - c)^{j-1}.$$

We require the probability of $k - j$ errors in S_1. One of these errors is implied in $[1 - p(ne)_2]$, since this probability implies a return to S_1 at some point. Once in S_1, the term $(ne)_1$ implies no more errors. The term $[1 - (ne)_1]$ therefore implies additional errors in S_1. For the $k - j - 1$ returns to S_1, we therefore use $[1 - (ne)_1]^{k-j-1}$, along with $(ne)_1$ for the point at which there are no more errors. The joint event of j errors in S_0 and $k - j$ errors in S_1 then has the probability

$$c[1 - p(ne)_2](1 - c)^{j-1}(ne)_1[1 - (ne)_1]^{k-j-1}.$$

We recognize that the j errors in S_0 can equal any number from 1 to $k - 1$. [The case where $j = k$ is represented in Eq. (7.50).] We shall therefore have to sum all of the probabilities represented in all of the possible values of j. This gives us Eq. (7.51) for the probability of k total errors.

$$P(T = k) = (1 - c)^{k-1}cp(ne)_2$$
$$+ \sum_{j=1}^{k-1} (1 - c)^{j-1}c[1 - p(ne)_2](ne)_1[1 - (ne)_1]^{k-j-1}. \quad (7.51)$$

We can restate Eq. (7.51) to make it easier to see the possibilities for convolution of the sum, and then carry out the convolution,

$$P(T = k) = (1 - c)^{k-1}cp(ne)_2$$
$$+ c[1 - p(ne)_2](ne)_1 \sum_{j=1}^{k-1} (1 - c)^{j-1}[1 - (ne)_1]^{k-j-1},$$

or

$$P(T = k) = (1 - c)^{k-1}cp(ne)_2$$
$$+ c[1 - p(ne)_2](ne)_1[1 - (ne)_1]^{k-2} \sum_{j=1}^{k-1} \left\{\frac{(1 - c)}{[1 - (ne)_1]}\right\}^{j-1}. \quad (7.52)$$

We can now carry out the sum implied in Eq. (7.52).

$$P(T = k) = (1 - c)^{k-1}cp(ne)_2$$
$$+ c[1 - p(ne)_2](ne)_1 \left\{\frac{[1 - (ne)_1]^{k-1} - (1 - c)^{k-1}}{c - (ne)_1}\right\}. \quad (7.53)$$

Equation (7.53) offers us the distribution of probabilities for all numbers of total errors.

Expected Number of Total Errors

To obtain the expected number of total errors, we can undertake the summation of Eq. (7.53) in a manner similar to our summation of Eq. (7.48), which gave us the expected value for the trial of the last error, in Eq. (7.49). However, this cumbersome route can be avoided, since we have $\pi_0'N$ in Eq. (7.13), which gives us the expected number of times in each state prior to absorption. We simply sum the expected number of times in states S_0 and S_1, and this offers us the expected number of total errors

$$E(T) = \frac{1}{c} + \frac{q}{\gamma}. \tag{7.54}$$

SEQUENTIAL STATISTICS

In Chapter Four, when analyzing the linear operator models, we derived equations for sequences of errors and successes. We can do this for the finite Markov chain model as well. We can use the theorems derived by Bush (1959) and explicated in Chapter Four for obtaining such statistics as the expected number of runs of errors without regard to size, called R_n in Eq. (4.66), and the expected number of runs of errors of length j, called r_{jn} in Eq. (4.65).

In Chapter Four, we defined the symbol

$$u_{jn} = \sum_{i=1}^{n-j+1} x_i x_{i+1} x_{i+2} \cdots x_{i+j-1}, \tag{7.55}$$

where x is a random variable equal to 1 or 0 in the case of error or success, respectively. The value of u_{jn} will therefore be 1 or 0 for each component of the sum in Eq. (7.55), depending on whether or not all i of the trials whose random variable values are being multiplied in each component of the sum yield an error, or whether even one of them yields a success (respectively). [It may help to point out that the sum in Eq. (7.55) is made up of products of precisely j random variable values. If $n = 10$, then the sequence being examined is 10 trials long, with 10 x values, each of which is either 1 or 0. We take the first of these and multiply it against $j - 1$ adjacent x values (to the right). That is one component of the sum. We then begin with the second x and multiply it against $j - 1$ adjacent x values (to the right) to obtain the second component in the sum; and so on. The process stops after we have begun with the $(n - j + 1)$st x value. That is the last value in a set of n values that will still have $j - 1$ values to the right of it.]

There are many ways in which j consecutive errors can occur. We sum the probabilities of all of them to obtain the probability of a sequence of errors j in length.

If the first error for the string of j x values being multiplied happens to occur in state S_1, then all of the following x values would naturally be expected to occur in S_1, since the system cannot return to S_0. So to obtain this probability, we obtain the product of the probabilities of the joint events necessary for the system to be in state S_1 on some trial k (that is, $i = k$) to be the first trial in the sequence of j trials (x values) being examined. We require the probability of being in S_1 on trial k [from Eq. (7.25)] and the probability of returning to S_1 $j - 1$ consecutive times [from Eq. (7.5)], which yields

$$P(S_{1k})[q(1 - e)]^{j-1}.$$

If the first error were to occur in S_0, we could similarly obtain the probability of j consecutive errors in S_0 as

$$P(S_0)(1 - c)^{i-1}.$$

We confront the need for a convolution when we attempt to sum all of the probabilities of some number of errors in S_0 and the remainder in S_1. The resulting equation to be summed by convolution would look like

$$
\begin{aligned}
E(u_{jn}) = {}& P(S_{0k})(1 - c)^{j-1} \\
& + P(S_{0k})(1 - c)^{j-2}cq + P(S_{0k})(1 - c)^{j-3}cq[(1 - e)q] \\
& + P(S_{0k})(1 - c)^{j-4}cq[(1 - e)q]^2 + \cdots \\
& + P(S_{0k})(1 - c)^{j-m}cq[(1 - e)q]^{m-2} + \cdots \\
& + P(S_{0k})cq[(1 - e)q]^{j-2} + P(S_{1k})[(1 - e)]^{j-1}.
\end{aligned}
\tag{7.56}
$$

We can separate out the first and last components of the sum in Eq. (7.56) and use the summation sign to simplify the equation.

$$
\begin{aligned}
E(u_{jn}) = {}& P(S_{0k})(1 - c)^{j-1} + P(S_{1k})[(1 - e)q]^{j-1} \\
& + cq \sum_{i=1}^{j-1} P(S_{0k})(1 - c)^{j-i-1}[(1 - e)q]^{i-1}.
\end{aligned}
\tag{7.57}
$$

For simplicity, we return to symbolizing

$$\alpha = [(1 - e)q].$$

We therefore restate Eq. (7.57) as

$$
E(u_{jn}) = P(S_{0k})(1 - c)^{j-1} + P(S_{1k})\alpha^{j-1} + cq(S_{0k}) \sum_{i=1}^{j-1} (1 - c)^{j-i-1}\alpha^{i-1}.
\tag{7.58}
$$

We can convolute the sum after the summation sign in Eq. (7.58).

$$\sum_{i=1}^{j-1}(1-c)^{j-i-1}\alpha^{i-1} = (1-c)^{j-2}\sum_{i=1}^{j-1}(1-c)^{-i+1}\alpha^{i-1}$$

$$= (1-c)^{j-2}\sum_{i=1}^{j-1}\left[\frac{\alpha}{(1-c)}\right]^{i-1}$$

$$= (1-c)^{j-2}\left\{\frac{1-[\alpha/(1-c)]^{j-1}}{1-[\alpha/(1-c)]}\right\}$$

$$= (1-c)^{j-2}\left\{\frac{[(1-c)^{j-1}-\alpha^{j-1}]/(1-c)^{j-1}}{[(1-c)-\alpha]/(1-c)}\right\}$$

$$= \frac{(1-c)^{j-1}-\alpha^{j-1}}{(1-c)-\alpha}.$$

Reentering Eq. (7.58) with this result, we have

$$E(u_{jn}) = P(S_{0k})(1-c)^{j-1} + P(S_{1k})\alpha^{j-1} + cqP(S_{0k})\left[\frac{(1-c)^{j-1}-\alpha^{j-1}}{(1-c)-\alpha}\right].$$

$$(7.59)$$

We wish the expected value of u_{jn} from $n = 1$ to ∞, over all starting trials k, to obtain expectations for the entire experiment. We therefore sum over all k for S_{0k} and S_{1k} in Eq. (7.59) [taking $\sum P(S_{0k})$ and $\sum P(S_{1k})$ from Eq. (7.13)], and obtain the expectation over all trials for $u_{j\infty}$ in Eq. (7.60).

$$\sum_{k=1}^{\infty} E(u_{j\infty}) = \frac{(1-c)^{j-1}}{c} + \frac{q\alpha^{j-1}}{\gamma} + \frac{q[(1-c)^{j-1}-\alpha^{j-1}]}{(1-c)-\alpha}. \qquad (7.60)$$

We can now use Eq. (7.60) to obtain the components needed for R_∞, $r_{1\infty}$, etc.

Obtaining the Total Number of Runs R_∞

From Eq. (4.72),

$$R_\infty = u_{1,\infty} - u_{2,\infty}.$$

From Eq. (7.60) we have

$$u_{1\infty} = \frac{1}{c} + \frac{q}{\gamma} + 0,$$

$$u_{2\infty} = \frac{1-c}{c} + \frac{q\alpha}{\gamma} + \frac{q[(1-c)-\alpha]}{(1-c)-\alpha}.$$

We now subtract the value of $u_{2\infty}$ from $u_{1\infty}$ to obtain R_∞.

$$R_\infty = \frac{1}{c} + \frac{q}{\gamma} - \frac{1}{c} + 1 - \frac{q\alpha}{\gamma} - q$$

$$= \frac{q}{\gamma} + p - \frac{q\alpha}{\gamma},$$

$$R_\infty = p + \frac{q(1-\alpha)}{\gamma}. \tag{7.61}$$

Equation (7.61) for R_∞ gives us the expected number of runs of errors of all sizes that we should anticipate in data expected to conform to this four-state Markov chain model of avoidance conditioning, implied in Eq. (7.5).

Obtaining the Total Number of Runs $r_{j\infty}$ of a Particular Size j

For runs of any single size, such as $r_{1\infty}$, which would be the number of occurrences of single isolated errors (errors surrounded by at least one success before and after), we would use Eq. (4.75).

$$r_{j\infty} = u_{j\infty} - 2u_{j+1,\,\infty} + u_{j+2,\,\infty}.$$

We enter Eq. (4.75) with the results of Eq. (7.60), applying this to deriving $r_{1\infty}$.

$$r_{1\infty} = u_{1,\infty} - 2u_{2,\infty} + u_{3,\infty},$$

$$r_{1\infty} = \left[\frac{1}{c} + \frac{q}{\gamma} + 0\right] - 2\left[\frac{(1-c)}{c} + \frac{q\alpha}{\gamma} + q\right]$$

$$+ \left[\frac{(1-c)^2}{c} + \frac{q\alpha^2}{\gamma} + \frac{q\{(1-c)^2 - \alpha^2\}}{(1-c) - \alpha}\right]$$

$$= \frac{q(1-\alpha)^2}{\gamma} - \frac{1}{c} + 2 - 2q + \frac{(1-c)^2}{c} + \frac{q[(1-c)^2 - \alpha^2]}{(1-c) - \alpha},$$

$$r_{1\infty} = c - 2q + \frac{q(1-\alpha)^2}{\gamma} + \frac{q[(1-c)^2 - \alpha^2]}{(1-c) - \alpha}. \tag{7.62}$$

Equation (7.62) can now be used to obtain the expected number of occurrences of single isolated errors in this model. Similarly, Eq. (4.75) can be used for obtaining all other desired sizes of error runs.

In our sequential analysis, we now have the means of obtaining the expected number of runs of errors of all lengths and the expected number of runs of errors of each particular length. Another interesting sequential statistic is the expected number of times that an error follows a success. (We should, for example, anticipate that such a statistic should have a larger expectation when successful trials contribute little to learning, or a correspondingly smaller value when successful trials are assumed to contribute a great deal to learning.)

Expected Number of Times That an Error Will Follow a Success

The logic for the derivation of this statistic is simpler than that for many of the preceding statistics. The only condition under which an error can follow a success is in the intermediate states. The total number of times in the intermediate states will be expected to be

$$\frac{p}{\gamma} + \frac{q}{\gamma} = \frac{1}{\gamma}$$

from Eq. (7.13). This can also be obtained by summing the probability of being in state S_1 or state S_2 (the sum of their respective probabilities) over all trials, from Eqs. (7.25) and (7.26). This will also come to $1/\gamma$.

The probability of having a success while in the intermediate states is p. This puts the subject in state S_2, and the probability of having an error while in S_2 is $q(1 - s)$. We then have, for each of the expected number of trials in the intermediate states, an expectation of $pq(1 - s)$ that there will be an error followed by a success. Multiplying this probability by the number of times that we expect the system to be in the intermediate states will give us the expected number of success followed by errors.

$$\bar{d}_1 = \frac{pq(1 - s)}{\gamma}. \tag{7.63}$$

Parameter Estimation

We looked at parameter estimation fleetingly in Chapter Two, when estimating c in Bower's model. We also estimated parameters in Chapter Four, for a linear operator model. We now illustrate parameter estimation in the current model.

For illustrative purposes, we shall use the data of the last 20 animals run by Theios and Brelsford in their control group. These data were presented in the Appendix of their 1966 article in the *Journal of Mathematical Psychology*, and are shown in Table 7.1.

ALGEBRAIC SOLUTIONS

We shall require the values of four parameters: p (from which we can obtain $q = 1 - p$), c, e, and s. We shall use a handy, though perhaps biased, empirical estimate of p, to reduce the number of more complexly estimated

TABLE 7.1

Last 20 Rats from the Control Group of Theios and Brelsford (1966)[a]

Rat		Rat	
147	1 0 1 1 1 1	157	1 1 1 0 0 1
148	1 1	158	1 1 1
149	1	159	1
150	1 1 1 1	160	1 1 1 0 1
151	1 1 1	161	1 1 1
152	1 1 0 0 0 1 0 0 1 0 1	162	1
153	1 1 1 1 1 1	163	1 1 0 0 0 1 0 1
154	1	164	1 1 1 1 1 1 1
155	1 0 0 1 1 0 1 1	165	1 1 0 0 1
156	1 1 0 0 1	166	1 1 1

[a] A 1 represents an error and a 0 represents a successful avoidance. Each animal was run to a criterion of 10 consecutive successful avoidances. A run of 10 zeros therefore follows all of the tabled data, and it is assumed that further testing would elicit only zeros.

parameters to three. Our estimate of p is based on our assumption that the subject cannot make a successful response until he is out of state S_0 and cannot make an error once he is in state S_3. The responses, then, between the first success and last error are responses in the intermediate states, where the probability of a correct response is p. We estimate p to be the proportion of these responses that are success responses.

The problem of bias is created by the fact that there can be a number of error responses that are in the intermediate states, but occur immediately and successively right after S_0, in an entrance into S_1 before any entrance into S_2. These errors would not follow a success, so would not be included in the tally of errors for our estimate, though they occur in one of the intermediate states. In addition, if the subject, while in the intermediate states, goes to S_2 and stays there for a succession of responses, and then goes from that state immediately to absorption in S_3, this last burst of successes will not be counted in the proportion of successes in the intermediate states, although they should also be included for an unbiased estimate of p. It is of course possible that these two sources of bias could cancel each other out. The proportion of successes between the first success and the last failure is more accurately equated with $[p(1-s)]/[1-(ps+qe)]$.† This is equal to

† This estimate is due to J. Greeno, cited in Bower and Theios (1964, footnote, p. 9), where a typographical error incorrectly presented the denominator term as a numerator.

p when $e = s$. Our explication of a technique for the estimation of the other parameters will be much clearer if we can assume the simpler equality. We can then get a direct empirical estimate of p, which we can use in the estimation of the remaining parameters.

From Table 7.1 we count the number of successes between the first correct response and last error for all subjects, and then the total of responses between the first correct response and the last error, and state this as a fraction for obtaining the proportion of correct responses.

There will be instances in which there will be no successes between the first correct response and last error. These subjects will simply not contribute to our estimate.

Let us look at Table 7.1. We begin *after* the first zero, and count all of the zeros thereafter, prior to the last number one (the last error). As an example, subject number 147 would have zero correct responses to contribute to the total of all subjects' correct responses between the first correct response and last error. However, he would have three responses to contribute to the total of all subjects' responses between the first correct response and last error. Subject 152 would have five correct responses to contribute to the number of correct responses for the numerator of our estimate of p, and a total of seven responses as the total of all responses to contribute to the pool of total responses for the denominator of our proportion. Proceeding in this way over all subjects, we would find that we had a total of 22 responses between the first correct response and last error, and 13 correct responses between the first correct response and last error. Therefore,

$$p = .59 \tag{7.64}$$

and

$$q = (1 - p) = .41. \tag{7.65}$$

We now proceed to develop estimates of the remaining three parameters. We require three equations for this purpose. We shall use Eqs. (7.41), (7.54), and (7.63). We shall equate theoretical values and empirical values of the quantities defined in those equations. With proper isolation of the parameters of interest within each equation, we shall find estimated values for the unknown parameters.

For Eq. (7.41), we require a count of the average number of errors before the first success, from Table 7.1. We find the total of such errors over the 20 subjects to be 51, giving an average number of 2.55. Therefore,

$$E(J_0) = 2.55. \tag{7.66}$$

We can also count the total number of errors $E(T)$. We find this to be 68. Taken over the 20 subjects, we have

$$E(T) = 3.40. \tag{7.67}$$

Finally, we can look at the number of successes that are followed by errors on the immediately following trial shown in Table 7.1. This turns out to be 12, which gives us the equation

$$\bar{d}_1 = .60. \tag{7.68}$$

Our next step is to isolate the parameters, to take advantage of these preceding statements of theoretical and empirical equivalence. We begin by combining Eqs. (7.41), (7.45), and (7.63) in the following way.

$$\frac{\bar{d}_1}{E(T) - E(J_0)} = p + qe. \tag{7.69}$$

Since we assume that we already have p (and q), we can use Eq. (7.69) to find the value of e. From Eqs. (7.64) through (7.68), we can restate Eq. (7.69) as

$$\frac{.60}{3.40 - 2.55} = .59 + .41e,$$
$$.71 - .59 = .41e,$$
$$e = .29. \tag{7.70}$$

We now have p, q, and e. To obtain c, we can restate Eq. (7.41) in a manner that isolates c. That is,

$$\frac{1}{c} = E(J_0) - \frac{q}{p + qe},$$
$$c = \frac{1}{E(J_0) - [q/(p + qe)]}$$
$$= \frac{1}{2.55 - [.41/(.59 + .41 \cdot .29)]}$$
$$= \frac{1}{1.97},$$
$$c = .51. \tag{7.71}$$

We now have all of the parameters except s. We can obtain s by restating Eq. (7.54):

$$\frac{q}{ps + qe} = E(T) - \frac{1}{c},$$
$$\frac{ps + qe}{q} = \frac{1}{E(T) - 1/c},$$
$$ps = \frac{q}{E(T) - 1/c} - qe,$$
$$s = \frac{q}{p}\left[\frac{1}{E(T) - 1/c} - e\right]. \tag{7.72}$$

From Eqs. (7.54), (7.64), (7.65), (7.70), and (7.71), we restate Eq. (7.72) as

$$s = \frac{.41}{.59} \left[\frac{1}{3.40 - 1.97} - .29 \right],$$

$$s = .28, \tag{7.73}$$

which completes our parameter estimations.

We can now place our parameter estimations into equations for which we have not yet computed the empirical values, and check the theoretical values against the empirical values. As an example, let us do this with Eqs. (7.10) and (7.49):

$$E(L) = \frac{1}{c} + \frac{q}{(ps + qe)(q + ps)}$$

$$= \frac{1}{.51} + \frac{.41}{(.59 \cdot .28 + .41 \cdot .29)(.41 + .59 \cdot .28)},$$

$$E(L) = 4.47 \quad \text{(predicted value)}. \tag{7.74}$$

We can now go on to Table 7.1 and compute the actual average trial of the last error. Totaling all of the trials of the last error, we obtain 89. Dividing by 20, we find that the result is

$$E(L) = 4.45 \quad \text{(empirical value)}. \tag{7.75}$$

Comparing Eqs. (7.74) and (7.75), we have to conclude that our prediction is quite close to the empirical value. A precise measure of good fit is discussed later.

We can test the predictions of other theoretical equations. For example, in our sequential analysis, we derived an equation for the expected total of all runs of errors (regardless of size) for each subject, in Eq. (7.61). We can again go to Table 7.1 for the empirical count of these events, divide the totals by 20, and obtain the empirical average. Then we can compare these empirical values with the values obtained by entering our parameter estimates into Eq. (7.61).

For Eq. (7.61) we would have

$$R = 1.61 \quad \text{(predicted value)},$$
$$R = 1.60 \quad \text{(empirical value)}.$$

Similarly, for Eq. (7.62), we would have

$$r_1 = .74 \quad \text{(predicted value)},$$
$$r_1 = .75 \quad \text{(empirical value)}.$$

The latter two predictions also support the model.

In the general literature, the four-state Markov model has tended to model the avoidance conditioning paradigm quite well (Bower and Theios, 1964; Theios and Brelsford, 1966). It is somewhat surprising, however, that we have been able to successfully predict details here with such accuracy, given such a small sample of data (20 subjects). A small sample implies a relatively large variance for a measure based on that sample. Therefore some of the predicted values should vary more from their empirical counterparts.

The method of parameter estimation used in our example was taken from Bower and Theios (1964). The method used by Theios and Brelsford (1966) was first discussed in detail by Atkinson and Crothers (1964). We shall give a brief description of this technique below. For the present model it has the advantage of avoiding the possible bias introduced by our simplified empirical estimate of p.

MINIMIZING CHI SQUARE FOR EXPECTED RESPONSE SEQUENCES

We begin by predicting the actual sequences of trials. That is, the theory yields the probability of an error on the first trial, the probability of an error on both the first and second trial, etc. We use the theory, then, to predict a set of of specific sequences. If we limit ourselves to a small enough number of trials, we can predict all possible sequences over those trials. For example, if we took a sequence of four trials, there would be 16 possible sequences of zeros and one. That is, since each trial has only one of two possible outcomes, there would be $2^n = 2^4 = 16$ sequences possible over $n = 4$ trials. The first trial in the experiment is always an error trial (in our theory and in our paradigm), so we can include the first five trials of the experiment in the $2^n = 16$ possible beginning sequences. Looking at Table 7.1, we see that the first five responses constitute a very large proportion of the data for sampling the patterns of responding.

Our 16 possible sequences would range from all errors to four correct, and include all combinations of $5 - k$ errors and k successes, with $0 \le k \le 4$, and an error on the first trial.

We can use the direct method to state the probability of each such possible sequence. For example, for five errors in trials 1–5, we would have

$$P_1 = P(1\ 1\ 1\ 1) = (1 - c)^4 + (1 - c)^3 cq + (1 - c)^2 cq^2(1 - e)$$
$$+ (1 - c)cq^3(1 - e)^2 + cq^4(1 - e)^3.$$

For four errors with a correct response on the fifth trial, we have

$$P_2 = P(1\ 1\ 1\ 1\ 0) = (1 - c)^3 cp + (1 - c)^2 cpq(1 - e) + (1 - c)^2 cqe$$
$$+ (1 - c)cq^2 e(1 - e) + (1 - c)cpq^2(1 - e)^2$$
$$+ cq^3 e(1 - e)^2 + cpq^3(1 - e)^3.$$

We then continue in like manner for all 16 possibilities from P_1 to P_{16}. Each of these 16 equations offers the probability of a particular sequence over the first five trials. Were we then to multiply each probability by the number of animals run in the experiment, we would have the expected number of times that that sequence should appear [according to the implications of Eq. (7.5) and assuming that we had the correct values for our parameters]. We can symbolize each such expectation as

$$E'(Y_i) = 20P_i,$$

where i is any number from 1 to 16 and Y is the number of occurrences of the ith sequence. [Our use of the coefficient of 20 applies to our example only. Usually, we would deal with larger amounts of data.]

Were we to subtract from each expectation $E'(Y_i)$ the observed number for each particular sequence $O(Y_i)$, we would have

$$E'(Y_i) - O(Y_i),$$

which we could state as the difference between the expected number of occurrences of a particular sequence and the observed number of times that that sequence occurred. We could then square this difference for each sequence, divide it by the expectation $E'(Y_i)$, and sum the results over all of the 16 sequences. We would then have, in Eq. (7.76), a value

$$\chi^2 = \sum_{i=1}^{16} \frac{[E'(Y_i) - O(Y_i)]^2}{E'(Y_i)} \tag{7.76}$$

which would distribute itself according to a known distribution, the chi-square distribution, with 11 degrees of freedom. (The basis of degrees of freedom is discussed later.) As long as the observed values $O(Y_i)$ are generated by (are sampled from) a distribution with expectation $E'(Y_i)$ for each i, then Eq. (7.76) will indeed be distributed as chi square. When this assumption is not met, Eq. (7.76) will most probably produce a value that will be seen to be unlikely, in a chi-square table.

The degrees of freedom include the number of sequences being compared (in our case 16) minus the usual 1, but additionally minus the number of parameters that had to be estimated (4 in our case), giving us the 11 degrees of freedom referred to in the preceding paragraph.

An important use of Eq. (7.76) is that it offers minimal values as $E'(Y_i)$ approaches $O(Y_i)$. By alternately fitting different sets of parameter values into the P_i values used in each $E'(Y_i)$, different values of chi square can be obtained. This suggests that a minimization of chi square is a means of obtaining "best fit" parameter values. The term best fit refers to finding parameter values for the theoretical expressions such that the predicted values $E'(Y_i)$ collectively come closest to the observed values $O(Y_i)$, in comparison with any alternative set of parameter values.

It is possible to program a computer so that it alternately tries different parameter values, arriving at a set of parameter values offering the minimal chi-square values for the set of equations $E'(Y_i)$ and the obtained data $O(Y_i)$. This method, then, offers an alternative way of obtaining parameter values.

Suppose that we had obtained a chi-square value of 19.7 in our example of 16 equations for all of the possible sequences for the first five responses (where we were estimating four parameters). Our model would be rejected at the .05 level, based on tabled significance values of chi-square for 11 degrees of freedom. Let us assume, however, that we had had to estimate only one parameter rather than four and had obtained the same chi-square value. The degrees of freedom would then be $16 - 1 - 1 = 14$. A chi-square table would then indicate a chance probability of between .10 and .20 at the now appropriate 14 degrees of freedom. Note that we are testing for any question as to the validity of the null hypothesis (of no difference between the observed and expected distributions). Therefore, we would probably consider an event that is as infrequent as once or twice in 10 samples from a distribution as a basis for questioning the theory's validity, despite the lack of statistical significance at more familiar criterion values.

It is possible to compare several theories, where each theory has achieved its parameter estimation by having reached its minimal chi-square value. This minimal chi-square value is the closest that the theory can come to the data (the obtained sequences) by appropriate manipulation of parameter values. Therefore, this obtained minimal chi-square value represents the best agreement that could be obtained between the theoretical and empirical facts for that theory and that particular listing of response sequences. The theory with the lowest chi-square value is thus the one that most closely mirrors the actual data. The use, then, of the minimal chi-square method for parameter estimation, using sequences of data, offers both the parameter estimates and a comparison among alternative theories of the same data.

When different numbers of parameters are estimated in the different theories, some allowance should be made for this. More parameters offer more chances for matching the data, offering more chances to reduce the chi-square value than in a theory with less parameters. Compensation for this can be obtained by entering the chi-square table with the obtained values at the appropriate degrees of freedom, and comparing probabilities of chi-square values rather than the actual chi-square values. More parameters reduce the degrees of freedom, making smaller values less meaningful. That is, a small chi-square value with, say, 7 degrees of freedom, is designated as more likely, in a chi-square table, than with 8 degrees of freedom.

Further Uses of Chi Square

Let us assume that there are additional data, beyond the first five trials, and that the parameter values are constant over the duration of the experiment. Then the parameters obtained by the minimization of chi square can be used to predict the values for additional theoretical equations, precisely as we did with Eq. (7.74), using our algebraically derived parameter estimates. If the parameter values derived from the first five trials of the experiment predict the trial of the last error, then, depending on how far past the five trials this predicted value is, to that degree the correct prediction would be impressive.

It is possible to use the parameters to predict distributions as well as only expectations. For example, we could use Eq. (7.48) for the distribution of the last error and enter it with our estimated parameters. Let us use the parameters that we obtained with the algebraic method, since the same parameters could, theoretically, have been obtained by both methods. The equation for distribution of the last error, with our parameters inserted into Eq. (7.48), would be

$$P(L = k) = (-.311)(.49)^{k-1} + (.457)(.289)^{k-1}. \tag{7.77}$$

In Table 7.2 we list the values of Eq. (7.77) for k equals 1 to 7 and above. Next to it, we list the number of subjects out of 166 subjects that are expected to have their trial of last error for each k value. We use 166 because that is the total number of subjects run in the Theios and Brelsford control group, and the method that we are examining would not be valid for only 20 subjects. [The reason it would not be valid is that we need more than one or two cases as the expected number in any class (for any k value). In fact, more than five

TABLE 7.2

Expected and Observed Frequencies for Trial of the Last Error

Trial of last error	Probability value from Eq. (7.77)	Expected number $E(Y_i)$	Observed number $O(Y_i)$
1	.146	24.2	22
2	.175	29.1	37
3	.159	26.4	32
4	.131	21.7	19
5	.102	16.9	15
6	.077	12.7	14
7	.058	9.6	7
>7	.148	24.6	20

is desirable. This is why, even with 166 subjects, we have combined the small expected frequency events ($k > 7$) into one class.]

The last column in Table 7.2 is the actual number of subjects out of the 166 in the Theios and Brelsford control group having each k value as the trial of the last error.

To recapitulate, we have taken all subjects run in an experiment and asked in which one of several mutually exclusive classes each subject fit (which trial of the last error). The discrepancies between observed and predicted frequencies in each class are then treated as in Eq. (7.76).

We use Eq. (7.76) to test whether the obtained data (the last column in Table 7.2) could reasonably be expected to have been generated by a theoretical distribution such as we obtained with Eq. (7.77). We sum Eq. (7.76) over all eight points in the distribution, and enter the chi-square table with $8 - 1 = 7$ degress of freedom. We find that our chi-square value of 5.75 is consistent with the distribution of Eq. (7.76): 50–75% of samples from such a distribution would be expected to give a chi-square value of 5.75 or more. Therefore, there is no reason to doubt the compatibility of our theoretical and empirical distributions.

Theios and Brelsford presented the predictions of their model for the expected number of total errors. As indicated above, they obtained their parameters by minizing chi square for response sequences over the first five trials. We present their predictions and the data for the distribution of the total number of errors per subject in Table 7.3.

We can again apply Eq. (7.76) to the discrepancies between the observed and expected values. The comparison is over eight points, suggesting 7

TABLE 7.3

Expected and Observed Frequencies for Total Errors per Subject[a]

Total number of errors	Expected number of subjects	Observed number of subjects
1	24.9	22
2	48.8	46
3	38.0	38
4	24.1	27
5	13.9	19
6	7.7	7
7	4.1	3
> 7	4.1	4

[a] Abstracted from Theios and Brelsford (1966, Table 7, p. 153).

degrees of freedom. However, much of the data used for the computation of Table 7.3 was also used in the minimization of chi square to obtain the four parameter estimates. This suggests that a conservative $7 - 1 - 4 = 3$ degrees of freedom might be more appropriate. Computing the chi-square value, we find it to be 3.08, which is within the expected range even with the more conservative degrees of freedom.

[Theios and Breksford used the Kolmogorov–Smirnov one-sample goodness-of-fit test instead of the chi-square test. The Kolmogorov–Smirnov test is described with great clarity in Siegel (1956). We have chosen to detail the chi-square test here because it is applicable to all of the examples in this section.]

Chapter Eight

Observable States and
Identifiable Parameters

In Chapter Two we indicated that one of the advantages of mathematical model analyses was that we could identify such things as the probability of entry into unobservable states (the value c in Bower's one-element paired-associate learning theory was the example used). A long battle has been waged between those psychologists who believe that the inner unobservable happenings are the most critical events for psychologists to study and those who believe that the unobservable is unacceptable in a science of psychology. The behaviorist revolution in psychology has, in a sense, been an attempt to see how far predictions could go, with the exclusion of postulated unseen events. Our psychodynamically oriented clinical colleagues have depended heavily on unobservable intervening variables to explain the observable. A position somewhere between these two is more generally found among most experimentalists, who (like Hull) are willing to allow intervening explanatory events, providing that these are unambiguously tied to observable events at both the stimulus and response ends of the experimental paradigms.

Since the invention of intervening variables does offer an easy way of rescuing any theoretical position from empirical embarrassment, there is legitimate cause for concern in its unrestricted use.

It is the possibility of observing inner events through changes in parameter values in models, changing their status from unobservables to observables, that gives mathematical models of theories such an important role in theoretical development. That is, a model will yield formulas for probabilities of

events, within which may be included parameters representing the probabilities of occurrence of some postulated inner events. Estimating these
inner-event parameter values, the experimenter can then manipulate the
experimental conditions in ways that his theory predicts should change the
probabilities of the unseen events. Reestimation of the parameter values subsequent to the experimental manipulations should offer either confirmation or
disconfirmation of the theory's assumptions as to factors affecting these inner
happenings. In this way statements about these intervening events can be
tested. When the probabilities of occurrence of "unseen" events can be
monitored, the events can then be considered to be under observation.

Parameter estimation, then, is a critical topic for those who wish to examine their theories with the aid of mathematical models. We gave some
examples of parameter estimation and illustrated some estimation techniques
in Chapter Seven. We shall explicate another technique in this chapter. Most
of the discussions of techniques for parameter estimation are contained within
the statistical literature, and extensive discussions can be found in any text
on mathematical statistics. A general discussion of parameter estimation that
is directly relevant to mathematical models in psychology has been written
by Bush (1963). There are also introductory discussions in Restle and Greeno
(1970, Chapter 9) and Atkinson, Bower, and Crothers (1965, Chapter 9).
An original and important discussion has been contributed by Greeno and
Steiner (1964; 1968) and Greeno (1968). The material following in this chapter
has relied heavily on the Greeno and Steiner work, and is an attempt to com-
municate the gist of their work without detailing their extensive proofs. Their
work is concerned with parameter estimation in paradigms analyzable with
Markov chain theory. This chapter can be seen as a further, more advanced
discussion of the Markov chain material presented in Chapters Six and
Seven.

A Theory with Nonobservable States

In Bower's one-element model of paired-associate learning, we had, in the
expanded matrix version, three states. They were the conditioned state (C),
the guessing without error state $(\bar{E} \cap G)$, and the guessing with error state
$(E \cap G)$. The matrix is reproduced in Eq. (8.1).

$$\mathbf{P} = \begin{array}{c} \\ C \\ (\bar{E}_n \cap G_n) \\ (E_n \cap G_n) \end{array} \begin{array}{cccc} C_{n+1} & (\bar{E}_{n+1} \cap G_{n+1}) & (E_{n+1} \cap G_{n+1}) \\ 1 & 0 & 0 \\ c & p(1-c) & q(1-c). \\ c & p(1-c) & q(1-c) \end{array} \qquad (8.1)$$

There are two parameters in the model (remembering that $p = 1 - q$), if
we can assume that the initial trial probabilities are $[0 \; p \; q]$.

Let us ask what the theory suggests as the various possible sequences of events when a subject is run in an experiment to which the theory would apply. The answer would consist of a set of sequences, where each sequence would be a sequence of two-tuples. That is, each sequence would be a sequence of couplets of random variable values (a variable value for guessing or conditioned, and a variable value for error or no error). The random variable values for each one of the two dichotomous possibilities could be taken as 0 or 1, yielding a pair of such values for each trial. Here we shall simply represent the variables by symbols for the outcomes. Any one trial could then have an outcome of (G, E) or $(G, \bar{E})$ or $(C, \bar{E})$, with (C, E) *not* being a possibility, according to the axioms of Bower's theory. One example of a sequence of events for successive trials would be

$$\{(G, E); (G, E); (G, \bar{E}); (G, \bar{E}); (C, \bar{E}); \ldots; (C, \bar{E})\}$$

and another would be

$$\{(G, E); (G, E); (C, \bar{E}); (C, \bar{E}); (C, \bar{E}); \ldots; (C, \bar{E})\}.$$

We could state all possible variations in sequences of two-tuples (assuming some finite number of trials to be run), and this would constitute the sample space of theoretical outcomes of the running of a subject. However, looking again at the two examples of sequences just given, you might recognize that there would be no *behavioral* distinction between the two theoretically different outcomes that we selected as hypothetical examples. That is, both examples would appear, in data form, as a sequence of one-tuples. They are both equivalent to

$$\{(E); (E); (\bar{E}); (\bar{E}); (\bar{E}); \ldots; (\bar{E})\}.$$

In fact, there are a number of theoretical sequences of two-tuples that would be behaviorally equivalent to the one-tuple sequence just presented.

What we have in this example is an instance in which a theory postulates one observable state [the guessing-with-error state, which would be indexed in a sequence of two-tuples as (G, E)] but also postulates two other states, which in some instances are not distinguishable from each other [behaviorally, we would, in many cases, confuse the two-tuples $(G, \bar{E})$ and $(C, \bar{E})$]. We can conclude that a subject was in the guessing-without-error state if at some point later in the sequence there is an error. But if the guessing without error occurs after the last error in the sequence, there is no way to determine when the guessing state has been left and the conditioned state entered. We cannot distinguish the two different states that could accompany a correct response, so that the two states are not observable. We therefore state that the theory is not an observable states theory.

It happens that in the case of finite Markov chain theories with some non-observable states, a behaviorally equivalent observable states theory can often be developed (Greeno and Steiner, 1964; Greeno, 1968).

An Example of Conversion to an Observable States Theory

We will examine a very general one-stage learning theory, with stationary transition probabilities, whose states are not all observable. The matrix of transition probabilities for the theory is shown in Eq. (8.2).

$$\mathbf{P} = \begin{array}{c} \\ L_n \\ E_n \\ S_n \end{array} \begin{array}{ccc} L_{n+1} & E_{n+1} & S_{n+1} \\ 1 & 0 & 0 \\ d & (1-d)t & (1-d)s \\ c & (1-c)q & (1-c)p \end{array} \tag{8.2}$$

where $t = (1 - s)$, and $q = (1 - p)$, and the initial probability vector = $[\pi_L \ \pi_E \ \pi_S]$.

State L refers to the subject having permanently learned (been conditioned), which is assumed to imply no more possibility of errors. State E refers to the subject having made an error. State S refers to the subject having been correct (successful) prior to having been conditioned. States L and S are not always distinguishable.

To develop the new observable states theory, we try to identify a set of states that will be a complete partitioning of all possible observable outcomes in the paradigm. At the same time, we attempt to relate each of these states to the original states, as shown in the following paragraph.

The foregoing description of states S, L, and E suggests that the success state S can be distinguished from the conditioned state L if there is an error later in the sequence that the experimenter is examining. Thus, *some* success state entries could be observed. (We assume that the experimenter will eventually have the complete sequence of responses available to him.) It is also clear that state E is observable at any point in the experiment. Consequently, in constructing an equivalent observable states model, we could include both an error state and a state for a success prior to the last error. Following Greeno and Steiner, we shall symbolize the new constricted success state as S' in our new theory and the error state as R. Our new theory then has all possible observable events categorized, with the exception of successful responses after the last error in the sequence of an individual subject's responses. We symbolize this remaining set of possible outcomes (a success after the last error) as A. (Note that state A consists of our old state L plus part of the old state S.) These three new states A, R, and S' are an exhaustive, mutually exclusive categorization of the observable events making up a sequence of correct and incorrect responses. We express the matrix of the transition probabilities between these states, in a very general way, in Eq. (8.3).

$$\mathbf{P} = \begin{array}{c} \\ A_n \\ R_n \\ S_n{}' \end{array} \begin{array}{ccc} A_{n+1} & R_{n+1} & S'_{n+1} \\ P_{aa} & P_{ar} & P_{as'} \\ P_{ra} & P_{rr} & P_{rs'} \\ P_{s'a} & P_{s'r} & P_{s's'} \end{array} . \qquad (8.3)$$

We now need to determine the transition probabilities of (8.3) for the model of this new observable states theory in terms of the parameters of (8.2). Much of the theoretical burden of the Greeno–Steiner work is to prove that the induced process (8.3) is also a Markov chain. We shall simply take this result for granted.

RECURRENT EVENTS RESET THE SYSTEM

By recognizing the components of the old states in the new states, we can state the transition probabilities for the new states in terms of the parameters of the old states. We begin by taking a look at the one observable state in the old theory, the error state E. Since the theory assumes stationary probabilities of transition, the occurrence of the error state means that the probabilities at any point at which an error occurs are precisely as they were at the very first occurrence of an error. When we have an observable state in a system with stationary probabilities, we can always make precisely the same predictions about future events in a sequence each time the observable state is entered. This reoccurrence of the observable state is therefore sometimes described as a "recurrent event" that "resets the system." This is a particularly apt description when, as in this case, all other states can still be entered following this observable state. Given stationary probabilities, any state entrance implies the same future probabilities, but only an observable state offers the possibility for this kind of *predictive* constancy. For example, in our old theory, if a success occurs and there are no more errors subsequent to that success, the system could conceivably be in state L or in state S. We could not simply turn to the matrix and state that the probability of a particular state on the next trial was one of the cells in the matrix. Rather, we would have to take into account the two alternative possible states for the current success. Thus we can see that only the observable state enables us to use the matrix for a direct reading of probabilities. In addition, the observable state can be defined in the same way for both the original and the observable states theory. Therefore, this recurrent event has the same status in both theories, and can be used as an indication of an equivalent point in the two models.

FINDING THE PARAMETERS FOR THE NEW MODEL

We shall need an equation for the probability of the recurrent event. In this instance, the probability of the recurrent event in the old model would also be correct for the new model. [In those instances where the old model does not have an observable state, we would have to construct the probability of a recurrent event in the new model in a slightly more complex fashion. See Problem 3 at the end of this chapter for an example of this.]

We shall symbolize the probability of the recurrent event as f_j, where j indexes the number of trials after the last occurrence of the recurrent event on which the recurrent event again occurs. That is, assuming the recurrent event occurred on trial n, the probability of it first occurring again on trial $n + j$ is

$$P_{r_n r_{n+j}} = f_j.$$

The probability of the recurrent event first occurring again on either the next trial *or* the trial following the next trial would be

$$P_{r_n r_{n+1}} + P_{r_n r_{n+2}} = \sum_{j=1}^{2} f_j,$$

and the probability of it ever occurring again would be

$$f = \sum_{j=1}^{\infty} f_j, \tag{8.4}$$

so that the probability of it never occurring again would be $1 - f$.

Let us now look at an equation for f_j, and then for f, derived from the transition probabilities of Eq. (8.2).

It is clear from the transition probabilities for the old theory [in Eq. (8.2)] that if an error has just occurred, the probability of it occurring again on the next trial is $(1 - d)t$, so that

$$f_1 = (1 - d)t. \tag{8.5a}$$

In Eq. (8.3) we can now fill in one cell, P_{rr}, which is the probability of going from state R to state R. (We can suppress the n and $n + 1$ notation within the matrix.) Consequently, we can state that

$$P_{rr} = (1 - d)t. \tag{8.5b}$$

In the same row, we would require $P_{rs'}$. Since our definition of state S' is that it is a state in which a success occurs, to be followed at some future (un-specified) time by an error, the transition probability $P_{rs'}$ would be the prob-ability of returning to an error state on any trial with the exception of the next trial. What would this be? We again look at the matrix of Eq. (8.2), and see that having just had an error, the probability of a success on the next trial that can be followed by an error later is $(1 - d)s$. The probability of that promised error occurring precisely j trials after the error, with repeated successes between, requires some $j - 2$ additional returns to state S, which has a probability $[(1 - c)p]^{j-2}$. The promised error, occurring from state S, will occur with a probability of $(1 - c)q$. Multiplying the probabilities of these three necessary events together gives us

$$f_j = [(1 - d)s][(1 - c)p]^{j-2}(1 - c)q \qquad \text{for} \quad j \geq 2. \tag{8.6}$$

Since $P_{rs'}$ implies the sum of all alternative values of $j \geq 2$ (an "or relation" of alternative numbers of trials till the promised error), we sum Eq. (8.6) and obtain

$$\sum_{j=2}^{\infty} f_j = \frac{(1 - c)(1 - d)qs}{q + cp}, \tag{8.7}$$

which gives us the proper transition value for cell $P_{rs'}$ in Eq. (8.3).

For P_{ra} in Eq. (8.3) we require the probability of no more errors, which would be $1 - f$. Equation (8.4) defines f as the sum of f_j over all values of j, and Eq. (8.7) is almost that, except for the absence of f_1 [Eq. (8.5a)] from the sum. We therefore obtain the value of f by summing Eqs. (8.5a) and (8.7), which yields

$$f = (1 - d)t + \frac{(1 - c)(1 - d)qs}{q + cp}$$
$$= (1 - d)\left[\frac{q + (t - q)c}{q + cp}\right] \tag{8.8}$$

and consequently

$$1 - f = d + \frac{(1 - d)cs}{q + cp}. \tag{8.9}$$

This completes one row of the transition matrix, which is shown in Eq. (8.10).

	A_{n+1}	R_{n+1}	S'_{n+1}
A_n	1	0	0
$\mathbf{P} = R_n$	$d + \left[\dfrac{(1 - d)cs}{q + cp}\right]$	$(1 - d)t$	$\dfrac{(1 - c)(1 - d)qs}{q + cp}$
S'_n	0	$q + cp$	$(1 - c)p$

$$\tag{8.10}$$

The row that is conditional upon moving from state S' is simpler than the row conditional upon state R. The observable states are defined so that movement from S' to A is not possible as a direct transition. This gives us

$$P_{s'a} = 0.$$

For the transition $P_{s's'}$ we have merely to look at the old theory's probability of return to the same success state (success without learning), which from Eq. (8.2) is $(1 - c)p$. Therefore

$$P_{s's'} = (1 - c)p. \tag{8.11}$$

There is only one other cell in that row that is nonzero. Since Eq. (8.3) defines a stochastic matrix, all rows must sum to 1. The remaining cell in row R is then obtained, from Eq. (8.11), as

$$\begin{aligned} P_{s'r} &= 1 - (1 - c)p \\ &= q + cp. \end{aligned}$$

The topmost row is the row conditional upon state A on trial n. The definition of state A (successes with no subsequent errors) implies that once in that state, the system is always returned to that state (since it can no longer be in that state if there are future errors, and if there are future errors, it is not yet in that state). We therefore have the familiar probability value of 1 on the diagonal and 0's in all remaining cells of the row. This completes the transition probabilities for our new observable states theory, as seen in Eq. (8.10).

INITIAL STATE PROBABILITIES FOR THE OBSERVABLE STATES MODEL

We might also want the vector of initial state probabilities for the new model.

For the probability π_R of beginning in state R, we would have the identical probability to that of beginning in state E in the original theory, π_E. We can therefore state that

$$\pi_R = \pi_E.$$

We would have two different ways that the probability of beginning in state A could occur, in terms of the parameters of Eq. (8.2) for the old theory. Either the subject could begin in the learning state, with probability π_L, or the subject could begin in state S, with probability π_S, and then never make any errors. The latter possibility could only occur by some consecutive number of times, say j times, in state S, followed by entry into state L. This would imply the probability

$$\pi_S[(1 - c)p]^{j-1} \cdot c$$

for beginning in state S, spending $j - 1$ additional trials in S, and then entering state L (with probability c). Since the event of entrance into state S with no errors thereafter could occur with j being any possible integer value (where j is the number of consecutive times in state S before learning), we would have to sum all of these different possibilities, along with the probability of beginning in state π_L. The resulting probability π_A would be

$$\pi_A = \pi_L + \pi_S \sum_{j=1}^{\infty} [(1 - c)p]^{j-1} \cdot c,$$

$$\pi_A = \pi_L + \frac{c\pi_S}{q + cp}.$$

Finally, we would want the probability for $\pi_{S'}$. For this event, in terms of the old theory, it is required that the subject begin in state S, remain there for some j trials, and then have an error. Again we have to sum all of the alternate possible times returned to state S, prior to an error, but this time ending in a transition to state E, which gives us

$$\pi_{S'} = \pi_S \sum_{j=1}^{\infty} [(1 - c)p]^{j-1} [(1 - c)q],$$

$$\pi_{S'} = \pi_S \left[\frac{(1 - c)q}{q + cp} \right].$$

Note that $\pi_R + \pi_A + \pi_{S'} = 1$, as required for a vector of probabilities.

Obtaining Identifiable Parameters

Equation (8.10) presents the matrix for the observable states model in terms of the parameters of the original theory. The 3×3 transition matrix for our observable states theory can be stated more simply. For example, in the bottom row (row conditional on S_n') there is one 0 cell, since transitions from S' to A are impossible. This means that whatever value one of the two remaining cells has as a transition probability, the final remaining cell is 1 minus that value, as we pointed out in developing Eq. (8.10). Let us use the symbols

$$P_{s'r} = w \qquad \text{and} \qquad P_{s's} = 1 - w.$$

From Eqs. (8.3) and (8.10), then, we have

$$w = q + cp \tag{8.12}$$

and

$$1 - w = (1 - c)p.$$

For the middle row of our simplified matrix (the row conditional upon R_n), we could have a probability

$$P_{ra} = u$$

where, from Eq. (8.10),

$$u = d + \left[\frac{(1 - d)cs}{q + cp}\right]. \tag{8.13}$$

Given that the system was not absorbed from state R into state A on some trial n, the system could either go into S' or return to R. That is, it would not go to A with probability $1 - u$, and conditional upon not having gone to A, it would go to either state R or state S' with some probabilities that we could symbolize as v and $(1 - v)$, respectively. To enter either R or S' from R a joint event would be required, suggesting the multiplication of two probabilities, so that

$$P_{rr} = (1 - u)v \qquad \text{and} \qquad P_{rs'} = (1 - u)(1 - v). \tag{8.14}$$

Combining Eqs. (8.5b) and (8.14), we can state that

$$v = \frac{(1 - d)t}{1 - u},$$

from which [with some algebraic manipulation using Eq. (8.13)], we would find that

$$v = \frac{t}{1 - [cs/(q + cp)]}. \tag{8.15}$$

The top row of Eq. (8.10) would not require simplification. The resulting restatement of Eq. (8.10) would be

$$\mathbf{P} = \begin{array}{c} \\ A_n \\ R_n \\ S_n' \end{array} \begin{array}{ccc} A_{n+1} & R_{n+1} & S'_{n+1} \\ 1 & 0 & 0 \\ u & (1 - u)v & (1 - u)(1 - v), \\ 0 & w & 1 - w \end{array} \tag{8.16}$$

where

$$u = d + \left[\frac{(1 - d)cs}{q + cp}\right], \qquad v = \frac{t}{1 - [cs/(q + cp)]}, \qquad w = q + cp.$$

Equation (8.2) has four parameters, c, d, p, and s. Our new theory as expressed in Eq. (8.10) maintained these four parameters. Note that our new matrix in Eq. (8.16) has only three parameters, u, v, and w.

There is the same empirical equivalent for each transition in the matrices of Eqs. (8.10) and (8.16). We could therefore equate both of these equations with Eq. (8.17), in which each N_{jk} refers to an actual observed number of times that subjects have had transitions from some state j to some state k.

$$\mathbf{P} = \begin{array}{c} \\ A_n \\ \\ R_n \\ \\ \\ S_n' \end{array} \begin{array}{ccc} A_{n+1} & R_{n+1} & S'_{n+1} \\ 1 & 0 & 0 \\ \dfrac{N_{ra}}{N_{ra} + N_{rr} + N_{rs'}} & \dfrac{N_{rr}}{N_{ra} + N_{rr} + N_{rs'}} & \dfrac{N_{rs'}}{N_{ra} + N_{rr} + N_{rs'}} \\ 0 & \dfrac{N_{s'r}}{N_{s'r} + N_{s's'}} & \dfrac{N_{s's'}}{N_{s'r} + N_{s's'}} \end{array} \qquad (8.17)$$

Because row sums must equal 1, and some of the values of Eqs. (8.10), (8.16), and (8.17) are already determined (as 0 or 1), we are left with only three cells that are "free." These 3 degrees of freedom mean that there are only three independent equations possible between theoretical values and empirical estimates of those values. Consequently, in equating u, v, and w from Eq. (8.16) with the corresponding values of Eq. (8.17), we would exhaust the number of independent equations that would be available for estimating the parameters. The specific equalities would be

$$u = \frac{N_{ra}}{N_{ra} + N_{rr} + N_{rs'}}, \qquad (8.18)$$

$$v = \frac{N_{rr}}{N_{rr} + N_{rs'}}, \qquad (8.19)$$

and

$$w = \frac{N_{s'r}}{N_{s'r} + N_{s's'}}. \qquad (8.20)$$

The empirical estimate of v in Eq. (8.19) is obtained by recognizing that our definition of v is the probability of going to state R from state R, given that the system goes to either state R or state S'. The frequency of transitions to state R from state R relative to the frequency of transitions from state R to either state R or state S' empirically defines the desired probability.

Substitutions of (8.18)–(8.20) in (8.16) yield (8.17), as expected.

Equations (8.13), (8.15), and (8.12) give us equalities between u, v, w, and the original parameters c, d, p, and s. Therefore, we can combine Eqs.

(8.13) with (8.18), (8.15) with (8.19), and (8.12) with (8.20) to obtain the estimates

$$d + \left[\frac{(1 - d)cs}{q + cp} \right] = \frac{N_{ra}}{N_{ra} + N_{rr} + N_{rs'}}, \tag{8.21}$$

$$\frac{t}{1 - [cs/(q + cp)]} = \frac{N_{rr}}{N_{rr} + N_{rs'}}, \tag{8.22}$$

and

$$q + cp = \frac{N_{s'r}}{N_{s'r} + N_{s's'}}. \tag{8.23}$$

Equations (8.21)–(8.23) give us three independent equations in four unknowns, and we therefore see the impossibility of finding unique values for the original four parameters that were incorporated into the original theory.

We label the theoretical parameters without unique solutions (c, d, p, and s) *nonidentifiable parameters*. We can contrast these with our three parameters u, v, and w, which we call *identifiable*. Our observable states allow simple counts of all transition frequencies, yielding probabilities of transition that can be equated with some set of parameters. When a set of parameters is uniquely determined by such probability estimates, we call that set of parameters identifiable.

Despite nonobservability of states and nonidentifiability of parameters, a theorist will often have specific psychological referents for the parameters of his original theory. Regardless of empirical limitations, he might still wish to postulate ongoing processes theoretically represented by nonidentifiable parameters. We therefore need to have some means of evaluating such parameters. The next section discusses some aspects of such a further analysis.

Working with Four Unknowns and Three Independent Equations

Equations (8.21)–(8.23) can be most easily solved for c, d, p, and s by assuming a value for one of the parameters. Note that the right-hand side in each of these equations has an empirical equivalent. Let us state these to have been found to be .40, .60, and .60, for the three equations, in that order. The parameter s represents the probability of being correct before conditioning on some one trial, given that an error was made on the last trial. The theorist might therefore consider s to be a guessing parameter and, as in Bower's one-element paired-associate learning model, he might assume its value to be the reciprocal of the number of alternative responses that are possible in the experiment. Let us assume two alternatives, so that $s = .5$. Having fixed one parameter, we can solve for the other three, based on this knowledge and (8.21)–(8.23). We next note that the value $q + cp$ is found to run throughout these equations, and Eq. (8.23) tells us that $q + cp$ is equal to our last empirical estimate; that is,

$$q + cp = .60.$$

We can now enter our assumed value and our empirical values into Eqs. (8.21)–(8.23), remembering that $p + q = s + t = 1$.

$$d + \left[\frac{(1 - d).5c}{.6} \right] = .40, \tag{8.24}$$

$$\frac{.5}{1 - (.5c/.6)} = .60, \tag{8.25}$$

$$q + cp = .60. \tag{8.26}$$

We solve Eq. (8.25) for c, which yields

$$c = .2.$$

We then insert the estimate of c into Eq. (8.24), which gives us

$$d = .28.$$

We finally insert c into Eq. (8.26) and obtain our last parameter estimate

$$p = .5.$$

Any other specific value assumptions that we might make about any other parameter would similarly yield a solution to the remaining parameters to be estimated.

In this specific case, note that we found that

$$s = p.$$

Such a finding would make sense if there were no reason to believe that guessing probabilities were different after successes than after errors.

Some relationships between parameters, such as the equality between s and p, can be tested without assuming any parameter values first. For example, we shall show below that if $w = v$, then $s = p$. Since w and v both have empirical estimates, their similarity, or dissimilarity can be directly observed.

We can restate Eq. (8.15) as

$$v = \frac{t(q + cp)}{q + cp - cs}. \tag{8.27}$$

Remembering that

$$t = 1 - s \quad \text{and} \quad q = 1 - p,$$

we can restate Eq. (8.27) as

$$v = \frac{(1-s)(q+cp)}{(1-p)+cp-cs}.$$

(8.28)

We know, from Eq. (8.12), that

$$w = q + cp,$$

so we can restate Eq. (8.28) as

$$v = \left[\frac{(1-s)}{(1-p+cp-cs)}\right]w.$$

(8.29)

If $s = p$, Eq. (8.29) can be restated as

$$v = \left[\frac{(1-p)}{(1-p+cp-cp)}\right]w$$

$$= w.$$

Therefore, if

$$s = p,$$

then

$$v = w.$$

Next we ask what the implications of Eq. (8.29) are if $v = w$. It would mean that

$$\frac{1-s}{1-p+cp-cs} = 1.$$

(8.30)

Restating Eq. (8.30) we have

$$1 - s = 1 - p + cp - cs,$$
$$p - cp = s - cs,$$
$$p = s.$$

In summary, Eqs. (8.12) and (8.27) imply Eq. (8.29), which in turn implies that if and only if

$$v = w,$$

then

$$s = p.$$

We can see whether or not $v = w$ by using the empirical estimates of Eqs. (8.19) and (8.20), and can thus see whether or not $s = p$ without actually knowing the values of s and p, and therefore not having to make any assumptions about parameter values. A test of the hypothesis $s = p$ is equivalent to a test of the hypothesis $v = w$. We discuss such a test below.

Comparing Two Models of the Same Theory

If it were true that

$$v = w,$$

then the matrix of Eq. (8.16) would reduce to

$$
\mathbf{P} = \begin{array}{c} \\ A_n \\ R_n \\ S_n' \end{array}
\begin{array}{cccc}
A_{n+1} & R_{n+1} & S_{n+1}' & \\
1 & 0 & 0 & \\
u & (1-u)v & (1-u)(1-v). & \\
0 & v & 1-v &
\end{array}
\qquad (8.31)
$$

An important implication of the difference between Eqs. (8.16) and (8.31) is that there are two different observable states models implied. The model having v equal to w implies that one less parameter is necessary to prediction of the observable sequences.

When first pointing out that the theoretically possible relationship of equality between s and p has an empirically identifiable concomitant expectation of equality between v and w, it was suggested that the data could be examined for the empirical identity. However, there is always error variance in data samples, so that identity of parameters might exist, but rarely would there be a numerical identity of estimated values. As is usually the case where error variance can obscure identities, we can turn to the literature of statistical inference for aid. We would find that the technique of maximum likelihood, and more specifically the use of a maximum likelihood ratio, would give us an excellent test of the tenability of the assumption of identity. Further, this test of identity between v and w would give us a test of the relative merits of the two different models implied with and without identity.

Maximum Likelihood

We shall pause in our exploration of the observable states theory of Eq. (8.10) to look at the use of maximum likelihood estimates and then at a use of maximum likelihood ratios. We shall apply the maximum likelihood ratio concept to a test between the two models of the observable states theory, comparing the model implied by Eqs. (8.16) with the model implied by Eq. (8.31). The question that we shall ask by such a test is whether the model with two parameters (just u and v) is as adequate for an explanation of the data as the model with three parameters (u, v, and w).

An Intuitive Estimate of p in the Binomial Distribution

Given a constant probability during guessing in some task, with only either success or error as possible outcomes on any trial, we have a Bernoulli series, for which the probability of j successes out of n trials is described by the binomial distribution. For the binomial, we know that the probability of some number j successes occurring out of n trials has a probability of

$$B(j; n, p) = \binom{n}{j} p^n (1 - p)^{n-j}. \tag{8.32}$$

Let us now assume that we had actually run a subject in such a circumstance, and discovered that he had 7 successes in a run of 10 trials. We would wish to know the probability of a success on any one of these trials.

We have an intuitive definition of p. Given that the probability of a success remains the same over all trials, having 7 successes in 10 trials suggests that the probability on any one trial is simply 7/10, the proportion of trials on which successes occurred. This is actually our operational definition of probability in general, and it applies readily in this example.

Maximum Likelihood Estimation of a Parameter

Given a finding of 7 successes in our example in the preceding section, we can substitute many possible values of p in Eq. (8.32) to find the probability of 7 successes in 10 trials, given each substituted value of p. We present a list of such probabilities in Table 8.1.

TABLE 8.1

p	$B(7; 10, p) = \binom{10}{7} p^7 (1 - p)^3$
.1	.0000001
.2	.0000066
.3	.0000750
.4	.0003539
.5	.0009766
.6	.0017886
.7	.0022236
.8	.0010008
.9	.0004783

We can see that the maximum probability obtained in Table 8.1 is .0022236, which is for $p = 7$. This tells us that among the set of values examined, .7 is the value of p that would make the finding of 7 successes out of

10 trials the *most likely* finding (thus "maximum likelihood"). But perhaps .75 or .65, neither of which is tabled, would have a greater likelihood. Rather than computing all possible probability values, we can use the method of maximum likelihood.

As in the intuitive example illustrated in Table 8.1, the method of maximum likelihood will have us maximize the probability value $B(j; n, p)$ in Eq. (8.32) over all possible values of p. We know from infinite calculus that if we obtain the derivative of a function, set the derivative equal to 0, and then solve the equation for the variable, we shall obtain an extreme value for the function. (If the second derivative is negative, as in the present equation, the obtained extreme will be a maximum.)

In the case of Eq. (8.32) we find the derivative to be†

$$\frac{dB}{dp} = \binom{n}{j} [jp^{j-1}(1-p)^{n-j} - (n-j)(1-p)^{n-j-1}p^j] \qquad (8.33)$$

$$= \binom{n}{j} p^{j-1}(1-p)^{n-j-1}(j-np).$$

Setting the derivative equal to 0 and then dividing both sides of the equation by $\binom{n}{j}(1-p)^{n-j-1}$, we have

$$0 = p^{j-1}(j-np) \qquad \text{or} \qquad np^j = jp^{j-1} \qquad \text{or} \qquad p = \frac{j}{n}.$$

The value of n is set experimentally (in our example it was set at 10). The value of j is normally identified from the data (in our example we simply stated that it was 7). Thus we have found the same value of $\frac{7}{10}$ through the method of maximum likelihood that we were led to intuitively. (Generally it is more convenient to find the derivative of the logarithm of the original equation. The log of an equation increases monotonically with the original equation, and the log is often easier to differentiate.)

In working with mathematical models, we shall generally have one or more parameters in our theory, and we shall wish to obtain estimates of the parameters. If we try to find the value of the parameters that will maximize the probability of the actual outcome of an experiment, we shall be using the method of maximum likelihood for that estimation. This is identical to our hypothetical example in which we allowed a sampling of 10 trials from a Bernoulli distribution and then tried to maximize the probability of obtaining seven successes in the 10 trials by varying the value of p in the formula for the

---

† If you have forgotten your calculus, you can simply take for granted that Eq. (8.32) implies Eq. (8.33). The remaining steps are just algebra.

binomial distribution. In general, we construct an equation for the probability of the event, and then find the value of the parameter which maximizes that probability.

For the theory implied by the matrix of Eq. (8.16), we would take the probability of each of the transitions that had taken place and then form a product of all of these transition probabilities. In this instance, we would have the product

$$L_1 = (u)^{N_{ra}}[(1 - u)v]^{N_{rr}}[(1 - u)(1 - v)]^{N_{rs'}}(w)^{N_{s'r}}(1 - w)^{N_{s's'}} \quad (8.34)$$

or

$$L_1 = (u)^{N_{ra}}(1 - u)^{(N_{rr} + N_{rs'})}(v)^{N_{rr}}(1 - v)^{N_{rs'}}(w)^{N_{s'r}}(1 - w)^{N_{s's'}}, \quad (8.35)$$

where N_{jk} is the number of times that the transition from state j to state k took place (and could conceivably be equal to 0). The factors in the equation are all taken from Eq. (8.16). (A more accurate likelihood function for the model would include the initial state probabilities π_i, where i equals R, S', or A, and each π_i would be raised to a power equal to the number of times that subjects began in the ith state. That would simply mean including three more factors in Eq. (8.34). We shall omit the initial trial probabilities in the following discussion to minimize the complexity of our equations.)

To obtain the parameter estimates of u, v, and w that would maximize our likelihood function, we would apply our maximum likelihood technique to Eq. (8.35). That is, we would take the logarithm of L_1, take the partial derivative for one parameter, and then set the differentiated logarithmic function equal to 0, solving for the parameter. We would then repeat this for each parameter, and would find that the maximum likelihood technique gives us precisely the same estimates that we have in Eqs. (8.18)–(8.20). Our parameter values then would be obtained simply by counting frequencies of the various transitions and entering these values into Eqs. (8.18)–(8.20).

Likelihood Ratios

If we had collected a set of data to test our observable states theory, we might want to know if the model implied by Eq. (8.16) is appropriate, or if the more parsimonious model of Eq. (8.31) would be sufficient. If the model of Eq. (8.31) were found to be sufficient, then any distinction between the parameters w and v would be without support. This would in turn throw doubt on any difference between the parameters s and p in our original theory. To make the comparison between the models, we would begin by developing two likelihood functions, one from each of the matrices. From Eq. (8.16), we have Eq. (8.35). For the matrix of Eq. (8.31), the likelihood function would again be the product of all transition probabilities in the matrix, each raised to a power equal to the number of times that each transition had occurred. That function would contain the parameters u and v but not w. We could obtain the maximum likelihood estimates of u and v by applying the maximum likelihood technique to that function. We would find the estimates to be

$$u = \frac{N_{ra}}{N_{ra} + N_{rr} + N_{rs'}},$$

$$v_2 = \frac{N_{rr} + N_{s'r}}{N_{rr} + N_{rs'} + N_{s'r} + N_{s's'}}. \tag{8.36}$$

Note that the estimate of u is identical to that of Eq. (8.18). However, the estimate of v_2 in Eq. (8.36) is different from the estimate of v in Eq. (8.19), which motivated our use of the subscript 2.

We present the likelihood function for the model implied by Eq. (8.31) in Eq. (8.37).

$$L_2 = (u)^{N_{ra}}(1 - u)^{(N_{rr} + N_{rs'})}(v_2)^{(N_{rr} + N_{s'r})}(1 - v_2)^{(N_{rs'} + N_{s's'})}. \tag{8.37}$$

(Note that again we have ignored first-trial probabilities.)

If the two models are equivalent; that is, if the data are equally likely to have been generated by a process analogized by either model, then -2 times the logarithm of the ratio of the two likelihood functions, employing their maximum likelihood estimators, will be distributed as chi square, assuming large sample data (Mood and Graybill, 1963, pp. 297–301). Chi-square distributions are dependent on degrees of freedom. The distribution of $-2 \log (L_2/L_1)$ is similarly dependent on the difference in the number of parameters between the two models. The function with fewer parameters is always placed in the numerator, and the difference between the numbers of parameters gives the value for the degrees of freedom under which we look in the chi-square table. In our example, the numerator has two parameters in the function and the denominator has three. Therefore, the chi-square with 1 degree of freedom would be the expected distribution (assuming that the data were actually generated from the simpler two-parameter theory). If the resulting value of $-2 \log(L_2/L_1)$ were unlikely under the appropriate chi-square distribution, then it would be assumed that the function with fewer parameters was not sufficient and not as adequate a model as the alternative model. Further, in this instance, we would assume that the parameters s and p of the original model are not equal.

Let us carry out a comparison of the type just discussed, with a specific example. Assume that we ran 50 subjects in an experiment in which each subject learned a paired-associate list of 10 letter–number pairs, each pair to a criterion of 10 consecutive correct responses. This would mean that 500 pairs were learned, so there would be 500 transitions T_{ra}. Given the criterion of 10 consecutive correct, there would be $(9 \times 500) = 4500$ transitions T_{aa}. The other numbers of transitions that we arbitrarily assume for the example are given in Table 8.2.

TABLE 8.2

		Artificial Data	
	A_{n+1}	R_{n+1}	S_{n+1}
A_n	4500	0	0
R_n	500	270	230
S_n'	0	390	360

We shall require two likelihood functions: L_1 from Eq. (8.16), which we obtained as Eq. (8.35); and L_2 from Eq. (8.31), which we obtained as Eq. (8.37). We shall assume independence of the different letter–number pairs and of the different subjects. We shall further assume that the same parameter values hold for each subject on each letter pair.

We want a ratio L_2/L_1. We can see that the factors

$$(u)^{N_{ra}} \qquad \text{and} \qquad (1 - u)^{(N_{rr} + N_{s'r})}$$

in Eqs. (8.35) and (8.37) are identical in our planned numerator and denominator terms, so we can cancel them out of the fraction. That would leave

$$\frac{L_2}{L_1} = \frac{(v_2)^{(N_{rr} + N_{s'r})}(1 - v_2)^{(N_{rs'} + N_{s's'})}}{(v)^{N_{rr}}(1 - v)^{N_{rs'}}(w)^{N_{s'r}}(1 - w)^{N_{s's'}}}. \tag{8.38}$$

We can extract the values N_{jk} from Table (8.2).

$$N_{ra} = 500, \; N_{rr} = 270, \ldots, N_{s's'} = 360.$$

Entering our N_{jk} values into Eqs. (8.36), (8.19), and (8.20), respectively, we obtain the estimates of v_2, v, and w.

$$v_2 = .53, \qquad v = .54, \qquad w = .52$$

Equation (8.38) can now be expressed with numerical values.

$$\frac{L_2}{L_1} = \frac{(.53)^{660}(.47)^{590}}{(.54)^{270}(.46)^{230}(.52)^{390}(.48)^{360}}. \tag{8.39}$$

We shall want the logarithm of Eq. (8.39).

$$\log \frac{L_2}{L_1} = 660(\log .53) + 590(\log .47) - 270(\log .54) - 230(\log .46)$$
$$- 390(\log .52) - 360(\log .48),$$

$$\log \frac{L_2}{L_1} = 660(-.2757) + 590(-.3279) - 270(-.2676) - 230(-.3372)$$
$$- 390(-.2840) - 360(-.3188),$$

$$\log \frac{L_2}{L_1} = -.087.$$

The final value that we seek, because of its expected distribution as chi square (assuming that the simpler, two-parameter theory is sufficient), is

$$-2 \log \frac{L_2}{L_1} = .174.$$

We now turn to a chi-square table as found in most statistics texts, and look under 1 degree of freedom. A value of 3.8 or larger would be required to reach the critical point of the distribution, if we identified as values belonging to the acceptance region only those that constituted the smaller 95% of the scores of the chi-square distribution. The value that we actually obtained is such that we would expect more than 50% of the chi-square distribution to be larger. The value of .174 is therefore not an unexpected value in that chi-square distribution, and we conclude that u and v alone are sufficient parameters to describe the data.

We can now return to our original question whether or not $s = p$. We can state that the data give us no reason to reject the hypothesis that

$$s = p.$$

More generally, we can state that there is no evidence that the model with three parameters [Eq. (8.16)] is any better as a predictor of the data than the model with only two parameters [Eq. (8.31)].

Problems

The following theory has been taken from Greeno (1970), and the questions have been abstracted from some of the material in Greeno (1968).

Let us assume a theory of paired-associate learning in which we conceive of two basic stages. The subject stores the pair, and then he learns to retrieve the pair. Initially, before the subject stores the pair, only errors are possible.

Subsequent to storage, the subject may alternate in some irregular fashion between retrieval and nonretrieval of the pair, until a reliable retrieval system has been learned. We symbolize the final state, in which the subject has learned to reliably retrieve the stored pair, as state L, the "learned state." The latter state is assumed to be an absorbing state. The initial prestorage state is designated as state O. The intervening possibilities are identified as state C on those trials on which the subject successfully retrieves the stored pair with his still unreliable strategy and as state E on trials on which the subject is unsuccessful in retrieving the stored pair. The matrix for the model of this theory is

$$
\mathbf{P} = \begin{array}{c} \\ L_n \\ E_n \\ C_n \\ O_n \end{array} \begin{array}{cccc} L_{n+1} & E_{n+1} & C_{n+1} & O_{n+1} \\ 1 & 0 & 0 & 0 \\ d & (1-d)q & (1-d)p & 0 \\ c & (1-c)q & (1-c)p & 0 \\ ab & a(1-b)e & a(1-b)(1-e) & 1-a \end{array}
$$

1. Which state or states are observable (if any)?

2. Present an equivalent observable states theory, giving a set of four states that would be a complete partition of the possible outcomes during the trials of a paired-associate experiment. The new states must all be observable.

See the answer to Problem 2 in order to understand the symbolism of the following questions.

3. Let us look at the recurrent probabilities for state R, the recurrent event of our observable states theory, using the symbol f_j defined in the next paragraph.

Define f_j as the probability of an error on trial $n + j$, and consecutive successes on trials $n + 1$ through $n + j - 1$, given the occurrence of state R on trial n.

Give the distribution for f_j, using the parameters of the original non-observable states theory (given in the matrix that was included in the introductory statement to these questions).

4. What would be the cell entry for the transition probability

$$
P_{r_n \, r_{n+1}}
$$

in terms of the parameters of the original nonobservable states theory?

5. What would be the cell entry for the transition probability

$$
P_{r_n \, q_{n+1}}
$$

in terms of the parameters of the original theory?

6. What would be the cell entries for the remaining two columns in the row of transition probabilities conditional on R_n?

References

Atkinson, R. C. Stimulus sampling theory. In R. D. Luce, R. R. Bush, & E. Galanter (Eds.), *Handbook of psychology*. Vol. II. New York: Wiley, 1963. Pp. 121–248.

Atkinson, R. C., Bower, G. H., & Crothers, E. J. *An introduction to mathematical learning theory*. New York: Wiley, 1965.

Atkinson, R. C., & Crothers, E. J. A comparison of paired-associate learning models having different acquisition and retention axioms. *Journal of Mathematical Psychology* 1, 1964, 285–315.

Bjork, R. A. Repetition and rehearsal mechanisms in models for short-term memory. In D. A. Norman (Ed.), *Models of human memory*. New York: Academic Press, 1970. Pp. 307–330.

Bower, G. H. Choice-point behavior. In R. R. Bush & W. K. Estes (Eds.), *Studies in mathematical learning theory*. Stanford, California: Stanford Univ. Press, 1959. Pp. 109–124.

Bower, G. H. Application of a model to paired associate learning. *Psychometrika*, 26, 1961, 255–280.

Bower, G. H., & Theios, J. A learning model for discrete performance levels. In R. C. Atkinson (Ed.), *Studies in mathematical psychology*. Stanford, California: Stanford Univ. Press, 1964. Pp. 1–31.

Bower, G. H., & Trabasso, T. Concept identifications. In R. C. Atkinson (Ed.), *Studies in mathematical psychology*. Stanford, California: Stanford Univ. Press, 1964. Pp. 32–94.

Burke, C. J., Estes, W. K., & Hellyer, S. Rate of conditioning in relation to stimulus variability. *Journal of Experimental Psychology*, 48, 1954, 153–161.

Bush, R. R. Sequential properties of linear models. In R. R. Bush and W. K. Estes (Eds.), *Studies in mathematical learning theory*. Stanford, California: Stanford Univ. Press, 1959. Pp. 215–227.

Bush, R. R. Estimation and evaluation. In R. D. Luce, R. R. Bush, & E. Galanter (Eds.), *Handbook of psychology*. Vol. I. New York: Wiley, 1963.

Bush, R. R., & Mosteller, F. *Stochastic models for learning*. New York: Wiley, 1955.

Bush, R. R., & Sternberg, S. H. A single-operator model. In R. R. Bush & W. K. Estes (Eds.), *Studies in mathematical learning theory.* Stanford, California: Stanford Univ. Press, 1959. Pp. 204–227.

Estes, W. K. Toward a statistical theory of learning. *Psychological Review,* **57**, 1950, 94–107.

Estes, W. K. Statistical theory of spontaneous recovery and regression. *Psychological Review,* **62**, 1955, 145–154.

Estes, W. K. Theory of learning with constant, variable, or contingent probabilities of reinforcement. *Psychometrika,* **22**, 1957, 113–132.

Estes, W. K. The statistical approach to learning theory. In S. Koch (Ed.), *Psychology: A study of a science.* Vol. II. New York: McGraw-Hill, 1959. Pp. 380–491.

Estes, W. K., & Burke, C. J. A theory of stimulus variability in learning. *Psychological Review,* **60**, 1952, 276–286.

Estes, W. K., & Straughan, J. H. Analysis of a verbal conditioning situation in terms of statistical learning theory. *Journal of Experimental Psychology,* **47**, 1954, 225–234.

Feller, W. *An introduction to probability theory and its applications.* Vol. I. (3rd ed.) New York: Wiley, 1968.

Freund, J. E. *Mathematical statistics.* Englewood Cliffs, New Jersey: Prentice-Hall, 1962.

Greeno, J. G. Identifiability and statistical properties of two-stage learning with no successes in the initial stage. *Psychometrika,* **33**, 1968, 173–215.

Greeno, J. G. How associations are memorized. In D. A. Norman (Ed.), *Models of human memory.* New York: Academic Press, 1970. Pp. 257–284.

Greeno, J. G., & Steiner, T. E. Markovian processes with identifiable states: General considerations and application to all-or-none learning. *Psychometrika,* **29**, 1964, 309–333.

Greeno, J. G., & Steiner, T. E. Comments on "Markovian processes with identifiable states: General considerations and applications to all-or-none learning." *Psychometrika,* **33**, 1968, 169–172.

Hull, C. L. *Principles of behavior.* New York: Appleton, 1943.

Kemeny, J. G., & Snell, J. L., *Finite Markov chains.* Princeton, New Jersey: Van Nostrand, 1960.

Kintsch, W. *Learning, memory, and conceptual processes.* New York: Wiley, 1970.

LaBerge, D. A model with neutral elements. In R. R. Bush & W. K. Estes (Eds.), *Studies in mathematical learning theory.* Stanford, California: Stanford Univ. Press, 1959. Pp. 53–64.

Miller, G. A. *Mathematics and psychology.* New York: Wiley, 1964.

Murdock, B. B. Short-term memory for associations. In D. A. Norman (Ed.), *Models of human memory.* New York: Academic Press, 1970. Pp, 285–304.

Mood, A. M., & Graybill, F. A. *Introduction to the theory of statistics.* New York: McGraw-Hill, 1963.

Restle, F. A theory of discrimination learning. *Psychological Review,* **62**, 1955, 11–19.

Restle, F. The selection of strategies in cue learning. *Psychological Review,* **69**, 1962, 329–343.

Restle, F., & Greeno, J. G. *Introduction to mathematical psychology.* Reading, Massachusetts: Addison-Wesley, 1970.

Siegel, S. *Nonparametric statistics for the behavioral sciences.* New York: McGraw-Hill, 1956.

Sternberg, S. Stochastic learning theory. In R. D. Luce, R. R. Bush, & E. Galanter (Eds.), *Handbook of psychology.* Vol. II. New York: Wiley, 1963. Pp. 1–120.

Theios, J. Simple conditioning as two-stage all-or-none learning. *Psychological Review,* **70**, 1963, 403–417.

Theios, J., & Brelsford, J., Jr. Theoretical interpretations of a Markov model for avoidance conditioning. *Journal of Mathematical Psychology,* **3**, 1966, 140–162.

Solutions to Problems

Chapter Two

1. From Eq. (2.48)

$$\sigma^2 = \sum_{k=1}^{\infty} k^2 p(k) - \left[\sum_{k=1}^{\infty} k p(k)\right]^2.$$

Therefore, for the distribution in question

$$\sigma^2 = \left(c + \frac{1-c}{N}\right)\left(1 - \frac{1}{N}\right)\sum_{k=1}^{\infty} k^2\left[\left(1 - \frac{1}{N}\right)(1 - c)\right]^{k-1} - \left(\frac{N-1}{Nc+1-c}\right)^2$$

$$= \frac{[c + (1-c)/N](1 - 1/N)\{1 + [(1 - 1/N)(1 - c)]\}}{\{1 - [(1 - 1/N)(1 - c)]\}^3} - \left(\frac{N-1}{Nc+1-c}\right)^2.$$

2. If we symbolize no more errors after trial n as $\bar{F}_n$ and an error on trial n as E_n, we can ask for the probability of the joint event $P(\bar{F}_n, E_n)$. But our theory is built around statements about states, from which errors and successes are predicted. It would therefore help to consider that a guessing state is necessary for this error. This would suggest the joint event

$$P(\bar{F}_n, E_n, G_n) = P(L = n).$$

Since we have a probability of no errors after a guessing state (b), we could readily obtain $\bar{F}_n$, given the guessing state on trial n. We therefore use the latter joint probability. Equation (2.16) gives us the probabilistic equivalent with this joint event. We then restate the equivalence with parameter equivalents from the theory.

$$P(\bar{F}_n, E_n, G_n) = P(\bar{F}_n | E_n, G_n) \cdot P(E_n | G_n) \cdot P(G_n),$$
$$P(L = n) = b \cdot (1 - 1/N) \cdot (1 - c)^{n-1}.$$

3. The expected trial of the last error would be the sum of each of the random variable values (each possible value of n) times its respective probability of occurrence.

$$E(L) = b(1 - 1/N) \sum_{n=1}^{\infty} n(1 - c)^{n-1}$$
$$= \frac{b(1 - 1/N)}{c^2}.$$

4. For $k = 0$: If the subject has his first success by guessing [Probability is g_1], then for an error to occur on the next trial, he must not be conditioned [Probability is $(1 - c)$], and must guess incorrectly [Probability is $(1 - 1/N)$]. This joint event [Probabillity is $g_1(1 - c)(1 - 1/N)$] is the only way that an error could occur immediately after the first success. Its complement is therefore the probability of 0 errors. Remembering that

$$\alpha = (1 - c)\left(1 - \frac{1}{N}\right),$$

we would have, for the probability of the random variable J_1 having the value 0,

$$P(J_1 = 0) = 1 - g_1\alpha.$$

Another way of coming to the same conclusion is to reason that, for 0 errors between the first and second success, (a) the subject did not have his first success by a guess [Probability is $1 - g_1$]; or (b) the subject had his first success by a guess [Probability g_1], but either he was conditioned during that trial, or not being conditioned, guessed correctly on the next trial [Probability is $1 - \alpha$], which suggests, via an "and" relation, Probability is $g_1(1 - \alpha)$. Routes (a) and (b) to 0 errors constitute an "or" relation, suggesting

$$P(J_1 = 0) = (1 - g_1) + g_1(1 - \alpha) = 1 - g_1\alpha.$$

For $k > 0$: (a) The first success had to occur by guessing, yielding

$$\text{Probability} = g_1$$

and (b) on the success trial (trial n) and $k - 1$ subsequent ones ($n, n + 1$,

$n + 2, n + 3, \ldots, n + k - 1$, totaling k trials), conditioning did not occur, yielding

$$\text{Probability} = (1 - c)^k$$

and (c) at the same time, on k subsequent trials $(n + 1, n + 2, \ldots, n + k)$, there are only errors, yielding

$$\text{Probability} = (1 - 1/N)^k$$

and (d) either the subject is conditioned on trial $n + k$, giving the second success, *or* the subject is not conditioned on $n + k$, *and* guesses correctly on trial $n + k + 1$ for the second success, yielding

$$\text{Probability} = c + (1 - c)(1/N).$$

Combining the four "and" related events yields

$$P(J_1 = k) = g_1(1 - c)^k\left(1 - \frac{1}{N}\right)^k\left(c + \frac{1 - c}{N}\right),$$

$$P(J_1 = k) = g_1\alpha^k(1 - \alpha), \qquad k > 0.$$

5. $E(J_1) = g_1(1 - \alpha)\sum_{k=1}^{\infty} k\alpha^k$

$$= \frac{g_1(1 - \alpha)\alpha}{(1 - \alpha)^2}$$

$$= \frac{g_1\alpha}{(1 - \alpha)}.$$

6. Here we have a situation of dichotomous events wherein on each trial we can have an occurrence or nonoccurrence of a response. This enables us to assign the random variable values 1 or 0, respectively. We can then simply sum the probabilities of the event of interest (response occurrence) over trials, to obtain the expected number of response occurrences. This is similar to the summation of the probability of an error on each trial in the Bower model. The summation then is simply

$$E(R) = P(R_1)\sum_{n=1}^{\infty} [(1 - e)(1 - s)]^{n-1},$$

$$E(R) = \frac{P(R_1)}{[1 - (1 - e)(1 - s)]}.$$

Chapter Three

1.
$$p_{n+1} = \alpha p_n + (1 - \alpha),$$
$$p_{n+1} - \alpha p_n = 0,$$
$$\mathbf{D}p_n - \alpha p_n = 0,$$
$$(\mathbf{D} - \alpha)p_n = 0,$$
$$\text{root} = \alpha.$$
$$\therefore p_n = \alpha^{n-1}C + \cdots.$$

$$(\mathbf{D} - \alpha)k = (1 - \alpha),$$
$$k - \alpha k = (1 - \alpha),$$
$$k = \frac{(1 - \alpha)}{(1 - \alpha)},$$
$$k = 1.$$
$$\therefore p_n = \alpha^{n-1}C + 1,$$

$$p_1 = \alpha^0 C + 1,$$
$$C = p_1 - 1,$$
$$p_n = \alpha^{n-1}(p_1 - 1) + 1,$$
$$p_n = 1 - \alpha^{n-1}(1 - p_1).$$

2. $P(R_n)$ = the probability that the subject is in the reminiscence state on trial n.

$P(F_n)$ = the probability that the subject is in the forgetting state on trial n.

(a) To obtain the recursive form, we need the same term on both sides of the equation, with the nth term in the sequence on the right and the $(n + 1)$st term in the sequence on the left. The probability in question is the probability of being in the reminiscence state. From probability theory as discussed in Chapter Two [see Eqs. (2.10) and (2.21)],

$$P(R_{n+1}) = P(R_{n+1} | R_n)P(R_n) + P(R_{n+1} | F_n)P(F_n).$$

Since there are only two states possible, the probability of one is the complement of the other. That is,

$$P(F_n) = 1 - P(R_n).$$

We can therefore state that

$$P(R_{n+1}) = P(R_{n+1} | R_n)P(R_n) + P(R_{n+1} | F_n)[1 - P(R_n)].$$

From the axioms of the little theory, this can be restated as

$$P(R_{n+1}) = \alpha P(R_n) + (1 - \beta)[1 - P(R_n)]$$
$$= \alpha P(R_n) + 1 - \beta - P(R_n) + \beta P(R_n)$$
$$= \alpha P(R_n) + \beta P(R_n) - P(R_n) + 1 - \beta,$$
$$P(R_{n+1}) = (\alpha + \beta - 1)P(R_n) + 1 - \beta.$$

(b) If

$$p_{n+1} = Ap_n + B$$

is solved as

$$p_n = A^{n-1}\left(p_1 - \frac{B}{1-A}\right) + \frac{B}{1-A},$$

then setting

$$A = (\alpha + \beta - 1) \quad \text{and} \quad B = 1 - \beta,$$

we have

$$R_{n+1} = (\alpha + \beta - 1)R_n + 1 - \beta$$

solved as

$$R_n = (\alpha + \beta - 1)^{n-1}\left[R_1 - \frac{1-\beta}{1-(\alpha+\beta-1)}\right] + \frac{1-\beta}{1-(\alpha+\beta-1)}$$

and, equivalently,

$$R_n = (\alpha + \beta - 1)^{n-1}\left[R_1 - \frac{1-\beta}{2-(\alpha+\beta)}\right] + \frac{1-\beta}{2-(\alpha+\beta)}.$$

3. $$p_{n+1} = (\alpha + \beta)^2 p_n + (\alpha + \beta) \quad \text{(recursive equation)},$$

$$\mathbf{D}p_n - (\alpha + \beta)^2 p_n = (\alpha + \beta),$$
$$[\mathbf{D} - (\alpha + \beta)^2]p_n = (\alpha + \beta),$$
$$\text{first root} = (\alpha + \beta)^2.$$

$$[\mathbf{D} - 1][\mathbf{D} - (\alpha + \beta)^2]p_n = [\mathbf{D} - 1](\alpha + \beta),$$
$$[\mathbf{D} - 1][\mathbf{D} - (\alpha + \beta)^2]p_n = (\alpha + \beta) - (\alpha + \beta)$$
$$= 0,$$
$$\text{second root} = 1.$$

$$\therefore p_n = C_1[(\alpha + \beta)^2]^{n-1} + C_2 1^{n-1} \quad \text{(general solution)}.$$

Using the form of the general solution, we have

$$p_1 = C_1 + C_2,$$
$$p_2 = C_1(\alpha + \beta)^2 + C^2,$$
$$p_2 - p_1 = C_1(\alpha + \beta)^2 - C_1,$$
$$p_2 - p_1 = C_1[(\alpha + \beta)^2 - 1].$$

Trivially,

$$p_1 = p_1.$$

Using the form of the recursive equation, we have

$$p_2 = [(\alpha + \beta)^2]p_1 + (\alpha + \beta),$$
$$p_2 - p_1 = [(\alpha + \beta)^2]p_1 - p_1 + (\alpha + \beta),$$
$$p_2 - p_1 = p_1[(\alpha + \beta)^2 - 1] + (\alpha + \beta).$$

Comparing general and recursive forms discloses that

$$p_2 - p_1 = p_2 - p_1,$$
$$C_1[(\alpha + \beta)^2 - 1] = p_1[(\alpha + \beta)^2 - 1] + (\alpha + \beta),$$
$$C_1 = p_1 + \frac{(\alpha + \beta)}{(\alpha + \beta)^2 - 1}.$$

From the general form

$$p_1 = C_1 + C_2;$$

$$\therefore p_1 = p_1 + \frac{(\alpha + \beta)}{(\alpha + \beta)^2 - 1} + C_2;$$

$$\therefore C_2 = -\frac{(\alpha + \beta)}{(\alpha + \beta)^2 - 1}.$$

Placing the solutions to C_1 and C_2 in the general solution form, we obtain

$$p_n = \left[p_1 + \frac{(\alpha + \beta)}{(\alpha + \beta)^2 - 1} \right][(\alpha + \beta)^2]^{n-1} - \frac{(\alpha + \beta)}{(\alpha + \beta)^2 - 1},$$

$$p_n = \frac{(\alpha + \beta)}{1 - (\alpha + \beta)^2} - \left[\frac{(\alpha + \beta)}{1 - (\alpha + \beta)^2} - p_1 \right][(\alpha + \beta)^2]^{n-1}.$$

4.
$$p_{n+1} = (\alpha \cdot \beta)^2 p_n + \beta^2.$$

Since

$$X_{n+1} = A X_n + B$$

implies

$$X_n = A^{n-1}\left(X_1 - \frac{B}{1-A}\right) + \frac{B}{1-A},$$

then with

$$A = (\alpha \cdot \beta)^2 \qquad \text{and} \qquad B = \beta^2$$

we have

$$p_n = [(\alpha \cdot \beta)^2]^{n-1}\left(p_1 - \frac{\beta^2}{1-(\alpha \cdot \beta)^2}\right) + \frac{\beta^2}{1-(\alpha \cdot \beta)^2}.$$

5. To prove:

$$X_n = [X_1 A + (n-1)B]A^{n-2}. \tag{1}$$

Defining equation

$$X_{n+1} = AX_n + BA^{n-1} \tag{2}$$

From the general form [Eq. (1)]

$$X_1 = [X_1 A + (n-1)B]A^{1-2},$$

$$X_1 = X_1 + 0 \cdot \frac{B}{A},$$

$$X_1 = X_1,$$
$$X_2 = [X_1 A + (2-1)B]A^0,$$
$$X_2 = X_1 A + B.$$

From the recursive form [Eq. (2)]

$$X_2 = X_1 A + B.$$

Therefore, Eq. (1) is correct for $n = 1$ and $n = 2$.

We now prove Eq. (1) is correct for $n = k + 1$, given it is true for $n = k$. Assume that for $n = k$

$$X_k = [X_1 A + (k-1)B]A^{k-2}.$$

From Eq. (2), the defining equation,

$$\begin{aligned}
X_{k+1} &= A[X_1 A + (k-1)B]A^{k-2} + BA^{k-1} \\
&= [X_1 A + (k-1)B]A^{k-1} + BA^{k-1} \\
&= [X_1 A + kB]A^{k-1} - BA^{k-1} + BA^{k-1}, \\
X_{k+1} &= [X_1 A + kB]A^{k-1}. \tag{3}
\end{aligned}$$

For $n = k + 1$, Eq. (3) is seen to be equal to Eq. (1).

6.
$$p_{n+1} = \alpha p_n + \beta \gamma^{n-1} + \delta,$$
$$p_{n+1} - \alpha p_n = 0,$$
$$\mathbf{D}p_n - \alpha p_n = 0,$$
$$(\mathbf{D} - \alpha)p_n = 0,$$
$$\text{root} = \alpha$$
$$p_n = \alpha^{n-1}C + \cdots,$$
$$(\mathbf{D} - \alpha)bk^{n-1} = \beta \gamma^{n-1},$$
$$bk^n - \alpha bk^{n-1} = \beta \gamma^{n-1},$$
$$bk^{n-1}(k - \alpha) = B\gamma^{n-1}$$

(isolating the desired term),

$$bk^{n-1} = \frac{\beta \gamma^{n-1}}{\gamma - \alpha}$$

(on the left-hand side of the equation, k represents γ; on the right-hand side, it becomes γ),

$$p_n = \alpha^{n-1}C + \frac{\beta \gamma^{n-1}}{\gamma - \alpha} + \cdots,$$
$$(\mathbf{D} - \alpha)d = \delta,$$
$$d - \alpha d = \delta,$$
$$d = \frac{\delta}{(1 - \alpha)},$$
$$p_n = \alpha^{n-1}C + \frac{\beta \gamma^{n-1}}{\gamma - \alpha} + \frac{\delta}{(1 - \alpha)},$$
$$p_1 = C + \frac{\beta}{\gamma - \alpha} + \frac{\delta}{(1 - \alpha)},$$
$$C = p_1 - \frac{\beta}{\gamma - \alpha} - \frac{\delta}{(1 - \alpha)},$$
$$p_n = \alpha^{n-1}\left[p_1 - \frac{\beta}{\gamma - \alpha} - \frac{\delta}{(1 - \alpha)}\right] + \frac{\beta \gamma^{n-1}}{\gamma - \alpha} + \frac{\delta}{(1 - \alpha)}.$$

7. The theory indicates what a probability will be on trial $n + 1$ only if we know what it will be on trial n. This statement of the theory in terms of conditional probabilities suggests that the axioms' implications can be stated mathematically with recursive equations.

Problem 7 is concerned with the probability of a refusal to answer. This is synonomous with being in the unlearned state (Axiom 4). We therefore want a recursive equation in $P(C_{0n})$. We begin by constructing an equation with $P(C_{0n})$ on one side and $P(C_{0,n+1})$ on the other.

From our probability theorems [Eqs. (2.10) and (2.21)] we can state that

$$P(C_{0,n+1}) = P(C_{0,n+1}|C_{0n})P(C_{0n}) + P(C_{0,n+1}|C_{1n})P(C_{1n}). \tag{1}$$

We wish to have $P(C_{0n})$ on the right side, rather than $P(C_{1n})$. This is arranged by taking advantage of the fact that there are only two states possible on trial n, implying that

$$P(C_{1n}) = 1 - P(C_{0n}),$$

which changes our probability statement [Eq. (1)] to

$$P(C_{0,n+1}) = P(C_{0,n+1}|C_{0n})P(C_{0n}) + P(C_{0,n+1}|C_{1n})[1 - P(C_{0n})]. \tag{2}$$

We now go to the axioms for our parameters. Since we have already noted that our theory makes its statements in a conditional form, you should recognize that we can make an immediate translation from the axioms to $P(C_{0,n+1}|C_{0n})$ (from Axioms 1 and 2) and $P(C_{0,n+1}|C_{1n})$ (from Axiom 3). We now restate Eq. (2) as

$$P(C_{0,n+1}) = [(1 - c) + cf]P(C_{0n}) + f[1 - P(C_{0n})]. \tag{3}$$

The coefficient of $[1 - P(C_{0n})]$ in Eq. (3) stems from Axiom 3, which indicates that

$$P(C_{0,n+1}|C_{1n}) = f. \tag{4}$$

For the coefficient of $P(C_{0n})$ in Eq. (3) we have to recognize that there are two ways that a subject in C_0 on trial n can still be there on trial $n + 1$. He can simply not be conditioned, which has a probability of $(1 - c)$ from Axiom 1, or he can be conditioned by the exposure to the response at the end of trial n (Axiom 1 again), but forget it before trial $n + 1$ (from Axiom 2), with a joint probability of cf. This gives two alternate roads to $C_{0,n+1}$ from C_{0n}, so that

$$P(C_{0,n+1}|C_{0n}) = [(1 - c) + cf]. \tag{5}$$

Equations (4) and (5) justify our restatement of Eq. (2) in the form of Eq. (3). We now simply rearrange Eq. (3) so that the recursive implication is more obvious.

$$P(C_{0,n+1}) = [(1 - c) + cf - f]P(C_{0n}) + f,$$
$$P(C_{0,n+1}) = (1 - c)(1 - f)P(C_{0n}) + f. \tag{6}$$

For the answer to Problem 7, we simply solve Eq. (6) in the manner suggested by either Table 3.1 or 3.5. It can also be obtained immediately by recognizing that $(1 - c)(1 - f)$ is analogous to A and f is analogous to B in Eq. (3.7), which yields the solution analogous to the one in Step 11 of Table 3.1. [Note that $P(C_{01}) = 1$, from Axiom 5.]

$$P(C_{0n}) = [(1 - c)(1 - f)]^{n-1} \left[1 - \frac{f}{f + c(1 - f)} \right] + \frac{f}{f + c(1 - f)},$$

$$P(C_{0n}) = [(1 - c)(1 - f)]^{n-1} \left[\frac{c(1 - f)}{f + c(1 - f)} \right] + \frac{f}{f + c(1 - f)}. \tag{7}$$

8. For the second trial as a trial with a refusal to answer, we would require $P(C_{02})$. Normally, we would quickly proceed to an equation such as

$$P(C_{02}) = P(C_{02}|C_{01})P(C_{01}) + P(C_{02}|C_{11})P(C_{11}), \tag{1}$$

since our axioms are stated as conditional probabilities, and there are only two states possible. However, we already know from Axiom 5 that

$$P(C_{01}) = 1 \qquad \text{and} \qquad P(C_{11}) = 0.$$

We can therefore restate Eq. (1) as

$$P(C_{02}) = P(C_{02}|C_{01}).$$

We found the parameter equivalent of this statement in the last example. It is, from Axioms 1 and 2,

$$P(C_{02}) = [(1 - c) + cf]. \tag{2}$$

For $n > 2$ we have to recognize that a subject would have to have been in the learned state on all trials between trial 1 and trial n for a second refusal to respond to have been delayed until trial n. Stating this probabilistically, we would have the joint event

$$P(C_{0n}; C_{1,n-1}; C_{1,n-2}; \ldots; C_{13}, C_{12}, C_{01})$$
$$= P(C_{0n}|C_{1,n-1}; C_{1,n-2}; \ldots; C_{13}, C_{12}, C_{01}) \cdot P(C_{1,n-1}|C_{1,n-2}; \ldots; C_{01})$$
$$\cdot P(C_{1,n-2}|C_{1,n-3}; \ldots; C_{01}) \cdots P(C_{12}|C_{01}) \cdot P(C_{01}). \tag{3}$$

This joint event then is seen to be the product of a number of conditional probabilities. Recognizing that our conditional probabilities are constant over all n, with no axioms concerning response sequences more than one trial previous, we can ignore all but the last conditional event in each conditional probability. Thus, for example,

$$P(C_{14}|C_{13}, C_{12}, C_{01}) = P(C_{14}|C_{13}).$$

We can therefore restate Eq. (3) as

$$P(C_{0n}; C_{1,n-1}; C_{1,n-2}; \ldots; C_{13}, C_{12}, C_{01})$$
$$= P(C_{0n}|C_{1,n-1}) \cdot P(C_{1,n-1}|C_{1,n-2}) \cdot P(C_{1,n-2}|C_{1,n-3}) \cdots P(C_{13}|C_{12})$$
$$P(C_{12}|C_{01}) \cdot P(C_{01}). \tag{4}$$

Reading from left to right on the right-hand side of Eq. (4), we have

$$= [f] \cdot [(1-f)] \cdot [(1-f)] \cdots [(1-f)] \cdot [c(1-f)] \cdot 1.$$

Carefully checking for the number of $(1-f)$ values in this product, we find that

$$P(R_2 = n) = cf(1-f)^{n-2}, \quad n > 2,$$

so that we have

$$P(R_2 = n) = \begin{cases} 0, & n = 1, \\ [(1-c) + cf], & n = 2, \\ cf(1-f)^{n-2}, & n > 2. \end{cases} \tag{5}$$

9. We first state the value that we desire in terms of our probability theorems.

$$P(C_{0,n+1}; C_{0n}) = P(C_{0,n+1}|C_{0n})P(C_{0n}). \tag{1}$$

Axioms 1 and 2 again give us the parameter equivalents of $P(C_{0,n+1}|C_{0n})$, following the logic of Problem 7. That is,

$$P(C_{0,n+1}|C_{0n}) = [(1-c) + cf], \tag{2}$$

which we place appropriately into Eq. (1).

For the parameter equivalents for $P(C_{0n})$, we turn to Eq. (7) in Problem 7. We then insert this into Eq. (1). In summary, the probability of two consecutive refusals to answer is the probability of a refusal to answer on trial $n[P(C_{0n})]$ multiplied by the probability of remaining in the unlearned state on trial $n+1$ given that the subject was in the unlearned state on trial $n[P(C_{0,n+1}|C_{0n})]$. The answer then looks like

$$P(C_{0,n+1}; C_{0n}) = [(1-c) + cf]^n \left[\frac{c(1-f)}{f + c(1-f)} \right] + [(1-c) + cf] \left[\frac{f}{f + c(1-c)} \right].$$

10. For this problem, we give the refusal to answer on any trial the random variable value 1 and an answer the random variable value 0. We then sum the random variable values over the m trials to obtain the expected number of refusals to answer. The equation to be summed is taken from the solution to Problem 7. The actual summation can be found in Table 2.1, with the symbol C in that table replaced with $[(1-c) + cf]$. The constant

$$\frac{c(1-f)}{f + c(1-f)}$$

would have to be multiplied against the answer. Also, m times $f/[f + c(1 - f)]$ would have to be added to that, since

$$\sum_{n=1}^{m} k = mk$$

if k is a constant. The answer then is

$$E(\text{total refusals}) = \sum_{n=1}^{m} P(C_{0n})$$

$$= \frac{1 - [(1 - c) + cf]^m}{f + c(1 - f)} \cdot \frac{c(1 - f)}{f + c(1 - f)} + \frac{mf}{f + c(1 - f)}$$

$$= \frac{1}{f + c(1 - f)} \left\{ \frac{1 - [(1 - c) + cf]^m c(1 - f)}{f + c(1 - f)} \right\} + mf.$$

11. In Problem 8 you were asked to find the probability of any trial n being the trial of the second refusal to answer $[P(R_2 = n)]$. Problem 11 asks for the expected value of the distribution of random variable values, derived as Eq. (5), in the solution to Problem 8. The expected value would be the sum of each of the random variable values, each times its respective probability, summed over these products. That would give, as the solution to Problem 11,

$$E(R_2) = \sum_{n=1}^{\infty} nP(R_2 = n),$$

which, from Eq. (5) in the answer to Problem 8, would give us

$$E(R_2) = 2[(1 - c) + cf] + cf \sum_{n=3}^{\infty} n(1 - f)^{n-2}. \tag{1}$$

The required summation in Eq. (1) cannot be found in Table 2.3. We therefore carry out the algorithm for finding the sum suggested in Chapter Two. In this case, it will be necessary to repeat the algorithm for the solution, somewhat like the example given as Figure 2.13.

$$S_n = \sum_{n=3}^{\infty} n(1 - f)^{n-2} = 3(1 - f) + 4(1 - f)^2 + 5(1 - f)^3 + 6(1 - f)^4 + \cdots,$$

$$(1 - f)S_n = 3(1 - f)^2 + 4(1 - f)^3 + 5(1 - f)^4 + 6(1 - f)^5 + \cdots$$

$$S_n[1 - (1 - f)] = fS_n = 3(1 - f) + (1 - f)^2 + (1 - f)^3 + (1 - f)^4 + \cdots,$$

$$(1 - f)fS_n = 3(1 - f)^2 + (1 - f)^3 + (1 - f)^4 + (1 - f)^5 + \cdots$$

$$S_n[f - f + f^2] = f^2 S_n = 3(1 - f) - 2(1 - f)^2$$
$$= (1 - f)(3 - 2 + 2f)$$
$$= (1 - f)(1 + 2f),$$

$$S_n = \frac{(1 - f)(1 + 2f)}{f^2}.$$

Returning to Eq. (1), we insert the solution to our summation procedure.

$$E(R_2) = 2[(1 - c) + cf] + \frac{cf(1 - f)(1 + 2f)}{f^2},$$

$$E(R_2) = 2[(1 - c) + cf] + \frac{c(1 - f)(1 + 2f)}{f}. \tag{2}$$

Equation (2) is then the solution to Problem 11.

Chapter Four

1. STEP 1. $V_{2,n+1} = C_3 V_{2n} + C_2 \bar{\alpha}^n + C_1.$
   STEP 2. $V_{2,n+1} - C_3 V_{2n} = 0.$
   STEP 3. $\mathbf{D}V_{2n} - C_3 V_{2n} = 0.$
   STEP 4. $(\mathbf{D} - C_3)V_{2n} = 0$ (root $= C_3$).
   STEP 5. $V_{2n} = C_3^n k_1 + \cdots$
             where k_1 symbolizes a constant.
   STEP 6a. $(\mathbf{D} - C_3)a^n k_2 = C_2 \bar{\alpha}^n$
             where both a and k_2 are constants, and we wish to find the term symbolized by $a^n k_2$ that, when operated upon by the root C_3, will yield the term $C_2 \bar{\alpha}^n$.
   STEP 7a. $a^{n+1} k_2 - C_3 a^n k_2 = C_2 \bar{\alpha}^n.$
   STEP 8a. $a^n k_2 (a - C_3) = C_2 \bar{\alpha}^n,$

   $$a^n k_2 = \frac{C_2 \bar{\alpha}^n}{\bar{\alpha} - C_3}.$$

   STEP 6b. $(\mathbf{D} - C_3)k_3 = C_1.$
   STEP 7b. $k_3 - C_3 k_3 = C_1.$
   STEP 8b. $k_3(1 - C_3) = C_1,$

   $$k_3 = \frac{C_1}{1 - C_3}.$$

   STEP 9. $V_{2n} = C_3^n k_1 + \dfrac{C_2 \bar{\alpha}^n}{\bar{\alpha} - C_3} + \dfrac{C_1}{1 - C_3}$ (general solution of the complete equation).

   STEP 10. $V_{2,0} = k_1 + \dfrac{C_2}{\bar{\alpha} - C_3} + \dfrac{C_1}{1 - C_3},$

   $$k_1 = V_{2,0} - \frac{C_2}{\bar{\alpha} - C_3} - \frac{C_1}{1 - C_3}.$$

   STEP 11. $V_{2,n} = C_3^n \left(V_{2,0} - \dfrac{C_2}{\bar{\alpha} - C_3} - \dfrac{C_1}{1 - C_3} \right) + \dfrac{C_2 \bar{\alpha}^n}{\bar{\alpha} - C_3} + \dfrac{C_1}{1 - C_3}.$

2. Analogously with Eq. (4.34b) and Table 4.2,

$$V_{m,n+1} = \pi_{11} \sum_k (\alpha_{11} p_{kn} + a_{11})^m p_{kn} P_{kn} + \pi_{12} \sum_k (\alpha_{12} p_{kn} + a_{12})^m p_{kn} P_{kn}$$

$$+ \pi_{21} \sum_k (\alpha_{21} p_{kn} + a_{21})^m P_{kn} - \pi_{21} \sum_k (\alpha_{21} p_{kn} + a_{21})^m p_{kn} P_{kn}$$

$$+ \pi_{22} \sum_k (\alpha_{22} p_{kn} + a_{22})^m P_{kn} - \pi_{22} \sum_k (\alpha_{22} p_{kn} + a_{22})^m p_{kn} P_{kn},$$

$$V_{m,n+1} = \pi_{11} \sum^m \binom{m}{l} a_{11}^{m-l} \alpha_{11}^l \sum_k^{4n} p_{kn}^{l+1} P_{kn} + \pi_{12} \sum^m \binom{m}{l} a_{12}^{m-l} \alpha_{12}^l \sum_k^{4n} p_{kn}^{l+1} P_{kn}$$

$$+ \pi_{21} \sum^m \binom{m}{l} a_{21}^{m-l} \alpha_{21}^l \sum_k^{4n} p_{kn}^l P_{kn} - \pi_{21} \sum^m \binom{m}{l} a_{21}^{m-l} \alpha_{21}^l \sum_k^{4n} p_{kn}^{l+1} P_{kn}$$

$$+ \pi_{22} \sum^m \binom{m}{l} a_{22}^{m-l} \alpha_{22}^l \sum_k^{4n} p_{kn}^l P_{kn} - \pi_{22} \sum^m \binom{m}{l} a_{22}^{m-l} \alpha_{22}^l \sum_k^{4n} p_{kn}^{l+1} P_{kn},$$

$$V_{m,n+1} = \pi_{11} \sum^m \binom{m}{l} a_{11}^{m-l} \alpha_{11}^l V_{l+1,n} + \pi_{12} \sum^m \binom{m}{l} a_{12}^{m-l} \alpha_{12}^l V_{l+1,n}$$

$$+ \pi_{21} \sum^m \binom{m}{l} a_{21}^{m-l} \alpha_{21}^l V_{l,n} - \pi_{21} \sum^m \binom{m}{l} a_{21}^{m-l} \alpha_{21}^l V_{l+1,n}$$

$$+ \pi_{22} \sum^m \binom{m}{l} a_{22}^{m-l} \alpha_{22}^l V_{l,n} - \pi_{22} \sum^m \binom{m}{l} a_{22}^{m-l} \alpha_{22}^l V_{l+1,n}. \qquad (1)$$

For $m = 2$, we reexpress Eq. (1) as

$$V_{2,n+1} = \pi_{11} \sum_l^m \binom{m}{l} a_{11}^{m-l} \alpha_{11}^l V_{l+1,n} + \pi_{12} \sum_l^m \binom{m}{l} a_{12}^{m-l} \alpha_{12}^l V_{l+1,n}$$

$$+ \pi_{21} \sum_l^m \binom{m}{l} a_{21}^{m-l} \alpha_{21}^l (V_{l,n} - V_{l+1,n})$$

$$+ \pi_{22} \sum_l^m \binom{m}{l} a_{22}^{m-l} \alpha_{22}^l (V_{l,n} - V_{l+1,n}),$$

$$V_{2,n+1} = \pi_{11} \left[\binom{2}{0} a_{11}^2 V_{1,n} + \binom{2}{1} a_{11} \alpha_{11} V_{2,n} + \binom{2}{2} \alpha_{11}^2 V_{3,n} \right]$$

$$+ \pi_{12} \left[\binom{2}{0} a_{12}^2 V_{1,n} + \binom{2}{1} a_{12} \alpha_{12} V_{2,n} + \binom{2}{2} \alpha_{12}^2 V_{3,n} \right]$$

$$+ \pi_{21} \left[\binom{2}{0} a_{21}^2 (V_{0,n} - V_{1,n}) + \binom{2}{1} a_{21} \alpha_{21} (V_{1,n} - V_{2,n}) \right.$$

$$\left. + \binom{2}{2} \alpha_{21}^2 (V_{2,n} - V_{3,n}) \right]$$

$$+ \pi_{22} \left[\binom{2}{0} a_{22}^2 (V_{0,n} - V_{1,n}) + \binom{2}{1} a_{22} \alpha_{22} (V_{1,n} - V_{2,n}) \right.$$

$$\left. + \binom{2}{2} \alpha_{22}^2 (V_{2,n} - V_{3,n}) \right],$$

$$V_{2,n+1} = \pi_{11}(a_{11}^2 V_{1,n} + 2a_{11}\alpha_{11} V_{2,n} + \alpha_{11}^2 V_{3,n})$$
$$+ \pi_{12}(a_{12}^2 V_{1,n} + 2a_{12}\alpha_{12} V_{2,n} + \alpha_{12}^2 V_{3,n})$$
$$+ \pi_{21}[a_{21}^2(1 - V_{1,n}) + 2a_{21}\alpha_{21}(V_{1,n} - V_{2,n}) + \alpha_{21}^2(V_{2,n} - V_{3,n})]$$
$$+ \pi_{22}[a_{22}^2(1 - V_{1,n}) + 2a_{22}\alpha_{22}(V_{1,n} - V_{2,n}) + \alpha_{22}^2(V_{2,n} - V_{3,n})],$$
$$V_{2,n+1} = (\pi_{21}a_{21}^2 + \pi_{22}a_{22}^2) + [\pi_{11}a_{11}^2 + \pi_{12}a_{12}^2 - \pi_{21}a_{21}(a_{21} - 2\alpha_{21})$$
$$- \pi_{22}a_{22}(a_{22} - 2\alpha_{22})]V_{1,n}$$
$$+ [\pi_{11}2a_{11}\alpha_{11} + \pi_{12}2a_{12}\alpha_{12} - \pi_{21}\alpha_{21}(2a_{21} - \alpha_{21})$$
$$- \pi_{22}\alpha_{22}(2a_{22} - \alpha_{22})]V_{2,n}$$
$$+ (\pi_{11}\alpha_{11}^2 + \pi_{12}\alpha_{12}^2 - \pi_{21}\alpha_{21}^2 - \pi_{22}\alpha_{22}^2)V_{3,n}. \tag{2}$$

We symbolize the following:

$$C_1 = \pi_{21}a_{21}^2 + \pi_{22}a_{22}^2);$$
$$C_2 = [\pi_{11}a_{11}^2 + \pi_{12}a_{12}^2 - \pi_{21}a_{21}(a_{21} - 2\alpha_{21}) - \pi_{22}a_{22}(a_{22} - 2\alpha_{22})];$$
$$C_3 = [\pi_{11}2a_{11}\alpha_{11} + \pi_{12}2\alpha_{12}a_{12} - \pi_{21}\alpha_{21}(2a_{21} - \alpha_{21}) - \pi_{22}\alpha_{22}(2a_{22} - \alpha_{22})].$$

Assume that

$$\alpha_{11} = \alpha_{12} = \alpha_{21} = \alpha_{22} = \alpha_{ij}. \tag{3}$$

Note that, from Eq. (4.61),

$$\pi_{11} = 1 - \pi_{12} \tag{4}$$

and

$$\pi_{21} = 1 - \pi_{22}. \tag{5}$$

Equations (3), (4), and (5) imply that the coefficient of $V_{3,n}$ in Eq. (2) is equal to 0. That is,

$$\pi_{11}\alpha_{11}^2 + \pi_{12}\alpha_{12}^2 - \pi_{21}\alpha_{21}^2 - \pi_{22}\alpha_{22}^2 = \alpha_{ij}(\pi_{11} + \pi_{12} - \pi_{21} - \pi_{22})$$
$$= \alpha_{ij}(1 - \pi_{12} + \pi_{12} - 1 + \pi_{22} - \pi_{22})$$
$$= 0.$$

We can now restate Eq. (2) as

$$V_{2,n+1} = C_1 + C_2 V_{1n} + C_3 V_{2,n}.$$

From Eq. (4.63)

$$V_{2,n+1} = C_1 + C_2[V_{1,\infty} - (V_{1,\infty} - V_{1,0})\gamma^n] + C_3 V_{2,n} \tag{6}$$

[where $\gamma = (\pi_{11}a_{11} + \pi_{12}a_{12}) - (\pi_{21}a_{21} + \pi_{22}a_{22}) + \alpha_{ij}$]. Equation (6) can be restated as

$$V_{2,n+1} = (C_1 + C_2 V_{1,\infty}) - C_2(V_{1,\infty} - V_{1,0})\gamma^n + C_3 V_{2,n}. \tag{7}$$

We then solve Eq. (7) by using the same steps that we used in solving the equation in Problem 6 of Chapter Three.

$$V_{2,n} = \frac{C_1 + C_2 V_{1,\infty}}{1 - C_3} - \frac{C_2(V_{1,\infty} - V_{1,0})\gamma^n}{C_3 - \gamma}$$

$$- \left[\frac{C_1 + C_2 V_{1,\infty}}{1 - C_3} - \frac{C_2(V_{1,\infty} - V_{1,0})}{C_3 - \gamma} - V_{2,0} \right] C_3^n \quad . \quad (8)$$

For the variance, we then use the second moment minus the square of the first moment [as in Eq. (4.42)]. That is,

$$\sigma^2 = V_{2,n} - (V_{1,n})^2,$$

where $V_{2,n}$ is taken as Eq. (8) and

$$V_{1,n} = V_{1,\infty} - (V_{1,\infty} - V_{1,0})\gamma^n.$$

3. $E(T_\infty) = p_1 \sum_{i}^{\infty} \alpha^{i-1}$

$$= \frac{p_1}{1 - \alpha}.$$

Empirical value of $p_1 = .9$; therefore, we assume this to be the true value.

$$E(T_\infty) = \frac{.9}{1 - \alpha}$$

Equating the theoretical and empirical total errors, we would have

$$4 = \frac{.9}{1 - \alpha}$$

(the value 4 was obtained by summing all errors and dividing by the number of subjects);

$$\alpha = .775.$$

The two parameters are then

$$p_1 = .9, \qquad \alpha = .775.$$

4. The probability of an error on any trial n is

$$p_n = \alpha^{n-1} p_1. \qquad (1)$$

We place the parameter values obtained in the solution to Problem 3 into Eq. (1).

$$p_n = (.775)^{n-1}(.9).$$

For trials 1 through 5, this yields

$$.90, \quad .70, \quad .54, \quad .42, \quad \text{and} \quad .32.$$

5. The expected total number of errors for a subject at the nth trial is

$$E(T_n) = \frac{p_1(1 - \alpha^n)}{1 - \alpha}$$

Using the parameter values obtained in solving Problem 3, we have

$$E(T_n) = \frac{(.9)[1 - (.775)^n]}{.225}.$$

For trials 1 through 7 this yields

$$0.90, \quad 1.60, \quad 2.14, \quad 2.56, \quad 2.88, \quad 3.13, \quad \text{and} \quad 3.33.$$

6. (a) We want the probability of the joint event $P(E_3, E_2, E_1)$, where E_j is an error on the jth trial.

$$P(E_3, E_2, E_1) = P(E_3 | E_2 E_1) \cdot P(E_2 | E_1) \cdot P(E_1).$$

The probability of an error on trial j is independent of previous responses; that is,

$$P(E_j | E_k E_m) = P(E_j | E_k) = P(E_j) = \alpha^{j-1} p_1.$$

Consequently,

$$P(E_3, E_2, E_1) = \alpha^2 p_1 \cdot \alpha p_1 \cdot p_1.$$

Using the parameters of Problem 3, we have

$$P(E_3, E_2, E_1) = .34$$

(b) Proceeding as we did for part (a), with C_j symbolizing a jth trial success, we would have

$$\begin{aligned}
P(C_3, E_2, E_1) &= P(C_3 | E_2 E_1) \cdot P(E_2 | E_1) \cdot P(E_1) \\
&= [1 - P(E_3)] \cdot P(E_2) \cdot P(E_1) \\
&= [1 - \alpha^2 p_1] \cdot (\alpha p_1) \cdot p_1 \\
&= .29.
\end{aligned}$$

7. The number of single (isolated) errors is $r_{1\infty}$. From Eq. (4.75), we have

$$r_{1n} = u_{1n} - 2u_{2n} + u_{3n}. \tag{1}$$

From Eq. (4.68), we have

$$u_{jn} = \sum_{i=1}^{n-j+1} x_i \cdot x_{i+1} \cdot x_{i+2} \cdots x_{i+j-1}. \tag{2}$$

We want the equation for the expected value of $u_{j\infty}$, so that we can obtain the expected value of $r_{1\infty}$. To obtain this, we turn to the model for its probability distribution for $P(x_i = 1)$. This is equivalent to the probability of an error. We therefore use Eq. (4.77),

$$p_n = \alpha^{n-1}p_1,$$

and form products of the probabilities of j consecutive $x_i = 1$ values, summed as suggested in Eq. (2), to obtain the expectation of the sum u_{jn}. That is,

$$E(u_{jn}) = \sum_{i}^{n-j+1} (\alpha^{i-1}p_1) \cdot (\alpha^i p_1) \cdot (\alpha^{i+1}p_1) \cdots (\alpha^{i+j-2}p_1). \qquad (3)$$

The sum in Eq. (3) is carried out as suggested in Eq. (4.83) and eventuates in Eq. (4.84),

$$E(u_{j\infty}) = \frac{\alpha^{[j(j-1)]/2}p_1^{\ j}}{1 - \alpha^j}. \qquad (4)$$

We can replace the n with ∞ under the assumption that we are modeling a paradigm where we have run the subjects to a criterion that assumes no more errors.

For $r_{1\infty}$, we have, from Eq. (1),

$$r_{1\infty} = \frac{\alpha^0 p_1}{1 - \alpha} - \frac{2\alpha p_1^{\ 2}}{1 - \alpha^2} + \frac{\alpha^3 p_1^{\ 3}}{1 - \alpha^3}.$$

Introducing the parameters from Problem 3, we have the result

$$r_{1\infty} = 4 - 3.14 + .63 = 1.49.$$

8. We use precisely the same logic as we used in solving the preceding problem. However, for Eq. (1) in the preceding solution, we substitute

$$r_{3\infty} = u_{3\infty} - 2u_{4\infty} + u_{5\infty}.$$

From Eq. (4) in the preceding solution, we have

$$r_{3\infty} = \frac{\alpha^{[3(3-1)]/2}p_1^{\ 3}}{1 - \alpha^3} - \frac{2\alpha^{[4(4-1)]/2}p_1^{\ 4}}{1 - \alpha^4} + \frac{\alpha^{[5(5-1)]/2}p_1^{\ 5}}{1 - \alpha^5}.$$

Substituting the parameters from Problem 3, we have the result

$$r_{3\infty} = .63 - .44 + .06 = .25.$$

Chapter Five

1. $\begin{pmatrix} k+e & k+1 \\ c+d & e+1 \end{pmatrix}.$

2. Define a matrix $\mathbf{E}$ having a 1 as the value of each and every component element of the matrix, and of the same order as $\mathbf{A}$. Then

$$\mathbf{B} = \mathbf{E} - \mathbf{A}.$$

3. $\begin{pmatrix} dq & dx \\ dy & dz \end{pmatrix}$

4.

$$\begin{pmatrix} c & 0 & 1-c \\ s[c + (1-s)] & (1-s)^2 & s(1-c) \\ ce + (1-e)[ps + e(1-p)] & (1-e)(1-s)p & e(1-c) + (1-e)^2(1-p) \end{pmatrix}$$

5. (a) Counting the columns from left to right and the rows from the top down: Add column 2 to column 3; subtract row 3 from row 2. The result will be

$$\begin{pmatrix} 1 & 0 & 0 \\ 0 & (1-c)p - d & 0 \\ c & d & 1-c \end{pmatrix}$$

The determinant is therefore $(1-c)[(1-c)p - d]$, the product of the diagonal elements. Other column and row operations could also lead to the same answer.

(b) Taking the determinants of the minors of the components in the top row and multiplying them against the components (eliminating two of them), we have

$$[(1-c)p](1-c-d) - d(1-c)(1-p) = (1-c)[p(1-c) - d].$$

6. $\mathbf{B}^{-1} = \dfrac{1}{|\mathbf{B}|} \mathbf{B}'_{cf}, \qquad \begin{aligned} |\mathbf{B}| &= bc - (1-b)(c-1) \\ &= b + c - 1, \end{aligned}$

$$\mathbf{B}'_{cf} = \begin{pmatrix} b & c-1 \\ b-1 & c \end{pmatrix}, \qquad \mathbf{B}^{-1} \dfrac{1}{b+c-1} \begin{pmatrix} b & c-1 \\ b-1 & c \end{pmatrix}.$$

7. $\begin{aligned} P^{k+1} &= [\mathbf{A}_1 + \mathbf{A}_2(a_{22} - a_{12})] \cdot [\mathbf{A}_1 + \mathbf{A}_2(a_{22} - a_{12})^k] \\ &= \mathbf{A}_1^2 + \mathbf{A}_1\mathbf{A}_2(a_{22} - a_{12})^k + \mathbf{A}_2\mathbf{A}_1 + \mathbf{A}_2^2(a_{22} - a_{12})^{k+1} \\ &= \mathbf{A}_1^2 + \mathbf{A}_2^2(a_{22} - a_{12})^{k+1} \qquad [\text{by Eq. (5.72)}] \\ &= \mathbf{A}_1 + \mathbf{A}_2(a_{22} - a_{12})^{k+1} \qquad [\text{by Eq. (5.73)}] \end{aligned}$

Chapter Six

1. $\mathbf{A}^{-1} = \dfrac{1}{|\mathbf{A}|} \mathbf{A}'_{cf}, \qquad |\mathbf{A}| = (1-a)(1-b)(1-c)$

(obtained as the product of the diagonal elements, since Matrix 2 is a triangular matrix),

$$\mathbf{A}_{cf} = \begin{pmatrix} (1-a)(1-b)(1-c) & -c(1-a)(1-b) & ac(1-b)-b(1-c) \\ 0 & (1-a)(1-b) & -a(1-b) \\ 0 & 0 & (1-c) \end{pmatrix}.$$

$\mathbf{A}_{cf}$ is then transposed and multiplied against the reciprocal of the determinant.

$$\mathbf{A}^{-1} = \begin{pmatrix} 1 & 0 & 0 \\ \dfrac{-c}{(1-c)} & \dfrac{1}{(1-c)} & 0 \\ \dfrac{ac(1-b)-b(1-c)}{(1-a)(1-b)(1-c)} & \dfrac{-a}{(1-a)(1-c)} & \dfrac{1}{(1-a)(1-b)} \end{pmatrix}.$$

2. $\mathbf{A}^{-1} = \dfrac{1}{|\mathbf{A}|} \mathbf{A}'_{cf}$,

$$|\mathbf{A}| = (1-a)(1-c)(1-d) - ad$$

[using Eq. (5.14a) and the first row of Matrix 3],

$$\mathbf{A}_{cf} = \begin{pmatrix} (1-a)(1-c)(1-d)-ad & -c(1-a)(1-d) & ac(1-d) \\ 0 & (1-a) & -a \\ 0 & -d & (1-c)(1-d) \end{pmatrix},$$

$$\mathbf{A}^{-1} = \dfrac{1}{(1-a)(1-c)(1-d)-ad}$$

$$\times \begin{pmatrix} (1-a)(1-c)(1-d)-ad & 0 & 0 \\ -c(1-a)(1-d) & (1-a) & -d \\ ac(1-d) & -a & (1-c)(1-d) \end{pmatrix}.$$

3. $\mathbf{N} = (\mathbf{I} - \mathbf{Q})^{-1}$,

$$(\mathbf{I} - \mathbf{Q}) = \begin{pmatrix} 1 - (1-c)(1-d) & -d \\ -a & a \end{pmatrix},$$

$$(\mathbf{I} - \mathbf{Q})^{-1} = \dfrac{1}{|\mathbf{I} - \mathbf{Q}|} (\mathbf{I} - \mathbf{Q})'_{cf},$$

$$|\mathbf{I} - \mathbf{Q}| = a - a(1-c)(1-d) - ad,$$
$$|\mathbf{I} - \mathbf{Q}| = ac(1-d),$$

$$\mathbf{N} = \dfrac{1}{ac(1-d)} \begin{pmatrix} a & d \\ a & 1 - (1-c)(1-d) \end{pmatrix}.$$

4. $\mathbf{H} = (\mathbf{N} - \mathbf{I})\mathbf{N}_{\mathrm{dg}}^{-1}$,

$$\mathbf{H} = \left[\left(\begin{array}{cc} \dfrac{1}{c(1-d)} & \dfrac{d}{ac(1-d)} \\[3mm] \dfrac{1}{c(1-d)} & \dfrac{1-(1-c)(1-d)}{ac(1-d)} \end{array} \right) - \begin{pmatrix} 1 & 0 \\ 0 & 1 \end{pmatrix} \right]$$

$$\times \left(\begin{array}{cc} \dfrac{1}{c(1-d)} & 0 \\[3mm] 0 & \dfrac{ac(1-d)}{1-(1-c)(1-d)} \end{array} \right),$$

$$\mathbf{H} = \left(\begin{array}{cc} 1-c(1-d) & \dfrac{d}{1-(1-c)(1-d)} \\[3mm] 1 & 1 - \dfrac{ac(1-d)}{1-(1-c)(1-d)} \end{array} \right).$$

5. We can use Eq. (6.32), which utilizes the $\mathbf{N}$ matrix, to obtain $\mathbf{K}[k]$. We can also use Eq. (6.31), which utilizes the $\mathbf{H}$ matrix. When we have obtained both the $\mathbf{N}$ and $\mathbf{H}$ matrices (as we did in solving Problems 3 and 4), it is most convenient to combine both equations. That is, we can use the first two factors in Eq. (6.31), $\mathbf{H}$ and $\mathbf{H}_{\mathrm{dg}}^{k-1}$, and then substitute $\mathbf{N}_{\mathrm{dg}}^{-1}$ for $(\mathbf{I} - \mathbf{H}_{\mathrm{dg}})$ in (6.31) as the last factor in the product [from the equality given in Eq. (6.35)]. Therefore, we can restate the equivalence with $\mathbf{K}[k]$ as

$$\mathbf{K}[k] = \mathbf{H} \cdot \mathbf{H}_{\mathrm{dg}}^{k-1} \cdot \mathbf{N}_{\mathrm{dg}}^{-1},$$

$$\mathbf{K}[k] = \left(\begin{array}{cc} 1-c(1-d) & \dfrac{d}{1-(1-c)(1-d)} \\[3mm] 1 & 1 - \dfrac{ac(1-d)}{1-(1-c)(1-d)} \end{array} \right)$$

$$\cdot \left(\begin{array}{cc} [1-c(1-d)]^{k-1} & 0 \\[3mm] 0 & \left[1 - \dfrac{ac(1-d)}{1-(1-c)(1-d)}\right]^{k-1} \end{array} \right)$$

$$\cdot \left(\begin{array}{cc} \dfrac{1}{c(1-d)} & 0 \\[3mm] 0 & \dfrac{1-(1-c)(1-d)}{ac(1-d)} \end{array} \right),$$

$\mathbf{K}[k]$

$$= \begin{pmatrix} [1 - c(1-d)]^k & \dfrac{d}{1-(1-c)(1-d)}\left[1 - \dfrac{ac(1-d)}{1-(1-c)(1-d)}\right]^{k-1} \\[3ex] [1 - c(1-d)]^{k-1} & \left[1 - \dfrac{ac(1-d)}{1-(1-c)(1-d)}\right]^{k} \end{pmatrix}$$

$$\cdot \begin{pmatrix} c(1-d) & 0 \\[2ex] 0 & \dfrac{ac(1-d)}{1-(1-c)(1-d)} \end{pmatrix} \cdot$$

Noting that

$$1 - (1-c)(1-d) - ac(1-d) = c(1-a)(1-d) + d,$$

we have

$$\mathbf{K}[k] = \begin{pmatrix} c(1-d)[1-c(1-d)]^k & \dfrac{acd(1-d)[c(1-a)(1-d)+d]^{k-1}}{[1-(1-c)(1-d)]^{k+1}} \\[3ex] c(1-d)[1-c(1-d)]^{k-1} & \dfrac{ac(1-d)[c(1-a)(1-d)+d]^{k}}{[1-(1-c)(1-d)]^{k+1}} \end{pmatrix}.$$

6. (a) $\mathbf{N} = (\mathbf{I} - \mathbf{Q})^{-1}$

$$\mathbf{Q} = \begin{pmatrix} 1-c-d & 0 & 0 \\ 0 & (1-c)(1-d) & 0 \\ 0 & 0 & 1-a-b \end{pmatrix},$$

$$(\mathbf{I} - \mathbf{Q}) = \begin{pmatrix} c+d & 0 & 0 \\ 0 & c(1-d)+d & 0 \\ 0 & 0 & a+b \end{pmatrix}.$$

Since $(\mathbf{I} - \mathbf{Q})$ is a diagonal matrix, we obtain its inverse by converting each diagonal element into its reciprocal. Therefore,

$$\mathbf{N} = (\mathbf{I} - \mathbf{Q})^{-1} = \begin{pmatrix} \dfrac{1}{c+d} & 0 & 0 \\[2ex] 0 & \dfrac{1}{c(1-d)+d} & 0 \\[2ex] 0 & 0 & \dfrac{1}{a+b} \end{pmatrix}.$$

(b) $\mathbf{H} = (\mathbf{N} - \mathbf{I})\mathbf{N}_{\text{dg}}^{-1}$,

$$\mathbf{H} = \begin{pmatrix} \dfrac{1-c-d}{c+d} & 0 & 0 \\ 0 & \dfrac{(1-c)(1-d)}{c(1-d)+d} & 0 \\ 0 & 0 & \dfrac{1-a-b}{a+b} \end{pmatrix}$$

$$\cdot \begin{pmatrix} c+d & 0 & 0 \\ 0 & \dfrac{1}{c(1-d)+d} & 0 \\ 0 & 0 & \dfrac{1}{a+b} \end{pmatrix},$$

$$\mathbf{H} = \begin{pmatrix} 1-c-d & 0 & 0 \\ 0 & (1-c)(1-d) & 0 \\ 0 & 0 & 1-a-b \end{pmatrix}.$$

In this problem, states S_3, S_4, and S_5 are not transient states, in that transient states can each be reached from each other (even if not directly). In the matrix of this problem, states S_3, S_4, and S_5 can only lead to S_1 or S_2, or return to themselves. This means that the probability of returning to a nonergodic state at least once is here equivalent to both the $\mathbf{Q}$ matrix and the $\mathbf{H}$ matrix. This explains why the $\mathbf{H}$ matrix and $\mathbf{Q}$ matrix are identical in this case. This identity would not hold with a set of transient states as properly defined.

(c) $\mathbf{B} = \mathbf{NR}$,

$$\mathbf{B} = \begin{pmatrix} \dfrac{1}{c+d} & 0 & 0 \\ 0 & \dfrac{1}{c(1-d)+d} & 0 \\ 0 & 0 & \dfrac{1}{a+b} \end{pmatrix} \cdot \begin{pmatrix} d & c \\ c & d(1-c) \\ a & b \end{pmatrix}$$

$$= \begin{pmatrix} \dfrac{d}{c+d} & \dfrac{c}{c+d} \\ \dfrac{c}{c(1-d)+d} & \dfrac{d(1-c)}{c(1-d)+d} \\ \dfrac{a}{a+b} & \dfrac{b}{a+b} \end{pmatrix}.$$

7. (a) The first interpretation is simply the matrix for the expanded Bower one-element paired-associate model. That is,

	Learned	Guessing with success	Guessing with error
Learned	1	0	0
Guessing with success	c	$p(1-c)$	$q(1-c)$
Guessing with error	c	$p(1-c)$	$q(1-c)$

(b) The second interpretation makes the assumption that learning can only occur on error trials. That is, the subject maintains his strategy as long as he is being reinforced. Therefore, if he has an incorrect strategy, so that he is simply guessing and he guesses correctly, he will not change his strategy for the next trial. This implies that learning cannot occur on a trial with a correct guess, and is represented in the matrix by a zero probability of transition from guessing with success to the learned state. On the next trial after guessing with success, he will still be guessing, and will therefore be successful with probability p and make an error with probability q. If he guesses and makes an error, either he can go to the learned state with probability c on the next trial, or with probability $p(1-c)$ he does not go to the learned state and guesses correctly, or with probability $q(1-c)$ he does not go to the learned state and guesses incorrectly. The matrix is therefore

	Learned	Guessing with success	Guessing with error
Learned	1	0	0
Guessing with success	0	p	q
Guessing with error	c	$p(1-c)$	$q(1-c)$

Chapter Eight

1. None of the states are observable.

2. We define a state I, which is the state for all errors prior to the first correct response.

We define a state S for any trial on which a correct response occurs, which is later followed by at least one error.

We define a state R for any trial on which there is an error after the first correct response has occurred. (This is a recurrent event.)

We define an absorbing state Q for all correct responses following the last error (or if there are no errors, this is the state beginning with trial 1).

3. We look at the matrix for the original theory, and we see that we must use the row conditional upon being in state E on trial n. It is required that we have successes on trials $n + 1$ through $n + j - 1$, which means that we must first go to state C, which has a conditional probability of $(1 - d)p$. Then, from state C we must return to state C on trials $n + 2$ through $n + j - 1$, which means $j - 2$ consecutive times. This yields a probability of $[(1 - c)p]^{j-2}$. Then, from state C we must go to state E, which has a probability of $(1 - c)q$. Combining these joint events, we have

$$f_j = [(1 - d)p][(1 - c)p]^{j-2}[(1 - c)q],$$
$$f_j = [(1 - c)p]^{j-1}[(1 - d)q]. \tag{1}$$

4. $P_{r_n r_{n+1}} = (1 - d)q.$

5. This would require going from an error to being continuously correct. This could occur by the subject going to state C of the original theory, staying there for some j trials, and then going to state L. The number of times that the subject can repeat in state C can vary from zero to infinity. We would therefore have a sum, beginning with

$$\sum_{j=0}^{\infty} [(1 - c)p]^j[(1 - d)p],$$

which would be multiplied by c for the probability of finally going to state L. There is also another possibility. The subject could simply go from state E to state L in the original model. That transition would have probability d. Therefore, summing all possibilities, the answer would be

$$P_{r_n q_{n+1}} = \sum_{j=0}^{\infty} [(1 - c)p]^j[(1 - d)p]c + d$$

$$= \left\{ \frac{[(1 - d)p]c}{1 - [(1 - c)p]} \right\} + d$$

$$= \frac{(1 - d)cp + d - (1 - c)dp}{1 - [(1 - c)p]},$$

$$P_{r_n q_{n+1}} = \frac{cp + dq}{q + cp}. \tag{2}$$

An alternative, and simpler, way to the same solution is to recognize that the transition $T_{r_n q_{n+1}}$ means a transition from error to no more errors. This would be equivalent to the complement of eventually having another error, so that

$$P_{r_n q_{n+1}} = 1 - \sum_{j=1}^{\infty} f_j. \tag{3}$$

Looking at the answer to Problem 3 for the parameter equivalent of f_j, we can see that by summing f_j as suggested in Eq. (3), we would obtain the same answer with $[1 - \sum_{j=1}^{\infty} f_j]$ as we had with Eq. (2).

6. State R can only be entered after at least one success. After the subject has had a success, however, he can no longer be in state I. Therefore,

$$P_{r_n I_{n+1}} = 0.$$

For $P_{r_n S_{n+1}}$ we can see that what we desire is a success right after an error, with the success eventually being followed by another error. Another way to phrase this is that we want an error that will occur on any trial in the future with the exception of the next trial. That would be

$$P_{r_n S_{n+1}} = \sum_{j=2}^{\infty} f_j$$

with f_j defined in Eq. (1) in the solution to Problem 3.

An alternative formulation is that we require the probability of going from state E in the old theory to state C in the old theory on one trial. That would suggest $(1 - d)p$. Having gone to state C, the subject must, at some future trial, have an error. That would require

$$P_{r_n S_{n+1}} = [(1 - d)p] \sum_{j=1}^{\infty} f_j.$$

The simplest procedure is to recognize that we can simply sum the remaining cell entries of the row of the new matrix (since we have all cells except one) and subtract that probability from 1.

All three of the suggested approaches lead to the same value,

$$P_{r_n S_{n+1}} = \frac{pq(1 - c)(1 - d)}{q + cp}.$$

Index